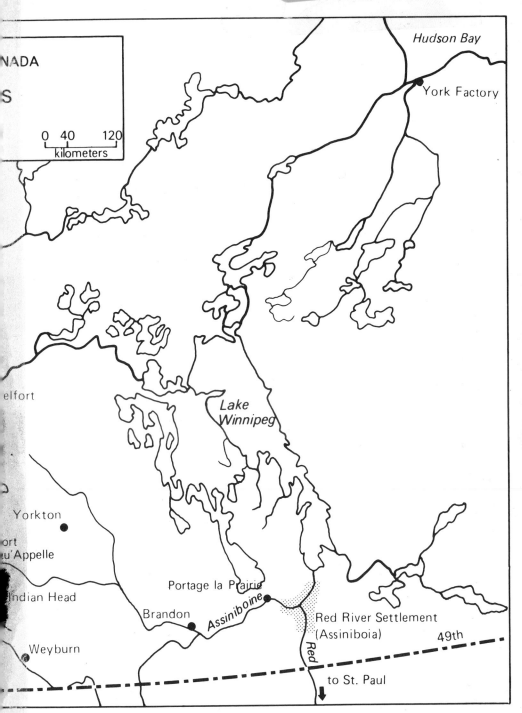

Hudson Bay

York Factory

NADA

S

0   40   120
kilometers

elfort

Lake
Winnipeg

Yorkton

ort
u'Appelle

Indian Head

Portage la Prairie

Brandon

Assiniboine

Weyburn

Red River Settlement
(Assiniboia)

Red

49th

to St. Paul

The Developing West

Lewis H. Thomas

The Developing West

Essays on Canadian History
in Honor of Lewis H. Thomas

edited by John E. Foster

 The University of Alberta Press

First published by
The University of Alberta Press
450 Athabasca Hall
Edmonton, Alberta
Canada T6G 2E8

Copyright © The University of Alberta Press 1983

ISBN 0-88864-035-8

Canadian Cataloguing in Publication Data

Main entry under title:
The Developing West

  ISBN 0-88864-035-8

  1. Prairie Provinces—History—Addresses,
essays, lectures. I. Thomas, Lewis H., 1917- *1983*
II. Foster, John Elgin.
FC3242.D48   971.2'02   C82-091094-5
F1060.9.D48

34,156   *C.1*

Cover photographs courtesy City of Edmonton Archives
Typeset by The Typeworks, Mayne Island, British Columbia
Printed by D. W. Friesen & Sons Ltd., Altona, Manitoba

Contents

Contributors

Brennan, J. William	Department of History, University of Regina
Cherwinski, W.J.C.	Department of History, Memorial University of Newfoundland
Clark, W. Leland	Department of History, Brandon University
den Otter, A.A.	Department of History, Memorial University of Newfoundland
Foster, John E.	Department of History, University of Alberta
Gilpin, John F.	Historic Sites Service, Alberta Culture, Edmonton, Alberta
Huel, Raymond J.A.	Department of History, University of Lethbridge
Luxton, Eleanor G.	Banff, Alberta
Regehr, T.D.	Department of History, University of Saskatchewan
Richeson, David R.	National Museum of Man, Ottawa, Ontario
Spry, Irene M.	Professor Emeritus, University of Ottawa
Stanley, George F.G.	Professor Emeritus, Mount Allison University and Royal Military College

Thomas, Lewis Gwynne	Professor Emeritus, University of Alberta
Van Kirk, Sylvia M.	Department of History, University of Toronto
Ward, W. Peter	Department of History, University of British Columbia

Acknowledgements

A passionate, almost consuming interest in all aspects of western and national history, together with diligence and thoroughness in research, are the scholarly qualities that come to mind when former students and colleagues speak of their associations with Lewis H. Thomas. Former students also recall hours of willing, patient, and helpful assessment and explanation. Colleagues recall a scholar whose enthusiasm for the "little man" in his subject matter never prevented him from empathetically and sympathetically perceiving views different from his own. All recall many acts of consideration and kindness of Lewis and his wife Margaret. It is in recognition of L.H. Thomas's contribution as scholar, colleague, mentor, and friend that this collection of essays is published.

In this *festschrift*, many colleagues and friends other than the contributors have played helpful roles. In particular I would note the suggestions, efforts, and encouragement extended by Rod Macleod, Doug Owram, David Breen, Don Blackley, Olive Dickason, David Hall, Bill Sampson, Stan Gordon, Betty Florchyk, and Eli Ives. Lillian Wonders and Kirsty Burt prepared the maps. At The University of Alberta Press, Norma Gutteridge and Katherine Wensel have been most patient and helpful. Shortcomings in the book are my responsibility alone.

The University of Alberta   John E. Foster
1982

Introduction

_____ John E. Foster

The diversity of subject matter in the essays in this volume emphasizes the variety of mechanisms involved in the metropolitan-hinterland relationship in western Canadian history. As well, these same essays show the value of metropolitanism as an interpretive context, usefully structuring the sequence of events and circumstances that express the western Canadian experience. Academics and laymen alike, more frequently by implication rather than by explication, have seen the facts of western history given meaning when viewed in terms of the region's relationship with institutions rooted in the metropolitan centres of the central provinces and in the national government. In terms of the nation's history, the metropolitan centres are seen as having secured the West for the "Dominion's purposes"[1] and as having the major role in directing the region's development. In terms of the region's history, the frustration of hinterland aspirations is seen as owing as much to the injustices arising out of The Transfer and the subsequent actions of central Canadian institutions and their agents as it is owing to the vagaries of a mid-continent climate and the extent of distances from national and world centres. Such historical interpretations seem to underlie not only the discussions of academics but the confrontations of politicians and the pontifications of editorial writers. Yet, to have scholarly value, such interpretations cannot simply describe the mechanisms of the metropolis-hinterland relationship: they must explain how such mechanisms relate to the sequence of events and circumstances that constitute the western experience.

Scholars have long recognized the West as an "environment that ... must change people and institutions greatly...."[2] Some would suggest that the various processes of change involved in adapting to a western environment have given expression to socio-cultural ways, some of which distinguish western Canadians from others. These distinctions arose because processes of change engendered individual experiences that were frequently shared with others. Over time, shared individual experiences coalesced as systems of belief and practice associated with particular communities. In many instances the collective nature of many shared experiences extended to encompass the people of the region. When the mechanisms of metropolis-hinterland relationships are cast in the light of these shared experiences, metropolitanism offers explanation as well as description to the facts of the western experience.

In comprehending changes in people and institutions as the shared experiences that gave expression to fundamental aspects of western history, the explanatory efficacy of metropolitan interpretations becomes more apparent. Significant works of scholarship, notably among them Lewis H. Thomas's *The Struggle for Responsible Government in the North-West Territories*, have demonstrated many, if not most, of the technological, economic, sociological, and political mechanisms that constitute the metropolitan relationship. In themselves these mechanisms evoke little discussion in studies concerned with their description: they seem to be viewed as the "basic stuff" of western history. Yet commentary on the nature and consequences of these mechanisms can call forth much divergent opinion. It is when these mechanisms of metropolitanism impinge directly on the shared experiences of the historical actors, both in the metropolis and in the hinterland, that images of each in the mind of the other take on critical importance. Metropolitanism, then, is as much image as it is mechanism: it is as both mechanism and image that it offers explanation to the western experience. The extent to which the essays in this volume further understandings of the mechanisms of metropolitanism in western history is one measure of their scholarly contribution. But the extent to which they clarify understandings of these images, arising out of the shared experiences involving these mechanisms, is the measure of their scholarly contribution to be emphasized.

Numerous sources have attested to the changing nature of the metropolitan relationship in the half-century preceeding The Transfer in 1870. At one time the relationship had rested upon the annual voyage of a few supply ships and their attendant flotillas of Yorkboats and canoes. In the years that followed the end of competition in the fur trade in 1820, additional routes to other metropolitan centres opened. At the same time as the pace of the industrial revolution accelerated in these centres, the nature of the various metropolitan relationships was continually and radically restructured.

In reflecting upon the responses of Old North-West communities to the "challenges" and "opportunities" arising out of the new relationships with world and continental centres, some authors conclude that the native people in particular lacked the technical and entrepreneurial skills needed to succeed in the new order. Irene Spry's essay, "The 'Private Adventurers' of Rupert's Land," suggests that for a significant number of inhabitants involved in merchandising, the principal problem of adjustment was not one of a lack of skills; rather it was a lack of socio-political ties with the increasingly numerous and assertive agents of metropolitan institutions. For the inhabitants of the Old North-West, technical competence in the ways of the newcomers would not count for much unless it was buttressed with adequate socio-political links to individual newcomers. Sylvia Van Kirk's essay provides a particularly poignant study of one family's encounter with the hinterland ramifications of the altered relationships with the outside. For members of the Alexander Ross family, instances of personal tragedy seemed to arise in major part from the lack of congruence between the image and the reality of metropolitan institutions in their lives.

In "Stony Indian Medicine," Eleanor G. Luxton[3] provides a vehicle for a few Stony elders to express some of their understandings of the impact of various changes on themselves and their people. As most of these men have been dead for a half-century, the article constitutes a valuable record of their views. At the same time it provides useful insight into the community of the author's family and their relations with the Stonys at Morley, Alberta, around the turn of the century and the years that followed.

Recent works have demonstrated the circumstances and the vehicles by which images of the hinterland were created in the central Canadian mind. Little attention, however, has been paid to vehicles by which images of the western hinterland were carried to the Maritimes. G.F.G. Stanley's essay, "New Brunswick and Nova Scotia and the North-West Rebellion, 1885," suggests one such vehicle. Military service exposed many young maritimers to the reality of the West while newspaper coverage drew the West to the attention of many thousands more. While the nature of the evolving western image in the maritime mind remains to be determined, the migration of a significant number of maritimers at various times suggests an impact of importance.

Andy den Otter in "The Hudson's Bay Company's Prairie Transportation Problem, 1870–85" and David Richeson in "The Telegraph and Community Formation in the North-West Territories" provide graphic examples of the problems involved in adapting technological advances originating in a metropolis to hinterland circumstances. Before The Transfer, the Hudson's Bay Company faced a variety of challenges to the ways and means that it conducted commerce in its territories. The key to the Company's success was the reduction of costs, principally labor and the turn-around time from the shipping of goods to the Company's posts to the sale of furs on the London market. In its efforts to reduce costs, steam power on the northern waterways, in time, proved particularly effective. The initial experiences on the prairie rivers, although less than successful, left a significant legacy for later development. The effective assertion of Canadian interests in the West required effective communication. The attempts to develop the telegraph as one such communication tool required solutions to both technological and administrative problems. Richeson suggests, however, that, in solving these problems and securing the West to the national interest, the telegraph also functioned as a mechanism by which the region shared experiences particular to itself.

An environmental factor of much consequence that historians have acknowledged, but do not seem to emphasize, is demography. W. Peter Ward's comparison of the demography of the prairie provinces West with the transmontane West since the turn of the century suggests the critical importance of this environmental factor in shaping the nature of the community that emerged. Ward's essay draws attention to the nature of the exploitable resources in each region and thus the particular demographic nature of the societies that developed in each region. Such demographic distinctions underline the differing nature of the social environments to which newcomers had to respond.

Land both as an exploitable resource and as a commerical commodity focussed much of the energies of governments, national and regional, corporations, and individuals. In its pursuit of the "Dominion's purposes," the national government took steps to further the more effective agrarian exploitation of western lands through the establishment of experimental farms. Yet, as W. Leland Clark demonstrates in his essay, it was land as a commercial commodity that made the question of the selection of such sites subject to the political concerns of patronage. In the author's opinion, such concerns were important but not sufficient to side-track or to destroy an effective response to problems associated with prairie farming.

John Gilpin in "Urban Land Speculation in the Development of Strathcona (South Edmonton), 1891–1912," emphasizes the importance of land as a commodity, particularly after the arrival of the railway more intimately tied Strathcona to other communities in the region and to outside centres. Outsiders associated with the railway subdivided the land not to serve the interests of the local community or to give physical expression to its aspiration and sense of itself, but to facilitate the marketing of land at minimum costs. The legacy of this commercial purpose is readily apparent today not only on Edmonton's southside but in other western communities. The role of Winnipeg-based entrepreneurs in this manipulation of land as a commercial commodity should be a subject of much interest in western history.

W.J.C. Cherwinski's study of the last of the British harvester movements in 1928 details an administrative nightmare for most of the participants: governments, railways, and harvesters alike. It marks the culmination of a practice originating a generation earlier that, with changing circumstances, no longer fulfilled its purpose at an acceptable cost. The British harvester movement of 1928 constituted a regional experience for westerners. One cannot help but wonder about its impact on the patchwork of sharply delineated ethnic communities. How did the nativistic views of English-speaking communities and their concern with the "foreign-born" adapt to the reality of social intercourse with their ethnic kindred, the unemployed British miners recruited as harvesters who frequently agitated "disruptively" for their Communist beliefs and aims? As a result of this experience, in part, did English-speaking westerners come to view their successful land-owning eastern European neighbors in a new light? In the eyes of westerners did they lose some of their faults and acquire new virtues, particularly when the 1920s marked the time when a large number of the second generation of the "foreign-born" were leaving school with a knowledge of the English language and a familiarity with fundamental community rituals?

The career of J.J. Maloney as recounted by Raymond Huel raises questions as to the "opportunities" Maloney perceived in the West for his anti-Roman Catholic crusade in contrast to Ontario, the locus of his initial successes. Huel demonstrates that Maloney enjoyed no small amount of favor in the West. Yet time and circumstance seemed to out-distance him. The success for which he yearned proved elusive, dooming him eventually to the obscurity many would feel he so richly deserved. The strengths and inadequacies of his personality and character as they altered over the years are obviously pertinent factors in explaining his successes and failures, but part of the explanation lies in the changing circumstances that Maloney encountered. An anti-Catholic crusade was possibly increasingly less meaningful in a society where communities re-defining "we-they" found regional collective interests an abiding concern.

C.A. Dunning's career stands in notable contrast to that of Maloney. J. William Brennan's study of this well-known western agrarian Liberal highlights the political aspects of the metropolitan relationship and the importance of political party in effecting western interests in a national context. The author rejects simplistic views of Dunning's career. While acknowledging the political gamesmanship involving Jimmy Gardiner, Brennan argues that Dunning's actions can be appreciated on the basis of Dunning's political assessment of circumstances rather than simply his personal ambition and vindictiveness. Likewise, in assessing his subject's work in the King cabinet the author finds that Dunning enjoyed much success in realizing western agrarian interests. Dunning's political path remained an option for westerners who would manipulate the metropolitan relationship in the region's interests. But as the 1930s unfolded, an increasing number of westerners were attracted to more radical and confrontationist political means for effecting these interests.

As a frontier, the West was a debtor area continually seeking credit on a basis that reflected the reality of its circumstances. While financial institutions other than the chartered banks were involved in the granting of western farm credit, Ted Regehr has chosen to study the chartered banks and their responses to the credit needs of a northern, mid-continent farming economy. The author views the actions of the banks as less than imaginative in several areas. Justifying their actions on the basis of "sound banking practices," which happened to be biased in terms of the metropolis rather than the hinterland, the banks were most laggard in responding to the particular credit needs of western farms. Yet in counterpoint, Regehr acknowledges the failure of western farmers to understand the importance of sound banking practices in sustaining their economy. The failure or success of western-based financial institutions in responding more recently to the credit needs of western farmers should provide some relevant criteria for comparison.

In recent years, westerners and Canadians elsewhere have appeared to become more cognizant of the West as a region. The concept of region in its socio-cultural context suggests distinctions from those of other regions, particularly the central provinces. The predominant view from the metropolis in the central provinces would appear to see western ways as but superficial distinctions in the commonality of the English-speaking Canadian experience. In the western hinterland, socio-cultural distinctions, while viewed as being "of degree" rather than "of kind," are seen as more substantive in nature. For westerners, answers to questions pertaining to socio-cultural distinctions lie in an understanding of the region's historical experience.

The relevant historical experiences were those shared in adapting individual and community ways to the evolving environmental circumstances in the West. Many of the shared experiences that emphasized a regional focus had their origin in one or more of the various metropolitan relationships. Such relationships were of equal or greater importance than the landscape and the climate in directing human adaptation to western circumstances. They were the mechanisms and the images that gave the West its regional experience. The essays in this volume demonstrate the range of subjects to be examined and the complexity of issues to be resolved before an understanding of the West's past can bear conclusively on current debates.

Notes

1. Chester Martin, "Dominion Lands" Policy. Edited and with an Introduction by Lewis H. Thomas (Toronto: McClelland and Stewart, 1973), p.10. While Martin's original phrase "purposes of the Dominion" was associated with lands policy, he clearly saw many of the broader implications arising out of such policies.

2. W.L. Morton, "Clio in Canada: The Interpretation of Canadian History," in A.B. McKillop, ed., *Contexts of Canada's Past: Selected History Essays of W.L. Morton* (Toronto: Macmillan, 1980), p. 109.

3. Eleanor Luxton's career is of interest in its own right. A long-time friend of Lewis H. Thomas, she was an honors graduate in English and History from the University of Alberta in 1930. She acquired, in subsequent years of the decade, a Bachelor of Education degree and a Master of Arts in History from the same university. After a brief stint teaching school in Alberta, she was employed by the Canadian Pacific Railway in Montreal in the design of steam locomotives. While with the C.P.R., she obtained a Bachelor of Science degree from Sir George Williams University. Serious illness forced Ms. Luxton to seek alternative employment, which included the management of a medical laboratory and lecturing at McGill University. In the mid-1950s she returned west to work as an historical researcher for the Glenbow Foundation (the Glenbow-Alberta Institute today) in Calgary. In the mid-1960s she returned to Banff, the community of her birth and childhood. She continues to write on aspects of her community's history and on the Stony Indians at Morley.

Lewis Herbert Thomas:
A Biographical Sketch

_____ Lewis Gwynne Thomas

Lewis Herbert Thomas was born in Saskatoon, Saskatchewan, on 13 April 1917. He was the only child of Robert Bremner Thomas (1867–1931) and Margaret Ross (1875–1931). Robert Bremner Thomas, a Nova Scotian of Welsh antecedents,[1] was, after a successful career in business,[2] ordained to the Methodist ministry and, at the time of his son's birth, had recently accepted a charge[3] near Saskatoon. His wife, Margaret Ross, was a daughter of a family long established in Cape Breton Island.[4] Soon the family moved to Bermuda,[5] an island of which they had such happy memories that Lewis H. was to revisit it during one of his sabbatical leaves. After two years they returned to Nova Scotia, where they remained for the remainder of their all too short lives.[6]

Their successive deaths left Lewis an orphan just after he had reached adolescence. For this reason, in 1931 he returned to Saskatoon, where his paternal aunt, Alice, and her husband, Dr. Herbert Weaver, had been long established. His high school and university years were thus spent in the Saskatchewan of the depression years. He graduated from the University of Saskatchewan in 1939 with High Honors in History and Economics. In spite of the depression, this was a period of great distinction for the University of Saskatchewan, when scholars like Arthur Silver Morton, MacGregor Dawson, and George Simpson were inspiring students like Hilda Neatby and Lewis H. to examine their roots in the Canadian past.

As his eyesight precluded service in the Armed Forces, Lewis continued his studies in Saskatchewan, and received his Master of Arts in History in 1941. He thesis, directed by Menzies Whitelaw, bore the title, "Constitutional Development of the North-West Territories,

1870–88." He then took a one-year high school teacher training course. He was awarded a fellowship by the Institute for International Education, and spent a year at the University of California, attracted there by the presence of three famous scholars, Frederick L. Paxson, John D. Hicks, and Herbert Eugene Bolton. From Berkeley he went to the University of Minnesota in Minneapolis. The University of Saskatchewan had received a grant from the Rockefeller Foundation to promote the development of archival work. Professor Simpson arranged for a grant to enable his former student to investigate the very fine archival facilities in Minnesota and the adjacent states. At the University of Minnesota, like Hilda Neatby before him, he prepared his doctoral dissertation under Professor A.L. Burt. Though his special interest was French Canada, Burt was, perhaps more than any other eminent Canadian scholar of his generation, interested in the ideas of Frederick Jackson Turner, ideas that had profoundly affected the development of the study of the history of the United States. The association with Burt was the basis of a lifelong friendship, which culminated in the publication of Lewis H.'s *The Renaissance of Canadian History: A Biography of A.L. Burt* in 1975. (*See* Appendix for a full bibliography of L.H. Thomas's writings).[7]

Under Burt's inspiration, Lewis H. chose as the field of his studies the political and constitutional history of the prairie West and as his thesis topic, "The Struggle for Responsible Government in the North-West Territories." Published by the University of Toronto Press in 1956, with a second edition in 1978, the book confirmed his reputation as a leading figure in the developing field of western Canadian history, complementing the earlier work of Arthur S. Morton and G.F.G. Stanley, and carrying the scholarly history of the region further forward in both time and space. Warmly received when it appeared, it remains one of the foundation stones of western Canadian studies. It was also the ground work for the view of the region developed in his later work, a view that, deep as his regional attachment has become, has never fallen into the manifest pitfalls of isolationism and provincialism.

Before he received his doctoral degree from Minnesota in 1953, and well before the appearance of *The Struggle for Responsible Government* (1956), Lewis returned to the University of Saskatchewan as a research assistant in the Department of History (1944–45). There, Professor Simpson, as part-time Provincial Archivist, was keenly interested in the appointment of a qualified full-time archivist. In 1946 Lewis H. was appointed Assistant Provincial Archivist of Saskatchewan, and in 1948 he became Provincial Archivist. Though the Saskatchewan Archives was built upon the devoted work of Arthur S. Morton and George Simpson, the institution as it emerged in the late 40s and early 50s as a model of its kind was very much the achievement of their pupil and successor. In the words of his former colleague Christine Macdonald, Legislative Librarian of Saskatchewan,

> working in his quiet way he was responsible for the excellence of the beginning of the Saskatchewan Archives, laying the foundation for the good reputation it has maintained over the years ... he was a very considerate person to work with and for, approachable when there were problems to be discussed, and willing to modify or change his opinion of methods to be employed when valid reasons were presented.... The Archives, as an example of what such an organization should be, was well enough known ... that a number of people from other countries were sent by an appropriate U.N. agency to survey it.[8]

His happy and fruitful years in the Archives at Regina were incomparably enriched by his marriage to Margaret Eleanor Telford in 1946. They met at the University of Saskatchewan, where she was a student from 1935 to 1938 and both were active in the Student Christian Movement. Brought up in Pelly, Saskatchewan, where her Ontario-born father was first a Baptist minister and then a lawyer,[9] Margaret had a grandstand view of the tribulations that beset the prairie West in the 1930s. Her mother, a graduate of McMaster, had earned the unusual distinction for those unliberated times of a master's degree in sociology from the University of Toronto.[10] Gertrude Telford threw herself with enthusiasm and zest into the reform movements then sweeping the prairies: temperance, the women's movement, and, above all, political reform as represented by the Progressives and, more to her advanced tastes, the C.C.F. in Saskatchewan. Her daughter, Margaret, after graduation from the University of Saskatchewan, went to the House of Commons secretarial staff in Ottawa in 1941 and then, from 1943 to 1946, was secretary to David Lewis. Mrs. Telford also worked in Ottawa from 1942 until 1944, when she returned to

Regina to live. She continued her lively interest in politics in Edmonton, where she made her home with Lewis and Margaret until she died in 1978 at the age of ninety-one.

This close association with prominent figures on the political left in Saskatchewan fed L.H.'s interest in the unique political history of the province and lies at the base of his most recent work, *The Making of a Socialist: The Recollections of T.C. Douglas* (1982). The years at the Archives in Regina were happy ones, marked for Lewis and Margaret by the birth of their two children, Jean Alice and Robert Telford. Their house on Angus Crescent, like their house in Windsor Park in Edmonton, always offered a warm welcome to a wide circle of friends. So deep and warm were the associations formed in Regina that Lewis H. has arranged to spend his retirement there. Lewis's activities in the field of archives, where he quickly earned a national reputation, were complemented by his work as Editor of *Saskatchewan History* from 1949 to 1957. This magazine from the first set high standards for its articles and reviews and was soon of far more than provincial interest.

In 1957, after better than a decade's devoted service to the Archives, years that had seen that institution assume an honored role among its peers, Lewis moved to the Regina campus of the University of Saskatchewan, later the University of Regina. Teaching was a natural extension of his vocation for history. As his work at the Archives and with *Saskatchewan History* had shown, he had a strong sense of the pastoral aspect of scholarship and much of his busy and active life has been spent in enabling others to pursue their scholarly goals. His publications, important as they have been and permanent as their value is, are only one aspect of the influence that he has had in his chosen profession of historian.

It was something of a surprise when in 1964 Lewis H. Thomas accepted the offer of an associate professorship in the Department of History at the University of Alberta. We had long been friends, indeed from the time when my supervisor at Harvard, Frederick Merk, had written rather plaintively to ask if it was true that I was then working on my Ph.D. at Minnesota under the supervision of Professor A.L. Burt. As I was then serving in the Canadian Navy, this first of many confusions because of the similarities of our names took some time to clear up.

By 1964 Lewis H.'s distinguished scholarship was well known to me and my colleagues at Alberta. We knew, too, of his remarkable accomplishments at the Saskatchewan Archives, to which we often pointed as a model for Alberta. We knew of the high repute in which he was held by eminent scholars like A.S. Morton and A.L. Burt in their generation and Hilda Neatby and Roger Graham in theirs. As I was to receive a sabbatical leave at the end of my six years as the Head of the Department, and as Lewis had expressed an interest in teaching at Alberta on a temporary basis, it seemed no breach of the informal agreement among the Heads of the four western Departments of History, not to poach in each other's preserves, to ask him to come as a visiting professor. When he suggested that he might be prepared to accept a permanent appointment, we were delighted. I suspect that Dr. Neatby was not altogether pleased, but she was too good a friend to bear malice.

As time passed we realized that Lewis H.'s commitment to scholarship and to his students and colleagues could be extended to embrace Saskatchewan's sister province. In his first year, the department was devastated by the tragic death of Barbara Fraser, an exceptionally promising young scholar who had quickly come to play an important part in our teaching of Canadian history. Lewis worked, humanely and effectively, to restore morale and in 1965 assumed the chairmanship, which he held until 1968 when his health obliged him to relinquish what was, in a difficult period of rapid growth, a taxing burden. By that time, he had, with the able assistance of Mrs. Beryl Steel, instituted an organization of the department's records and procedures that has been a blessing to his successors and the envy and model of other departments. He continued to serve as the wisest of counsellors in the department and gave generously to other aspects of the university's development, particularly to the establishment of the University of Alberta Archives. He was an active member of the Historical Society of Alberta in both its Edmonton and Alberta aspects and served as president of the Edmonton chapter, at once broadening the range of the society's interests and intensifying the interest in its activities of its academic constituency.

He served with particular distinction from 1968 to 1977 as Alberta's representative on the National Historic Sites Board of Canada. A passionate traveller with a devotion to the Canadian landscape and the Canadian culture reflected in his interest in Canadian arts and crafts, and especially in painting, he brought to the Board a view of the country and its history of singular breadth. He could respond with warmth and appreciation to every facet of the Canadian mosaic, intolerant only of the misuse of the cultural interest to serve the advantage of social or political ends. Himself an effective and skilled administrator, he has always been impatient with bureaucratic fumbling and has the true Socialist's contempt for the use of government powers of intervention to work against the common good. His curiosity about the environment, and especially about the more inaccessible parts of the mountains, and of the North, has led him into expeditions that appeared to challenge the powers of younger and apparently more robust companions, but from which he always emerged modestly and unobtrusively triumphant. It is not surprising that during his tenure, the Board, which previously seemed to some of its critics close to moribund, was able to instigate and support some changes that had a significant effect not only on Canada's historic sites but on its national park policy.

At the centre of L.H.'s career is his concern for scholarship that sees no dichotomy between teaching and research and embraces both the creation and transmission of man's knowledge of himself and his environment. At the University of Alberta he has played a major part in the development of the department's offerings in the field of Canadian history. While recognizing that the effective teaching of history depends upon the student's ability to relate the external world to his own experience, and thus to give the past a present meaning, he has consistently resisted any tendency to narrow possibilities of expanding that experience. When to know a great deal about very little has become a temptation not merely to the scholar but to the job seeker, he has always encouraged his students, his colleagues, and his friends to enlarge their horizons. Thus, when language departments resisted the introduction in the university curriculum of oriental languages, specifically Chinese, he lent his considerable support to the institution in the Department of History of a course called Historical Chinese, which now lies at the base of the work of the Department of East Asian Languages and Literature. Similarly, he has insisted that students who embark upon a specialization in western Canadian history must know, or be prepared to find out, a great deal about British social history, especially of the nineteenth century. His own ability to respond appreciatively to the traditions that have come together to form the country and the region in which he has spent most of his life is one of his most precious gifts to his students and his friends. This is set in a broad knowledge of a world to which he has always had the capacity to respond with excitement, whether as a reader or a traveller.

This openness in response to ideas makes it difficult to assign Lewis H. Thomas to any of the categories of historical thought that have been suggested for the convenient cataloguing of Canadian historians. His appreciation of the British contribution to world civilization does not make him uncritical of many British policies in relation to Canada and he is certainly far from the "Blood is thicker than water" school discerned by J.M.S. Careless. Though no historian of the Canadian West can escape the influence of Frederick Jackson Turner and his followers in the frontier school, Lewis H. has always been too conscious of the importance of the cultural baggage supporting or encumbering the settler to accept the westward movement as even beginning to describe, let alone explain, Canadian development. Yet his thinking reflects his sensitivity to the environment that he has missed no opportunity to explore at first hand.

The attitude of mind that runs most consistently through his writing is a reasoned outrage against the exploitation of man by his fellows and a sense of the dignity of the victim. This appears in his writing as early as *The Struggle for Responsible Government* as a muted protest against Canadian policies that, no matter how well intentioned they appeared to be, militated against the ultimate interest of the region that he had chosen as the focus of his view of history. The attitude may well be discerned in all his later work, whether it be his article on the Welsh migration of 1902 from Patagonia to Assiniboia or his various writings on Riel, the archetypal figure of the West as victim. It is apparent in his ability to take a fresh and dispassionate view of William Aberhart in *William Aberhart and the Social Credit in Alberta* (1977), a view that, briefly expressed though it is, does more to illuminate the tragedy of his relationship with Alberta than some of the volumes in the Social Credit series. Lewis H.'s unique perspective will also be recognized in his latest book, *The Making of a Socialist.*

His attitude is rooted in the theology of a man deeply influenced by the Christian tradition. A son of the parsonage, he has maintained a close relationship to the church. He was an active member of the Student Christian Movement as an undergraduate at Saskatchewan and has retained, through all the turmoil that has enlivened the life of the denominations that are commonly seen as part of the Canadian religious establishment, a calm, if gently critical, assurance that Christianity has an ultimate relevance.

The relationship of L.H.'s religious convictions to his conduct of his life has been admirably expressed by Brian Heeney, a close friend and colleague during his early years at Alberta, who shared the conviction that the role of the scholar, or indeed of any professional, is essentially pastoral:

> My recollections of Lewis in my time in Edmonton are really three-fold: as chairman, churchman and friend. His special character in the first role was a combination of strength and gentle consideration. He would go to almost any length, to great personal inconvenience and labour, in order to help his colleagues achieve their personal ends and to ease their burdens. On the other hand, there were limits to the absurdities he would tolerate, and I think all his colleagues were grateful for the shape to departmental life that these limits helped to provide. Lewis is a theologian of no mean calibre, and a Christian of high quality; as an Anglican clergyman I felt the support of this United Church layman on many occasions. The most striking of Lewis' many qualities of personal friendship in my experience is his warm loyalty. He can be absolutely relied upon for a warm welcome, for an expression of interest, and for certain support.[11]

His convictions are often implicit in his choice of subject, and I think they clearly affect the standards against which he examines human conduct. They do not, however, constitute a theory of history, though they have everything to do with the way he writes and teaches, two activities that are difficult to separate. Conviction is in no way irreconcilable with a scrupulous objectivity, which is concerned, not with conclusions, but with the way conclusions are reached. A passage in a recent paper, "The C.C.F. Victory in Saskatchewan, 1944," is revealing in its frankness. Here, L.H. examines the literature that discusses the C.C.F. in Saskatchewan in terms of social science:

> One glaring defect in the works of sociologists and political scientists is the failure to assess the impact of the social gospel on the ideology of the Saskatchewan CCF and of its record in office. All these writers are secularists, who are probably incapable of either

appreciating the significance of the social gospel and Christian Socialism, or of realizing its influence on the more important leaders of the CCF....[12]

There could scarcely be a franker expression of the writer's own convictions, but what is more significant is the demand that every consideration be taken into view and the implicit assertion that the historian must be capable of a sympathetic understanding of many points of view. Otherwise he will ignore a substantial body of evidence that bears upon his topic and thus fail in his primary purpose, the intellectual reconstruction of the past, and its objective presentation.

Lewis H. has been a central figure in the scholarly re-examination of western Canada's history at a time when that field has been attracting a new generation of Canadian historians. No one has a more thorough knowledge of the resources for its study and interpretation; he has, indeed, himself been an unfailing and invaluable resource to everyone involved in the field. No biographical sketch would be complete without a reference to his role at the various meetings and conferences that are so much a part of Canadian academic life, and perhaps particularly important to western historians — "western" in the geographic sense as well as in the sense of regional specialization — because of their relatively small number and their relative isolation in terms of the distance of one department from another. His contribution to the network of communications that now exists between them, many of whom are his former students, would be difficult to exaggerate.

The centrality of his contribution to the development of western Canadian studies in the last thirty years was never more apparent than at the annual meeting of the Canadian Historical Association in Saskatoon in 1979. The University of Regina had awarded him the degree of Doctor of Laws in 1972[13] and, in 1979, he was the guest of honor, as the first full-time Provincial Archivist of Saskatchewan, at a dinner given by the Saskatchewan Archives Board to celebrate its thirty-fifth anniversary. The next day, the incoming President of the Canadian Historical Association, Professor R. Craig Brown of the University of Toronto, presented him with the rarely awarded distinction of an Honorary Life Membership, a presentation greeted with a standing ovation. On 5 June he read a warmly received paper, "Socialism in Saskatchewan, 1944." The cordiality and warmth of the meetings, and the high standard of the papers in the field of western Canadian history, were less formal but equally real tributes to the contribution of Lewis Herbert Thomas.

It has been suggested earlier that it is not easy to assign L.H. Thomas to any specific school of Canadian historians. It seems to me that to do so would be to misread the man and to misrepresent the quality of his scholarship. He has devoted his life, in all its aspects, to a search for an understanding of the complexity of Canada, with its many regions, its varied cultural inheritance, its complicated and indeed unique relationships with the world beyond its borders, its inheritance of displacement, its vast natural wealth, and its harsh physiographic realities. To the many interpretations of the Canadian experience that have been presented by Canadian scholarship, he has been open and appreciative insofar as they can cast new illumination on the scene that he loves so well, but I think he is not convinced that any holds the only key to unlock the riddle of the Canadian identity. The fruitful course of his life, and all that it has meant to his family, his friends, and his students, suggests that the way of the pilgrim, though it may be hard, is not without reward.

Notes

1. His father, Lewis Thomas (1842–80) came from Lallaston, Wales, to Nova Scotia, where he married Elizabeth Bremner (1843–1934).

2. He was for eighteen years an agent of the Canadian Express Company.

3. His responsibilities included the towns of Fleming, Cupar, and Hazenmore.

4. Her father, Dr. Jeptho G. Ross, was of a family that had come from Skye to Cape Breton in the 1820s. The family of her mother, Margaret Salter, came originally from Ireland.

5. As Officiating Clergyman to Wesleyans in the Army and Navy, Ireland Island, Bermuda.

6. The Thomases resided at Granville Ferry (1926–29), Port Hood (1929–30), and Collingwood (1930–31), all in Nova Scotia.

7. L.H. Thomas was at the University of Minnesota from 1942 to 1944. In 1942 he received a fellowship for one year's graduate study in the United States from the Institute of International Education, New York.

8. Christine Macdonald to Lewis G. Thomas, 13 April 1981.

9. John M. Telford was born at Valens, near Galt, Ontario, in 1878 and died in 1963. In 1944 he went to Regina as Clerk of the Executive Council and a lawyer in the Department of Social Welfare. He also acted as Chief Electoral Officer. He retired in 1958.

10. Gertrude Sarah Steinhoff was born at Simcoe, Ontario, in 1887 and died in 1978. Her thesis topic was "Livingstone (No. 331–Saskatchewan) A Rural Survey."

11. W.B.D. Heeney to Lewis G. Thomas, 11 November 1980.

12. Lewis H. Thomas, "The CCF Victory in Saskatchewan, 1944." *Saskatchewan History*, vol. XXXIV (Winter 1981), no. 1, p. 1.

13. Among the many publications that established Lewis H. Thomas as a leading authority on the history of Saskatchewan is *The University of Saskatchewan 1909–1959* (1959).

The Hudson's Bay Company's Prairie Transportation Problem, 1870–85

_____ A. A. den Otter

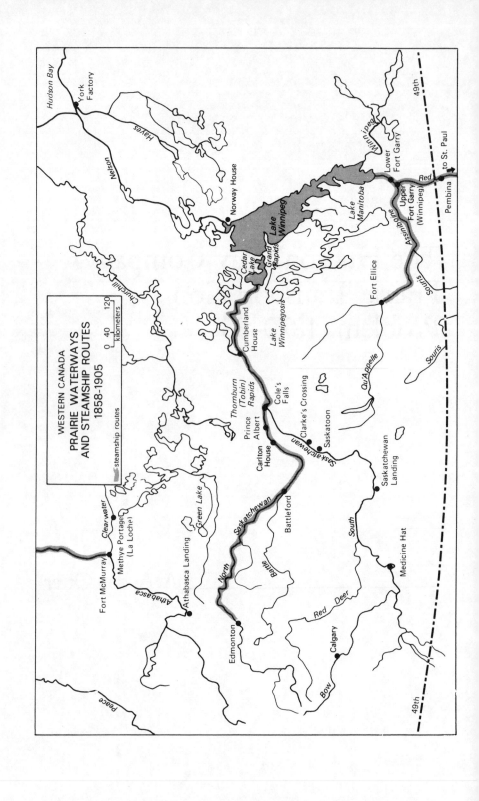

WESTERN CANADA
PRAIRIE WATERWAYS
AND STEAMSHIP ROUTES
1858-1905

0 40 120
kilometers

▬▬ steamship routes

Hudson Bay

York Factory

Hayes

Nelson

Churchill

Norway House

Lake Winnipeg

Grand Rapids

Cedar Lake

Cumberland House

Lake Winnipegosis

Lake Manitoba

Lower Fort Garry

Upper Fort Garry (Winnipeg)

Assiniboine

Red

Pembina

to St. Paul

49th

Fort Ellice

Souris

Souris

Qu'Appelle

Thornburn (Tobin) Rapids

Cole's Falls

Prince Albert

Carlton House

Clarke's Crossing

Saskatoon

Saskatchewan

Saskatchewan Landing

Battleford

North Saskatchewan

Battle

South

Medicine Hat

Red Deer

Bow

Calgary

Edmonton

Green Lake

Athabasca Landing

Clearwater

Methye Portage (La Loche)

Fort McMurray

Athabasca

Peace

49th

The 1869–70 Red River insurrection was the catharsis forcing the Hudson's Bay Company to come to terms with the new order imposing its ways upon the Canadian Northwest. Riel's confrontation with the first major wave of the new technological society was a clear warning that the tradition-bound fur business might succumb unless it adopted the techniques of the modern business world. With American railways reaching the Upper Mississippi, and with Canadian surveyors criss-crossing the prairies in search of a suitable railway route, the Company could no longer afford to rely on old and well-tried carrying methods. The complex Yorkboat shuttle, from York or Moose factories on Hudson Bay, or alternatively from Fort Garry and the Red River via Norway House to the outlying plains and forests of the northwestern territories, was too slow and expensive. At best, four years were required to realize a return on capital invested in trade goods. In 1869 and again in 1870, valuable furs were left in the country, accumulating interest charges and thus eroding profits. Moreover, this fragile system depended upon Indian and Métis tripmen, who were expensive to hire and feed, who were very difficult to recruit for the backbreaking work, and who, as the uprising and previous incidents demonstrated, were able to cripple the entire system at whim.[1] In such circumstances the Company had to prepare to meet the competition of newcomers well versed in the techniques and tools of the modern business world. To meet the challenge, the Hudson's Bay Company had to reduce operating expenses: transportation appeared among the most obvious areas in which to increase efficiency and consequently reduce costs.

To the men in the field, the answer was steamboats. In the summer of 1870 a council of chief factors instructed Donald A. Smith, the newly apppointed chief commissioner, to get permission from the governor and committee in London to build a steamer on Lake Winnipeg and another on the Saskatchewan River. They also wanted a tramway to skirt the turbulent Grand Rapids on the Saskatchewan River near Lake Winnipeg. By utilizing steamboats on the prairie waterways in conjunction with existing rail and steamer connections between England and the Red River, the factors hoped that all trade goods could be shipped into the country in a single season, thereby avoiding the customary, costly winter storage at Norway House.

The London directors, swayed by the promise of quicker returns on their capital, decided to apply nineteenth-century industrial technology to the Hudson's Bay Company's transportation problem. The committee was even willing to invest a considerable amount of money in order to reduce excessive transportation costs and to free the Company from dependence upon "fickle voyageurs."[2] After conducting a feasibility study, the board authorized the construction of a new steamer, which was launched on 7 May 1872 and christened the *Chief Commissioner* in honor of Donald Smith. Commenting on the successful launch, Sir Stafford Henry Northcote, the Hudson's Bay Company governor, noted that the new lake steamer and American railways would allow a much faster turnover of trade goods and thus improve profits.[3]

Donald Smith, the driving force behind the steamer scheme, advocated the Lake Manitoba-Winnipegosis rather than the Lake Winnipeg route to the Saskatchewan River. He argued that the distance was shorter and the navigation season longer, and believed that with only three inexpensive canals, the route would eliminate costly portages, particularly the infamous Grand Rapids. Low water on the Dauphine River foiled the *Chief Commissioner,* however, and the following year the federal government refused to assume the cost of constructing the canals. Both incidents were ominous portents of the future. The *Chief Commissioner* was shunted to the rough waters of Lake Winnipeg for which the keelless vessel was ill-suited.[4]

Lack of proper planning continued to plague the efforts of the Company. In 1873 it built a river steamer just above the Grand Rapids. Poorly designed, the boat was not powerful enough to ascend the Demi-Charge Rapids near Cedar Lake. While the still unnamed vessel was being warped up the rapids she struck a rocky shoal and foundered.[5] Thus, the Company's second ship also proved unsuitable for its task.

The next summer an American crew constructed a better vessel. An exact replica of the familiar Mississippi stern-wheelers, the 150-foot *Northcote* commenced its maiden voyage late in August 1874. "If she is successful," James A. Grahame, the new chief commissioner, wrote his superiors, "the relief to our transportation business will be immense and with the proper boat on Lake Winnipeg our Interior Districts can be fully supplied with goods at a shorter time and less expense."[6] The plan worked this time and the *Northcote*, after ten days' steaming, reached Carlton House with a cargo of trade goods. Although the ship had recouped much of its cost in a single trip, James Grahame insisted on utmost frugality. The *Northcote* would have no passenger accommodation and provide no furniture for the crew. In future, only the officers could be American; the remainder of the crew had to be recruited locally for the shipping season only.[7]

Despite the *Northcote*'s successful maiden voyage, steam technology did not replace traditional methods in 1875. To be sure, the stern-wheeler completed a dramatic voyage to Edmonton on 22 July laden with cargo that had left Lower Fort Garry an unprecedented thirty-three days earlier. But once back at Grand Rapids, the river boat had to wait a full month for the next load. The *Chief Commissioner* had crossed Lake Winnipeg early in the spring but the trip had weakened her hull so severely that she was unsafe for another voyage. Her replacement, the *Colvile*, did not reach Grand Rapids until 3 September, too late in the season for the *Northcote* to travel beyond Carlton. To continue the flow of goods, Chief Commissioner Grahame commanded a flotilla of twenty-eight small boats and one schooner to ferry supplies and returns between Red River and Grand Rapids, York and Grand Rapids, and between Grand Rapids and La Loche Portage by way of Cumberland House. Although at times the boats were laden with three tons of goods, the shuttle service employed a crew of well over a hundred men for an entire summer and hinged on precision timing with no appreciable delays. In addition to this armada, the company also chartered an expensive army of four hundred carts to transport the *Northcote*'s cargo to destinations beyond Carlton House.[8]

Despite the many problems, the limited use of steamboats in 1875 demonstrated their cost efficiency in relation to Yorkboats and overland routes. And, as the general depression of the 1870s drove down fur prices, Company officials were ever more determined to reduce operation expenses by improving their transportation network. In fact, Chief Commissioner Grahame recognized that transportation was his most pressing problem. He resolved to establish Carlton House as the steamboat supply depot for the northern trade. The previous summer he had already employed a crew to reopen the trail from Carlton to Green Lake, and for 1876 he planned to improve the La Loche Portage, and place a small steamer on the Clearwater River and a larger boat on the Athabasca River.[9] These plans gained urgency when a group of Winnipeg merchants formed the North West Trading Company for the purpose of placing steamers on the Lake Winnipeg-Saskatchewan River run. Although Grahame believed that the Hudson's Bay Company could outlast an upstart competitor, he nevertheless fretted that several seasons of cutting freight rates would have a devastating effect upon the Company, especially once the railway from St. Paul was completed.[10] Therefore, as the accoutrements of civilization moved into the Hudson's Bay Company's old domain, Grahame resolved to meet the challenge by utilizing the most modern techniques the Company could afford.

In keeping with this policy, Grahame called for a substantial investment to eliminate one of the major obstacles to the efficient use of the steamboats—the Grand Rapids portage. Just before the Saskatchewan River emptied into Lake Winnipeg, a steep limestone channel entrapped the river and in less than two miles dropped it a turbulent seventy-four feet. Portaging the rapids was a time-consuming, laborious task and from the very beginning of the steamboat program, Hudson's Bay Company officials had talked about building a tramway around the rapids. As early as 1872 the Company had surveyed and obtained title to small parcels of land at both ends of the rapids and in 1876 acquired a lease to a fifty-foot right-of-way. Commissioner Grahame stockpiled construction materials during the summer of 1876 and the following year hired Walter Moberly, a civil engineer, to build the three-and-a-half mile, narrow-gauge rail line equipped with four horse-drawn wagons. For an expenditure of $20,000, Grahame removed a major bottleneck.[11]

Although there were repeated pleas from Company directors for cost-cutting measures in order to meet the severely depressed fur market, Graham continued to invest in transportation improvements. In

1876 he arranged the purchase of a new steamer, the *Lily,* from the Clyde shipyards of Yarrow and Company. Built at a cost of £4,000, the two-decked vessel had a steel hull and represented a departure from the typical American river steamer. It was an ill-fated and expensive experiment. Grahame intended the vessel to operate on the Carlton-Edmonton run and thus wanted her assembled above Cole's Falls. The various sections of the *Lily* arrived too late on the Saskatchewan to be shipped upriver, however, and she was assembled above the Grand Rapids.[12] The following spring, she took aboard part of the Athabasca and Mackenzie outfits but, because of low water, could not take them beyond Cumberland. Although faster than any other sternwheeler, she drew four more inches of water than planned. She could not be used again that year, nor did she do better in 1878. After extensive engine modifications she finally travelled up to Edmonton in 1878 but hit a rock on the way back. Repairs to the damaged hull put her out of commission for the rest of the season.

The *Northcote* was hardly more successful. While she had been effective in 1877, she made only a few voyages in the low waters of 1878 and severely damaged her hull while descending Cole's Falls. Although repaired in time for the 1879 season, low water again frustrated her progress. On her third trip that summer, the *Northcote* failed to ascend Cole's Falls; she was beached for the year and her cargo forwarded by carts to Carlton. After eight years of planning and vigorous action, steamship technology had not yet conquered the capricious North Saskatchewan.

The lacklustre performance of the steamboats coincided with the general economic depression of the 1870s. At a time of dismal profits, the Hudson's Bay Company found itself committed to an expensive capital investment program that failed to improve its cumbersome transportation system.[13] Naturally, the committee began to look for a scapegoat and found it in James A. Grahame. The chief commissioner had come into office at the start of the decline in fur prices and during the past five years had been unable to restore the Company's fortunes. Although he labored tirelessly to cut overhead expenses by continuously exhorting his charges to lower their inventories and tariffs, by ruthlessly abandoning unprofitable ports, and by boldly risking the steamboat scheme, he had not produced tangible improvements. That Grahame could not control the level of water on the Saskatchewan nor stem the fall of prices in Russia was of little concern to those who missed their dividends. Factors, shareholders, and directors demanded new ideas and novel concepts; they wanted fresh faces and different approaches. James A. Grahame, who had joined the company in 1843 and served as factor in a number of important posts, was too closely identified with the fur trade and the old way of doing business. He was seen as being unable to provide dynamic leadership in a new era. "The rapid changes that are passing over ... [Winnipeg] since the Railway connection [to St. Paul] has been made are enough to make one pause," he wrote the board secretary, "If I am overcautious I would prefer being thought so rather than act rashly."[14] In 1879, when railways were advancing upon the Northwest, heralding a new age, it was not a confession the board wanted to hear. They fancied a confident executive – someone familiar with colonization, general merchandising, and especially someone at home in the complex politics of railways.[15]

Despite their wish to embrace the new order, Governor Goschen and his committee clung to the vestiges of their old paternal system. When Donald Smith resigned his land commissionership in February 1879, the committee readily accepted the unsolicited application of Charles J. Brydges, the recently dismissed general superintendent of government railways. Brydges appeared to be the ideal candidate. For the past twenty-six years he had been involved in every major railway undertaking in Canada, including the Great Western, Grand Trunk, and Intercolonial. He had meticulously cultivated close friendships with senior bureaucrats and leading politicians of all persuasions. Moreover, he was a friend of John Rose, a member of the Hudson's Bay Company's governing committee. Curiously, the board gave Brydges shared responsibility with the chief commissioner but never informed Grahame of this fact.[16] In keeping with tradition, the Company preferred not to fire a trusted old employee, but instead, replaced him surreptitiously.

If the Company welcomed a whirlwind of reform, they could not have chosen a better man. Brydges' computerlike mind immediately set out to create order and system out of the casual, sometimes haphazard, ways of the Smith and Grahame team. After an exhausting 2,500-mile tour of the Northwest, the new commissioner began a shake-up of the senior administration, initiated a comprehensive survey of the Company's land holdings, and created the complex bureaucratic structure needed to administer this real-estate empire. Recognizing Winnipeg as the future metropolis of the Northwest, he moved his office there and eventually centralized the Company's Canadian operations in that city. Every nook and cranny of the Company's domain felt the impact of Brydges' technocratic obsession for organization and expansion; in every way, his appointment signalled the beginning of a new era.[17]

As instructed, C.J. Brydges also turned his attention to the prairie transportation problem. His first objective was the removal of the most troublesome physical impediments to efficient river navigation. Within months of taking office, Brydges, who was accustomed to massive government railway subsidies, asked the Public Works Department to remove boulders from various rapids on the Saskatchewan River, to construct warping piers and wing dams at some of the major falls, and to dredge the mouth of the Red River. When the department did not respond immediately, Brydges repeated his request, adding that the Hudson's Bay Company had opened its steamers to public traffic and reduced its freight rates, thereby benefitting the North West Mounted Police and the Indian Department. He also promised to spend $100,000 "to put two additional steamers on [the Saskatchewan River and Lake Winnipeg]... provided we can have the assurance that the river will be put into such a condition as will enable the boats to run with safety."[18] After Hector Langevin, the Minister of Public Works, balked at the proposal, Brydges scrapped the idea of wing dams and offered to have the Company build the piers, leaving the government to spend $20,000 on other improvements. To bolster his bid, he asked his personal friend, Sir John A. Macdonald, to prod his colleagues into action. In October 1879 the cabinet agreed to spend $2,000 immediately to dredge the Red River and promised to seek appropriations for boulder removal during the coming session of Parliament.[19]

While the government's obligations were relatively minor, those of the Hudson's Bay Company were not. In fact, Brydges' unauthorized promise to spend $100,000 alarmed the governor's committee and they quickly vetoed his wholesale expansionist plans. Chastened, Brydges carefully explained that the idea for additional steamboats had come from Governor Colvile and Chief Commissioner Grahame, and that he personally preferred to build one or two barges to be towed by the *Colvile*.[20] Fortunately, the government had not yet begun the dredging work and thus Brydges could still back out of his offer. "When the [Red River] bar is dredged," he informed Langevin, "and sufficient depth of water provided, the question of building another steamer will, of course, be carefully considered, should the growth of traffic prove to be more than the present steamer and barges can handle."[21]

As promised in his appeals for government help, Brydges opened the steamboats to public traffic. This drastic change in policy brought him in conflict with Chief Commissioner Grahame, who had developed the steamboats primarily for the fur trade. Brydges, however, argued that the failure to open the boats to general cargo could lead to the establishment of rival lines on the river. Brydges wrote his superiors:

> I have represented to Mr. Grahame very strongly indeed, that unless the company is prepared to make its boats available for public traffic and especially in regards for the Indian Department, that there will undoubtedly be an opposition line of boats put upon the river, which will have the effect of opening up the whole of the northern country for supplies for fur trading purposes in direct opposition to the Hudson's Bay Company.[22]

It was a telling argument, not lost on Grahame. In fact, three years earlier he had authorized the *Northcote* to transport some government goods. The following spring Grahame warned the board that the Company had to be careful about carrying government supplies because the *Northcote* had experienced difficulty in meeting the contract. Nevertheless, he asked permission to compete with the Montana-based firm of I.G. Baker for the Mounted Police and Indian department contracts. The committee, horrified by the prospect of large capital expenditures on additional ships at a time of retrenchment, vetoed the idea. Since the board had not informed him of a reversal in policy, Grahame naturally opposed Brydges, and when the land commissioner bid on several government contracts without consulting him, he protested that Brydges was exceeding his authority.[23] The board upheld Brydges' argument that unless the Company took on government contracts, it would encourage competing lines, but instructed him to work more closely with Grahame.

Accordingly, the two men worked out a policy for the carriage of public goods and passengers. They prepared a schedule of rates for points west of Winnipeg low enough to discourage the government from subsidizing other carriers yet sufficiently high to earn the Company a good profit. Grahame, who was still worried that low water might hamper the fleet, insisted first on a stipulation that higher rates would prevail should the Company have to resort to land transportation and, second, on a disclaimer from any rigid delivery deadlines. To meet the anticipated increase in traffic, Grahame had a wooden sheath placed around the *Lily*'s vulnerable steel hull and had a passenger saloon installed on the *Northcote*.[24]

The Hudson's Bay Company's new policy did not eliminate all competition. Since the Company could hire steamers only as far as Fort Ellice on the Assiniboine River, it had to surrender the southwestern corner of the prairies to the I.G. Baker firm in Fort Benton, with their own well-established transportation network.[25] Of greater concern to the Company was the rumor that no less than two companies planned to take advantage of the steady growth of population along the Saskatchewan River by establishing rival steamboat lines. While the Hudson's Bay Company willingly ceded the Southwest to I.G. Baker, it would not surrender its hold on the Saskatchewan, the gateway to its fur domain. To meet the threat from competing steamboats, the Company became actively involved in both ventures and eventually merged its own transportation interests with them. It was to be a last-ditch effort to control access to the fur empire before the Canadian Pacific Railway would open the fur forest to all comers.

The policy of maintaining a controlling interest in rival transportation concerns was not a new departure for the Hudson's Bay Company. Within months of Captain Anson Northup's successful voyage down the Red River in 1859, the Company had bankrolled J.C. Burbank & Co. to buy his *Anson Northup* and monopolize river traffic. The arrangement was kept secret because American law forbade foreign companies to own property on United States soil.[26] Subsequently, the Company transferred the management of the *Anson Northup*, and a second vessel, the *International*, to its agent, Norman W. Kittson, who maintained an intermittent service throughout the next decade. By 1871, however, when the Northern Pacific reached the Red River at Moorhead and the St. Paul and Pacific arrived at Breckenridge, the Hudson's Bay Company once again felt the hot breath of competition. James J. Hill, the ambitious partner of the St. Paul firm of Hill, Griggs & Company, launched the *Selkirk* and, after the Hudson's Bay Company refused his services, declared that a congressional law permitted only American ships to carry goods on rivers within the United States. The British company successfully thwarted Hill by transferring the ownership of the *International* to Kittson, who was an American citizen. Competition, however, served only to reduce rates and profits; therefore, in 1872 the two rivals founded the Red River Transportation Company, which set preferential tariffs for the Hudson's Bay Company and ruled the river virtually unchallenged until 1878.[27] It was to be an extremely lucrative monopoly. In 1878, for example, the Red River Transportation Company paid a dividend of 80 percent to all its shareholders, including the Hudson's Bay Company.[28]

The two active principals in the Red River Transportation Company, J.J. Hill and Norman Kittson, as well as their mutual friend and Hudson's Bay Company employee, Donald Smith, had more faith in the future of railways than of steamboats. In the spring of 1877 the three men persuaded George Stephen, president of the Bank of Montreal, to help them buy out the defunct St. Paul and Pacific Railway with the object of extending the line to Winnipeg and across the plains to Puget Sound. The complex deal, finally completed a year later, required that both Hill and Kittson sign over all but a few of their Red River Transportation Company shares to the venture.[29] The resuscitation of the railway company with the steamboat shares meant that the Hudson's Bay Company was linked to the new railway, renamed the St. Paul, Minneapolis and Manitoba. In March 1878 Grahame predicted that the day of the Red River steamboats would soon be over and he recommended a more extensive amalgamation with the railway firm. The extravagant ambitions of Hill went far beyond the capital resources of the Hudson's Bay Company, however, and in the end the Company retained only a very small stake in the St. Paul railway.[30] The Company might have been successful in controlling the relatively inexpensive steamboat mode of transportation, but it could not afford to dominate the very costly field of railway technology.

The completion of the rail link between St. Paul and Winnipeg rang the death-knell for the Red River steamboats, but it also established Winnipeg as the distribution centre for western Canada. In 1878 a group of Montreal, Winnipeg, and St. Paul business men formed the Winnipeg and Western Transportation Company to operate steamships in western Canada. They purchased the *Alpha* and *Cheyenne* from the Red River Transportation Company and operated them on the lower Red River and the Assiniboine. Within two years the new company also acquired the Red River Transportation Company's *Manitoba* and *Minnesota*, lengthened them both by fifty feet, and rechristened the latter the *City of Winnipeg*. By then the C.P.R. had decided to follow the southern route across the prairies parallel to the Assiniboine River. Since steamboats could not compete with fast, year-round rail service, the Winnipeg and Western Transportation Company decided to transfer its ships to the Saskatchewan River, in direct rivalry with the Hudson's Bay Company's steamers.[31]

While the C.P.R. confined its operations to the southern prairies, the North Saskatchewan appeared wide open for steamboat investments. A Scottish enterprise, the Dundee Mortgage and Trust Investment Company represented by the Montreal and Winnipeg firm of Drummond Brothers and Company, proposed to duplicate the Hudson's Bay Company's system by placing a steamer on Lake Winnipeg and another on the Saskatchewan River. The seemingly well-financed proposal caused considerable concern among Hudson's Bay Company officials. In November 1880, C.J. Brydges suggested to C.S. Drummond that they work out an agreement for "mutual action and concert [which] would be better than strong competition."[32] Brydges suggested the formation of a new company, to be capitalized at $200,000 and called the North West Navigation Company. He proposed that the new company purchase from the Hudson's Bay Company the *Lily, Northcote, Colvile*, the derelict *Chief Commissioner*, the Grand Rapids tramway, and all warehouses and barges for $100,000 in shares. Further, he proposed that the Hudson's Bay Company have an option to buy an additional 25 percent of the shares and enjoy a 33 ⅓- percent rebate on freight rates. Lastly, Brydges recommended that the proposed company build two new steamers, one for the Saskatchewan, and the other for Lake Winnipeg.

In principle, James Grahame liked the idea. It meant that the boats would be managed by professional staff rather than by fur traders, but still give the Hudson's Bay Company preferential treatment over those "who might try to tap our Northern Districts."[33] He was less enthusiastic about the construction of new ships and believed the value of the Hudson's Bay Company facilities at $100,000 to be too low. With the express approval of the board he took charge of the negotiations, assigning Brydges an advisory role. By February 1881 Grahame and the Drummonds had increased the capitalization of the new company to $250,000, left the evaluation of the Hudson's Bay Company plant in abeyance, but reached a stalemate on the rebate issue. The negotiations collapsed when Peter McArthur, a Winnipeg lumber baron and owner of an Assiniboine freighter, the *Marquette*, announced he would build a large vessel, the *North West*, to ply the North Saskatchewan. The prospect of competition frightened the Drummonds and their associates. With lower profits a distinct possibility, they balked at giving the Hudson's Bay Company a guaranteed one-third rebate on all future freight rates. Despite Grahame's repeated assurances that, without access to the Grand Rapids tramway no company could challenge the Hudson's Bay Company's hegemony, the Drummonds refused to promise more than a 10-percent freight rebate. Even though no final agreement was reached before the North West Navigation Company was incorporated in 1881, Grahame and Brydges were named to the board of directors, and the company commissioned the construction of a new lake steamer, the *Princess*.[34]

The break in the impasse came in June 1881 when the Winnipeg and Western Transportation Company, which was planning to transfer its fleet to the Saskatchewan River, offered the Hudson's Bay Company a 15-percent rebate on its freight and an amalgamation accord. At first, Grahame wanted to defer consideration of the proposal until he had concluded his talks with the North West Navigation Company, but he changed his mind. The previous year, he had sold the Hudson's Bay Company's interest in the St. Paul, Minneapolis and Manitoba Railway and purchased a small share in the Winnipeg steamboat firm.[35] He also realized that an amalgamation of the two existing fleets would save the Hudson's Bay Company costly investments in new boats. By late summer he and Brydges had worked out the details. The Winnipeg and Western Transportation Company increased its capitalization to $250,000, took over the Hudson's Bay Company fleet and tramway for $100,000 in shares, and laid plans to place the *Manitoba* and *City of Winnipeg* on the Saskatchewan River. The Hudson's Bay Company also bought 2,763 shares for $38,150 and thus ensured a controlling interest in the amalgamated firm. James Grahame was appointed president, while C.J. Brydges and Alexander Christie, a chief factor at Red River, were named directors.[36]

The new arrangement did not enjoy an auspicious start. In September 1881, the 190-foot *City of Winnipeg* left Selkirk, towed by the new *Princess,* for the perilous journey across Lake Winnipeg. The keelless boat was ill-suited for lake travel, particularly in the stormy fall season. Indeed, a violent storm battered the fragile vessel to pieces, and after she was cut loose from the *Princess,* she foundered on the rocky lake shore. An angry Grahame calculated the loss at $15,000 and blamed Brydges for finalizing the amalgamation agreement before the boats were safely docked above the Grand Rapids. His annoyance was eased somewhat by the knowledge that the machinery of the *City of Winnipeg* had been removed prior to the journey and that the Winnipeg and Western Transportation Company had just paid the Hudson's Bay Company a $2,500 dividend.[37]

The accident did not end the attempt to monopolize steamboating in western Canada. In fact, it spurred the Winnipeg businessmen to seek closer co-operation. A general freighting alliance was given even greater urgency as the C.P.R. progressed across the prairies. As Grahame explained, once the C.P.R. bridged the South Saskatchewan River, the usual steamboat routes would be obsolete. Instead of docking at Grand Rapids, the river steamers would load at the river crossing, sail down the South Saskatchewan to the Forks, and steam up the North Saskatchewan. It would be foolish, Grahame argued, to operate two competing fleets on both the river and the lake when a simple division of territory was more efficient and, of course, more profitable. As president of the Winnipeg and Western Transportation Company and a director of the North West Navigation Company, he had little difficulty concluding an agreement. The Winnipeg and Western Transportation Company agreed to sell the *Colvile* to the North West Navigation Company and promised to stay off Lake Winnipeg for the next three years. In return, the North West Navigation Company pledged not to work the Saskatchewan River. In the face of such a clear division of territory, Peter McArthur could not remain aloof. He sold both his *North West* and *Marquette* to the North West Navigation Company and joined the Winnipeg and Western Transportation Company as managing director. In the final step of the arrangement, the North West Navigation Company sold the *North West* to the Winnipeg and Western Transportation Company. The Hudson's Bay Company assumed the responsibility of transferring the vessel to the Saskatchewan,[38] a task it completed in the summer of 1881. The

Marquis and *Manitoba* followed the *North West* that same summer. In a relatively simple way, with no heavy capital expenditures on ship construction, Grahame created a monopoly on both Lake Winnipeg and the Saskatchewan, won a preferential position for the Hudson's Bay Company, maintained general control over a fleet of five river and three lake steamers, and delegated management responsibilities to experienced personnel.

The collusion was not as profitable as the negotiators had envisioned. The agreement rested on the assumption that the Canadian government would improve navigation on the Saskatchewan. It was an idle presupposition. Although the government had agreed to spend $20,000 on river improvements, it was in no hurry to act. It did nothing in 1881, ostensibly because its engineer had no time to make the required preliminary studies. This bureaucratic procrastination angered C.J. Brydges, who noted ruefully, "Unfortunately there are no political results likely to follow the removal of boulders from Cole's Falls."[39] To speed matters, he proposed that the Hudson's Bay Company do the work provided the government covered the expenses. The administration still did not accept the offer until July 1882, much too late in the season to commence the project.

When finally carried out, the river improvements were only minor, and, significantly, confined entirely to the North Saskatchewan. During the summer of 1882, the Hudson's Bay Company employed one barge to remove the largest boulders from Cole's Falls and another to clear out an eighty-mile section below Edmonton. The following summer a small crew continued the work on Cole's Falls, made a survey of the North Saskatchewan, and placed navigational aids on several islands. The cost for two years of work, carried out by the Hudson's Bay Company, totalled only $25,000. The government spent another $35,000 in subsequent years, most of it on Cole's Falls.[40] Compared to the massive subsidies to prairie railways, the expenditures on river improvements were miniscule and clearly indicated the government's priorities.

Without extensive work on the falls and rapids of the Saskatchewan River, navigation was not reliable and therefore not competitive with railways. Despite its monopoly, the Winnipeg and Western Transportation Company was unsuccessful. The first year was a disaster. First of all, the river remained at its lowest level since 1878. Second, the navigation channel near Cumberland House had ruptured the previous year, spilling its valuable water into nearby swamps and seriously reducing water levels below the lake. Finally, the *Lily* sank on its way back from an exploratory trip to Medicine Hat. The company never recovered from this calamitous year. The failure to deliver vital merchandise caused hardships among the settlers along the Saskatchewan, and destroyed the confidence of wholesalers and merchants.[41] Even the Hudson's Bay Company deserted the steamboats in favor of the C.P.R., which completed its prairie section by 1883. The following year, and again in 1885, the Hudson's Bay Company shipped most of the Edmonton and some of the Mackenzie and Athabasca outfits by way of Calgary.[42] Although the overland route was more costly, it was much faster, and finally enabled the Company to distribute its trade goods in a single season. In a highly competitive business based on luxury goods and fluctuating prices, speed and reliability were of the essence. The steamboats delivered neither, the C.P.R. both.

Caught in the vicious cycle of low water, missed delivery dates, and skeptical customers, the fortune of the Winnipeg and Western Transportation Company deteriorated rapidly. In 1884, after another difficult year, the company reduced the value of its shares by another 30 percent in order to keep them attractive to possible buyers. The Riel Rebellion sparked a flurry of activity and good profits, but the remainder of the season produced little traffic; consequently, the company once again reduced the value of its shares.[43] Its boats, too, were victims of circumstance. The *Manitoba* was crushed by spring ice in 1885; the *Northcote* was beached in 1886, permanently trapped by the low waters at Cumberland; and the *Marquis* was gouged by rocks in the Thornburn Rapids in 1886, briefly refloated, but never again sailed commercially. Only the *North West* maintained a sporadic tramp service until its demise in a flood at Edmonton in 1899. Two years later, the Winnipeg and Western Transportation Company wound up its affairs and transferred its assets to the Hudson's Bay Company, its only creditor.[44] The Saskatchewan River had foiled the clever schemes of enterprising business men. Waiting too long to conquer the Saskatchewan River, they had too little time to be innovative and to adapt the technology of steamboats to the peculiar problems of the river. They had allowed another transportation technique to catch up and defeat them.

Another casualty of the dawning of the railway age in western

Canada was James A. Grahame. Even though Governor Colvile had publicly praised Grahame as recently as 1881 for successfully controlling expenses during an especially difficult period, only two years later he asked for the chief commissioner's resignation. He explained that the Hudson's Bay Company needed a younger and more vigorous man. Grahame complied, but the board, which apparently was not informed of Colvile's request, balked at the suddenness of the dismissal. Nevertheless, Grahame's days were numbered and a year later the committee accepted his resignation.[45] The post of chief commissioner was abolished and his replacement, Joseph Wrigley, sent fresh from England, was named trade commissioner. The whole Canadian operation was placed under a sub-committee consisting of two board members who resided in Canada. Clearly, the fur trade was taking second place to the Company's concern with the settlement of the prairies.

Grahame and his fellow officers had embarked upon the steamboat scheme even though they were fully cognizant of the possibilities of railways. As early as 1871, Donald A. Smith, a close associate of Grahame, was one of the partners in an attempt to secure rail charters from Pembina via Fort Garry to Thunder Bay.[46] Seven years later, Smith was a prime mover in the revitalization of the St. Paul and Pacific, and still later, became a prominent backer of the Canadian Pacific. Grahame, too, had always used rail whenever possible and for a short time toyed with the idea of a full amalgamation with the St. Paul railway. But, railways, unlike steamboats, could not be used to shut competitors out of the fur domain. In fact, railways depended on expanding commerce and growing settlement, the very antithesis of the fur trade. Moreover, railway technology was beyond the financial resources of the Hudson's Bay Company. Obviously, the Company could not afford to purchase a controlling interest in such an enormous undertaking, nor could it alone generate the traffic to warrant such a massive investment. Thus, time and circumstance caught up with the Company and forced it to accept the most dramatic revolution in its history. For the first time ever, it lost exclusive control over the transportation of trade goods, one of the most vital aspects of its operations.

The Hudson's Bay Company might have lost control over its transportation system, but it could try for a special arrangement with the C.P.R. In its favor were the size of its shipments and distances involved. So, too, was Donald Smith, who, as the company's largest shareholder, was also a C.P.R. director. Smith, however, was only a director and but one of the policy-makers in the large corporation. Moreover, his interest in the railway company would preclude the Hudson's Bay Company from using American railways to reach the Canadian West. Consequently, mutual interest suggested that the Hudson's Bay Company ship by steam to Montreal, use the C.P.R. to its stations in western Canada, and in return receive a modest rebate to offset the cost of the National Policy tariffs. In February 1885, trade commissioner Wrigley travelled to Montreal and negotiated a secret agreement with William Van Horne. The C.P.R. agreed to give the Hudson's Bay Company the best rate possible from Montreal and western Canada as well as a rebate on the section east of Winnipeg. Federal laws, regulating the western monopoly, barred rebates for the western section, but officials of both companies felt that the eastern rebates were sufficient to cover the entire route. Haggling over details consumed several more months. The C.P.R. at first refused a rebate on eastbound furs because they supposedly did nothing to build up the western economy and because the C.P.R.'s special insurance on this valuable cargo was in itself a subsidy. The C.P.R. also refused to include flour exports in the rebate scheme because the rate on flour was already low and because it was not about to give an advantage to the Hudson's Bay Company in this very vital industry. Eventually, the C.P.R. yielded on the fur issue; it gave the Company a 12½-percent discount on all freight except flour.[47]

By 1885, therefore, the completion of the C.P.R. forced the Hudson's Bay Company to accept the reality of western settlement. As Colvile noted at the spring general meeting, the C.P.R. would "bring the western country, in which we are all so much interested, within a very measurable distance not only of England but of the, I will not say the civilized, but the older and better settled portions of Canada."[48] For two centuries, the Hudson's Bay Company had ruled its western territories, keeping its trading monopoly intact by controlling transportation into the region. A royal charter together with innovations like the Yorkboat were the techniques the Company used to restrict access to the Northwest.[49] The steamboat experiment represented a last-ditch effort in a traditional policy of using modern technology to monopolize transportation and communication on the prairies and thereby minimize the impact of the outside world on its fur preserve. This decision came too late. By 1885 the effort proved in vain.

Notes

1. Hudson's Bay Company Archives, Public Archives of Manitoba [Hereafter cited as H.B.C.A., P.A.M.], Report of the Governor and Committee of the Hudson's Bay Company, 22 November 1870 and 28 June 1871; A6/44, f167, Smith to Smith, 1 November 1870.

2. H.B.C.A., P.A.M., Proceedings of the General Court of the Hudson's Bay Company, 28 June 1871.

3. H.B.C.A., P.A.M., Proceedings of the General Court of the Hudson's Bay Company, 28 June 1872; Report of the Governor and Committee of the Hudson's Bay Company, 22 November 1870; A6/44, f346, Armit to Smith, 1 August 1871; *Manitoban*, 18 May 1872. The report cited above noted the appointment of Cyril Grahame, formerly an expert with the Colonial Office, as the consultant for the feasibility study.

4. Bruce Peel, *Steamboats on the Saskatchewan*, (Saskatoon: Western Producer Prairie Books, 1972), pp. 14–16. *See also* Fortescue to Smith, 28 December 1871, cited in Beckles Wilson, *The Life of Lord Strathcona and Mount Royal*, vol. 1 (Boston: Houghton Mifflin Company, 1915), p. 512.

5. Peel, *Steamboats*, pp. 19–23; Theodore Barris, *Fire Canoe: Prairie Steamboat Days Revisited* (Toronto: McClelland and Stewart, 1977), p. 43. Warping was the process by which a steamboat was moved by a small engine and capstan, which pulled in a rope attached to a boulder on shore. The ships also had a elaborate system of poles and ropes by which the ship could be raised and literally walked across shoals.

6. H.B.C.A., P.A.M., D13/1, f51, Grahame to Armit, 7 September 1874.

7. H.B.C.A., D14/1, f34, Grahame to Clarke, 27 July 1874; f60, 21 September 1874; f271, Grahame to Aymond, 8 December 1874.

8. H.B.C.A., P.A.M., A12/16, f609, Grahame to Armit, 28 July 1875; D14/1, f275, Grahame to Belanger, 10 December 1874; D14/2, f423, Grahame to Clarke, 15 May 1875; f471, Grahame to Hamilton, 12 June 1875; Peel, *Steamboats*, pp. 33–36.

9. H.B.C.A., P.A.M., Report of the Governor and Committee, 29 June and 10 November 1875; D12/16, f812, Grahame to Armit, 20 December 1875; D14/2, f307, Grahame to McMurray, 7 April 1875; f423, Grahame to Clarke, 15 May 1875; A12/16, f699, Grahame to Armit, 30 October 1875.

10. H.B.C.A., P.A.M., A12/16, f333, Grahame to Armit, 11 February 1875; f422, 17 March 1875; f657, 4 August 1875; f754, 16 November 1875.

11. Ron Vastokas, "The Grand Rapids Portage," *The Beaver* (Autumn 1961), pp. 22–26; Canada, *Sessional Papers*, no. 139, 1882.

12. H.B.C.A., P.A.M., A12/17, f289, Grahame to Armit, 25 August 1876.

13. According to the books, the steamboats were losing money. (*See* Table I below). Of course, it must be noted that without the steamboats, the Company would have had to charge the fur trade the more costly overland rates for transportation.

Table I: Losses on Steamboat Operations, 1879

		Expenditures			Revenues	Losses
	Insurance	Wages	Repairs and Supplies	Depreciation		
Colvile	$1,278	$3,793	$10,235	$4,766	$10,235	$9,837
Northcote	1,278	7,352	7,277	4,851	20,407	351
Lily	1,789	2,835	5,874	6,396	2,718	14,176
Total	4,345	13,980	23,386	16,013	33,360	24,364

Source: H.B.C.A., P.A.M., A12/48, f15, Grahame to Armit, 12 January 1880.

14. H.B.C.A., P.A.M., A12/47, f300, Grahame to Smith, 16 September 1879.

15. Hartwell Bowsfield, ed., *The Letters of Charles John Brydges 1879–1882: Hudson's Bay Company Land Commissioner*, introduction by Alan Wilson (Winnipeg: Hudson's Bay Record Society, 1977), pp. xxxvi–xl. In his introduction, Wilson judges Grahame's tenure as chief commissioner too harshly. Perhaps his evaluation is exaggerated by his attempt to place the administration of C.J. Brydges in an extremely favorable light.

16. Ibid., p. xl.

17. Alan Wilson, "'In a Business Way': C.J. Brydges and the Hudson's Bay Company, 1879–1889," in *The West and the Nation: Essays in Honour of W.L. Morton*, ed. by Carl Berger and Ramsay Cook (Toronto: McClelland and Stewart, 1976), pp. 118–23.

18. Canada, *Sessional Papers*, no. 138, 1885, Brydges to Langevin, 28 September 1880.

19. Ibid., Order-in-Council, 15 October 1880.

20. Brydges to Colvile, 1 November 1880, cited in Bowsfield, *Letters of C.J. Brydges*, pp. 103–5.

21. Canada, *Sessional Papers*, no. 138, 1885, Brydges to Langevin, 2 November 1880.

22. Brydges to Armit, 8 January 1880, Bowsfield, *Letters of C.J. Brydges*, p. 47.

23. H.B.C.A., P.A.M., A12/17, f720, Grahame to Armit, 16 November 1877; A6/507, f538, Armit to Grahame, 27 June 1877; A12/47, f170, Grahame to Armit, 5 August 1879; f85, Grahame to Armit, 24 April 1879.

24. H.B.C.A., P.A.M., A12/48, f125, Grahame to Armit, 22 Janaury 1880; f196, 26 February 1880.

46 / *A.A. den Otter*

25. Ibid., f327, Grahame to Armit, 14 May 1880, Paul F. Sharp, *Whoop-Up Country: The Canadian-American West, 1865-1885* (Norman: University of Oklahoma Press, 1973), pp. 207-28.

26. Alvin C. Gluek, Jr., "The Minnesota Route," *The Beaver* (Spring 1956), pp. 44-50.

27. Albro Martin, *James J. Hill and the Opening of the Northwest* (New York: Oxford University Press, 1976), pp. 76-84; Barrie, *Fire Canoe*, pp. 25-40. The Hudson's Bay Company may have had about 800 shares worth $40,000 in the Red River Company. *See* H.B.C.A., P.A.M., A12/17, f304, Grahame to Armit, 1 November 1876.

28. H.B.C.A., P.A.M., A12/46, f115, Grahame to Armit, 28 March 1878.

29. Martin, *J.J. Hill*, pp. 125-49.

30. The negotiations for the conversion of steamboat into railway shares were extremely complex and revolved around D.A. Smith's desire for greater Hudson's Bay Company involvement, Stephen's ambivalent attitude, and Grahame's belief that the railway would not be able to compete with the C.P.R. When completed, the transaction converted $40,000 of steamer shares into $50,000 of railway shares, which amounted to a mere 0.5 percent of the total capitalization of the railway. *See* H.B.C.A., P.A.M., A12/46, f103, Grahame to Armit, 21 March 1878; f190 Grahame to Armit, 29 April 1880. The correspondence between Grahame and Kittson and between Grahame and Stephen in A12/47 is also enlightening.

31. John Macoun, *Manitoba and the Great Northwest* (Guelph: World Publishing Co., 1882), pp. 582-85; Peel, *Steamboats*, pp. 76-78.

32. H.B.C.A., P.A.M., A12/48, f463, Brydges to Grahame, 25 November 1880.

33. H.B.C.A., P.A.M., A12/49, f177, Grahame to Armit, 27 January 1881.

34. H.B.C.A., P.A.M., A7/5, f19, Colvile to Brydges, 6 January 1881; A12/49, ff1, 120, 195, 279, and 310, Grahame to Armit, 3 and 27 January, 7 March, 30 May, and 11 August 1881; Peel, *Steamboats*, pp. 78-79.

35. H.B.C.A., P.A.M., A12/49, f289, Grahame to Armit, 10 June 1881.

36. H.B.C.A., P.A.M., A12/48, f439; Grahame to Armit, 5 November 1880.

37. H.B.C.A., P.A.M., A12/64, f342, Grahame to Armit, 1 October 1881.

38. H.B.C.A., P.A.M., A12/50, f95, Grahame to Armit, 16 March 1882.

39. Brydges to Armit, 5 January 1882, Bowsfield, *Letters of C.J. Brydges*, p. 227.

40. Canada, *Sessional Papers*, no. 138, 1885.

41. Ibid., Petition of the Merchants of Prince Albert.

42. H.B.C.A., P.A.M., A12/51, f243, Grahame to Armit, 2 August 1883; A12/27, f195, Wrigley to Armit, 20 February 1885.

43. H.B.C.A., P.A.M., A12/27, f170 and f460, Wrigley to Armit, 12 January and 17 November 1885. The devaluation of shares was largely a bookkeeping arrangement and the Hudson's Bay Company lost only $7,000 on the deal.

44. Peel, *Steamboats*, pp. 142–214. The North West Navigation Company did better; while the *Colvile* was lost to fire at Grand Rapids in 1894 and the *Princess* sank in a storm on Lake Winnipeg in 1906, the Company built and operated other steamers on Lake Winnipeg well into the twentieth century.

45. H.B.C.A., P.A.M., A2/40, Minutes of the General Court of the Hudson's Bay Company, 29 June 1881; A12/52, f227, Grahame to Armit, 14 July 1884; A7/5, f108, Colvile to Grahame, 11 June 1884.

46. Leonard Bertram Irwin, *Pacific Railways and Nationalism in the Canadian-American Northwest, 1845–1873* (New York: Greenwood Press, 1968), p. 169.

47. H.B.C.A., P.A.M., A12/27, f87, Wrigley to Armit, 3 November 1884; f183, 2 February 1885; f302, Kerr to Wrigley, 14 April 1885; f303, Wrigley to Kerr, 16 April 1885; f304, Kerr to Wrigley, 16 April 1885; f349, Kerr to Wrigley, 3 June 1885; f351, Wrigley to Kerr, 6 June 1885; f353, Kerr to Wrigley, 8 June 1885; f354, Wrigley to Kerr, 9 June 1885; f354, Kerr to Wrigley, 10 June 1885.

48. H.B.C.A., P.A.M., Proceedings of the General Court of the Hudson's Bay Company, 30 June 1885, p. 7.

49. John A. Alwin, "Mode, Pattern and Pulse: Hudson's Bay Company Transport, 1670–1821" (Ph.D. diss., University of Manitoba, 1978).

The "Private Adventurers"
of Rupert's Land

_____ Irene M. Spry

Author's Note:

In 1957 the Saskatchewan Archives, then under the direction of Lewis H. Thomas, was making a collection of Palliser material by way of celebrating the 100th anniversary of the start of the Palliser Expedition. When the Palliser home in County Waterford, Ireland, was burnt down in "The Troubles" in 1923, the family papers were destroyed, but perhaps relevant documents might exist elsewhere. Dr. Thomas asked Graham Spry, then Agent-General for Saskatchewan in Britain, to see if anything could be found. Graham and I remembered seeing filing cabinets labelled "Upper Canada" and "Lower Canada" in the Commonwealth Relations Office. The helpful staff introduced me to the rich collections of the Public Record Office, which include records of the old Colonial Office and other government departments. Miss Alice Johnson, the Archivist of the Hudson's Bay Company, also put me on the track of Palliser material. A trip for the Associated Country Women of the World to Australia enabled me to study the Sir James Hector Papers at the University of Otago in New Zealand and, in the course of a long hunt, described in Saskatchewan History *(XII, 2, Spring 1959), other scattered items came to light.*

This search introduced me to such remarkable characters as James Sinclair and James McKay and led to a lasting interest in Rupert's Land and its people, for which I owe a debt of gratitude to Lewis H. Thomas. That debt has been much increased by the generous hospitality that Lewis H. and Margaret Thomas have given me over the years to facilitate research in Edmonton.

Women of Red River gives a picture of a friendly, cheerful society in the middle decades of the nineteenth century. A child growing up there later remembered a world of "comfort and happiness."[1] Aspirations to refinement and elegance were in evidence, such as kid gloves and hoop skirts, books and British periodicals, music and pianos—even a harp—and balls where the polka was danced.[2]

Besides the Governor of Assiniboia, the officers of the Hudson's Bay Company at Upper and Lower Fort Garry, and the resident clergy, this society was made up of the families of the "principal settlers" and a few independent merchants. Its economic basis was largely the wealth accumulated by former chief factors and chief traders while they were in the service of "the Honourable Company," now settled on large grants of land.[3] Such was the means of support of leading families like the Birds, the Logans, the Prudens, and the Bunns, supplemented in some cases by the emoluments of public office. Former Chief Factor James Bird, for example, was Collector of Import and Export Duties, and Alexander Ross was Sheriff of Assiniboia.[4] In addition, some retired Hudson's Bay men supplemented their incomes with trade, milling, and freighting ventures, notably John Inkster,[5] Robert Logan[6] and William Hemmings Cook.[7] A few "private adventurers" (as Governor George Simpson called them)[8] built up sufficient wealth to become part of the élite of Red River Settlement. Outstanding among them were Andrew McDermot, James Sinclair, Augustin Nolin, Narcisse Marion, John Inkster, and A.G.B. Bannatyne.

The sons and grandsons of this social and economic élite, born in Rupert's Land and mostly of mixed descent, faced the problem of achieving sufficient affluence to support the gentlemanly status of their progenitors. With the exception of such rare career women as "The Misses Nolin,"[9] their sisters depended on finding eligible husbands for "ultimate respectability."[10] A few, such as the flirtatious and fascinating Margaret Sinclair,[11] found mates among visitors from the outside world. Miss Sinclair married Lieutenant Darling of the Sixth Regiment of Foot, who in due course became a general in the British Army. A number of girls were married off to clerks and officers in the service of the Company, some happily, but some much against their will. The rest had to find husbands among the natives of the country.

This problem of marriage added greatly to the pressure on young Rupert's Landers to find lucrative occupations, as is evident in the sad story of young William Cook. In love with the daughter of a well-to-do family, he realized that he could never hope to attain sufficient prosperity to claim her as a bride, went mad, and drowned tragically.[12] Another case is recorded by Alexander Ross. When a leading half-breed aspired to the hand of a young lady "accustomed ... to the first society," his suit was brusquely rejected by her guardian. This drove the "English half-breeds" into alliance with the French Métis. The native origins of the suitor, "a comely, well-behaved young man, of respectable connections," and favored by the girl,[13] would undoubtedly have been overlooked if his economic prospects had been good enough. James Sinclair, for example, who was of mixed descent, married James Bird's daughter, Elizabeth,[14] and held an unassailable position as one of the élite of Red River.

Some natives of Rupert's Land might look for a career in the great Company in which their fathers and grandfathers had been officers, but in the early days of the "Little Emperor's" reign, very few of them got even a foothold on the ladder of promotion.[15] Even the few enlisted as clerks faced a long and uncertain climb to the higher ranks. In 1831, Chief Factor John Stuart wrote to Governor Simpson about William Sinclair II, James Sinclair's oldest brother, that, though he had the capacity, he "had but little chance of being promoted."[16] The creation of a special category for the recruitment of half-breed lads as apprentice postmasters may have allowed more natives to join the Company, but it certainly did not improve their prospects of advancement.[17]

Despairing of a worthwhile career in the service of the Company, some young Rupert's Landers sought (or their fathers sought for them) more promising opportunities in Britain, Canada, the United States, or west of the Rocky Mountains. A.K. Isbister, for instance, left the service of the Company, in which he had been a clerk, to get a better education. He graduated from the University of Aberdeen and stayed in Britain, where he was a persistent and powerful advocate of the interests of the natives of Rupert's Land. He became a man of substance and ended his career as principal of the College of Preceptors.[18] "Captain" William Kennedy, of Arctic fame, allied himself with Canadian entrepreneurs who were interested in developing communication with and exploiting opportunities in the Red River colony and the plains beyond.[19] George Gladman, Jr., led, in its first season, the Canadian expedition sent to explore the canoe route from Lake Superior to Red River and the territory to the Northwest.[20] James Ross, before his ill-fated return to Red River, worked on the Toronto *Globe*.[21] Still others sought opportunities on the westward advancing American frontier. For a time Peter Garrioch held a post with an American fur trading concern, while Louis Goulet served as a scout in the American army.[22] James Sinclair even became an American citizen[23] with a view to settling in the Oregon Territory. The hope of making "a lucky strike" drew more than one Rupert's Lander across the Rocky Mountains to the gold diggings in California, the Fraser Valley, and the Cariboo. James Sinclair made £1,300 in a single week in California[24] and Peter Erasmus, Jr., brought back "a snug little sum of money" from the "gold Mines," which he subsequently lost, with his accumulated savings, when the Commercial Bank failed.[25] He noted cynically how the possession of this modest fortune changed his status with the Company. At Fort Pitt, on his way back from the mines to Red River, he shared the "menu reserved for high-ranking officials of the Company... Apparently as a man of substance, my native antecedents were entirely removed."[26]

Both the young Rupert's Landers who made forays into the outside world but came back to the land of their birth, and those who never left, had to find what economic opportunities they could in the country of their birth. Most of them, "trained up in the school of idleness and wild freedom," as that stern Presbyterian, Alexander Ross, remarked,[27] were content to live by the hunt, the trap line, the fishery, the boat brigade or the cart line, "wintering over" in Red River or in some camp out on the plains near the buffalo herds,[28] perhaps practicing a little desultory farming and cattle raising and, when opportunity offered, engaging in trade on the side. This way of life offered constant change and variety; the excitement of the chase, possible encounters with the Sioux, of running dangerous rapids; bursts of concentrated effort that challenged a man's strength, endurance, and skill; and long periods of leisure, or idleness as it seemed to most missionaries.[29] The hunt and winter camp gave ample opportunities for socializing as well as for music, dance, and other creative and artistic pursuits. The plains rang with the sound of fiddle music, song, and the thud of moccasined feet stamping out the rhythm of the Red River jig.[30] Such a gregarious, exciting, and interesting life was eminently suited to the tastes of most Métis and mixed-bloods alike; in adopting it they behaved as rationally as any economist might assume they would, notwithstanding the missionaries' view that their "erratic habits" were irrational.[31] Not only did it satisfy their own leisure and artistic preferences, but it took advantage of the most rewarding economic opportunities available.[32] Simpson's 1824 expectation that an increase in agriculture and cattle raising would displace the buffalo hunt and leave the hunters without employment[33] had not been realized. The hunt went on as long as the herds survived. Agriculture, a prey to floods, late and early frosts, grasshoppers, and drought, was a most uncertain source of livelihood, while lack of a market limited any possibility that farmers would get rich. The buffalo hunt offered larger and more dependable returns. Though the hunt sometimes failed, at least locally, the mobile native population could move with the herds, supplementing plains provisions with other game and fish when need arose.[34] The buffalo hunt, as Lionel Dorge has pointed out, [35] was, in fact, the basis of the first great industry of western Canada. That it was carried on on the open plains, not in a factory, did not make it any less an industry. Once the buffalo were killed, the carcasses had to be butchered, the meat dried or made into pemmican, shaganappi and sinews processed, and the robes and hides prepared for use. All the functions of a modern packing plant and tannery were performed by the hunters and their wives and families, using traditional labor-intensive methods.

As the scale of the hunt grew and as it drew further away from Red River, the problem of providing supplies to the hunters and delivering their products to the market increased. This created an opportunity for those ambitious Rupert's Landers who were not content with the simple material standards of most of their countrymen.

As early as 1824, Andrew McDermot had seen the possibilities of the plains trade. In the same spirit of "wild adventure" as the hunters, he went with them to the plains. He gradually established a monopoly of the provision trade, and after ten years he settled in Red River.[36] Meanwhile, young James Sinclair, back in Rupert's Land after attending school in Scotland, became his partner,[37] developing unexcelled plains skills and using a small legacy left him by his father as the basis of a fortune totalling £4,500 when he left Red River.[38] Others followed suit, among them Joe McKay,[39] Norbert Welsh, "The Last Buffalo Hunter," and Moïse Goulet and his son, Louis.[40] These men and many others joined in the hunt; traded with the hunters and Indians; and organized freighting services to bring supplies of tea, sugar, ammunition, tobacco, knives, blankets, and, above all, liquor[41] to them and to carry away the harvest of the hunt to market. Some, notably Moïse Goulet, became employers, hiring people to process robes and to make coats and moccasins and other goods, for which there was a ready market.

Trade in the products of the buffalo hunt went hand in hand with trade in furs. After an early attempt to stamp out private trading in furs, Simpson had hit on the plan of licensing private traders to collect furs along the American border in competition with American traders, instead of setting up new Company posts. He wrote in 1825:

> The Indian trade of this District [Red River Settlement] continues to be conducted on the plan adopted last year and is found to answer our expectations, that of having no dealings with Indians ourselves, attaching Nettley Creek to Bas de la Rivière, and permitting Settlers outfitted by us for ready money and duly authorised to trade, to collect the hunts of those Indians who frequent the frontiers and which would in all probability fall into the hands of the Americans; for which we give a fair and reasonable price.[42]

Among the authorized traders were Andrew McDermot and later James Sinclair and Augustin Nolin.[43] When the system was discontinued in 1844, on the grounds that licences to trade "might give the Settlers a taste for the Fur Trade,"[44] it was already too late; a great many Rupert's Landers were by then involved in "trafficking in furs." This change in policy precipitated a conflict between the private traders and the Company.[45]

Another type of private business activity that had at first been approved by the Company was freighting between Red River Settlement and York Factory. As the population grew, and, with it, the needs of the settlers, the Company found it increasingly troublesome to transport what the settlers and the multiplying retail traders[46] required. "Private adventurers" were therefore encouraged to do their own freighting, to undertake freighting for their fellow colonists, and, eventually, to carry freight for the Company itself.[47] As in the case of licensed fur trading, what was at first helpful to the Company began to create problems. Large freighters, especially McDermot and Sinclair, seeking to cut costs, began to hire Indians, who were thus diverted from working for the Company. A new clause in freighting contracts prohibited their employment.[48] Even so, Simpson felt that the freighting business gave McDermot and Sinclair a dangerous influence among "the lower class."[49] Their contracts were cancelled without the year's notice specified,[50] and insult was added to injury by the transfer of Sinclair's contract to his brother, Thomas.[51]

The Company faced yet another threat when a group of aspiring young entrepreneurs—Peter Garrioch, Henry Cook, Alexis Goulet, Peter Hayden, James Sinclair, and two others named Roulette and St. Germain— began to develop a "cartline" to St. Paul for the importation of American goods. They refused to pay the import duty and a controversy followed about "taxation without representation."[52] A petition from importers of American goods (Charles Laurence, Dominique Ducharme, Peter Garrioch, Henry Cook, Peter Hayden, and Alexis Goulait [Goulet]) came before the Council of Assiniboia on 16 June 1845. Three days later, the Council arrived at a compromise arrangement whereby payment of duties was to be enforced but substantial duty-free concessions were approved.[53]

Meanwhile, efforts by Rupert's Land entrepreneurs to develop new types of business venture were being frustrated. A project for a local distillery (recommended by Simpson but disallowed by the governor and committee in London) came to nothing.[54] The export of tallow, a by-product of the buffalo hunt, was nipped in the bud, this time by Simpson despite approval by the governor and committee.[55]

To this accumulation of frustrations, the Company, suspecting that a clandestine trade in furs was developing, added a series of punitive countermeasures.[56] Using its control of ships, and so of imports from Britain, as well as bills of exchange and currency, and its position as landowner, the Hudson's Bay Company attempted to stop exports of furs across the border to American traders such as Norman Kittson. After a visit to Red River Settlement in 1843, Kittson had set up a trading post in 1844 just south of the border at Pembina.[57]

The measures taken by the Company gave impetus to the very export trade in furs they were intended to prevent. Sinclair wrote to Governor Christie on 25 August 1845:

So many obstacles of late years have been thrown in the way of not only my advancement but the settlers in general that I do not see how I can in any manner support myself and family except by entering into such business as may interfere with the interest and privileges of the Hudson's Bay Co....[58]

Kittson had written on 6 February 1845 that Sinclair had refused an invitation to smuggle furs to him.[59] Now, Sinclair and McDermot began to explore possibilities for the sale of furs independently of the Company. They looked into the question of chartering a ship to ply the Bay route.[60] McDermot negotiated with Kenneth McKenzie of Fort Union on the Missouri as a possible purchaser of his furs[61] and Sinclair became involved with the Garrioch group in smuggling furs across the border to Kittson.[62]

The struggle between the Company and the emerging class of independent entrepreneurs was, however, wider and deeper than a dispute about the Company's claim to a monopoly of the fur trade. The traders of Rupert's Land challenged the Company's domination of business activity in the territory, the necessity of Company approval for virtually any business venture, and the limits set on any attempt to explore economic opportunities other than those offered or at least authorized by the Company.

Sinclair and his fellow entrepreneurs pressed the issue first with the authorities in Rupert's Land and then with the Imperial government. Chief Factor Alexander Christie, Governor of Assiniboia, replied in 1845 to an inquiry by Sinclair and his colleagues that the rights of natives of the country were the same as those of any British subject and, therefore, constrained by the Charter rights of the Company.[63] Sinclair then took two memorials challenging the domination of the Company to London, one in English and one in French. With the help of A.K. Isbister, these petitions were forced on the attention of a reluctant government, which, after inquiries among official informants, concluded that there were no grounds for action. None the less, the petitions and related correspondence came before the House of Commons in 1849.[64]

Meanwhile, in Rupert's Land, the free trade issue remained the focus of continued conflict, which came to a head in the same year. McDermot had been reconciled with the Company in 1846.[65] The arrival of the Sixth Regiment of Foot at Fort Garry, also in 1846, created short-lived opportunities for business prosperity outside the fur trade,[66] but when the troops were withdrawn in 1848 the unresolved conflict over freedom of trade flared up again. Local officials decided on decisive action. Pierre Guillaume (William) Sayer and three other Métis were brought to trial for illicit fur trading.[67]

The court house was surrounded by angry Rupert's Landers who threatened violence. A delegation, with Sinclair as spokesman for the prisoners, was admitted to the trial. Sayer was pronounced guilty, but no penalty was imposed on him and when the case against his colleagues was dropped, there were joyful shouts of "Le commerce est libre!" From then on the "Honourable Company" did, indeed, abandon its efforts to enforce monopoly privileges. Instead, it countered opposition by attempting to out-compete the free traders.[68]

Sinclair and his fellow entrepreneurs had won the right "to try to make an honest livelihood out of the staple of the Country," for which McDermot had pleaded four years earlier.[69] Free traders now roamed the plains in increasing numbers. William Traill stated that by the late sixties, "most of the hunters were also fur traders, taking out goods in the spring and fall to trade for robes, furs and pemmican."[70] American sources of trade goods and American outlets for furs multiplied. Nevertheless, the Company still wielded immense power and influence, so much so that when James Sinclair decided to leave Rupert's Land for Oregon, he took service with it.[71] In 1841 he had successfully led a party of twenty-three emigrant families from Red River to the Columbia.[72] In 1854, as the secret agent of the Company,[73] he again undertook the long journey across the plains and through the mountains with another band of emigrants, this time accompanied by his own family.[74] In 1850 he had spent some time trying to find a rumored better pass than the one by which he had crossed the Rockies in 1841.[75] He reached the Pacific Coast,[76] though which pass he used is not known. In 1854 he tried yet another new route, probably Elk Pass, which leads out of the Kananaskis Valley.[77] At Walla Walla, besides carrying on Company business, he embarked (with Simpson's acquiescence) on his own ranching and timber trading projects,[78] but his enterprising and adventurous career was cut short in 1856 when he was killed in an Indian battle on the Columbia River at the Cascades.[79]

Other Rupert's Landers continued to seek out and pursue business opportunities in their native land. For three decades after 1849, the fur trade and the buffalo hunt remained their major concerns. The number of entrepreneurs and the scope of their operations expanded rapidly.[80] Many of them got their supplies from and sold their furs, robes, and pemmican to merchants in Red River Settlement, such as A.G.B. Bannatyne[81] and the Inksters.[82] Others dealt directly with American suppliers and outlets.[83] Contact between Rupert's Landers and the merchants of St. Paul and at trading posts strung along the Missouri River quickly multiplied when there was no longer need for clandestine dealings.

Even the Hudson's Bay Company began to use the American route to Rupert's Land and to collaborate with former American opponents, including Kittson, who became an agent of the Company. A secret agreement was made by the Company to help finance experiments in steam navigation on the Red River, and in the stage-coach and wagon service established by the Burbank Brothers of St. Paul, to connect steam ship services on the Mississippi and Red rivers. Sir George Simpson himself made his last annual trip to Rupert's Land by way of Minnesota instead of by the usual canoe route.[84] Improved transport facilities between Rupert's Land and St. Paul and other American centres enlarged markets and sources of supply for Rupert's Landers but, as Dr. John Rae noted in 1861, with the shift from cart train and trail to steamship and stage-coach, "the transport of goods and passengers which had formerly been carried on by the [Red River] settlers themselves in boats and carts, was now done by the steamer and by waggons from St. Pauls, to which place, the money went, instead of being retained in the Colony."[85]

As the American frontier advanced westward, after the interruptions caused by the Sioux Uprising of 1862 in Minnesota and the Civil War, American markets, sources of supply, enterprise, and capital became increasingly important in Rupert's Land and the Indian Territory north of the 49th parallel.[86] The acquisition of Hudson's

Bay Company stock by the International Financial Society in 1863 foreshadowed the Deed of Surrender of 1869.[87] Already, outsiders—missionaries, big game hunters, miners, explorers, and Canadian adventurers, notably Dr. John C. Schultz—had been introducing new ideas and creating new business opportunities in the old fur trading and buffalo hunting wilderness.[88] In that wilderness new settlements were growing up at St. Albert, Victoria [Pakan], Prince Albert, Duck Lake, St. Laurent, and Portage la Prairie. New types of freighting businesses developed to serve the needs and transport the produce of sedentary agriculturalists. New kinds of enterprise were in demand, such as grain milling, sawing, operating ferries, and trading in cattle and horses, which were perennially in short supply.[89] When Rupert's Land and the Indian Territory became part of Canada in 1870, they ceased to be a preserve for fur trading and buffalo hunting. Manitoba and the North-West Territories became a valuable expanse of real estate open to entrepreneurs from the outside world. New settlements, such as Battleford, grew up, and land speculation became a way of life. Steamboats on the Saskatchewan and Assiniboine rivers changed the pattern of transportation. Now freight for the interior could be shipped by steamboat to Fort Ellice and then taken overland by Red River cart trains or, increasingly, by wagon, to such destinations as the Qu'Appelle Valley.[90] Telegraph and railroad connection with the United States in the 1870s, and eventually direct contact with central Canada, when the Canadian Pacific Railway was completed, brought further changes in patterns of freight and passenger traffic. Trail and cart train became feeders to the new trunk lines.[91] Boundary, geological, land, and railway surveyors traversed the wilderness.[92] The North-West Mounted Police made their historic march west and established posts and patrols.[93] Liquor might no longer be lawfully traded in the North-West Territories. Indian treaties were negotiated and the Indians settled on reserves.[94] Buffalo herds dwindled and disappeared[95] and other formerly plentiful resources, such as wood and fish, became scarce.[96] Prospective settlers, as well as new traders with new kinds of goods to meet their wants, began to arrive.[97] Government was organized, first in Manitoba and then in the North-West Territories.[98] A new life came rushing "at breakneck speed."[99]

The plains traders and fur traders of Rupert's Land had to change with all these changes. They showed extraordinary adaptability.[100] As the buffalo herds dwindled, freighting became more profitable than the plains trade. As the Indians were settled on reserves, the Indian trade, especially at treaty-paying time, replaced the fur trade. As loads of robes and pemmican grew scarce, loads of flour and timber took their place. When the Carlton Trail was superseded by the C.P.R., freighters worked out new routes between the railway and settlements it did not serve. When buffalo hunters had to switch from the chase to digging snake-root, the traders met their needs. Nothing was too insignificant for them to try: scouting for the Boundary Survey Commission,[101] construction work, cutting timber, ranching, guiding mounted police officers on special missions, freighting supplies for teams of surveyors or crews of railroaders—every new opportunity was explored.

Despite these initiatives, not all the old Rupert's Land business men made the transition successfully from the old life to the new one. Joe McKay, for example, had been among the élite of the plains traders in the heyday of the buffalo hunt, but he ended his days in poverty. Recalling his "happy days," he said: "I rode the finest and fastest of buffalo horses in the hunts. I wanted nothing then. I had everything a man could wish for in abundance." As he spoke, he was trudging beside a slow ox-cart laden with firewood in Prince Albert. Like other plainsmen he had sustained losses in the second Riel Rising.[102] Many more suffered sad reverses when the buffalo disappeared.

There were some, however, whose restless energy and innovative ingenuity enabled them to make the most of the opportunities that came with the new order. Pre-eminent among them was "Big Jim" McKay, alias the Honorable James McKay of Deer Lodge.[103]

Born in Edmonton, the son of a noted steersman and a Métisse mother, he left the service of the Company in 1860 to set up in business on his own. The "ablest guide in the country,"[104] he took charge of parties of wealthy young British sportsmen, such as those of Sir Frederic Johnstone, Baronet, and Henry (later Viscount) Chaplin in 1861,[105] and Lord Dunmore in 1862.[106] He looked after Lord and Lady Dufferin in Manitoba in 1877.[107] Besides his thriving business in outfitting and guiding "pleasure parties,"[108] he undertook a wide variety of transport assignments. For a time he was manager of a section of the Dawson Route.[109] When a public postal service was started in the West, he carried the mails.[110] Railroad construction gave him a chance to freight supplies for the contractors' crews.[111] When immigrants began to come into the country, he advertised "The Saskatchewan Express" from Winnipeg to Battleford and Edmonton, carrying passengers and mail "at reasonable rates," forwarding freight and making special arrangements for immigrants as well as for hunting parties.[112] This was all in addition to important public service. He was on the Council of Assiniboia, 1868–69; a member of the Executive Council of Manitoba, 1871–76, and its President, 1871–74; a member of the Provincial Legislative Council, 1871–76, and its Speaker, 1871–74; as well as Manitoba's first Minister of Agriculture. From 1873 to 1875 he was a member of the Council of the North-West Territories. He headed the committee set up to make plans for conservation of the buffalo. Speaking English, French, Cree, Ojibway, and Sioux, he got on well with the Indians and played an important part in relation to policy concerning Sioux refugees and in negotiation of five of the Indian treaties concluded in the 1870s, serving as a commissioner for Treaties Five and Six.[113] He bred horses and raced them; he established a herd of tame buffalo. He helped to initiate newcomers, like James Ashdown and the Alloways, into western ways and was famous for his generosity and cheerful hospitality. His wife was the daughter of Chief Factor John Rowand. Her wealth and social status helped him to attain a position among the élite of Rupert's Land and Manitoba, which his own character and qualities did so much to earn.

An advertisement he published in an immigration pamphlet in 1879 spanned the gulf between the buffalo hunting, fur trading days and the advancing frontier of settlement and agriculture, between the wilderness and the "civilized" world. In the same year this "prince of travellers",[114] the great buffalo hunter and plainsman turned business man, died.

McKay's death marked the end of an era, the end of the restless individualism of the native entrepreneurs of Rupert's Land. They had accumulated their own personal capital. Those who achieved wealth, status, and influence had done so on the basis of their own ambition, courage, initiative, energy, and shrewd intelligence and also of their prowess in the chase, on the trail and in boat brigades, and their intimate knowledge of the plains and the peoples of the plains. Now strangers were arriving in increasing numbers. Some of them, like their predecessors, were full of ambition, initiative, energy, courage, and intelligence. They had yet to learn how to live, travel, and trade on the plains,[115] but they brought with them new and different skills — sophisticated commercial[116] and technical skills—and had access to outside sources of capital,[117] to partners with funds, to corporate finances, or to bank loans. Despite the coming of capital-intensive technology—steam boats in place of boat brigades, flat boats, or canoes; railroads in place of Red River carts and pack ponies; packing plants in place of family butchering and processing of plains provisions; and ranching in place of the buffalo hunt—there was still scope for individual enterprise as witness the "Edmonton Trader" from Ontario or Pat Burns, but increasingly, economic initiative in Manitoba and the North-West Territories was to fall into the hands of newcomers, farmers and a new generation of business men, who were attuned to the new ways that were replacing the old roving life of the plains on which the success of the private adventurers of Rupert's Land had once been based.

Notes

1. W.J. Healy, *Women of Red River* (Winnipeg: Russell, Lang and Co. Ltd., 1923), p. 15.

2. Ibid., especially chapter III and pp. 18, 20–21, 26–28, 32, 35, 42, 102, 195.

3. These ranged from 500 acres (for example, W.H. Cook) to 1,000 acres (for example, James Bird). Hudson's Bay Company Archives (hereafter H.B.C.A.) E.6/1–16, Land Register Books and other documents.

    Material from the Hudson's Bay Company Archives is used by kind permission of the Company.

4. E.H. Oliver, *The Canadian North-West; Its Early Development and Legislative Records; Minutes of the Councils of the Red River Colony and the Northern Department of Rupert's Land,* 2 vols. (Ottawa: Government Printing Bureau, 1914–15), vol. I, pp. 58, 61, 314.

5. *Dictionary of Canadian Biography* (*D.C.B.*), X. Many of the individuals mentioned in this essay may be found in *D.C.B.*

6. Oliver, vol. I, p. 59.

7. H.B.C.A., D.4/3, fos. 70–70d, Simpson to D. McKenzie, 5 July 1824.

8. H.B.C.A., D,4/5, fos. 37–37d, Simpson to J.G. McTavish, 1 June 1825.

9. Donald Chaput, "The 'Misses Nolin' of Red River," *The Beaver* (Winter 1975), pp. 14–17.

10. The title of an article by Jennifer Brown, "Ultimate Respectability: Fur-trade Children in the 'Civilized World'," *The Beaver*, part I (Winter 1977), pp. 4–10; part II (Spring 1978), pp. 48–55.

11. Healy, p. 26 and M.A. MacLeod, *Letters of Letitia Hargrave* (Toronto: Champlain Society, 1947), pp. 206–7 and 231–32.

12. P.A.M., Garrioch Papers, MG2 C38, entries in Journal for 24 July and 21 August 1844.

13. Alexander Ross, *Red River Settlement* (London: Smith, Elder and Co., 1856; reprinted, Edmonton: Hurtig Publishers, 1972), pp. 238–39.

14. H.B.C.A., E.4/1a, Register of Marriages, 3 December 1829.

15. Carol Judd, "Native Labour and Social Stratification in the Hudson's Bay Company's Northern Department, 1770–1870, *Review of Canadian Sociology and Anthropology*, vol. XVII, no. 4 (Autumn 1980), pp. 305–14; and "Employment Opportunities for Mixed Bloods in the Hudson's Bay Company to 1870," paper presented to the American Historical Association, 1978.

16. H.B.C.A., B.4/b/1, C.F. John Stuart to Simpson, 26 May 1831. In fact William Sinclair II eventually became a Chief Factor in the service of the Company. *D.C.B.*, IX.

17. Judd, "Employment Opportunities," pp. 18–21.

18. In addition to the *Dictionary of National Biography* and *D.C.B.*, XI, *see British Parliamentary Papers* (Shannon, Ireland: Irish University Press, 1969), vol. 18, *1849, Colonies, Canada, Correspondence Relating to the Red River Settlement and the Hudson's Bay Company*, pp. 293–432, and vol. 3, Report from the *Select Committee on the Hudson's Bay Company, 1857*, pp. 120–37 and 353–56.

19. Alvin C. Gluek, Jr., *Minnesota and the Manifest Destiny of the Canadian Northwest* (Toronto: University of Toronto Press, 1965), pp. 123–25.

20. Canada, Legislative Assembly, *Report on the Exploration of the Country Between Lake Superior and the Red River Settlement* (Toronto: John Lovell, 1858).

21. Sylvia Van Kirk, "What if Mama is an Indian?" in this volume.

22. Guillaume Charette, *Vanishing Spaces: Memoirs of Louis Goulet* (Winnipeg: Editions Bois-Brûlés, 1977), pp. 90–97, translated by Ray Ellerman from the original French edition, *L'Espace de Louis Goulet* (Winnipeg: Editions Bois-Brûlés, 1970.)

23. Sinclair's declaration of intention to become a citizen of the United States was sworn to and subscribed before John K. Humphrey, Clerk, District Court, 9 May 1850, Ramsay Co., Minnesota Territory. The declaration states that he first entered the U.S.A. in October 1849.

24. Public Archives of British Columbia (hereafter P.A.B.C.), Add. MSS 635, file 88, John Lee Lewes, Edmonton (where he had just arrived from the Columbia), 20 December 1848. Thomas Sinclair, in conversation with Manton Marble, confirmed that James had gone to California in 1848. "To Red River and Beyond," part III, *Harper's New Monthly Magazine*, February 1861, p. 313.

25. Peter Erasmus, *Buffalo Days and Nights*, as told to Henry Thompson (Calgary: Glenbow-Alberta Institute, 1976), pp. xx-xxi.

26. Ibid., p. 134.

27. Ross, p. 237.

28. For a vivid picture of this life, *see* Charette and Mary Weekes, *The Last Buffalo Hunter*, in which she recorded the reminiscences of Norbert Welsh (New York: Thomas Nelson and Sons, 1939; Toronto: Macmillan of Canada, 1945).

29. The Rev. William Cockran, for example, considered the way of life of the half-breeds to be "idle gossiping, extravagant, and licentious." John Foster, "Missionaries, Mixed-bloods and the Fur Trade: Four Letters of the Rev. William Cockran, Red River Settlement, 1830–1833," *Western Canadian Journal of Anthropology*, vol. III, no. 1 (1972), p. 105.

30. *See* Charette; Weekes; Erasmus, chapter XIII; Katherine Hughes, *Father Lacombe: The Black-Robe Voyageur* (Toronto: Wm. Briggs, 1914), p. 33; and Father G.A. Belcourt's description of the hunt in H.R. Schoolcraft, ed., *Historical & Statistical Information Concerning the History, Condition and Prospects of the Indian Tribes of the United States*, 6 vols. (Philadelphia: Lippincott, Grambo and Co. for the Bureau of Indian Affairs, 1852–57), part IV, pp. 101–10.

31. Cockran, for instance, wrote: "if they became agriculturalists, they would be rational beings." Foster, p. 116.

32. Belcourt stated that in one hunt, 55 Métis families made £1,700 (less £200 in expenses) in two months. Schoolcraft, ed., p. 110.

33. H.B.C.A., D.4/8, fo. 9d, Simpson to Governor and Committee, 5 June 1824.

34. C. Herman Sprenger, "The Métis Nation: The Buffalo Hunt vs. Agriculture in the Red River Settlement (Circa 1810–1870)." *Western Canadian Journal of Anthropology*, vol. III, no. 1 (1972), pp. 159–78. Charette's and Weekes's accounts confirm Sprenger's views.

35. "The Métis and Canadian Councillors of Assiniboia," part I, *The Beaver* (Summer 1974), pp. 12–13.

36. Ross, pp. 400–403.

37. Healy, p. 17.

38. H.B.C.A., B.235/d/34, "Winnipeg Settlers and Retired Servants Accounts, 1827–28," p. 12; D.5/25 (1849), fo. 607, John Ballenden to Simpson, 20 August 1849.

39. Weekes, pp. 15–26. He was one of the "Little Bearskin" McKays, descendants of John Richards McKays; his family is not to be confused with that of James McKay and his brothers. Their father, another James, was a noted boat brigade guide in the service of the Hudson's Bay Company.

40. Weekes recounts Welsh's experiences and Charette those of Moïse and Louis Goulet.

41. As well as numerous reference in Weekes and a few in Charette, *see* Isaac Cowie, *The Company of Adventurers* (Toronto: William Briggs, 1913).

42. H.B.C.A., A.12/1, fos. 187d–188, Simpson to Governor and Committee, (?) August 1825.

43. H.B.C.A., D.5/15, fo. 134, McDermot to Alexander Christie, 4 August 1845; A.12/2, fo. 659d; Sinclair to Christie, 25 August 1845; A.12/1, fo. 396, Simpson, 18 July 1831.

44. H.B.C.A., A.12/2, fo. 388, Simpson, 20 June 1844.

45. W.L. Morton, Introduction in E.E. Rich, ed., *London Correspondence Inward from Eden Colvile 1849–1852* (London: Hudson's Bay Record Society, 1956), pp. lxiv-lxvi.

46. Ross, pp. 155–57.

47. H.B.C.A., D.4/5, fos. 37–37d, Simpson to J.G. McTavish, 1 June 1825. The Winnipeg Account Books in the H.B.C.A., B.235/d series show how important freighting contracts were to the entrepreneurs of Red River Settlement.

48. H.B.C.A., D.4/23, fo. 121d, Simpson to Alexander Christie, 20 February 1838.

49. H.B.C.A., A.12/2, fo. 544, Simpson to Governor and Committee, 20 June 1845.

50. H.B.C.A., A.12/2, fos. 652–654, Sinclair to Christie, 18 July 1845. The contracts are in H.B.C.A., B.235/z/3, fos. 57, 59, 60, and 62. I am indebted to the Keeper of the Hudson's Bay Company Archives for this reference.

51. Morton, in Rich, ed., *Colvile's Correspondence,* p. lvii.

52. P.A.M., Garrioch Papers, MG2 C38, Journal for 1845.

53. Oliver, I., pp. 314–15, 318–20.

54. H.B.C.A., A.12/1, fo. 421, Simpson to Governor and Committee, 10 August 1832; A.12/2, fo. 181, Simpson, 21 June 1843; and fo. 206d, Simpson to Sir J.H. Pelly, 28 July 1843. *See also* E.E. Rich, *The History of the Hudson's Bay Company 1670–1870,* 2 vols. (London: Hudson's Bay Record Society, 1959), vol. II, p. 480.

55. H.B.C.A., A.12/2, fos. 389–389d, Simpson to the Governor and Committee, 20 June 1844.

56. For one account of these measures, *see* Morton, in Rich, ed., *Colvile's Correspondence,* pp. liv-lxvii. Morton, perhaps, overemphasizes Christie's role. Simpson appears to have instigated and managed the attack on McDermot and Sinclair, probably on the advice of Thom.

57. Gluek, chapter III.

58. H.B.C.A., A.12/2, fo. 659d.

59. Minnesota Historical Society, H.H. Sibley Papers, Kittson to Sibley, 6 February 1845.

60. H.B.C.A., A.12/2, fos. 647–648d, Simpson, 11 November 1845.

61. H.B.C.A., A.12/2, fo. 662, Kenneth McKenzie to McDermot and McLaughlin, 14 March 1845.

62. P.A.M., Garrioch Papers, MG2 C38, "The Pleasures of Smuggling."

63. For the letter from Sinclair et al dated 29 August 1845 and Christie's reply of 5 September 1845, *see* Lewis G. Thomas, ed., *The Prairie West to 1905* (Toronto: Oxford University Press, 1975), pp. 56–59.

64. These memorials are published (but without the signatures to the one in French) in *British Parliamentary Papers*, vol. 18.

65. Morton, in Rich, ed., *Colvile's Correspondence*, p. lxxiii.

66. Ross, pp. 402–3.

67. Ross, pp. 372–77, and St. George Stubbs, *Four Recorders of Rupert's Land* (Winnipeg: Peguis Publishers, 1967), pp. 26–29.

68. Dr. Hector of the Palliser expedition, for example, describes William McMurray's efforts to out-compete free traders at Jack Fish Lake in December 1857. Irene M. Spry, ed., *The Papers of the Palliser Expedition* (Toronto: Champlain Society, 1968), pp. 190–91.

69. H.B.C.A., A.12/2, fos. 656d–657. McDermot to Christie, 4 August 1845.

70. Mae Atwood, ed., *In Rupert's Land, Memoirs of Walter Traill* (Toronto: McClelland and Stewart, 1970), p. 57.

71. H.B.C.A., D.5/37. pp. 603–5. Sinclair to Simpson, 28 and 29 August 1853, and D.4/74, pp. 20–22, Simpson to Sinclair, 8 October 1853.

72. William J. Betts, "From the Red River to the Columbia: The Story of a Migration," *The Beaver* (Spring 1971), pp. 50–55; George Simpson, *Narrative of a Journey Round the World*, 2 vols. (London: Henry Colburn, 1847), vol. I, pp. 66, 76, 78–79, 82, 88–90, 92–93, and 126; and H.B.C.A., D.4/57, p. 48.

73. H.B.C.A., D5/37. pp. 603–4, Sinclair to Simpson, 28 August 1853.

74. Healy, 37, and P.A.C., MG19 E8, Diary for 1854 of Dr. William Cowan, Sinclair's son-in-law.

75. P.A.B.C., Add. MSS 635, file 196, Rowand, 15 December 1850, and file 26, Clouston, 17 December 1850.

76. P.A.B.C., E/B/Si6, Sinclair to McDermot from San Francisco, 19 March 1851.

77. John V. Campbell, "The Sinclair Party–An Emigration Overland...in 1854," edited by William S. Lewis, *The Washington Historical Quarterly* VIII, no. 3 (June 1916), pp. 187–201; P.A.B.C., E/B/Si6, Sinclair from Canal Flats, 24 October 1854, says the party went up the Strong Current River and down the Kootenay to Canal Flats. The Strong Current is clearly today's Kananaskis. It seems unlikely that even Sinclair could have got 250 head of cattle over either Kananaskis Pass, but the Elk Pass, also leading out of the Kananaskis Valley, is much easier and the Elk River might easily be mistaken for the Kootenay. It does not lead to Canal Flats but there is a connection by way of Bull River. Its outlet is marked "Emigrants Pass" on a map by Thomas W. Blakiston of the Palliser Expedition.

78. Healy, p. 37, and H.B.C.A., D.4/75, p. 509, Simpson to Sinclair, 1 March 1855. The Company was to supply Sinclair with 200 head of cattle.

79. Healy, p. 37, and H.B.C.A., B.223/b/41, pp. 212–13, Dugald Mactavish, 5 April 1856.

80. Irene M. Spry, "Free Men and Free Trade," unpublished paper submitted to the Canadian Historical Association meeting in 1979.

81. Moïse Goulet bought his trading stocks at Fort Garry and when he fell ill sold his whole outfit to "Ballantyne" (Bannatyne), Charette, pp. 60, 67–68.

82. Peter Erasmus traded with his old school friend, "Inkster," probably John Inkster's son, Colin. Erasmus, pp. 190–92 and other references.

83. Gluek, chapters 4,5,7, and 8. For contacts between Fort Benton and the southwestern Canadian plains, *see* Paul F. Sharp, *Whoop-Up Country,* 2d edition (Helena: Historical Society of Montana, 1960; orig. ed., Minneapolis: University of Minnesota, 1955).

84. Gluek, pp. 140–50, 162.

85. Irene M. Spry, ed., "A Visit to the Red River and to the Saskatchewan, 1861, by Dr. John Rae, FRGS," *The Geographical Journal,* vol. 140, part I (February 1974), p. 16.

86. Gluek and Sharp.

87. Rich, *History of the Hudson's Bay Company,* II, pp. 816–48, 850–900.

88. Irene M. Spry, "The Transition from a Nomadic to a Settled Economy in Western Canada, 1856–96," *Transactions of the Royal Society of Canada,* vol. IV, series IV (June 1968), section II, 187–201, and "Early Visitors to the Canadian Prairies," in Brian V. Blouet and Merlin P. Lawson, eds., *Images of the Plains* (Lincoln: University of Nebraska Press, 1975) pp. 165–80.

89. Spry, "Transition"; Weekes; and Charette.

90. Weekes, pp. 206–7, 208.

91. Louis Goulet, for example, established a freighting business between Troy (Qu'Appelle) and Prince Albert. Charette, p. 104.

92. Don W. Thomson describes survey activities in *Men and and Meridians: The History of Surveying and Mapping in Canada*, 3 vols. (Ottawa: Queen's Printer, 1966–69), vol II, chapters 3,5, 6, 7, 10, 13, and 18.

93. John Peter Turner, *The North-West Mounted Police, 1873-1893*, 2 vols. (Ottawa: King's Printer, 1950).

94. Alexander Morris, *The Treaties of Canada with the Indians of Manitoba and the North-West Territories* (Toronto: Belfords, Clarke and Co., 1880); Canada, *Indian Treaties and Surrenders*, 3 vols. (Ottawa: Queen's Printer, 1891; reprinted, facsimile ed., Toronto: Coles Publishing Co., 1971); and Weekes, p. 201.

95. For the effect on the Indians, *see* Hugh A. Dempsey, *Crowfoot* (Edmonton: Hurtig, 1972), chapters 10, 11, and 12.

96. Irene M. Spry, "The Great Transformation: The Disappearance of the Commons in Western Canada," in Richard Allen, ed., *Man and Nature on the Prairies* (Regina: Canadian Plains Research Centre, 1976).

97. Men like Hillyard Mitchell, whose account books are in the Saskatchewan Archives, Saskatoon. He sold exotic canned goods and other delicacies.

98. W.L. Morton, *Manitoba: A History* (Toronto: University of Toronto Press, 1957), pp. 144–50; and Lewis H. Thomas, *The Struggle for Responsible Government in the North-West Territories 1870–1897* (Toronto: University of Toronto Press, 1956).

99. Charette, p. 102.

100. Both Norbert Welsh and Louis Goulet, for example, describe a series of new ventures undertaken as the buffalo hunt and plains trade waned, and as new opportunities developed, such as freighting flour, instead of pemmican, and carrying supplies to survey parties instead of to the hunters. Weekes and Charette. By 1865 there was more money to be made in freighting than in trading. Weekes, p. 72.

101. John E. Parsons, *West on the 49th Parallel: Red River to the Rockies 1872-1876* (New York: William Morrow and Co., 1965), pp. 53–54.

102. Weekes, pp. 23–25.

103. N. Jaye Goossen, "A Wearer of Mocassins: The Honourable James McKay of Deer Lodge," unpublished, documented paper and *The Beaver*, (Autumn 1978), pp. 44–53; *D.C.B.*, X; Mary McCarthy Ferguson, *The Honourable James McKay of Deer Lodge* (Winnipeg: By the Author, 1972); Spry, ed., *Palliser Papers*, lxvi–lxvii; and P.A.M., Inkster Papers, "The Honourable James McKay of Deer Lodge," typescript.

104. Spry, ed., "Rae's Visit," p. 9.

105. Ibid., pp. 9–14.

106. Lord Dunmore, "Log of the Wanderers on the Prairies in Search of Buffalo Bear Deer &c, North American Prairies, August, September, October, 1862," MS in the possession of Lady Dunmore.

107. The Marchioness of Dufferin and Ava, *My Canadian Journal 1872-9....* (London: John Murray, 1881), pp. 336-37, 339, 341-43, 359-62, 365, and 367.

108. Advertisement published by McKay in Thomas Spence, *The Prairie Lands of Canada: Presented to the World as a New and Inviting Field of Enterprise for the Capitalist, and Superior Attractions and Advantages as a Home for Immigrants Compared with the Western Prairies of the United States....* (Montreal: Gazette Printing House, 1879).

109. Parsons, p. 35.

110. Advertisement in Spence, *Prairies of Canada.*

111. Goossen, 1978, p. 53. In partnership with William F. Alloway, McKay secured contracts to freight supplies to crews working on the railroad.

112. Advertisement in Spence, *Prairies of Canada.*

113. On this aspect of his career, *see* especially Goossen.

114. *The Nor'Wester,* 1 July 1861.

115. James G. MacGregor, *Edmonton Trader* (Toronto: McClelland and Stewart, 1963) describes the sometimes difficult process of plains eduction that John A. McDougall had to undergo.

116. The importance of the new commercial skills, even in the Hudson's Bay Company, is evident in *The Letters of Charles John Brydges 1879-1882,* edited by Hartwell Bowsfield (Toronto: Hudson's Bay Records Society, 1979).

117. For example, McDougall secured a loan on the basis of funds expected from Ontario (MacGregor, pp. 20-21), and Pat Burns secured a loan from William Mackenzie (Grant McEwan, *Pat Burns: Cattle King* (Saskatoon: Western Producer Prairie Books, 1979), pp. 120-21.

New Brunswick and
Nova Scotia and the
North-West Rebellion, 1885

_____George F.G. Stanley

I

On 27 and 28 March 1885, Canadian newspapers carried the story that a group of Métis, led by Louis Riel, had defeated a force of North West Mounted Police and Prince Albert Volunteers at an obscure site in Saskatchewan known as Duck Lake. Among the twenty-three casualties was Inspector Joseph Howe, a Nova Scotian and a nephew of the well-known politician of the same name.[1]

This "sensational"[2] news came as a surprise to the people of Canada's maritime provinces, perhaps because any outbreak of shooting in anger seems to come as a surprise to Canadians. Not that maritimers in 1884 and 1885 were wholly unaware of Louis Riel's return to the Saskatchewan valley in 1884, or of his political activities among the white and mixed-blood settlers of St. Laurent and Prince Albert, but rather, armed "rebellion" seemed so unlikely in 1885. The situation was different from 1869 to 1870 in Red River, when Louis Riel and his halfbreed associates had organized armed resistance to the incorporation of their homeland, Manitoba, into the Canadian union until positive guarantees had been given by Ottawa. In 1884 and 1885 telegraphic communication existed between the North-West Territories and the rest of Canada. Canadians in all parts of the country were therefore aware that Riel had been invited to leave Montana and lead a protest movement in the Northwest, and that he had been interviewed by the Winnipeg *Sun,* which considered him "an intelligent and shrewd man, a born agitator, yet cool and calculating and a natural leader of men."[3] And not only was there a telegraph line, a transcontinental railway was in the process of construction.

Nova Scotians, if one may judge from the infrequency with which news items relating to the Northwest appeared in the local newspapers, were really not very interested in Riel or in the general discontent to be found on the Canadian prairies. They were far more concerned about local politics, teachers' salaries, Ned Hanlan's defeat in the world championship rowing match in San Francisco, possible union with the West Indies, and the victory of the Liberal "repealer," W.S. Fielding, over his Conservative opponent, John Payzant, in the Halifax county by-election in July 1884. When they did look farther afield, it was to read about the insoluble Irish question in the United Kingdom, or to discover if Mrs. Belva Lockwood of Washington was really going to run as a Women's Rights candidate in the United States presidential election. Of course, some Nova Scotians, if they were Conservatives, might read about Sir Hector Langevin's reception in the city of Winnipeg in September 1884, or listen to A.N. Burgess, the Deputy Minister of the Interior, who visited Halifax and talked about the crop prospects in the West, the demise of the Farmers' Union, and his belief that the ranchers were not, despite statements to the contrary, opposed to farm settlement on the plains.[4] But there was very little to read regarding the grievances of western farmers, the halfbreeds, or even Riel himself.

Despite Inspector Howe's wounding, Nova Scotians were not alarmed at the news of Duck Lake. Not, at least, for several weeks. Duck Lake might conjure up visions of Indian massacres in the imaginations of white settlers living in isolated prairie communities; it might prompt the immediate dispatch of the Winnipeg militia (the Ninetieth Rifles) to Qu'Appelle, the nearest point on the railway line to Riel's headquarters at Batoche; but in Halifax it merely afforded the Conservative *Morning Herald* new opportunities to cross verbal swords with its Liberal rival, the *Chronicle*. According to the editor of the *Morning Herald*, "the Grits" had been largely responsible for Riel's actions, having aided and abetted the Métis, whose "disturbance" would, "like Joseph's gourd ... disappear in a day."[5] Looking for possible explanations for the Métis' actions, the *Morning Herald* speculated upon the possibility that the "riot" had been engineered by "those two sources of Grit Policy," the Northern Pacific and the Grand Trunk railways. They were obviously responsible for "Mr. Riel's latest pranks."[6] The *Morning Herald*, admitting that the Métis might possibly have "reasonable" grievances and that the federal government could possibly have been "slow" in looking into them,[7] could see no chance of a successful rebellion on the part of the halfbreeds. How could these miserable people hope "to give the Dominion of Canada very serious trouble"[8] when the Canadian Pacific Railway could transport the Royal Irish Rifles, complete with arms and stores, from Halifax to the Northwest in less than a week? After all, this was 1885, not the days of the Red River Insurrection of fifteen years earlier, when Wolseley's troops took several months to travel to Fort Garry by steamboat, canoe, and on foot.

New Brunswickers were no better informed about the Northwest than were the Nova Scotians. They did, however, read that the Canadian Pacific Railway was planning to ship cattle to the Northwest from Moncton, Sussex, and Sackville, and that the railway was building special cars that would travel over Canada displaying North-West Territories produce, including Red Fife wheat, oats, cabbages, turnips, mangels, potatoes, cauliflower, native grasses, and coal.[9] Not until the telegraph wires carried the word of the victory of Riel's men over Superintendent L.N.F. Crozier's force at Duck Lake did news from the Northwest become a daily feature of the newspapers of New Brunswick.[10] Even then, however, the members of the Legislative Council and the Legislative Assembly did not consider it worth their while to make any reference to what was happening in the Northwest. The session in Fredericton closed in April without the name of Louis Riel ever being mentioned in the debates.[11]

New Brunswick journalists, like their Nova Scotian colleagues, once they did become aware of the serious nature of developments in the Northwest, tended to follow the line adopted by the political party with which they were associated. At first, New Brunswickers adopted a low-key approach. They limited themselves largely to reprinting reports and articles that had already appeared in the press of the upper provinces, particularly in Toronto and Montreal, and in the Winnipeg newspapers. These last were regarded with suspicion; perhaps they were too close to the events and were, in consequence, less reliable. For the most part, news items were short factual statements unaccompanied by political comment, although, according to the Moncton *Times,* itself given to occasional bursts of political hysteria, the Grit papers were prone to publish "doctored" and "coloured" reports.[12] There was a great deal of searching for answers to the question of why the halfbreeds had taken up arms. The *Sun* of Saint

John wondered if Russia was responsible for the troubles in the Northwest, and whether Russian agents had engineered the whole thing in an effort to prevent Canada from helping England halt Russia's growing imperialism.[13] Other journalists wondered if the rebellion was designed to stop the dispatch of Canadian troops to the Sudan or Afghanistan where they might be required by the Mother Country. The Fredericton *Evening Capital* expressed the view that the troubles in the Northwest were clearly the outcome of clandestine Fenian activities. The I.R.A. was sending money and arms to Riel![14] Accurate reporting was not an editorial long suit, particularly when one considers *The New Brunswick Reporter*'s description of Riel as a man who had "snugly ensconced himself in the Chair of a Professorship in a Western College" in which he "should have remained satisfied with this condition of life."[15]

Despite these flights of editorial fancy, it is fair to say that, at the outset, the New Brunswick newspapers were disposed to play down their political bias, showing a remarkable degree of non-partisanship in their reports.[16] Upon one point they all agreed, namely, that the rising, or "rebellion" as they always called it, should be suppressed.

Unlike Nova Scotia, New Brunswick had a considerable number of French-speaking inhabitants, in addition to an Anglophone population made up largely of English and Irish settlers. Expelled in 1755 by the British authorities from the region known as Acadie, many of the original French settlers had returned to their homeland after 1764, when the Lords of Trade gave them permission to do so. They could not re-occupy the farm lands from which they had originally been driven. These had been purchased, seized, or squatted upon by settlers from England and New England. Therefore, they had to find new homes. They settled in Cape Breton and in southwest Nova Scotia, in western Prince Edward Island, and more particularly in New Brunswick, along Chaleur Bay and the northeast coast, extending from Restigouche to Westmorland counties. A glance at the map of the maritime provinces will reveal that the Francophone communities in New Brunswick possessed a greater geographical and, in consequence, cultural cohesion than those of Nova Scotia. It is hardly surprising, therefore, that, as the Acadians became more politically and culturally self-aware, the dynamic should have come from the Acadians of New Brunswick rather than those of Nova Scotia or Prince Edward Island. This was the case particularly after the founding of St. Joseph College at Memramcook in 1864. Some years later, a number of Acadians were invited to take part in the great national demonstration at Quebec organized by the Société St.Jean-Baptiste. This was followed in 1881 by a national convention of Acadians at Memramcook, the first of several such national gatherings, which led to the establishment of a national Acadian society, the selection of a national flag, a national hymn, and a national holiday.[17] Here, then, in the early 1880s, was a distinct ethnic and cultural group, striving for self-identification and recognition; a group that, within the limits of New Brunswick, resembled the French Canadians of Quebec within the larger limits of Canada. New Brunswick was a microcosm, culturally and politically, of the whole of Canada. Would it not have been natural for the Acadians to show sympathy, if not active support, for Louis Riel and the Métis who also constituted a distinct ethnic and cultural group, struggling for self-realization and recognition within the boundaries of western Canada?

Neither in 1884, nor in the early months of 1885, did the Acadians see in Riel and the Métis movement a parallel to their own historical development. *Le Moniteur* of Shediac, the sole French-language newspaper in the province at this time, had virtually nothing to say about Louis Riel prior to the engagement at Duck Lake. Politically, the allegiance of the newspaper was Conservative; for the Conservatives, ever since the alliance of John A. Macdonald and George E. Cartier, had been looked upon by the Francophone population of Canada as being more sympathetic to their aspirations than the Liberal party of the Francophobe Ontarian, George Brown. After the shots were fired at Duck Lake, *Le Moniteur* reported events in the Northwest without comment. The source of *Le Moniteur*'s information was the Conservative French-language press in Quebec, usually *La Minerve*. When the editor did, occasionally, express his opinion, it was to observe cautiously that the Métis had been neglected by the federal authorities and had, in a moment of exasperation, yielded "aux conseils peu sages de quelques chefs."[18] It is possible that *Le Moniteur*'s lack of enthusiasm for Riel may have come from Riel's break with the Roman Catholic church in March 1885. The same lack of support for Riel on the part of a number of newspapers in Quebec derives from this source. The Toronto *Globe* summed up an attitude that, at least at the outset of the Saskatchewan troubles, was fairly widely held by maritimers and Canadians alike: "Riel is not the whole half-breed population."[19]

II

The Canadian militia was not prepared for the problem presented by Duck Lake, probably because the government had never expected that western political discontent would lead to armed rebellion. As far as Canadian defence was concerned, it had been seen essentially as a response to an external rather than internal threat. And external defence was looked upon as Great Britain's responsibility, with the Canadian militia playing only a back-up role. Accordingly, in 1885, Ottawa had to improvise every step at the last moment. It is astonishing that everything went off as well as it did. On 22 March, Major General Frederick Middleton, a British professional soldier who had wangled the command appointment in Canada as an undemanding post for his last quiet years before mandatory retirement, was told to go to the Northwest to look over the situation. He was not quite sure why, but admitted, "I am inclined to think that there must be something serious or Sir John would not have consented to my being sent up."[20] Early on 27 March, a few hours after the news of Duck Lake had gone over the telegraph wires, Middleton arrived in Winnipeg. Meanwhile, a company of the Ninetieth Rifles (Winnipeg) had been mobilized and additional Manitoba troops were called out for service. This was followed by the dispatch of the two regular batteries from Kingston and Quebec, a company of the Infantry School Corps (later the Royal Canadian Regiment) from Toronto, and militia artillery from both Ontario and Quebec. Despite the reference in the Halifax *Herald* to the possible use of the Royal Irish Rifles, a British regiment stationed in Halifax for the defence of H.M. Dockyard, it was the intention of the Department of Militia to use only Canadian soldiers.[21] For that reason no assistance was requested from Great Britain. Instead, militia units in the maritime provinces were placed on the alert late in March.

In Halifax, Lieutenant Colonel J.J. Bremner, commanding the Sixty-sixth Princess Louise Rifles, was eager to lead his troops in battle. On 30 March, acting through the local Deputy Adjutant-General, the "elderly and somewhat fussy" Lieutenant-Colonel John Barton Taylor, he offered the services of the Fusiliers to the Adjutant-General in Ottawa. This officer, Colonel Walker Powell, replied by asking Bremner to hold his men in readiness to proceed to the Northwest on short notice. Bremner was delighted. Instructions were immediately issued for the officers and men of the Sixty-sixth to parade in full dress at the drill shed on the afternoon of 1 April. The response was good and on 2 April the officers and men of the regiment were informed that they were now "on active service" and that it was "no longer a matter of choice."[22] To bring the regiment up to full strength, an active recruiting campaign was undertaken.

Not all Haligonians were as military-minded and as pro-Canada as Colonel Bremner. Separatism in Nova Scotia had not died when Joseph Howe accepted an appointment in the federal cabinet. "Repealers" were still active in Nova Scotia politics in 1885, and even the provincial premier, the Honorable W.S. Fielding, was disposed to flirt with the idea of separation from Canada. It is hardly surprising, therefore, to discover a number of Halifax employers proposing to dismiss their employees should they continue to turn out for militia parades. Of course, there was an economic argument to justify these threats. The absence of the workers from their jobs would slow down or even halt production. But there was also a political bias behind the economics, which became obvious when some merchants argued that the federal government had "no business to call upon the Militia in Halifax to go to the North West to fight Half-Breeds and Indians" and that "this rebellion in the western part of Canada" was "none of our funeral down here."[23] In the local legislature, Otto Weeks, the anti-Confederate member for Guysborough, rose from his seat in Province House on 1 April to demand if any communication had been received from Ottawa ordering Nova Scotians into military service. Was this call compulsory or voluntary? "When it comes to be known," Weeks told his fellow-members,

> that out of one establishment in this city ten men had been required to present themselves at the drill shed, and that the sons of some of our wealthiest and most respected citizens had been required to present themselves, it would be seen that it was important to ascertain whether the necessary steps had been taken to give the order calling out these men validity.

Developing his argument that the call was illegal, Weeks declared that "Her Majesty alone could call upon the Militia in particular districts to serve outside the limits of such districts," and that he had "yet to see any requisition from Her Majesty the Queen calling upon the Militia

of this province to serve in suppressing the North West Rebellion."
Surely, he added, the upper provinces had "a sufficient number of men
available for the purpose." Nova Scotia had "nothing to do" with the
rebellion, which could have been avoided had the government in Ottawa taken the "proper precautions."[24]

Weeks's argument was fallacious. Even the premier was prepared
to admit as much when he pointed out that the British North America
Act gave the federal authorities complete jurisdiction over the
militia. One of the members of the Assembly had to be restrained
from administering a corporal rebuke to Weeks. And the Halifax *Herald* reported that Weeks had made "a bad speech" and suggested that
"the Speaker of the Assembly should shut that man's mouth."[25] Weeks
tried to defend his position in the House of Assembly the next day,
falling back on the familiar argument of "free speech." He resented the
inference that he was a "traitor"; he believed that he was simply expressing the views of those Nova Scotians who were opposed to using
the people of the Maritimes to fight Canada's battles in the Northwest
"before Militia nearer the scene had been exhausted."[26]

Nevertheless, Weeks was not alone in his opposition to Nova Scotian participation in the federal attempt to suppress the North-West
Rebellion. He had the support of a number of Halifax merchants, and
James Crosskill Mackintosh, the Mayor of Halifax, with a municipal
election in the offing, found himself in the awkward position of having to mediate between the merchants distressed at the thought of losing employees to the militia[27] and the pro-Canadian militia group an-
noyed at the anti-Confederate sympathies of those who opposed sending Nova Scotian soldiers to the Northwest. Mackintosh could appreciate the merchants' point of view—they might have to close some
of their shops and factories—but if he were to take any steps that
might discourage recruiting, he would be charged with disloyalty.
And in any electoral contest between patriotism and profit—especially in wartime—Mackintosh suspected that the blare of the trumpet
would sound more loudly than the tinkle of the cash register.[28]
Mackintosh was particularly alarmed when he received a telegram
stating that a bulletin had been posted in Montreal to the effect that
the men of the Halifax militia had refused to go to the Northwest.
Mackintosh's correspondent, J.L. Harris, asked if what was going on
in Halifax indicated "a want of patriotism in the people" and demanding it be "contradicted promptly if false as it surely must be."

Mackintosh replied to Harris that the report was "exaggerated" but admitted that some employers were threatening "to dismiss men if they turn out." He also sent a note to the *Gazette* and to the *Herald* in Montreal stating that "Nova Scotia won't fail in her duty to the Queen and country."[29] When he met the merchants in his office, Mackintosh waved in their face the telegrams he had received—from Montreal of all places—questioning the loyalty of Haligonians, and told them that "public opinion would not tolerate such a state of matters." But Mackintosh was politician enough to realize that a compromise would be the best solution to his problem; rather than send the Sixty-sixth Fusiliers, perhaps a composite Nova Scotian battalion could be organized. Those members of the Fusiliers who were unfit or who were essential for the conduct of the business concerns with which they were associated might be excused duty, their places being taken by drafts from other regiments. This suggestion was received with widespread acclaim. The merchants liked it. So, too, did those volunteers anxious for the excitement of military service, especially when it was accompanied by a promise to form a soldiers' relief association to look after the families of the men who would be far from home and unable to support them on a private's pay. According to the Halifax newspaper, after Mackintosh put forward his suggestion, "the copperheads slunk away to the rear, and the loyalty and enthusiasm of the people asserted itself." Poking fun at the "repealers," the editor of the *Herald* wrote,

> It is said that the "repeal" leaders in the North West are frightfully disgusted with their comrades in Nova Scotia. Poundmaker, Red Pheasant, Yellow Calf and Riel have written the "repealers" in Nova Scotia asking them why they are so afraid to go to the country.... they have "gone to the country" and they demand that Croaking Jim, Big Fury and Little-Man-with-the-gun down here by the sea, should do likewise.[30]

While Mackintosh was exercising his political talents in Halifax, telegrams were on their way to Ottawa putting forward his suggestion of a composite battalion.[31] On 3 April it was officially announced by Deputy Adjutant-General Taylor that the Minister of Militia, the Honorable Adolphe Caron, had sanctioned the formation of a provisional battalion that would be made up of the Sixty-sixth Princess

Louise Fusiliers, the Sixty-third Halifax Rifles, and the Halifax Garrison Artillery.[32] There was some doubt in the mind of Colonel Taylor as to the suitability of J.J. Bremner of the Sixty-sixth to command the battalion under active service conditions. He was a fussy, cranky, indecisive man but he had good connections and so he remained in charge of the new Provisional Halifax Battalion.[33] Fortunately, in Taylor's view, Major Charles John MacDonald, the local Post Office Inspector, would be able to carry most of the load. Meanwhile, the officers and men of the new battalion continued to weed out the paper soldiers. Everything was going well. For the moment at least, the merchants were silent. So, too, were the hard-line "repealers," although here and there in the provincial press there were indications of hostility to Nova Scotian participation in the fighting in the Northwest. Writing to his mother on 5 April, William Tupper, the son of Sir Charles (who had enlisted in the Sixty-sixth so that people would not be able to say that "young Tupper funked his duty and is a coward" and would be shamed by the thought that Edward Blake's son and nephew had gone "to the front" but that neither of the Tuppers had done so) stated that "although the Grits in Halifax are showing the white feather," the son of A.G. Jones, one of the province's leading Liberals, had turned up on parade.[34]

Finally, on 10 April, orders came from Ottawa that the Halifax Battalion would proceed at once to the western plains. Guns were fired from the Citadel and the troops mustered at the drill shed on Spring Garden Road. Each man received three blankets and twenty rounds of ammunition. William Tupper's brother brought him a "splendid pair of water-tight boots," which were to stand him in good stead. On the morning of the next day, crowds gathered to speed the troops on their way, and accompanied by the bands of the two militia regiments, the Sixty-sixth and the Sixty-third, the Halifax Provisional Battalion marched from the drill shed to the station. According to Tupper, "there was no business done that day in Halifax, but everyone was beside himself with enthusiasm for the Hfx Battalion."[35] To the cheers of the crowd the troops entrained in the second-class carriages of the special train drawn up at the platform. The officers had a first-class carriage to themselves. Stacking their rifles and their swords, cartridge belts, and other military impedimenta wherever they could, the troops settled down for a long journey to Winnipeg. There was no sleeping accommodation and nothing to do. But perhaps the rest was

better than spending several hours a day drilling on the parade at nine-
ty cents a day and paying for one's own rations. Now they were getting fifty cents with rations provided; and Colonel Bremner had
received four hundred dollars a month to furnish meals.[36]

All along the railway line, crowds gathered to cheer the troops as
the train sped past: Moncton, Campbellton, and finally Montreal the
next day, where, during a brief stopover of fifteen minutes, the mayor
of the city delivered a short patriotic address. Then, on again to Ottawa, where the troops changed trains and acquired sleeping cars
"just like Pullman's except they have no cushions or padding."[37] Then
on to Pembroke, Mattawa, and Biscutasing to the end of the railway
line. Borne in open sleighs, they journeyed all day to cover the next
twenty-five miles in deep snow; then, on flatcars, with no more protection from the elements than that afforded by a few board railings
on the sides. After sixty miles of this, another gap of twenty-five miles
had to be covered by most of the men on foot. Once more back to the
open flatcars as far as Jack Fish Bay, where there was a stopover to
enable the battalion baggage to catch up. The cold, the damp, the
wind, the physical discomfort, and then, at long last, Winnipeg. Some
old soldiers who had served with the British Army against the Rus-
sians declared that the journey to the Canadian Northwest imposed
greater hardships "than they had ever experienced in the Crimea."[38]
Few of Halifax soldiers would ever experience anything like it again.
And yet, they survived in good health—most of them.

The Halifax Provisional Battalion never saw action against the
Métis or against the Indians. Instead they found themselves manning
the lines of communication along the Canadian Pacific Railway between Swift Current and Medicine Hat[39] under the command of
Major-General J. Windham Laurie, an ex-British regular army officer,
who had settled in Halifax and for several years was in charge of the
Nova Scotia militia. Laurie, because his seniority would have been a
source of embarrassment to Major-General Middleton, was not given
an active command. Instead he was given the official title of Com-
mander of the Base and Lines of Communication and sent to Swift
Current, a small community that had no military role other than that
served by its location on the Canadian Pacific Railway as the closest
point to the South Saskatchewan River. From his headquarters at
Swift Current, Laurie was to organize and supervise the movement of
men and supplies by boat to the seat of the insurrection downstream.

Neither Laurie nor the Nova Scotian soldiery acquired much distinction in their dull but essential role. In a letter to his mother, young Tupper wrote on 13 June, "We are here doing no earthly good, except wasting Gov't Money." A week later, Tupper remarked, "We are all heartily sick of the regular routine of military life."[40] On 21 June there was strong protest from the troops when they were kept working instead of given a holiday to celebrate Halifax's natal day. At least some of them found relief from boredom by visiting the Rocky Mountains. William Tupper was one of the lucky ones. Along with several of his friends in the regiment, he travelled to Calgary, Canmore, and Banff. Crossing the Bow River at Banff on a raft, the young Nova Scotians entered the cave in Sulphur Mountain and bathed in the warm water. "It reminded me of Dante's Inferno," wrote Tupper, "as it was dark, hot, and sulphurous and we all looked like devils in the weird light."[41]

At last, orders were issued to prepare the return home, and in mid-July the Halifax Provisional Battalion moved to Winnipeg; there, on 17 July, the troops embarked on the east-bound train that was to take them over the Grand Trunk line via Sarnia to Toronto and Montreal and then home to Halifax. In Halifax, preparations were being made to receive the heroes of the North-West campaign. There would be music and speeches, of course, and fireworks and food, and a long march through the city streets from the railway station along North, Brunswick, Jacob, Argyle, Buckingham, Granville, George, Hollis, and Pleasant streets. Along the whole route, banners would be hung bearing the names Saskatchewan Landing, Medicine Hat, Swift Current, Moose Jaw, just as if they were battle honors. When on 24 July, the "brave and successful" soldiery detrained at the station, they were greeted by Lieutenant-Governor Richey, the Provincial Secretary, J.W. Longley, Mayor Mackintosh, and members of the city council. At the Exhibition Building, food was served and the

> Moose Jaw Minstrels, dressed as Indians, put on a show. The whole reception was concluded with a display of fireworks and the burning of Louis Riel in effigy. On the following Sunday, prayers of thanks were offered up in the various churches for the safe return of the volunteers.[42]

III

At least the Nova Scotia Battalion reached the Northwest. The volunteers in New Brunswick never got beyond their camp at Sussex. Not even the regulars of the Infantry School Corps at Fredericton left the province. While their comrades from Toronto were being blooded by Poundmaker's Crees at Cutknife, the Fredericton Company of the Infantry School Corps remained in barracks waiting for their movement order. That did not come until 11 May. On that day Lieutenant-Colonel George Maunsell, the Deputy Adjutant-General for Military District No. 8, received a telegram from Ottawa, asking for a battalion of infantry comprising the regulars and eight companies of militia "for immediate service in the North West."[43]

Anxious to avoid the kind of problems that had occurred in Halifax, Maunsell decided to draw his men, not from any one city corps in Saint John, but from several units scattered throughout the province. He therefore split the Infantry School Corps into two companies, and for the remainder drew his men from the Sixty-second Saint John Fusiliers, the Sixty-seventh Carleton Light Infantry, the Seventy-first York Regiment, the Seventy-third Northumberland Regiment, the Seventy-fourth New Brunswick Rangers, and two companies of the Eighty-second Queen's Country Regiment from Prince Edward Island. On 16 May the newly formed composite battalion was ordered to proceed to Sussex. "Immense crowds," according to local press report, assembled at Fredericton and at Saint John to wish "God Speed" to the troops "en route" for the Northwest.[44] In number they totalled 429 officers and men. With them was their chaplain, the Reverend G.G. Roberts of Fredericton and formerly of Westcock near Sackville, the father of the poet, Sir Charles G.D. Roberts.[45]

Meanwhile, the final military engagement of the North-West Rebellion had been fought at Batoche, on the banks of the South Saskatchewan River. After a three-day battle, Riel's men, lacking ammunition and bodies, yielded to Middleton's militia army. On 15 May Riel gave himself up to two of Middleton's scouts. Still another battle remained to be fought by Major General T.B. Strange against the Cree Chief, Big Bear, at Frenchman's Butte on 28 May; but when Riel surrendered, to all intents and purposes, the rebellion was at an end. There was no further requirement for troops from eastern Canada, and the New Brunswick soldiers assembled at Camp Sussex were paid off on 26 May. On the following day they quietly returned home.[46]

IV

With the shooting war over, the political war began. It was a war over Métis rights, real or imaginary, valid or illegitimate, but, above all, over what was to be done with the Métis leader, Louis Riel. During the political war, the abstention from bickering, and the solidarity and unity that had generally characterized Canadian attitudes from one end of the country to the other during the weeks of the actual rebellion, began to disintegrate when the fighting came to an end. Canada became divided. The division was not strictly along religious lines, Roman Catholic versus Protestant Orangemen; nor was it even strictly along racial lines, French versus English. It was political, with ethnic overtones.

The official Conservative line was that Louis Riel had led the Métis in armed revolt against the Crown and had encouraged the Indians to participate. He should therefore be punished. And the penalty for treason was death. The Liberal opposition took the view that Riel had, admittedly, led an armed uprising; but the Conservatives were to blame. Their attitude to halfbreed grievances had provoked the native peoples into taking up arms. During the next few months, these arguments were repeated day after day in the columns of the newspapers and on the hustings.

The Conservative newspapers, such as *The Mail* in Toronto and the *Gazette* in Montreal, *The Times* in Moncton, the *Sun* in Saint John and *The Morning Herald* in Halifax, gave full support to the federal government's policy as expressed in Parliament. Making allowance for regional differences, on the issue of the trial and execution of Louis Riel they all read very much alike; largely because of the accepted practice of the provincial papers of copying articles and news items directly from the metropolitan dailies. By the same token, the Liberal papers, *The Globe* in Toronto, the *Herald* in Montreal, *The Transcript* in Moncton, the *Globe* in Saint John and the *Chronicle* in Halifax, were easily identifiable by the anti-government tenor and content of their editorials on the Riel issue.[47]

As the weeks passed, the editorials grew sharper and more strident. Journalists in Canada in the 1880s were not disposed to pull their punches and, even if more biased than the colorless "independent" reporters to which Canadians have become accustomed a century later, they produced lively prose. *The Times,* for instance, did not hesitate to suggest that there would be no pardoning of Riel merely because he was of French extraction, and the *Maritime Farmer* demanded that the gallows be erected at once so "the murderer" could swing for his sin of shedding innocent blood and for despoiling the western country. The *Herald,* aiming a blow at Edward Blake, who on 6 July delivered a devastating but excessively dull seven-hour speech condemning the "neglect, delay and mismanagement in matters affecting the peace, welfare and good government of the country,"[48] remarked dryly that the Grits had "an unfortunate faculty of getting in the same boat with rebels, traitors and enemies of the country of every kind, and of doing so at the most unfortunate times."[49] The Nova Scotia secessionists had little to say. They had burned their fingers by opposing the dispatch of Nova Scotian troops to the Northwest and were not anxious to identify themselves with Riel's cause once the Métis leader had been defeated. One of the "repealers," J.W. Longley, simply remarked that Riel was a Tory;[50] Richardson, the judge at Riel's trial, was a Tory and the lawyers for the prosecution were Tories. And Longley did not like Tories. In 1886, W.S. Fielding's Liberal administration went to the electorate on the issue of the repeal of the British North America Act, arguing the case for provincial fiscal autonomy (how familiar that sounds today!), objecting to federal taxes to support public works in the "barren" West.[51] Fielding won his election, but his victory was mollified eight months later, when Sir John A. Macdonald won fourteen of twenty-one Nova Scotian seats in the federal election. And of the seven Liberals elected, only two were "repealers." Perhaps the most restrained newspaper in the Maritimes was *The Transcript,* which argued that Riel, whatever he might have done, was entitled to a fair trial and to competent counsel. And when the death sentence was pronounced, *The Transcript* spoke out strongly in favor of commutation.

Another Anglophone who favored clemency for Riel was the Nova Scotia-born Principal of Queen's University in Kingston, Ontario, George Monro Grant. Grant had travelled across Canada in the early seventies and published his *Ocean to Ocean* in 1873. He knew the western scene and he knew the Métis. In a public lecture delivered in Halifax on 28 August 1885, Grant took a strong stand about Riel, arguing that to hang him "would be criminal on our part.... it would not only be a crime but a blunder.... Rather than hang him, I would open his prison doors and let him go free."[52] With what would almost seem to be prophetic foresight, Grant predicted that Riel's execution would "embitter the half-breeds against us permanently. They would complain that the English had hanged the man who had gone to their relief." His was not a popular point of view in English-speaking Canada at that time, and the vote of thanks stressed Grant's courage more than his judgement. But Grant, it should be remembered, was not a party man. The editor of the Halifax *Chronicle*, however, was a party man and although he was not prepared to accept Grant's suggestion tht Riel should be set free, he did explain that in "keeping silent on Riel's fate" he was "following good precedents and complying with the dictates of common decency": "We deem it by no means a duty to howl for Riel's blood. However much we may think him deserving of the greatest punishment known to the law, we still do not consider it proper or even decent to join in the cry for his death."[53]

In Saint John, New Brunswick, the *Telegraph* took the stand that the death sentence should be commuted, not because the editor felt any particular sympathy for Riel, but because he was alarmed by the political overtones of the Riel issue in Canada. Why execute a man if the cost in terms of Canadian unity was too great? At the same time, however, the Moncton *Times* was demanding that the sentence be carried out. "Not for a moment," stated *The Times*, "would a pardon be tolerated by . . . patriotic citizens." The Saint John *Sun*, by way of contrast, was beginning to question the advisability of the death sentence, admitting quite frankly that its change of attitude was not because it disliked Riel less, but because it loved Canada more, and feared that Riel's execution would only make a "martyr" of him. In prison, Riel would be forgotten—better, then, that the death sentence be commuted. The *Globe* in Saint John never came out openly for a commutation, but concentrated its editorial attacks upon Sir John Macdonald as the man really responsible for precipitating the whole crisis. The Moncton *Transcript* constantly argued that the execution of Riel was not just a legal matter; it was basically a political one, and politics demanded the commutation of the death sentence. But if some of the principal dailies were inclined toward life imprisonment rather than death, there were others that adhered strictly to the legalistic approach, urging that Riel should swing from the gallows since the courts had condemned him to hang. Among those clamoring for the legal pound of flesh were the politically independent *Union Advocate* and the *Miramichi Advance*.

In view of these differences of opinion, it is interesting to note that most of the maritime newspapers, after Riel's execution on 16 November 1885, quickly ceased to comment upon what had happened. For a few weeks the Riel issue continued to provide the press with opportunities to play the political war game, and for a few days after the execution, newspapers all over Canada played it to the limit. The *Chronicle*, for instance, parroting the Toronto *Globe*, asserted that Macdonald's trip to England at this time was the action of a "terrified" person who had "skulked out of Canada like the guilty man he is" in a futile effort to escape the consequences of his actions. At intervals, the two Halifax dailies exchanged verbal blows on the matter of half-breed claims. But Riel, dead, quickly ceased to be news in the English-speaking regions of maritime Canada, and for the most part, both the Nova Scotian and the New Brunswick newspapers returned to the kind of items that had filled their columns in the months prior to Duck Lake. Stewart Parnell took Riel's place in the minds of maritimers as the political bad boy. And when not commenting upon the Irish question, Anglophone editorial writers directed the attention of the public to trade with the United States, the problems of the fishermen, the elections in England, the death of King Alfonso of Spain, and the advisability of vaccination for smallpox.

The sharp lines that characterized most of the English-language press in Canada became somewhat blurred in the case of the French-language press, largely as a result of the emergence of the "national" issue, that is, by the identification of Louis Riel and the western Métis with the French Canadians of Quebec. Although Métis "nativism" was the real source of the Métis consciousness of their own identity, many French Canadians in Quebec were inclined to see the half-breed rising as a manifestation of Franco-Latin "nationalism" on the western plains. The result was that the Conservative press and their pro-government supporters at the constituency level found themselves faced with a conflict of loyalties: to the Conservative party (backed by hierarchy) and to their French cultural background, and even loyalty to their province. *La Minerve*, the principal Conservative French-language paper in Quebec, felt compelled to soften its earlier anti-Riel stand as the date for Riel's execution approached. It might even have come out whole-heartedly for Riel had it not been for Riel's religious apostacy.

The opposition of the church derived from Riel's religious unorthodoxy, which dated back to his days in Longue Pointe and Beauport. Riel's idea of setting up a new, reformed Catholic church in western Canada, his abrupt defiance of R.P. Moulin at Batoche, and the murder of the two Oblates, Marchand and Fafard, at Frog Lake by Big Bear's Indians, alienated many of the clergy; and in so doing, prevented Riel's fate becoming a matter of religious as well as political controversy. What Orangeman could attack Riel as a Roman Catholic, while at the same time the Roman clergy were attacking him as a lapsed Catholic? Admittedly, whenever the church has come in conflict with the "national" idea in Quebec, the "national" idea has invariably emerged on top. And it was Quebec's "national" sympathies that dominated the response of the French-language press in Quebec.

The same, however, cannot be said of the French-language press in the Maritimes. Here, in the nineteenth century, Catholicism and Acadian "nationalism" were mutually supportive. That is why both *Le Moniteur* and *Le Courrier des Provinces Maritimes* avoided editorializing on the fate of Louis Riel. It was sufficient for them to copy articles and news items from the Quebec newspapers, and to give them front-page publicity. *Le Moniteur* would go no further than to deplore the "ignorance" and "fanatisme" of the Moncton *Times*; *Le Courrier* merely regretted Riel's "triste exécution." The result was that in New Brunswick, the racial tension that marked political developments in Quebec and Ontario and gave strength to Honoré Mercier, never attained the same degree of intensity as in the upper provinces.

V

During the summer and autumn of 1885, voters in the Maritimes had only limited opportunities to express their views on the federal government's policy in western Canada and on the fate of Louis Riel. Two by-elections were held in the autumn following Riel's trial, but prior to his execution. In the New Brunswick port city of Saint John, the sitting Liberal member, Isaac Burpee, died. He had been elected as a supporter of Edward Blake in 1882, defeating the Conservative candidate, Charles A. Everett, by a majority of 534 votes. In October 1885 Everett once more offered himself as a pro-government candidate. The Liberal candidate was George MacLeod. This time Everett had no difficulty in winning the Saint John seat. His opponent endeavored to introduce other issues into the political campaign, but it was soon clear that the dominant theme was the federal government's policy in the Northwest. According to Everett, a vote for the Conservative party was a vote for Canadian unity, and a vote for Blake was a vote in support of rebellion. It was an argument the Liberals found hard to answer. The Roman Catholic vote, which, under normal circumstances, was inclined to go to the Liberals, was turned away by the recollection of Riel's apostasy.[54] How could any convinced Catholic vote for the party that sympathized with an apostate?

The Conservative victory in Saint John was repeated in the constituency of Antigonish, Nova Scotia. Here, John Sparrow Thompson was persuaded by Sir John A. Macdonald to leave the bench, to which he had been appointed in 1882, to run as the government candidate in a constituency that he had previously represented in the provincial legislature. As the appointed Minister of Justice in succession to Alexander Campbell, Macdonald's one-time law partner in Kingston, Ontario, Thompson was a strong candidate. A convert to Catholicism, he was not popular with the Orange order; but no Orangeman could conscientiously support a party that sympathized with the man who had been responsible for the death of Orangeman Thomas Scott in Red River in 1870. And Antagonish was largely a Catholic constituency. With the strong support of Bishop Cameron of Antigonish, Thompson had little difficulty in being elected over his opponent, Dr. McIntosh. There is no evidence to show that the Métis rebellion played any significant part in the election campaign (McIntosh, incidentally, ran as an independent in what had previously been a Liberal seat), although the Halifax *Chronicle* tried to inject Riel into the campaign by expressing the hope that Thompson might see his way clear to commute the sentence of death. The editor even suggested that such might be Thompson's intention, writing, "The Honourable Gentleman is to be congratulated if there is any truth in the rumour that the Riel case has been disposed of by commutation of the sentence."[55]

But the commutation of Riel's sentence was not, at this time, part of the government's policy. The fate of Riel was decided by the courts and by a special Insanity Commission appointed by Macdonald. The verdict of the court in Regina was upheld by the Judicial Committee of the Privy Council, which refused to hear the appeal. Early in November, the medical commissioners, restricted by the guidelines laid down by the McNaghten rules, could report only that Riel was legally sane and was fully aware of what he was doing. His execution was, in consequence, carried out. Thus it fell to the lot of John Thompson, the new Minister of Justice and Member of Parliament for Antigonish, to defend the federal government's decision to reject the recommendation for mercy advanced by the Regina jury and proceed with the penalty as read by Hugh Richardson on 1 August 1885.

No sooner did Thompson arrive in Ottawa than he was faced with the problem of examining the sentences passed on the Métis and Indians convicted of participation in the North-West Rebellion. Letters suggesting life imprisonment rather than hanging poured into his office. Thompson's wife sent an appeal urging him to be sure that the Riel hanging did not take place on 10 November, the date of Thompson's birthday.[56] From Thompson's correspondence, it is obvious, however, that at no time did he ever seriously consider any mitigation of Riel's sentence. He had no sympathy for Riel or for those French Canadians who were clamoring on behalf of a "paltry hero who struggled so long and so hard for the privilege of hanging."[57] It was his opinion that the agitation in Quebec would continue only so long as Riel was alive. Once the Métis leader was in his grave, the frothy excitement stirred up by Mercier and his ilk would soon subside.

The parliamentary session opened on 25 February 1886. Thompson hoped that public tempers would have cooled by then. On 11 March, however, Philippe Landry, a Quebec Conservative from Montmagny, moved that the House should "express its deep regret that the sentence of death passed upon Louis Riel, convicted of high treason, was allowed to be carried into execution."[58] The Liberal case was presented by Wilfrid Laurier in a speech that many of his contemporaries considered his greatest oratorical triumph. Several days later, John Thompson replied. His maiden speech in Parliament, it was a powerful defence of the government's decision to allow the law to take its course in the case of Riel. It was a lawyer's speech, an unemotional, methodical reply to all the arguments in favor of clemency, replete with legal precedents culled from British history. As Thompson progressed from point to point, the government supporters became jubilant. Here was a man who could do more than hold his own with Edward Blake. Blake had, indeed, met his match.

Several other maritime Members of Parliament added their arguments to those of Thompson. Pierre-Amand Landry, the Acadian from Memramcook, representing Kent county in New Brunswick, while admitting that the Acadian people were disturbed by the execution of Riel, "the unfortunate rebel chief," strongly disapproved of rebellion as a means of redressing grievances and deplored the inflammatory language of many of the Quebec newspapers, such as *L'Electeur* and *La Presse.* Landry denied that Riel was entitled to be considered as a "martyr," that distinction being reserved only for those who died in a French or Catholic cause. Drawing a parallel with the Acadians, Landry argued that the latter would never have made any political progress in New Brunswick had there been any recourse to violence on their part. He was a firm believer in political gradualism, not in armed revolution. "I do not believe in inflammatory speeches" he said, "and if we condemn inflammatory articles and speeches, let us condemn them when they are made by the minority as well as the majority." [59] John Costigan, the Irishman from Victoria county, New Brunswick, and C.E. Kaulback from Lunenburg, Nova Scotia, also spoke on behalf of the government, the former denying that Riel was executed as a result of pressure from the Orange order, [60] and the second to praise the response of the Haligonians of the Sixty-sixth Regiment and "the flag that braved a thousand years, the battle and the breeze." Hurling his clichés at the opposition benches, Kaulback urged westerners to beat their swords into ploughshares and their spears into pruning hooks, and to use these implements in the development of the Great North-West "so boundless in its extent and so inexhaustible in its richness." [61]

When, finally, the vote was taken on 24 March, the Philippe Landry motion was defeated 146 to 52. Four maritimers voted for the motion, thereby indicating their opposition to Riel's hanging; thirty-two opposed it, thus supporting the government's policy. One maritimer, the Honorable Peter Mitchell, paired with Sir John A. Macdonald. [62]

VI

When the North-West Rebellion broke out in 1885, maritimers were compelled to look at their country, Canada, for the first time in national rather than in regional terms. Lacking direct contact, politically or economically, with the western prairies, maritimers had not been greatly interested in what went on in the western part of the continent. When they did direct their attention to the West, it was with a source of grievance that their money was being used to pay the price demanded by the Hudson's Bay Company for the sale of the Territories, to construct the C.P.R., and to provide public works for the Territories. Even as late as 1885, Senator David Wark of Richibucto was asking why the federal government would not reserve certain western lands to reimburse other provinces, and particularly the Maritimes, for debts incurred in developing the West. When maritimers did give some thought to the West it was to conclude that the new territories might bring some economic benefit to Ontario, but to the Maritimes? None at all. This largely explains the lack of interest displayed by maritimers in western Canada until the actual outbreak of fighting at Duck Lake.

The rebellion brought to the Maritimes a new awareness of the country beyond the Canadian Shield. Despite some slight opposition on the part of Nova Scotian separatists to maritime participation in the suppression of the rebellion, maritime troops did play a role, albeit modest, in the army sent to the prairies by the federal government. Not only did they serve alongside soldiers from other provinces, they also had a chance to see the Territories they had complained of helping to support. Some of them even went as far as the Rocky Mountains, returning home with a new vision of what a confederated Canada really meant in terms of size and economic potential.

In making maritimers think of Canada as a vast political entity extending from sea to sea, the rebellion also made maritimers more aware of Canada's political problems. Maritimers had never been really aware of the French-English problem as an historical factor in Canada's growth and development. They had not seen Confederation in 1867 in terms of a bi-racial, bi-cultural compact as did the French Canadians of Quebec and the Anglo-Canadians of Ontario. Admittedly, there was a Francophone population in the Maritimes, but Franco-Maritimers or Acadians had remained politically dormant. The North-West Rebellion brought the racial problem to the attention of every maritimer, and promised new and exciting developments in the future. Maritimers, no more than other Canadians, could not afford to ignore the fact that Canada was a bi-cultural nation.

Broadly speaking, historians have been inclined to oversimplify the attitudes of Canadians toward the Riel issue as a factor in the English-French confrontation in Canada. The impression is usually left that French and English Canadians thought entirely along racial and religious lines. It should always be remembered that there were Francophones who opposed Riel, and Anglophones who sympathized with him. Nevertheless, in broad terms, the generalization holds true that Canadians were split along racial lines in their attitude to the North-West Rebellion. The same is not true of the maritimers. The Acadians were less vocal and less politically active than the French Canadians; and the English, Scots, and Irish, in Nova Scotia and New Brunswick, divided their sympathies along party lines. Political parties, however, were organized on a national as well as provincial basis, and maritimers, whether they wanted to or not, were forced to view the rebellion from a national perspective. In this way, the North-West Rebellion was, at one and the same time, a divisive and a unifying factor in Confederation.

Notes

1. J.F. Turner, *The North-West Mounted Police 1873–1893*, 2 vols., (Ottawa: E. Cloutier, King's Printer, 1950), II, p. 115.

2. *The Mail* (Toronto), 24 March 1885.

3. *The Morning Herald* (Halifax), 4 July 1884.

4. Ibid., 18 September 1884.

5. Ibid., 26 March 1885.

6. Ibid., 24 March 1885.

7. Ibid., 30 March 1885.

8. Ibid., 26 March 1885.

9. Ibid., 22 October 1884.

10. A contemporary account of the events leading up to Duck Lake will be found in a letter by Harold Ross in C.B. Fergusson, "A Glimpse of 1885," *Saskatchewan History* (Winter 1968): 24-29. Ross, the son of George and Mary Ross of New Ross, N.S., joined the Mounted Police in 1878. Retiring in 1884, he became deputy sheriff of Prince Albert. He was captured by Gabriel Dumont prior to Duck Lake on 26 March 1885 and remained a prisoner until the capture of Batoche by the militia. On one occasion he was saved from summary execution by Riel's intervention.

11. *See* New Brunswick, House of Assembly, *Debates*, 1885, "Synoptic Report."

12. *The Times* (Moncton), 31 March 1885.

13. *The Daily Sun* (Saint John), 4 April 1885. For this and other quotations from the New Brunswick press, *see* Sheila Betty Carr, "New Brunswick Reaction to the North West Rebellion—A Study in Regionalism and Ethnicity" (M.A. thesis, University of New Brunswick, 1971).

14. *The Evening Capital* (Fredericton), 4 April 1885.

15. *The New Brunswick Reporter* (Fredericton), 23 May 1885. A teacher in a small one-room school in St. Peter's Mission in Montana, Riel would never have recognized himself in this description!

16. *The Times* (Moncton), 31 March 1885, blamed the North-West troubles on the dull winter, the scarcity of food, and the suffering of those it called "the treacherous half-breeds." *The Transcript* (Moncton), 1 April 1885, was closer to the mark when it blamed the government's "bungling land policy" and indifference to the warnings frequently given that serious discontent existed.

17. *See* G.F.G. Stanley, "The Flowering of the Acadian Renaissance" in D.J. Bercuson and Phillip Buckner, eds., *Eastern and Western Perspectives*, (Toronto: University of Toronto Press, 1981), pp. 28-29.

18. *Le Moniteur* (Shediac), 1 avril 1885.

19. *The Globe* (Toronto), 18 May 1885. It should be noted that while there was some grumbling in the French-language press about Canadians being sent to fight Canadians, nobody came out publicly in support of Riel at the outset of the rising. When two militia regiments were mobilized in Montreal and Quebec and sent to the Northwest, large crowds turned out to see them on their way. *See* Desmond Morton, *The Last War Drum*, (Toronto: A.M. Hakkert, 1972), p. 37. *Also see* R. Rumilly, *Histoire de la Province de Québec, Louis Riel*, (Montreal: B. Valiquette, [1940]), p. 23. Rumilly wrote, "Le fait majeur à souligner est que nul ne refusait la quote-part de sa province. Nul ne prenait d'emblée le parti de Riel."

20. Morton, p. 28.

21. Desmond Morton and Reginald H. Roy, *Telegrams of the North West Campaign* (Toronto: Champlain Society, 1972), p. xciii.

22. *The Morning Herald,* 1 April 1885.

23. Ibid., 2 April 1885.

24. Nova Scotia, House of Assembly, *Debates and Proceedings,* 1885, p. 298.

25. *The Morning Herald,* 2 April 1885.

26. Nova Scotia, House of Assembly, *Debates and Proceedings,* p. 305.

27. Bremner believed that the opposition to the Nova Scotia participation in the Northwest militia force was based entirely on politics. He sent a telegram to the Minister of Militia, Adolphe Caron, on 4 April, 1885 stating: "Some disloyal Grits did everything they could to prevent the regiment going, threatening their employees with immediate dismissal if they attended a single parade...." *See* Morton and Roy, p. 139.

28. A.C. Dunlop, "Willie Goes to War," *Nova Scotia Historical Quarterly* 5 (March 1975), pp. 1–20.

29. *The Morning Herald,* 3 April 1885.

30. *The Morning Herald,* 4 April 1885.

31. Morton and Roy, p. 60: Tupper to Caron, 1 April 1885.

32. J.J. Bremner of the Sixty-sixth was in command. The other officers included Majors C.J. MacDonald (66th), Walsh (63rd), Captains B.A. Weston (66th), C.H. MacKinley (66th), R.H. Humphrey (66th), W. Bishop (63rd), James Fortune (63rd), H. Heckler (63rd), James Curran (H.G.A.), L.J. Beard (H.G.A.), and Lieutenants James Bremner (66th), Alfred Whitman (66th), J.A. McCarthy (66th), Bowman Boggs (66th), Herbert Hensley (66th), C.E. Cartwright (66th), J.T. Twining (63rd), H. Sinclair Silver (63rd), T.O. Jones (63rd), Charles Fletcher (63rd), C.J. Mackie (63rd), C.K. Flake (H.G.A.), R. Skimmings (H.G.A.), Maxwell (H.G.A.), Arthur Hare (H.G.A.); Captain and Adjutant, L.G. Kenny; Surgeons, Drs. Tobin and Harrington (66th), Quartermaster, Captain Corbin (63rd); Paymaster, Captain Garrison (H.G.A.).

33. Bremner notified N.B. Daly and J.F. Stairs (the first, the federal member for Halifax, and the second, the provincial member) that there should be no delay in sending the Halifax Provisional Battalion to the Northwest. On 7 April Taylor telegraphed Caron stating that to remove Bremner would only "cause delay." *See* Morton and Roy, pp. 126, 130.

34. Dunlop, p. 4.

35. Ibid., p. 10.

36. *The Morning Herald,* 11 April 1885.

37. Dunlop, p. 12: Tupper to his mother, 24 April 1885.

38. Ibid., p. 16.

39. Morton and Roy, p. 306: Jackson to Caron, 20 May 1885.

40. A.C. Dunlop, "Letter from a Soldier Tourist," *Alberta History* (Summer 1975): 24.

41. Ibid., p. 27. The present cave and basin in Banff, Alberta

42. *The Morning Herald*, 24, 25, and 27 July 1885.

43. Canada, *Sessional Papers*, XIX, 1886, p. 38: Report of Military District 8, H.Q. Fredericton, 9 November 1885.

44. Ibid., p. 39.

45. The officers of the New Brunswick composite battalion included, in addition to Colonel Maunsell who was commanding officer, Major Gordon (I.S.C.), Captains E. Sturdee, H.J. Godard, J.F. Hegan, and M.B. Edwards, (62nd Fusiliers); Captains J.W. Baker (67th), W.T. Howe (71st), Bedford Harper (74th), Wm. Mc-Naughton (73rd), Daniel Stewart and T.S. Macleod (82nd). The Adjutant was Captain Hugh McLean (62nd). The lieutenants included Gregory, Godard, Fraser, Ruel, Thompson, Lordly, Churchill and McMillan (62nd); Lieutenants Carman and Brown, (67th), Loggie and Johnson (71st), McFee (74th), Wedderburn (8th Yeomanry Calvary), Hanning and Russel (I.S.C.). The Surgeon was T. Clowes (I.S.C.), the Quartermaster Major Devlin (62nd), the Paymaster Major McCully (73rd) and the Sergeant Major Sergeant McKenzie (I.S.C.). The adjutant was Lieutenant T. Young (I.S.C.). *See* W.T. Baird, *Seventy Years of New Brunswick Life, Autobiographical Sketches*, (Saint John: Day, 1890), pp. 299–300.

46. Baird, p. 300.

47. The quotations in the succeeding paragraphs are taken largely from Sheila Carr's thesis referred to in note 13. For an analysis of Ontario and Quebec press opinion, *see* R.E. Lamb, *Thunder in the North*, (New York: Pageant Press, 1957).

48. G.F.G. Stanley, *The Birth of Western Canada*, (Toronto: University of Toronto Press, 1960), p. 402.

49. *The Morning Herald*, 8 July 1885.

50. Interestingly enough, *The Morning Herald* on 14 August referred to Riel as a "half crazy Grit, with a faculty for jabbering and scribbling." After the Red River affair, Riel had run for Parliament as a Conservative.

51. C.D. Howell, "W.S. Fielding and the Repeal Elections of 1886 and 1887 in Nova Scotia," *Acadiensis*, vol. VIII, no. 2, 1979, p. 35. *See also* Bruce Fergusson, *The Hon. W.S. Fielding, The Mantle of Howe*, vol. 1, (Windsor: Lancelot Press, 1970), p. 79.

52. *The Morning Herald*, 29 August 1885.

53. *The Morning Chronicle*, September 1885.

54. P.A.C., Macdonald Papers, part 1, p. 277: Tilley to Macdonald, 21 October 1885.

55. *The Morning Chronicle*, 17 October 1885.

56. John P. Heisler, "Sir John Thompson, 1844–1894" (Ph.D. thesis, University of Toronto, 1955), p. 42.

57. Ibid., p. 43.

58. Canada, House of Commons, *Debates*, 1886, p. 59.

59. Ibid., p. 223.

60. Ibid., p. 310.

61. Ibid., p. 324.

62. Ibid., p. 367.

Stony Indian Medicine

_____ Eleanor G. Luxton

Author's Note

This short paper is composed of legends and facts, excerpts taken from a book to be published at a future date. The research was done in the 1920s and 30s when the Indians I interviewed were old men and women. I was fortunate in having a mother who spoke Cree and Stony fluently and a father who spoke Stony.[1] My mother was closely associated with Indians all her life, as was my father. They worked among and with the Indians. Both parents (and later I) hunted and travelled with them because we were interested in their way of life and their lore, but above all, we recognized the Indians as individuals and respected their beliefs and knowledge.

In what follows, I have tried to use facts and stories that show the strong belief of the Indian in the Great Spirit and in the true aspects of Indian Medicine. The subjects of religion, philosophy, and medicine were so closely linked in the Indians' lives that it is sometimes difficult to tell where one began and the other ended. The phraseology of the original storytellers has been retained in an effort to keep the events and philosophies of the Indians in their proper context.

In daily life, the Indians accepted the legends of their beginnings passed down by word of mouth for generations. Likewise, they accepted the Medicine Man as an intermediary between the Great Spirit and themselves. They also sought his ministrations as a healer of physical ills. He was the one who told the youths the course to pursue that they might become braves and find a name by which they would be known.

The Indian was not only a believer in the mystical, he was a realist. Accidents happened and wounds were suffered when the Indian was hunting or fighting enemies. Then the Indian had to be healed by his mother or his wife, who used what resources she had at the time. If one became ill far from the band, only a knowledge of plants, trees, and bushes would save a life.

When some catastrophe occurred to change an Indian's life he felt that he had displeased the Great Spirit in some way. After destroying his Medicine, he went to the woods or to a mountain or a stream or even a rock where he fasted and dreamed. He prayed and waited for the Great Spirit to speak to him through an animal, a bird, the wind in the grasses, or the trees. Having received his message, he returned to his family and started to collect new Medicine and live as he had been instructed.

The first story reflecting aspects of Stony medicine is the legend of how the Stony tribe, who are Assiniboines, a branch of the Sioux nation, came into existence.

_____ Origins

The story of how the Sioux nation began was told to me by Peter Wesley,
an old Chief and Medicine man of the Stony tribe, as we sat on top of
Devil's Head Mountain.[2]

It was during the age of the earth when the Gods were sorting the species of all creation into their proper channels, that the Indian people
became a recognized race. Animals and birds were numbered as the
stars in the heavens, trees and flowers as the clouds in the skies, but all
so mixed by crossing and breeding that not even the greatest hunters
of the time could tell who had been sired or mothered by which.

The Gods were greatly put to it, for their job was to purify each
species, as nature had intended; to destroy all crosses of animals and
birds that did not conform to their original being. Literally, earth was
crowded with many misshaped and terrible monsters, monstrosities
that might have the two legs of a buffalo or a bear, wings of an eagle;
another with the tail of a lion and the body of a horse. Of the human
species, they were little better, as they had already commenced to
breed themselves to some favorite four-footed friend or bird. Which
way to turn? How to sort all this muddle out? The Gods were sadly at
their wits' end.

One race of the humans had stayed close to their original form, so
to them the Gods made supplication, promising rewards and compensation such as these people had never imagined. They would be the
Gods' chosen people, all things on earth would be theirs to command,

never would they be hungry, cold, or forgotten and all the land and waters would be theirs for evermore. These people were known as "Indians" and of all the species that then inhabited the earth, they came closest to the images of the Gods. These people were tall, six feet or more, walked on two legs that could carry them swiftly over land, water, or brush, and had two arms and hands that could perform miracles like none of the other species.

To all this the Indian species listened and promised their aid as the Gods would command. First, the Gods created an animal so huge in stature it took a fast-running Indian part of a morning to cover the ground from his tail to his nose and so high in proportion that he shadowed the sun for miles beyond him. Teeth he had, like nothing ever seen before, and claws beyond description on all four feet. To this creature the Gods commanded: "Dig and pile the earth into huge ranges of rock and matter, that the earth might give forth, make canyons and pitfalls of perpendicular walls that nothing can get out." Though there were hundreds of these huge creatures that the Gods had created, it took many years to form these mountains, stretching from far to the north and many days' travel south, all down one side of the earth. So high and mighty was the earth piled, it could be seen afar off, and this still remains today, the greatest of all the Gods' creations.

The Gods commanded the Indians to walk as far east as twelve moons would take them, when they would right-about turn, join hands, and sweep before them all the species of the earth, letting none escape behind them, except those that had the true formation of their species. The Indians formed a line so long that from one end to the other none could see it. So across the earth as a living fire it swept all before, the very monstrosities themselves helping the huge drive onward, for, panic-stricken, they became weaker and weaker and many were trampled to death. No time was taken for sleep or drink. Into the mountains they were driven tumbling and terrified. The huge drive went on. None but the truebloods were left behind. Into the canyons and pitfalls these misborn things of nature tumbled for days and days, until nothing of their kind was left behind. The earth was cleansed of all its early evil and sinful performance and the Indian tribes were left in charge, for the Gods had departed for the Moon and the Sun to see that they kept on shining.

Ages and aeons passed away and the Indians, as the Gods promised, became the masters of all the earth and everything on it. All living things that were true increased in tremendous numbers and scattered to all corners of the universe, learning how to use the gifts the Gods had given them. Some Indians prospered while others became indolent and lazy, abusing their privileges. To these people the Gods one day returned and asked for an accounting. Woe to them who had not played the game. One tribe in particular had wasted and abused all the things of the earth that they had been commanded to care for and on these people the Gods visited their wrath and displeasure. Putting them into a sleep like unto death itself, the Gods removed every woman and child of this nation, only leaving the young men and the old men of the tribe. On awakening, so sound had been the sleep of forgetfulness, that none of the men remembered the women and the children, thinking they were the only humans in creation. Now you know, an Indian is of little use to himself without the aid of his woman and in no time, where these men had been fat and lazy, they became thin and hungry. They were continually looking for something to eat and for something to cover their nakedness, for the Gods had arranged it so that it was hard for the hunters to find anything to kill. As the years passed these men became more and more desolate, and were even hunted by their own kind as they took on less the appearance of humans and more that of the animals. Desolate was their state in the most afflicted manner. When the first snow came that fall they were happy for it would give them good tracking to follow the game they needed so much.

It was decided that each hunter would go his separate way and report at the council fire that night on his day's findings, so that if large herds of game were found they would bunch the hunters and kill the meat. As the sun set the following day, all the hunters turned campward and around the fire that night, belts were drawn tight, for no meat pots were on the fires. Much game had been seen but none close enough to be killed. One man only had a different story to tell.

"I left camp this morning early. My Medicine seemed to direct my footsteps in a straight line to the rising sun and I walked until it was two hands high, when I sat down to rest and smoke awhile. Suddenly I heard the grunting of a buffalo and, climbing to the top of the little hill I was on and looking over it, there, right below me and within easy shooting distance were many, many buffalo. Without thinking of our arrangement to have a mighty hunt by all the tribe, I at once strung my bow, and in twenty arrows I killed twenty buffalo. My arrows seemed to be guided by the Gods themselves, for every one of them spoke death to the heart of each buffalo. More I killed, when I changed my position, all with equal results to the first killing. Yes, quite forty dead buffalo to my one bow, more than any one man has done in the entire history of the tribe. My Medicine was strong and it could not miss."

The lone hunter stopped talking and all his companions thought surely he was crazy or dreaming. "But where is all the meat?" they cried.

"When I got to the first kill," the young hunter said, "to open it up and prepare it for stripping, suddenly to my ears there came a sound that turned me hard as stone. For long I could not move—only my ears were alive—such sounds in all my life I have never heard. It was music such as the trees make on the highest mountains when lightning has blasted from them all their leaves and then the gentle breezes woo them and tell them from whence they have come; such sounds as running waters and their echoes leave in the canyons deep; yes, softer sounds than the grass and the flowers make when creeping through the earth to seek the sunshine. Louder, louder, the sounds came closer. Then out from the winding hills, quite suddenly and not far from me, there came creatures stranger than anything I had ever seen. They were not men, nor were they animals walking on four legs, they walked as we do. Some were much larger around and many smaller and all more lithe and light than the deer when it is at play.

"I watched these strange creatures when they suddenly discovered my kill. All was silence for a moment, then quietly as the shadows disappear when the sun sets, they faded away into the cover of the hills and trees. Perhaps you may say I am crazy with hunger and want, perhaps I was dreaming and never went on this hunt, but all I can tell you is that my moccasins are worn through and my quiver is empty. But let me tell you something that happened as I watched; there came to me a feeling that I have never had before—a sensation and impressions that no Indian words can talk. Tomorrow we will see."

In the morning, it was decided that twelve men would go with the lone hunter and spy out what they could, then return that night to give a report on their findings. About noon that day the spies reached the country where the buffalo had been killed. All was silent with the exception of the crows who were enjoying a great feed on the dead buffalo. There was not a sight of anything but many, many tracks of moccasins all much smaller than those of the parties studying them. The men walked carefully and quietly into the hills where the tracks led them. Then came to the hunters' noses the smell of smoke and what was much better, the smell of cooking meat. Carefully approaching the brow of the hill, they looked into a very large camp made up of many teepees, hides drying on racks, large fires burning, and only one strange creature in sight who was tending the fires and turning the hides. The spies watched for a long time, then by signs it was decided to send the lone hunter into the camp to talk to the creature. Leaving behind all his hunting equipment and weapons, he approached the camp from the trees that were closest to the fires. Not until he was but a few feet from the big round creature did it look up and discover him. There they stood, only a few feet apart: eye to eye they looked, and neither one afraid. Then, again, the hunter had the same sensations that had seized him the day before and he stood as a rock that is a pillar unto itself. Only when the creature made signs for him to sit down did he come to himself. As he sat, almost at once he was served with fresh-cooked buffalo, wild tea, and dried berries, on plates and in a cup made from the antlers of a moose and the horns of a wild sheep.

So the lone hunter ate as he had not eaten for many a day, with hardly a thought of his companions on the hill. Many times were his plate and cup filled and it was only when he could not possibly force another mouthful down his gullet that he pushed aside his plate and cup.

Hardly was he through eating when a pipe was handed to him and a live ember applied to the sweetest Kin-nick-in-ic[3] he had ever tasted. As if at the command of an unseen master, once more the sound of the beautiful music drifted through the trees; and then in a long procession there appeared twelve more creatures dressed in feathers and buckskins, tanned to the finest of softness, and it was they who were making the music. Along the fires they softly stepped, keeping time to their own voices, circling and dancing—it was a scene long to be remembered. Then in a row opposite to him they squatted.

From the top of the hill his twelve companions came, with wonder and startled faces to take their positions beside the lone hunter. They sat in silent amazement. Long it seemed before anyone spoke, when, suddenly to his feet the lone hunter jumped, and to all present shouted: "You have what we haven't got; we have what you haven't got; you want what we want and we want what you want." Thus was the beginning of the Sioux Nation.

_____ The Naming of Walking Buffalo

As an exception to the usual practice of a man taking a name when he felt himself ready to become a brave, George MacLean, whose Indian name was Walking Buffalo, told me of the particular circumstances associated with his name. MacLean's and the community's belief in the story signified a sense of a special relationship between Walking Buffalo and the Great Spirit that endured throughout his life.

One fall day about 1875 the Stony people were camped where the town of Mirror, Alberta, is situated today, some thirty miles east of Red Deer. The hunters had had a wonderful day among the buffalo and enough meat had been secured to see the tribe into the late winter months. The women would be busy for many a day, tanning and making robes and teepees of the hides. Suddenly from the north one of the very sudden blizzards came sweeping across the prairies, blotting out everything beyond a few yards' visibility. All the teepees were made snug and tight and the tired hunters were no doubt glad that the hunt had ended so early in the day, for everyone was accounted for and no one had to worry.

During the late evening after the men had smoked the last pipe and most of them had gone to their beds, knowing that lodge fires had been properly banked to keep them warm for the next four or five hours, only a few of the women were finishing the last chores in the lodges. In one of the teepees pitched farther out on the prairie, the woman of the lodge paused suddenly in her banking of the fire to listen. Yes, she could hear it again, a noise of the crying of a child. No noise of the wind or the driving of the snow could make a sound that every mother must know, the wailing of a baby in distress. Wakening her husband, she told him what she had heard, when once again to prove her story, they both heard the sound and this time there was no doubt.

Removing the storm barricades in front of the lodge door, they both rushed out into the storm and all but collided with a very large shaggy monster. At first they thought it was one of their horses but when they tried to drive it away, it showed fight and charged them. Then they discovered it was not a horse but a buffalo cow.

The enraged animal chased the man around one side of the teepee, while the woman ran around the opposite direction, only to meet her man as he made the circle. Both were glad to once more get into the shelter of their teepee, but they were no sooner inside than they again heard the crying.

Quietly leaving his lodge, the man hurried to some of the nearest teepees and soon had several of the hunters out into the storm, with their one or two guns and their bow and arrows. All this took considerable time and no doubt, if it had not been for the bravery of the woman, the buffalo cow would have been lost in the blizzard. Quietly following the sound of the crying, the woman managed to keep in touch with the animal from which the noise seemed to come. Finally the men reached her. It was not an easy killing, several shots as well as arrows fired at the cow who in turn, kept repeatedly charging the brave hunters. It was some time before this furious animal was dispatched.

Then a different hunt began. Because of the blowing snow and the wind it was some time before the woman found the child. He was perhaps two years old, quite naked and almost as cold as the very storm that had brought him—the baby Indian boy, Walking Buffalo, as he came to be known—to the lodges of the Stony people.

_____ Stony Medical Practice

My father, N.K. Luxton, offered to me some observations from his experiences concerning what the white man would consider medical practice. Even when the mysterious element is removed from these stories they give reason to pause and to reflect on the ways of the Stonys.

Like all races, the American Indian had his "fakirs," but no more than past or present-day whites. That true Indian doctors existed and still exist is as much a fact as the medical profession today.

From personal observation I have seen the sleight-of-hand work of the Medicine Man who appeared to remove large stones from the belly of a suffering Indian. The Medicine Man was sufficiently clever to fool the relatives and friends of the patient, but nonetheless failed to save his patient. Neither were the loud wailing and prayers of an entire tribe led by the Medicine Man to any avail in saving the drying-up of the only village spring. Thus both in a fake and in a serious ceremony, their faith and supplications offered to the Great Spirit were defeated.

Medicine used and practised a few hundred years ago in Europe was no less terrifying and absurd than some of that practised by the American Indian. The everyday life of the Indian hunter has led us to think that he knew more about the anatomy of the human body than the average European. Nonetheless, the Medicine Man of America didn't have as much surgical knowledge. In surgical work he was limited to the tools that nature had provided, such as flint, stone, shell, bone, and wood. As far as antiseptics were concerned, he was as ignorant as the European. The sharpest tools the Indian could make were the fire-pointed stick or thorn, the chipped-off edges of flint, the hard bone of a rib ground down for a knife blade, or the shin bone of a moose made into a jagged-edged scraper or saw. These, with a bone needle and sinew, comprised his surgical instruments. Even with such crude tools the Indian Medicine Man worked wonders. The amputation of fingers and toes, the splicing and setting of broken limbs, the replacing of dislocations, and the cleaning and treating of most desperate wounds were all handled with great success. Medicine men were ignorant of antiseptics, but certain herbs, they knew, kept the wounds open for necessary drainage while other herbs stimulated healing at the proper time.

Tapping the chest to drain away fluids was practised by the Indians. The tourniquet was not new to the Indians when the first white man showed it to them. For years the Medicine Man had been using this effective way to stop the bleeding of terrible wounds suffered in warfare or hunting. All Indians knew first aid in so far as it went. Splints of the most ingenious patterns were used and may be seen in some of the old Indian collections. Some of these were wood-slats laced apart, so treatment would be given to a compound fracture; also, rawhide, shaped when wet, made an ideal splint when it dried. Stiff gumbo clay was used as plaster of Paris.

I have seen more than one patient return to the reserve when the white doctor's skill could not cure him. One in particular was a tuberculosis case. This doomed native took his wasted body, thin as a shadow, to the Medicine Man of his tribe. Inside of a year this man was married and raising a family and became one of the healthiest men on the reserve. Many similar instances could be recited of cases of successful surgical work, as well as other medical practices, from many Indian reserves all over America.

_____ More Stony Medical Practices in the Life of Jobin Two-Young-Men or Mountain Lion

Jobin was an Indian of over fifty years when my father first met him in 1903, and much older when I knew him. Dressed in a blue serge suit with brass buttons, wearing a round Christy Stiff,[4] carrying a cane, and wearing the Queen Victoria Treaty Number Seven medal, Jobin was very much the Indian Councillor, with all the dignity of his race.

He could tell the most startling yarns about the old men of his tribe. He claimed that as a wee child he saw the first horses ever seen by his band. They were ridden by white men and caused consternation in the camp. One, he said, had long ears and at first they thought it was a moose. Jobin said the horses were the biggest help the white man ever brought to the Indian.[5]

Some ten years before my father knew him, Jobin had a terrible pain in his side that, in spite of herbs and sweathouse treatment, got worse. He and his wife Sarah had been hunting a hundred miles from civilization. After consulting with her, Jobin decided a cut in the side was the only remedy to save his life. The only thing she had to use was one of the old Hudson's Bay Company knives. The blade, of the best steel, was quite eight inches long by two-and-a-half inches wide. With herbs, Sarah kept the wound open for some time to let the pus drain, and when it was all gone, used other herbs in grease to heal it. Such an operation sounds pretty drastic to a white man, but Jobin said it was not too bad because after all, the old Indians knew every part of the human body as well as they did the organs of the animals. At a later date a noted white doctor commented most favorably on the skill with which this appendectomy had been conducted.

When we said good-bye, on one occasion Jobin told my father he would not see him again because he was dying, the doctor had told him, of an old injury he had received while hunting buffalo. He did not die that night, however, because my father saw him again several times. My father told me Jobin's last story as follows.

One Sunday when I was visiting Jobin, he was sitting on the floor of his house propped up by pillows. Suddenly he said to his son in Cree, "I want to tell you and the Indian trader a story." Though quite capable of telling it in English, he told it in his own language, while his son translated:

"Once when I was a young man, that is a long time ago, the sun went out of my eyes and for seven days I never saw the earth. I was camped close to where Cochrane, Alberta, is today, and I could hear the wolves howling all around me but could not see them until the eighth day when I took off the bandages from my eyes and the bright snow was gone. Though I had little to eat, I was not sick. We never got sick in the old days and we had nothing to eat but meat. That's all," he ended. So his son and I thanked him for his story.

Like all native peoples, the Stony Indians used natural barks, roots, flowers, and leaves of trees, bushes, and plants for medicine. I personally had experience with this aspect of Indian medicine. From my mother I heard of remedies that Old Mary used for her, when she was a growing child. Mary Chiniquay was the woman who delivered my mother, when my grandmother was alone and a hundred miles from a doctor. When Mary and Mother would be walking on the prairies or in the woods, Mary would pick a flower or berry or point to a bush or tree and tell her what it would cure.

One day Mother and I were pulling white yarrow from the flower beds and she told me that Old Mary had boiled the dried flowers of it to get the juice to cure a toothache by putting a few drops onto the tooth. In this way I learned of other remedies. The boiled liquid from juniper leaves and kin-nick-in-ic was taken in small quantities to cure dysentery. To clean cuts, Mary always had dried Saskatoon bark and dried balsam bark, one of which she would boil in water to get the antiseptic fluid. The juice from the three or four inches of stock above the root of the fireweed was prepared in the same way, but to heal wounds, not keep them clean.

If a cut became swollen from an infection it was cleaned with the an-

tiseptic then a poultice of powdered balsam bark and grease was applied to draw the poison. This poultice would bring swellings or boils to a head until they broke and the pus ran out. They were then washed with the antiseptic and the healing poultice applied. There were many more remedies, such as boiled choke-cherry bark to make a tea for coughs, but they are too numerous to list.

My father had much respect for Stony Medicine as medicine and equal respect for Stony Medicine as religion.

"Indian Medicine," how easily these words are so often misconstrued or badly explained! There is nearly always a certain amount of superstition attached to Indian Medicine, and, thus, it is difficult to understand. Try for a minute to think of the Indian's view. He is not superstitious in our meaning of the word, because he knows that his "Medicine" is good or bad, and helps or hinders him in all his undertakings. When it ceases to help him he throws it away for new. The very manner in which he secured that Medicine is proof enough for him that it is "medicine," so it is up to him to keep that Medicine working in his favor; there is no hesitation on his part—it is or it is not—no doubting.

This Medicine might be some small animal he has adopted into his family as an emblem to provide him with inspiration, or a dried snake skin or whatever. Possibly he found that Medicine when, as a youth, he was going through an ordeal to be accepted into his tribe as a brave—the recognition of a grown man. Perhaps the ordeal called for his absence from the tribe and all humans for days in some secluded spot where nature alone lives. Here, day after day and night after night, alone, he waited for something to happen. Invariably, it came in the shape of a dream. Half-delirious for want of food, water, and companionship, he slipped off into dreamland. There he talked with some animal, fish, bird, or tree—always something to do with nature. Whatever it might be, he accepted it as his future Medicine. White people are equally superstitous—what about that lucky pocket-piece that you would not take ten dollars for, or that horseshoe that lies in your road, or wishing on a new moon, and ten hundred supposed good and bad omens?

The Indian lives very close to nature. He knows more of the meaning of the noises and signs of nature, its animals, its birds, its hills, its trees, its mountains than all the white man's knowledge put together. The Indian has meanings and understandings that are impossible for any white man to comprehend.

Similar to the revival meetings of Christian believers, when yearly meetings are held and their hearts are laid bare to their God, so the American Indian meet in early spring. When everything is turning green and the migration of the birds is over, the tribes gather in a selected spot, build a huge lodge of trees and brush and there give thanks to nature and the Great Spirit for all the good things the earth has supplied.

This gathering of the tribes is usually called the Sun Dance, which embraced a much larger meaning a few years ago than it does now. One or more of the Medicine Men or Medicine Women prepared themselves days ahead for the ordeal and perished their bodies. Having starved themselves of food and water to mere shadows of their normal condition, they sat in the Sun Lodge to receive the sick and the lame. In this emaciated condition, they believed that they were more of the spirit than of the earth, and were in better mind to take the troubles of their tribe to the Great Spirit, who could cure all ills, and thus, they were his disciples. Is this Indian belief of intercession any more strange than the white man who takes his worries to his priest, or in silent meditation and prayer lays his troubles before his Maker?

Singing and dancing are part of the Sun Dance rites. Thanks are given to nature for its abundant offerings: to the grass that is green, to the good trees that make wood, to the never-drying springs and rivers, to the game that is plentiful, to increasing grain fields, and to the bounteous herds. All this is expressed in dance, song, and prayer to the Medicine Man who passes it on to the Great Spirit. Such is the Sun Dance—the joy and thanksgiving of the tribe! To his last cent, the Indian will contribute to the feast of the Sun Lodge and to its decorations of trade cotton and bunting that proudly hang on the ceremonial pole.

Ask one of the Rocky Mountain Foothills Indians what it all means. He will likely tell you it is his church, that he is glad to be of the earth, which is so full of all he needs and that he is thanking everything that grows and lives so he will have little to worry about tomorrow.

Sarah's Survival

Early missionaries experienced numerous examples of the abiding faith of the Stonys in their traditional medicine. As well, they experienced very practical demonstrations of adaptations to the new circumstances and opportunities. The story of Sarah's survival through a difficult winter was related by a missionary acquaintance.

Jobin Two-Young-Men died during the winter of 1932–33. His wife, Sarah, went to live with her son, Jacob Two-Young-Men, who then was Chief of the Chiniquay Band of the Stony. One winter the moose had moved their browsing grounds and the best hunters of the Stony tribe had failed to find them in sufficient numbers to feed all the hungry people during the winter. Sarah went to her missionary, the Reverend Edward J. Staley, informing him that she would go out and cut willow wood for the mission stoves. Mr. Staley told her he had all the wood he wanted for many moons to come. This did not daunt the woodcutter by any means and she told him this woodcutting had always been part of her life's work and no man would take it from her. She went on to say she would also cut some hundred fence pickets and though the Reverend gentleman assured her he already had several thousand of these and needed no more, she just nodded "yes." What could he do against this little eighty-year-old bag of explosives? He could only give in and ration her food for a job he did not want done. She also told him she had good help, and on his asking who, she gave the names of two more ladies quite as old as herself. Of course, the wood and the pickets were delivered and Sarah successfully survived another short period of hunger in her life.

Stony Medicine in the Life of Hector Crawler or Calf Child

Perhaps no better insight into Stony Medicine can be gained than viewing Medicine in the life of a man who seemed to experience all of its dimensions. My father narrated Hector Crawler's story to me many years ago.

It is something over forty years ago since I first met this man, who was in his early fifties at the time [*ca. 1903*] and looked all of ten years younger. Hector Crawler or Calf Child was a full-blood Stony living at Morley, Alberta. He had a manner that was not common to his people, an appeal so strong, that as long as you were in his company you just kept on finding something new in his character. He was small of stature, size fives would fit his feet, and his hands were such that the average white woman would love to have them. He had high cheekbones and a not-too-pronounced eagle nose, his mouth matched the rest of his features and it told you he was all you had discovered, that he loved a joke, and that he was happy. There were lights in his eyes that you might see in those of few other men—men who had lived life and finally understood it.

Forty years ago, Hector was the best hunter and trapper on his reserve—foxes, martin, mink, and beaver all came to his traps. He was a man of means, his horses numbered into the hundreds, and his house was the largest in the Chiniquay band. He was the first Indian on the reserve to own a cookstove and he had more white man's furniture than any ten families. Up to about his fortieth year he was a very happy soul, with a fine wife and children, who were the envy of all the girls and boys; for like their father, they possessed all his good looks and his gracious nature. His goods and wealth were always at the command of his friends and neighbors. Then his reverse came.

One early fall, coming toward the village of Banff from trapping and hunting over Simpson Pass, a terrific blizzard with a heavy snow caught him far from camp. Eventually, after hours of wading through snow and breaking trail, his pack train of seventy-five head of horses struggled on to the right-of-way of the Canadian Pacific Railway. Here, the snow plows had brushed the deep drifts away, and it would be easy going into Banff, some five miles distant, for himself and the half-dozen families Hector always took along with him when he went trailing. Hardly had they got the packs straightened and balanced after the heavy plunging of the horses through deep snow, when around the bend in the railway, out of the blizzard, came a fast freight. Hector could see that it would be impossible to get his ponies through the drifts piled along the sides of the tracks. He commanded the men to work fast. They barely had time to throw the women, children, and babies off the horses' backs across onto the far sides of the drifts, when along came the iron monster, literally plowing through horses and packs. Not one horse was left alive or not so seriously injured that it had to be destroyed. Apart from bruises and fright, the people all escaped.

This disaster Hector never could forget, for in his Indian way he could only figure that it was a warning he had done or not done something. Surely his Medicine was angry with him or it would never have dealt him such a blow. Hector's hunting expeditions became fewer and his horses had no more delight in his pleasure, so that in a few years, he was only one of many of the poor Indians on the reserve.

Then one night in a dream, there came to him the Great Spirit, who said: "Into the mountains you will go, and for four days and nights you will dream and sleep. Four nights will the thunder clap over your bed of boughs, and each time the thunder rolls, you will cover your cheeks with the ochre of the Indian paint. The fifth day you will return to your people and teach to them, through the Medicine Bundle, the faith of the tribes of long ago. Power to you will be given; through your touch, breath, and song you will be a great healer and to all the tribes for miles around you will be as famous as the Medicine Men of old."

Acting on these instructions, Hector first destroyed all his old Medicine, then for four successive nights slept on top of a mountain that was part of his reserve. As the Great Spirit foretold, the storm came, the thunder rolled, and the lightning was as day, but strengthened by the words of the Great Spirit he was never once afraid. He was happy, not like the old days, but happy that he was travelling in the shadow of the Great Spirit. Such was his happiness that it could not be expressed, but it possessed his entire being. Then he gave a great dance, where all the tribes assembled. His fame spread as one of the chosen of the Great Spirit. He became so famous for his healing ability that Indians came from far and wide, Crees from the north, Flatheads from Montana, and all the tribes in between became his patients. For, as the Great Spirit in his dream had said, he healed with his hands, his breath, and his song.

During the First World War, I moved to the Reserve at Morley and there became better acquainted with my friends the Stonys, even to being accepted as a blood-brother and later as a chief. Hector became one of my greatest friends, and always was I welcomed to his teepee in summer and his comfortable log cabin in winter. He had by this time become one of the councillors for his band. Sound was his advice and reasoning, never did he give a decision until he had consulted with the Great Spirit, either in the woods, along the streams and rivers or on the mountain tops, and seldom was his Medicine wrong.

Then came the flu epidemic of 1918–19. Many were dying and doctors were hard to find forty miles from the nearest city. For a week I was the only white man among these people to give them what relief was possible. Twenty percent of the three Stony bands died. Hector was always on the job, so that between the faith that our patients had in Hector and the bottles of Johnny Walker scotch whisky that I served with aspirin, we no doubt saved many a flu case. One day Tom Powderface died. He had been one of the philosophers of his tribe and his words were always listened to by everyone with great respect; his going was a blow to the morale of the tribe. The morning after his death I could see that any of the little cheerfulness they had was gone. Strange to say, that very night I had dreamed of Tom. Well, I told those Indians my dream, and perhaps elaborated on the vision. It was a vision of a very happy Tom living in a country full of game, among old friends. I even described old chiefs and early missionaries that I had known and who had departed years before. I told how each arrival was welcomed by them. Suddenly I saw Hector looking at me with wonder in his eyes. I was abashed at my imagination running away with me, so there I stopped. However, my story had done its good work and from that time on they were in better spirits. The doctors and nurses finally arrived and I did not see the tribe again for some time, for the flu had me.

Thereafter Hector was a closer friend and more of a teacher. To me he told most intimate things that many years of previous friendship had never disclosed. It seems from his earliest boyhood it was the passion of his father to teach him all that an Indian boy should know. It was always a great source of pride that he was able, even as a very young fellow, to supply his nomadic people with a large share of the food that gave them life. His early teaching stood him in good stead, and more than once his well-developed natural ability of reading the signs, no matter how obscure, saved his life.

When he was still in his teens, alone on a hunting expedition, in the wide valley of the Highwood, he saw the flicker of a shadow, which was quickly followed by another, dodging in an out of the willow-grown banks of the river. At once his senses told him they were human beings and, in all probability, not his friends. He knew that he had been seen, but also told me, he knew that they did not know that he was aware of them; so on he walked, striding toward where he was expected to go. This country was rolling with many hills, each of which might make an acre or more in size. One large hill, which had obstructed the view for some time, was the last between him and the river and on the other side of this hill he knew that enemies awaited his approach. Upon reaching the bottom of the hill, he quickly circled its base to a quarter way around and there, sure enough, were the two shadows in the shape of two Indians, that he recognized as people from far west and deadly enemies.[6] Hector's only weapon was his bow and arrows. Just as fast as a man could pull a trigger, Hector shot his two arrows, each to the death of these ancient enemies.

Another time, he discovered he was being followed through the actions of a mountain sheep he was stalking. He quietly faded away to one side of his game, and taking up a safe place of observation, he soon saw a half-dozen of the tribe's enemies, still stalking along after the sheep, thinking that Hector was ahead of them. This time Hector did not do any shooting but quietly departed to "a more healthy country."

In all these different experiences, Hector told me, he took the greatest delight. Whether he was staking his ability as a hunter or a warrior against animal or Indian, he never once had the thought that he would come out second-best. Nature and its signs were to him as simple to read as the white man reads his letters, and nature to him in his quiet moments was the most beautiful thing in his whole life. Never until he had changed his Medicine and the Great Spirit had spoken to him, had he really enjoyed living. It was then that all things spoke to him, telling him of the past, telling him of the present, and telling him what was to come.

Hector, of course, was a pagan in every sense of the word as the white man understands it. He attended the mission church on his re-serve, possibly more often than many who professed the white man's faith, but his attendance was made only in the hope that he might understand this faith of his white brothers. Talk and printed books, even in his own language, could never convert him. He could never look at the white man as a savior nor accept his God. Hector was a modern Indian seer, with all the old traditions of his people brought to him by the Great Spirit. He always lived in hope that he would someday restore those old beliefs to his people. Hector did admit that some of the talk of the white Medicine Man was good and he had no hesitation in taking that part and putting it with his own teachings, for he claimed this made his Medicine that much stronger. To him, the white man's God was like looking for something in a very dark night, while in contrast his belief was with him no matter where he went. It was not only with him but all around him. Look where he would, it was always there—the entire universe and all that was on earth—and from all this wonder he drew his Medicine.

Hector died in his eighty-fourth year defending a cow from a dozen worrying dogs. He slipped and fell on ice, and the cow charged him and fractured his skull. In 1934 Hector had been one of the few left among the Stonys who could remember their people as the crudest of nomads, following game wherever it went with only dogs to do the packing. Every moment they were watching and listening with an intentness that became second nature, either to ward off death or to secure something to eat. This latter objective, Hector would note, was always the hardest. Then came horses and guns in much greater numbers, and life became easier. The missionaries came to teach of another life and brought the schools. They were followed by the settlers. "None of the changes," Hector said, "not even the automobile or the flying bird ever took me as close to my God as when I go to commune with the trees, the rivers, and the mountains, at night or in the day. With them I am close to where I will be sometime when I am dead, just like moving my camp to another valley where the grass is green, the water is good, and there is plenty of game." So ended the story.

Notes

1. *Editor's note:* The author's mother, Georgia Elizabeth McDougall, was the daughter of Annie Mackenzie McDougall and David McDougall, a well-known Indian trader and merchant. His brother John was the noted Methodist missionary. Georgia McDougall was born at Fort Victoria North, N.W.T. (now Pakan, Alberta) on 28 October 1872 and died in Banff, Alberta, on 29 March 1965. The author's father was Norman Kenny Luxton, an Indian trader and businessman in the Banff region. He was the son of Sarah Jane Edwards Luxton and William Fisher Luxton. He was born at Upper Fort Garry (now Winnipeg, Manitoba) on 2 November 1876 and died in Calgary, Alberta, on 26 October 1963.

2. The present Devil's Head Mountain near Banff is only the neck of the Mountain. The "Head," a balancing rock, succumbed to unknown forces of nature, falling with a crash and reverberations that were heard and felt from distances of several miles. My mother recalled the event happening in the early 1880s.

3. Kin-nick-in-ic is a creeping shrub found in the foothills and mountain regions. The leaves were used as a tobacco and the bark was and is used as a medicine.

4. A phrase used to refer to a bowler hat.

5. *Editor's note:* Jobin Two-Young-Men's statement regarding the "first horses" lends weight to the view that the Stonys at Morley, a few miles east of Banff originated from among the "Thickwood Assiniboines." During the era of the fur trade the bulk of the Assiniboines adopted a plains way of life with its extensive use of the horse. A few bands continued as trappers and hunters in the forest regions. At the end of the eighteenth century the Thickwood Assiniboines were found in the boreal forest to the north and west of Fort Edmonton. During the succeeding century some of these bands appear to have moved southward along the foothills. Two-Young-Men's age suggests a date circa 1855 for his comment. This date is compatible with known events. With increasing frequency and in greater numbers, bands of Cree and Métis were crossing the Battle River to hunt buffalo on lands the Blackfoot identified as their own. It would appear that the Stony band with whom Jobin lived at the time were taking advantage of the plasticity of circumstances to acquire horses and add, or increase, a prairie dimension to their annual cycle of hunting activities. Circa 1740 is the date usually assigned to the first appearance of the horse on the Canadian Plains in what is today southwestern Alberta.

6. Probably Kootenays, possibly Flatheads from west of the Rockies. In the incident in the succeeding paragraph the details do not suggest an identity for "the tribe's enemies."

"What if Mama is an Indian?"
The Cultural Ambivalence
of the Alexander Ross Family

_____Sylvia M. Van Kirk

Recent historical studies of the mixed-blood people of western Canada have concluded that within this broad category, there were specific groups who can be differentiated on the basis of ethnicity, religion, and class. In the period before 1870, there was a discernible Anglophone mixed-blood group, sometimes known as the "country-born."[1] These people exhibited a cultural orientation quite distinct from that of the larger Francophone mixed-blood group or Métis. There is considerable truth to Frits Pannekoek's assertion that the principal aspiration of this "country-born" element was assimilation into the British, Protestant world of their forefathers.[2] As Jennifer Brown has emphasized, this was due in large measure to an active and pervasive paternal influence within many of these British-Indian families.[3] Much work remains to be done, however, in analyzing the actual impact of this process of enculturation on the children of these families. In a useful article about the children of Chief Factor Roderick McKenzie and his Ojibway wife Angèlique, Elizabeth Arthur has suggested that the pressures to succeed in their father's world imposed severe psychological distress upon them, especially the sons.[4]

This paper provides a case study of another prominent British-Indian family, the Alexander Ross family of Red River. In determining the success of the program of enculturation that British fathers, aided by church and school, mapped out for their children, it is useful to focus on the élite, for these fathers (usually retired Hudson's Bay Company officers) had the desire, along with sufficient rank, wealth, and education to secure the enculturation of their children as members of the British Protestant community in spite of their birth in a distant and isolated part of the Empire. The Alexander Ross family appears to have been one of the most successfully enculturated British-Indian families in Red River. Yet, ultimately, an outstanding younger son, James, suffered an "identity crisis" so profound that it destroyed him. The tragedy of his life is representative of the Anglophone mixed-blood group as a whole. Owing to the irreconcilable conflicts of enculturation they experienced, they lacked the Métis sense of a cultural identity based on an acceptance of their dual racial heritage.

When the young Scots Presbyterian Alexander Ross first emigrated to the Canadas in 1804, he earned his livelihood as a school teacher. After several years, this profession yielded so few monetary and social benefits that he decided to try his fortune instead in the fur trade. As a clerk with the Pacific Fur Company, he helped to establish trade with the Okanagan Indians of the Upper Columbia River. Shortly after, around 1813, he wed *à la façon du pays* an Okanagan chief's young daughter whom he called Sally. Their first child Alexander was born in 1815, followed by three girls, Margaret (b. 1819), Isabella (b. 1820), and Mary (b. 1823). Although Ross had a high regard for the Okanagan people, as his family grew, he felt it best to remove them from the world of fur trade post and Indian camp. In 1825, he retired from the trade and settled his wife and children on an extensive land grant in the Red River colony. There he hoped they would be able to receive "the Christian education" he considered the best portion in life that he could give them.[5]

In time, the Ross family numbered twelve children in all—four boys and eight girls. For the eight youngest children, Red River was the only home they had ever known; they never had any contact with their mother's kin across the Rocky Mountains. We don't know what Sally Ross felt on taking leave of her father's people for the last time, but there is certainly evidence that her loving maternal presence considerably strengthened the Ross children's sense of family. Yet, as a Christianized Indian, the extent to which she transmitted her native heritage to her children appears to have been limited. That some Indian expressions were used in the family circle is evidenced by the little endearments James penned to his mother in later years, and the older girls were proficient in Indian crafts such as making moccasins.[6] But such attributes were almost completely overshadowed by the Scots Presbyterian influence of the father.

As the patriarch of "Colony Gardens," Alexander Ross shaped the upbringing of his half-Indian children. It was he who determined their religious and secular education, and who later gave land to his sons to establish their own households or provided succor for widowed daughters.[7] Ross's most ardent desire was that his family be imbued with the precepts of Christianity. Although disappointed that there was as yet no Presbyterian minister in the settlement, Ross had his wife and children baptized in the Anglican church. He and his wife were also formally married by the Reverend William Cockran in 1828. But while religious observances had to be made at the Anglican church, Ross kept his staunch Presbyterianism alive through regular family gatherings for Bible reading and prayers. All the while he campaigned to bring a Presbyterian minister to Red River, which was at last achieved in the person of the Reverend John Black, who arrived in 1851. Religion emerged as one of the most formative influences in the lives of the Ross children. Their sincere religious conviction gave them a sense of purpose—they subscribed to the Presbyterian view that God had put them on this earth to be instruments of His purpose and that He would reward those who diligently applied their talents.[8]

The application of the benefits of secular education seems to have been somewhat more uneven. With the exception of two of the younger ones, little formal education was bestowed upon the girls, most of whom married in their teens. But the sons, who were to carry on the family name, received the best education that Red River had to offer. William (b. 1825) was a very creditable graduate of the Red River Academy, while his younger brother James (b. 1835) was such an outstanding pupil of Bishop Anderson's that he was sent to further his education at the University of Toronto in 1853. The education of the youngest Ross children was taken over by the Presbyterian minister John Black. Sandy Ross (who was named in memory of his eldest brother who had died in 1835) was one of a class of six young scholars. Privately, Black tutored Henrietta (b. 1830), who later became his wife, and undertook to improve upon the superficial girls' school education that her younger sister Jemima (b. 1837) had received.

For the girls, marriage to a man of consequence in their father's opinion was practically the only route to assimilation. Significantly, four out of the six Ross daughters to reach adulthood married white men. In 1838, Margaret Ross married Hugh Matheson of Kildonan, and she was eventually listed in the Red River census as white. Henrietta's marriage to the Reverend John Black, while it helped to seal the family's identification with the Scots Kildonan community, also emphasized the family's orientation toward newcomers, for Black had but recently come from Canada. Isabella Ross's second husband was James Stewart Green, an American free trader who arrived in the settlement in the 1840s. Finally in 1860, the Canadian connection was further extended when the youngest Ross girl, Jemima, married William Coldwell, who had arrived the year before to start the colony's first newspaper.

These marriages to white men not only underscore the Ross family's desire to be viewed as "British," but they symbolize the way in which the family identified with the forces of "progress" in Red River. It was a measure of the family's success that its sons were equipped and ready to play a leadership role in the colony, to bring about a new order based on the benefits of civilization. Old Alexander Ross had every reason to be proud of his son William. By the early 1850s, William had succeeded to all his father's public offices, which included Councillor of Assiniboia, Sheriff, and Keeper of the Jail. "Is it not very pleasing to see a son step into the shoes of his father and do ample justice to all of these offices?" the old patriarch enthused.[9] William, who could not have been unaware that his station in the colony depended in large measure on the good will of the old Company establishment, did not publicly criticize the rule of the Hudson's Bay Company; yet, like many of his peers, he chafed under the old regime. He wrote to his brother James in 1856:

> You know the fact that Red River is half a century behind the age—no stirring events to give life and vigour to our debilitated political life—The incubus of the Company's monopoly—the peculiar government under which we *vegetate*... all hang like a nightmare on our political and social existence.... Such a state of things cannot last forever, sooner or later the whole fabric must be swept away.... We ought to have a flood of immigration to infuse new life, new ideas, and destroy all our old associations with the past, i.e. in so far as it hinders our progress for the future—a regular transformation will sharpen our intellects, fill our minds with new projects and give life and vigour to our thoughts, words, and action—when that day comes along you may rest assured that there will be no complaint.[10]

Just what role William Ross would have played in the turbulent years that followed must remain a matter of speculation, for a few months after he wrote these words he was dead, cut down at the age of thirty-one.

James Ross, however, emerged as an ardent champion of the cause of Canada in Rupert's Land. It is scarcely surprising that from young James's point of view, Canada was the land of opportunity. He performed brilliantly at Knox College, winning an impressive array of scholarships and prizes. His father, highly gratified, exclaimed, "What will they say of the Brûlés now?"[11] Socially, James's acceptance also seemed to be complete, for in 1858 he married Margaret Smith, the daughter of a respected Scots Presbyterian family in Toronto. To marry a white woman represented a considerable achievement for a British-Indian man, and was almost unheard of in Red River. Both of James's brothers, for example, had married well-connected British-Indian women.[12]

On the surface, the children of Alexander Ross were extremely successful in terms of criteria derived from their father's world; yet they were not immune to social gossip that was essentially racist in nature. Instances of racial prejudice were evident in the community's reaction to Henrietta's marriage to the Reverend John Black. It was intimated that his marriage to a native would prove detrimental to his ministry.[13] Indeed, at least some members of the predominantly white congregation resented the prominent position of this "halfbreed" family—they occupied three out of the six prestigious square pews. The ears of young Jemima Ross were stung by remarks that Mr. Black must feel rather ashamed to see all his "black" relations when he stepped into the pulpit.[14] Although she tried to make light of the situation, it is evident that Jemima was wounded and began to feel ambivalent about having an Indian mother. Although privately she might have been quite devoted to her mother, she became increasingly embarrassed to be seen in public with her. Ambivalence toward their native mothers, which was in essence an ambivalence toward their own Indian blood and heritage, was evidently not uncommon among British-Indian children. James Ross himself lamented that "halfbreed" children often did not show enough respect to their Indian mothers. He feared that some of his brothers and sisters might succumb to this temptation, especially after the death of their father, which prompted his anguished admonition, "What if Mama is an Indian?"[15] While James loved his mother, it is difficult to interpret this statement as a positive defence of his mother's Indianness. What the statement does signify is that, *even* if their mother was an Indian, she was a most exemplary mother and for that reason was entitled to the love and respect of her children. Her simple Christian virtue, he argued, was far more worthy of esteem than the superficial accomplishments of some white ladies held in such high regard in Red River. But the fact that he felt moved to make such a comparison indicates the social strains to which the younger members of the family in particular were exposed.

James's own response to racial prejudice, to which he appears to have been quite sensitive, was to work diligently to prove that one could rise above the derogatory stereotypes of mixed-blood people perpetrated in non-native circles in nineteenth-century Red River.[16] Indeed, these stereotypes were uncomfortably close to home. On reading his father's book, *The Fur Hunters of the Far West,* James was disconcerted to find that his own father made unflattering generalizations about halfbreeds, characterizing them as "fickle" and "destitute of steady purpose." "I think some of your statements about Halfbreeds unnecessarily harsh," James could not help telling him, and he vowed that his father would never be able to accuse him of being guilty of such behavior.[17]

In fact, James Ross seems to have been almost obsessed with the desire to make his father proud of him. He could not fail. The pressure on him increased unexpectedly when in 1856 not only his elder brother but his father died. Within a few short months, the Ross family had suffered a double blow—not only had they lost their guiding head, but also the one who had been groomed to take his place. In a British-Indian family where the family's welfare and status was so dependent upon the father, his demise could be catastrophic. Again James Ross acknowledged that "halfbreed" families generally dwindled into insignificance after the patriarchs died.[18] He fervently believed that the same must not happen to the Ross family. In a moving letter to his siblings, he exhorted them to a standard of conduct that would ensure the family's standing and respectability within the community.

After completing his B.A., James Ross returned to Red River with his Canadian bride in the summer of 1858. In assuming the mantle of family leadership, he was considerably proud to be chosen to follow in the footsteps of his father and brother by being appointed Sheriff and Postmaster. Unlike his brother, however, James Ross felt compelled to speak out against the Company. In the late 1850s, agitation for a Canadian takeover was growing and it found widespread support in the Anglophone mixed-blood community. In 1857, for example, the mixed-blood sons of the late Chief Factor Alexander Kennedy had obtained hundreds of signatures to a petition appealing to the Legislature of the Province of Canada.[19] James Ross was ideally placed to continue this campaign and he found his vehicle for expression in *The Nor'Wester*, of which he became co-editor in 1860. But Ross was to learn that although the Company might be weakened, it had not yet lost all power. In 1862, after publishing a petition that ran counter to the one being promoted by the Hudson's Bay Company on the question of defence for Red River, Ross found himself summarily divested of his appointed offices. Shortly afterward, he became heavily involved in the sordid Corbett case; along with a significant sector of the British-Indian community, he seemed to feel that the unhappy minister was being persecuted because of his anti-Company stance.[20] By 1864, with his prospects tarnished, Ross, perhaps at his wife's urging, decided to return to Canada.

So promising did Canada seem that James urged other members of the family to emigrate. William and Jemima Coldwell and young Sandy Ross with his mixed-blood wife Catherine Murray arrived in Toronto the following year. It was not a happy interlude. Although he had previously spent some years at Knox College, Sandy was so homesick that he and Catherine returned to Red River within twelve months. Jemima Coldwell also did not adapt well to her new surroundings. Although she had a fine house, she may have shared her sister Henrietta's apprehension that a "dark halfbreed" like herself would never really be acceptable in Canadian society.[21] In any event, Jemima grew increasingly melancholy, especially after the death of her eldest daughter, and she herself died in Toronto in 1867.

Only James seemed to thrive—his list of accomplishments was increasingly impressive. He completed his M.A. degree and articled at law, coming first in the class when he was admitted to the bar. He quickly attracted the attention of George Brown, and later became a lead writer and reporter for *The Globe*. As Jennifer Brown has pointed out, Canada could absorb a few talented native sons, isolated as they were from their fellows.[22] Doubtless, James Ross would have prospered had he stayed in Canada. Instead he returned to Red River on

the eve of momentous change. He had been encouraged by the lieu-
tenant-governor-to-be, William McDougall, who advised him that the
new Canadian possession would need leaders like himself. Indeed, few
could match his credentials. A man of striking mien and persuasive
speech, he was fluent in both English and French, devoted to Red
River, but with influential and sympathetic ties to Canada. Ross had
always felt that his destiny was somehow bound up with the colony.
Here was the golden opportunity—the longed-for time that his
brother had not lived to see. The Anglophone mixed-blood community was apparently ready to secure the promise of their British Protestant heritage through union with Canada, and Ross intended to lead
them to it.

For James Ross, however, the Red River Resistance proved to be
not only a political but a personal crisis of great magnitude. It
essentially destroyed him. Instead of providing consistent leadership,
Ross vacillated. At first the ardent champion of the Canadian cause, he
ended up as Chief Justice of Riel's provisional government. Ross was
won over by Riel's appeal to racial unity—the Métis were not fighting
solely for their rights, but for the rights of all the indigenous people of
Red River. As anglicized as he might be, Ross could not ignore the
Indian dimension of his heritage; indeed, he was far more Indian by
blood than was Riel. The bond of their native ancestry made Ross
anxious to avoid taking up arms against the Métis. Nothing was worth
a civil war against "brothers and kindred."[23] As a result, Ross's course
throughout the resistance was to try desperately to maintain peace
and prevent the clash that he feared might result in the massacre of the
English sector of the community.[24] Yet his course was a tortured one;
as a darling of the Canadian cause, it was not easy to be allied with
Riel. Friends and relatives in Canada suspected Ross of treasonous
conduct and British-Indian countrymen who remained opposed to
Riel accused him of being a self-seeking rogue.[25] In turmoil, Ross was
driven to drink. His feelings of ambivalence and guilt must have been
profound. Hopelessly torn between the Canadians and the Métis, he
was quite unable to deal with this polarization of his heritage. All his
life he had believed that he could transcend the limitations of his
origins; but one suspects that the events in Red River had made him
begin to doubt McDougall's assurances that native rights would be
respected. It must have hurt him deeply when even his beloved *Globe*
printed disparaging remarks about renegade halfbreeds, tarring the
entire mixed-blood community with the same brush. Ross and others

were horrified at the violence of the Canadian troops. The Anglo-phone mixed-blood community experienced a real sense of disillu-sionment with the Canadians when they actually arrived, realizing that they, too, could fall victim to racist attacks.[26]

In the summer of 1870, James Ross took a trip to Toronto to settle some business affairs. It was in some sense a pilgrimage, a reaffirm-ation of his ties with Canada. He was able to pull himself together and returned to Red River with renewed purpose. He hoped to escape the stigma of his association with Riel and be called upon to serve in the new administration of Governor Archibald. Instead, he suffered the mortification of seeing himself passed over in favor of Canadian new-comers.[27] Whether he would ever have been able to fulfil his outstand-ing promise remains conjecture; he died in September 1871.

After James's death, the youngest son, Sandy, did not take over as head of the Ross family. Although not much is known about him, he was the most insecure of all the sons and never found his niche. Death claimed him early, too, at the age of thirty-one. The leadership of the Ross family passed to the white sons-in-law, the Reverend John Black, who remained concerned for the family's welfare even after the death of Henrietta in 1873, and especially William Coldwell, who married Jemima Ross (née McKenzie), William Ross's widow, in 1875.

In spite of their great promise, an air of tragedy hung over the chil-dren of Alexander Ross. By 1874, they were all dead (except one daughter), most having died in their thirties. Like other mixed-blood families, they were susceptible to lung diseases, but one wonders to what extent psychological stress contributed to their poor health. It seems that the degree of psychological dislocation was proportional to the degree to which they attempted to imitate the ways of the newcomers.

The ones who fared best were the daughters, perhaps partly be-cause there was less pressure on them to succeed. Yet even here the most well-adjusted seem to have been those who were not forced to completely suppress their Indian heritage. Mary Ross, for example, who married the mixed-blood Orkneyman George Flett, eventually helped her husband establish a Presbyterian mission among the Riding Mountain "Chippewas" or Saulteaux. There her familiarity with the Indian language and customs was an advantage, not a detriment.[28] Her younger sisters who married prominent whites had to confront prejudice more directly. Henrietta was able to weather the racial jibes of the Kildonan community, being greatly assisted by a

134 / *Sylvia M. Van Kirk*

loving and supportive husband, but Jemima, who was the youngest and most upwardly mobile, had a great deal of trouble coping with her situation.

The sons suffered most. Their fate is important, for in the 1850s and '60s, talented young Anglophone mixed-bloods like themselves were emerging as important leaders in Red River.[29] In 1861, according to fellow countryman A.K. Isbister, British-Indians occupied nearly all the important and intellectual offices in the colony. Most prominent among them was James Ross.[30]

Indeed, the pressure on Ross must have been enormous, for he was held up as an example to all. Yet James Ross's crisis in 1869–70 is really symbolic of an inherent flaw in the enculturation process to which Anglophone mixed-blood children were subjected. The Red River Resistance polarized the settlement into two elements—white and Métis. British-Indian leaders such as James Ross, discovering that they were really neither, were essentially paralyzed by their own ambivalence. Ultimately, the cultural biases of the newcomers, often racist in nature, denied to this group the successful integration into white society that they desired.[31] Significantly, the new élite of Winnipeg soon bore little resemblance to the old Red River élite that had given Isbister so much satisfaction. Yet, leaders such as James Ross could not be Métis, even though they might have felt a bond of kinship with the French-Indian community. Unlike the Métis, the Anglophone mixed-bloods lacked a distinct cultural identity based on the duality of their heritage, and this made it difficult for them to build upon their uniqueness as a people of mixed racial ancestry. In 1869–70, the Métis were secure enough in their own identity to champion the cause of native rights and would henceforth emerge as the strongest of the mixed-blood community. The particular tragedy of the "British-Indian" people of Rupert's Land was that, in the end, they were neither white nor Métis.

Notes

1. The phrase "country-born" was first brought into use by John Foster in his Ph.D. thesis, "The Country-born in the Red River Settlement, 1820–50" (University of

Alberta, 1972). Other terms include "Hudson's Bay English" and "Red River Halfbreed." I am grateful to Irene Spry for suggesting the designations Anglophone and Francophone in reference to mixed-bloods.

2. *See* Frits Pannekoek, "The Churches and the Social Structure in the Red River Area 1818–1870" (Ph.D. thesis, Queen's University, 1973).

3. Jennifer Brown, *Strangers in Blood: Fur Trade Families in Indian Country* (Vancouver: University of British Columbia Press, 1980), pp. 216–20.

4. Elizabeth Archer, "Angelique and her Children," *Thunder Bay Historical Museum Society, Papers and Records* VI: 30–40.

5. Alexander Ross, *The Fur Hunters of the Far West* (London: Smith, Elder and Co., 1855), vol. 2, p. 233.

6. Public Archives of Manitoba (hereafter P.A.M.), Alexander Ross Family Papers, James to his father, 31 December 1853; Alexander to James, 11 June 1854; James to his father, 1 July 1854.

7. The Ross family seems to have conformed to the patriarchal household described by Frits Pannekoek in his article, "The Demographic Structure of Nineteenth Century Red River" in L.H. Thomas, ed., *Essays on Western History* (Edmonton: University of Alberta Press, 1976), pp. 83–95.

8. P.A.M., Ross Family Papers, James to his father, 1 July 1854.

9. Ibid., Alexander to James, 25 August 1854.

10. Ibid., William to James, 9 February 1856.

11. Ibid., John Black to James, 9 February 1854. *Bois Brûlés* was a term used originally to apply to the Métis. It could be translated as "mixed-blood" or "halfbreed."

12. William Ross married Jemima McKenzie, a daughter of former Hudson's Bay Company officer Roderick McKenzie, and a grand-daughter of Chief Factor James Sutherland. The youngest son, Sandy Ross, married Catherine, the daughter of prosperous Kildonan settler Donald Murray and his mixed-blood wife Catherine Swain.

13. Hudson's Bay Company Archives, D. 5/38, Jas. Sinclair to Simpson, 11 December 1853, f. 342 and Jn. Bunn to Simpson, 16 December 1853, f. 372d–373.

14. P.A.M., Ross Family Papers, Jemima to James, 9 November 1854.

15. Ibid., Jas. Ross to siblings, 25 December 1865.

16. For a discussion of the growth of these stereotypes, *see* Brown, *Strangers in Blood.*

17. P.A.M., Ross Family Papers, James to his father, October 1856. James may well have thought that his father was ashamed of his half-Indian family. Significantly, their existence is never mentioned in Alexander Ross's later volume, *The Red River Settlement.*

18. Ibid., James Ross to siblings, 25 December 1856.

19. "Petition of Inhabitants" in L.G. Thomas, ed., *The Prairie West to 1905* (Toronto: Oxford University Press, 1975), pp. 59–61.

20. For a discussion of this episode, *see* Frits Pannekoek, "The Rev. Griffiths Owen Corbett and the Red River Civil War of 1869–70." *Canadian Historical Review* LVII, 2, pp. 133–49.

21. P.A.M., Ross Family Papers, Henrietta to James, early 1854.

22. Jennifer Brown, "Ultimate Respectability: Fur Trade Children in the 'Civilized World'," *The Beaver* (Spring 1978): pp. 48–55.

23. W. L. Morton, ed., *Alexander Begg's Red River Journal* (Toronto: Champlain Society, 1956), p. 422.

24. P.A.M., Ross Family Papers, James to his wife, 24 September 1870.

25. Morton, *Begg's Journal*, p. 351; P.A.M., Ross Family Papers, Jas. Smith to Maggy, 30 November 1869; Rev. John Laing to Ross, February 1870.

26. P.A.M., Ross Family Papers, James to his wife, 29 September 1870; Matthew Cook to Jas. Ross, 22 November 1870.

27. Ibid., James to Governor Archibald, 11 March 1871.

28. P.A.M., William Coldwell Papers, Draft notes about Mary Ross Flett.

29. Frits Pannekoek has suggested in his thesis that the "country-born" or Anglo-Indian community was not able to produce its own leaders. The evidence does not seem to support this. Men such as William Hallett, James Sinclair, and the Kennedy brothers, in addition to the Ross brothers, were leaders and more attention needs to be given to their role.

30. W.L. Morton, *Manitoba, A History,* (Toronto: University of Toronto Press, 1967), p. 90.

31. Consider the fate of William Hallett, for example. An ambitious man, he was to suffer racial prejudice in his attempt to succeed in white society. He committed suicide after the failure of the "Canadian party" to overthrow Riel.

The Telegraph and Community Formation in the North-West Territories

_____David R. Richeson

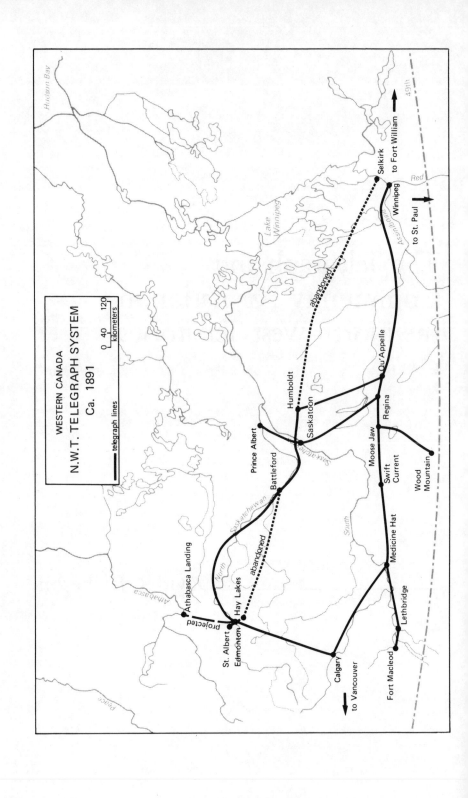

WESTERN CANADA
N.W.T. TELEGRAPH SYSTEM
Ca. 1891

▬▬ telegraph lines

0 40 120
kilometers

to Fort William
49th
Red
to St. Paul
Selkirk
Winnipeg
Assiniboine
Qu'Appelle
Regina
Humboldt
Saskatoon
abandoned
Moose Jaw
Swift Current
Wood Mountain
Prince Albert
Battleford
Saskatchewan
South
Medicine Hat
abandoned
Hay Lakes
St. Albert
Edmonton
projected
Athabasca Landing
Athabasca
North
Saskatchewan
Lethbridge
Fort Macleod
Calgary
to Vancouver
Lake Winnipeg
Hudson Bay
Peace

The electric telegraph was the most effective communications tool of the nineteenth century. Its use for economic, social, political, and military purposes could greatly diminish the problems created by both distance and time. Wherever it was introduced, the telegraph had the effect of stimulating and accelerating the exchange of ideas among communities. The existence of this communications tool was particularly important in the Canadian Northwest, where vast distances and often difficult weather conditions produced challenging communication problems. An examination of the history of the introduction of telegraphy to the North-West Territories between 1870 and the turn of the century indicates that it had a particular impact upon certain significant elements involved in community formation — particularly the press. The telegraph service, which emerged from a combination of Dominion government and private company initiatives, was introduced in response to a combination of national and regional needs and objectives.

The need for improvement in communications in the Northwest was apparent when the region was acquired by Canada. In the 1860s, the Hudson's Bay Company had considered the construction of an electric telegraph. Dr. John Rae had carried out a feasibility survey of the entire route in 1864 and materials had subsequently been assembled at Red River to begin construction.[1] Changes in the priorities of the Company and The Transfer negotiations had stayed commencement of the project. The assembled materials were finally utilized in 1871, not for a telegraph line across the Northwest, but rather for a telegraph connection constructed by the North Western Telegraph Company between Fort Garry and the Company's lines in Minnesota.[2]

The communications system saw no additional improvement until 1874 when the government of Alexander Mackenzie, as part of the plan for a Pacific railway, had private contractors build an electric telegraph line along a projected railway route selected by Chief Engineer Sandford Fleming's numerous survey parties in the Northwest.[3] Fleming's concept for development of internal communications in frontier areas called first for a telegraph line followed by a trail, then a wagon road, and, finally, a railway. Fleming believed that "telegraphy will act as the spinal cord" for the finished system.[4] Unfortunately for the economic success of the telegraph, and contrary to Fleming's principles, the projected railway line missed nearly all existing trading posts and settlements in the Northwest – probably in an effort to diminish land speculation. The electric telegraph was thus constructed, largely between 1874 and 1878, along a route from Fort William, north of Winnipeg, and along the North Saskatchewan River to Hay Lakes, south of Fort Edmonton. The contract for an Edmonton-Kamloops connection via the Yellowhead Pass was cancelled after a season's work, perhaps as a result of increasing uncertainty about the future of the railway.[5] By 1880, $1,024,640 had been spent for 1,222 miles of telegraph line that worked sporadically at best.[6]

The Winnipeg office of the Canadian Department of Public Works had been requested in September 1878 to send weekly "test" telegraph messages west over the Dominion telegraph line. The first message directed to Edmonton on 5 October was followed by a second on 15 October. On 28 October a third message was sent in an attempt to determine the fate of the earlier two. A response from Edmonton finally arrived on 11 November indicating that the first message had gone to Battleford by telegraph and on to Edmonton by mail; the second two messages were accepted for the telegraph but were sent by mail because the line was down.[7] The test demonstrated what numerous complaints had already established: the government's attempt to provide a communication system in the Northwest, based on a telegraph line constructed, operated, and maintained by subsidized private contractors, was not working. It still took weeks for messages of any type to reach destinations in the Northwest. The population remained nearly as isolated from the outside world as it had been a decade earlier.

A series of inspections of the telegraph line revealed a multitude of problems. D.E.R. Lucas had reported in 1877 that the usually inoperative section of the line west of Battleford, constructed and operated by Richard Fuller, used inadequate poles "more like wigwam or hop poles," which in some instances were held up only by the wire. The line wandered across the parkland and normally avoided all obstacles, but occasional sections of wire were "beautifully festooned in trees." He concluded that "no attempt has been made to build the line properly."[8] Fuller's contract had called for the line to be maintained "in good running order for a period of five years. – This he seems to consider something different from good working order," reported the Public Works staff in Winnipeg.[9] It was reported in addition that Fuller's maintenance staff of five men also managed his Battleford store and a farm.[10]

Contractors, once they were paid for construction of the line, found there was little profit to be made in the operation of the telegraph. Maintenance costs soared owing to a variety of factors, including inferior materials (undersize poles, light wire, unthreaded insulators on "green" wooden brackets, which dried and fell off) and inexperience (the wire frequently broke in cold weather because the slack was insufficient to permit contraction). Other contributing factors were: destruction of the line by frequent prairie fires, lightning strikes, and serious flooding, particularly north of Winnipeg where nearly half of the line that ran through dry areas in 1875–76 was in standing water by the end of the decade.[11] Since railway construction had not followed, little business was done by the telegraph. Notoriously unreliable lines and isolated offices made its use for administrative purposes, personal communication, or for business both difficult and expensive.[12] The *Saskatchewan Herald* reflected upon the route of the telegraph: "It is a striking commentary upon the selection of the route for the railway upon which the telegraph was built that along its whole length, from Battleford to Selkirk on the east to Edmonton on the west, there is not a single settler."[13]

While a new Canadian Pacific railway policy was being considered, Sir John A. Macdonald's Conservative government initiated an extensive administrative reorganization and consolidation in the communications area, which resulted in the creation of a Dominion Government Telegraph and Signal Service in 1879. The objectives of the new service were to provide communication facilities to sparsely populated areas not served by private companies and to "provide telegraph facilities to the frontier areas of the nation."[14] One of the first duties of newly appointed Superintendent Fredrick N. Gisborne, a pioneer in Canadian telegraphy in Atlantic Canada,[15] was a personal inspection of the moribund Dominion telegraph line in the Northwest. Following his inspection, Gisborne informed the minister that unsuitable materials had been used in the pioneer line between Fort William and Edmonton, and that it was "thus almost valueless for all practical purposes."[16] Gisborne recommended that the government terminate the contracts, take over the line, and consider rebuilding it entirely.

After a period of indecision and unsuccessful attempts to sell the Dominion telegraph line, the government finally decided to abandon a major portion of the old line east of Humboldt, to turn the Fort William section over to the new Canadian Pacific Railway, which had a charter provision to operate a telegraph service, and, finally, to rebuild and relocate much of the remaining line.[17] "As it had in many other areas, the federal Government took a direct role in developing the West." Along with this involvement "was its control of decisions and policy with regard to that area."[18] For the first time, the federal government had a policy on communications in the Northwest and in other areas of Canada, as well an an effective administrative structure to meet policy objectives.

This new government initiative was greeted enthusiastically by merchants, settlers, and newspapers in areas of the Northwest far removed from the new southern route of the Canadian Pacific Railway. It was hoped that the days when "the one-horse cart comes rattling along with the 'very latest—twenty days from Winnipeg'" were over.[19] In addition, "the creation of a telegraph line, post offiice, or other government presence added to the attractiveness of a town and, as in the case of North Battleford, increased its chances for further growth and prosperity."[20] The *Saskatchewan Herald* concluded that completion of the new line would mean "that business will receive an impetus and an additional interest [will] be evoked in the affairs of the outside world."[21]

Interest in the affairs of the outside world had prompted the residents of Edmonton to establish the *Bulletin* on a subscription basis. It featured weekly summaries from Winnipeg "giving the most notable occurrences in the world at large and matters concerning the Northwest Territories in particular," local news from the upper Saskatchewan country, and "opinions on matters and things connected with the Northwest."[22] The prospect of a more reliable telegraph service prompted the residents of Prince Albert to petition for an extension of the proposed new line and, similarly, to create a subscription newspaper.[23] The content of the Prince Albert *Times and Saskatchewan Review* during the completion of the telegraph line indicates the importance of outside news. The editor informed his readers that "with no telegraph to communicate with the great outside world and a mail only once in three weeks (as is now the case) it will be a hard matter to find material to supply our columns with matter of general interest to our readers." The immediate possibility, however, for "these two great feeders of the press" to be improved held the prospect for raised standards.[24] In the meantime, the newspaper printed a lengthy novel in installments and reported arrivals and departures of Prince Albert travellers in detail.

An examination of newspaper formation in the North-West Territories, in communities that had grown to a population of six hundred or more by 1901, indicates that in only two of fourteen communities was a newspaper established prior to the arrival of telegraph service. The exceptions were Prince Albert, where the telegraph was anticipated shortly, and Ford Macleod, which had a *Gazette* supported by merchants and the N.W.M.P.

Number of
Communities[25]   *Chronological Pattern of Development*

4	Telegraph ⟶ Newspaper ⟶ Railway
7	Railway/Telegraph ⟶ Newspaper
1	Telegraph ⟶ Railway ⟶ Newspaper
2	Newspaper ⟶ Telegraph ⟶ Railway

In the North-West Territories, a telegraph connection to the news of the world at large was a precondition for a successful newspaper. Newspapers, therefore, developed from a non-political tradition, unlike the pattern in central Canada and Atlantic Canada. This factor may well have additional importance in explaining the formation of a sense of "district consciousness" in the Northwest and the nature of this region's relationship with central Canada.

Although the Dominion government was committed to improving the basic communication system, a degree of financial support was required from many individual communities. Edmonton residents paid for the extension of the line from Hay Lakes to the Fort; Prince Albert residents paid for and transported the poles needed to make the connection with the main line. Similar conditions were fulfilled by the Saskatoon settlement of the Temperance Colonization Society, which also freighted the wire at no cost. In general terms, the Dominion government responded effectively to local concerns and petitions for improved telegraph communications following the formation of the Government Telegraph and Signal Service.

Local financial involvement by communities could, however, lead to problems, as proved by the 1883 situation in Prince Albert. Anticipation for improved services was great, as the editor of the Prince Albert Times wrote: "To have to wait three weeks for our letters and newpapers, and no telegraph to inform us of the doings of the great outside world, may have suited the last decade, but will not do for this generation. So move along ye Government officials. . . . "[26] After patiently waiting through a series of construction delays for the long awaited connection to the telegraph, Prince Albert residents "waxed exceeding wroth" when it was found that the office for the telegraph was placed at the Hudson's Bay Post at the river landing rather than in "that part of the settlement which had given the heaviest bonus, and which appeared to promise the largest share of business."[27] The Prince Albert Telegraph Pole Committee held "an indignation meeting" where resolutions were passed "defining the position of the pole committee, the position of the poles, the position of the lots, and the position of the telegraph superintendent in the estimation of those assembled at the meeting."[28] The meeting then broke up amid "wild enthusiasm," and a number of telegraph poles were removed and an effigy burned of the regional Telegraph Superintendent, Hartley Gisborne. Damage charges were drawn up and then dropped as local passions cooled. The government responded by temporarily establishing a second Prince Albert telegraph office (a first in the North-West Territories)![29] A magistrate's investigation of the affair concluded that there had been a simple misunderstanding, but it resulted in a telegram of apology from the federal Minister of Public Works.[30]

The telegraph also featured in misunderstandings of another sort, often resulting from severely abbreviated telegraphic accounts of events in the Northwest that were received and then embellished in eastern Canada and the United States. An example is an exaggerated

Chicago newspaper story regarding an Indian raid at Prince Albert in 1879, which prompted the *Saskatchewan Herald* to comment, "When it was said of any one a few years ago that 'he lied like the telegraph' it was considered nothing worse could be said."[31] The *Saskatchewan Herald* had earlier stated sarcastically that "owing to the telegraph line being down we are at a loss to know what Indian outrages are being perpetrated in our midst, as well has how matters are progressing in the outer world."[32]

In the absence of regular news-gathering correspondents in the Northwest, items of sensational news often originated from the telegraphers. The Sharphead "uprising" at Hay Lakes in 1881, reported in the Edmonton *Bulletin,* resulted from destitute Indians attempting to obtain food from a frightened telegrapher at Hay Lakes.[33] The early 1880s were times of increasing unrest and movement among Indians in the Northwest experiencing food shortages, although reports of Indian uprisings could emanate from the most innocent incidents. An interesting example was the Indian uprising reported at Battleford in April 1884. Under a heading of "False Reports" the *Saskatchewan Herald* noted: "A considerable degree of excitement was occasioned in the Eastern Provinces lately by a telegram from Qu'Appelle sent out on the 16th April, to the effect that there had been an Indian uprising at Battleford, and that the operator here reported two thousand Indians marching on the town." The newspaper concluded that the story grew from an incident in which the telegrapher answered a question on the number of Indians near the town – followed by a break in the telegraph line.[34] Newspapers in the Northwest recognized that such stories would inhibit immigration and settlement and perpetuate an unfavorable frontier image.

Events surrounding the 1885 Rebellion, however, had enough sensational content that little embellishment was needed. In September 1884 the government telegraph line had been extended to Duck Lake near Batoche's Crossing.[35] Within the first hours of the clash between the N.W.M.P. and the Métis, this line and the line to Prince Albert were cut. Shortly after, sections of the line between Battleford and Edmonton, and Clarke's Crossing and Humboldt, were also removed, effectively heightening tension and apprehension among the inhabitants of these communites.[36] Somewhat ironically, for several days in March 1885, the beleaguered residents of Battleford were in the dark about the state of events at nearby Duck Lake, Batoche, and

Prince Albert, but were kept up to date by telegraph of the efforts of the British forces in Egypt and the Sudan to quell the Mahdi's uprising.[37]

The telegraph played an essential role in the Canadian effort to settle the Saskatchewan Rebellion. The Canadian field forces were served by telegraphers in various support capacities. Special guard detachments were placed at isolated telegraph stations, such as Humboldt, that were open night and day. In general, the Canadian forces moved along the telegraph lines toward Batoche ensuring effective co-ordination of supplies and manpower.[38] After their initial steps to cut the lines, there is no indication that Louis Riel's forces made any effort to disrupt telegraphic communications behind the Canadian forces. Routine repair and maintenance of the lines, however, became dangerous during the rebellion, particularly as bands of hostile Indians were moving about the region of the North Saskatchewan River. One telegraph repairman was murdered and a second held prisoner by Indians for the duration of the rebellion.[39]

Fears of unrest among the Blackfoot in the Southwest prompted the government to embark on rapid construction of several new telegraph lines to sensitive points. Orders-in-Council were approved in April 1885 for the construction of telegraph lines from the main line of the C.P.R. to Fort Macleod, which also linked the Lethbridge mines, and to the N.W.M.P. Post at Wood Mountain. Both lines were paid from the appropriation for military operations in the Northwest.[40] In addition, the C.P.R. built a sixteen-mile telegraph line between Swift Current and Saskatchewan Landing on the South Saskatchewan River.[41] The residents of Edmonton, cut off from all news except by courier, demanded during the height of the rebellion that a telegraph connection be established to Calgary. Major General Strange supported this request, writing that an Edmonton-Calgary telegraph was essential as the Edmonton-Battleford line was in the hands of "hostiles." He added that such a line would save the cost of the couriers currently being used, each of which cost seven dollars per day.[42] Although construction estimates were prepared, events at Batoche brought an end to the rebellion before a separate telegraph line was built.

Following the rebellion, work resumed on government plans to reconstruct major portions of the northern telegraph line between Humboldt and Edmonton—this time connecting settlements, Indian reserves, and N.W.M.P. posts. The line was to be built of first-class materials, and to include the innovative use of galvanized metal telegraph poles on a major section west of Battleford in an attempt to lessen the damage from recurring prairie fires.[43] The route selected followed roughly along the Victoria Trail between Battleford and Edmonton. Fears of continuing Indian unrest prompted extensions of the telegraph to reserves such as Onion Lake, Saddle Lake, and Stony Plain. Such developments reflected an ongoing apprehension of trouble and an appreciation of the value of communications in meeting any emergencies. Other work by the Government Telegraph Service involved extensive relocation of telegraph lines along road allowances, since most lines built earlier were erected without any reference to survey lines and merely followed the route with the fewest obstructions. Maintenance of telegraph lines in treeless areas remained a problem as travellers persisted in "shaving" telegraph poles for wood to use as fuel.[44]

The Government Telegraph Service emphasized improvement of existing facilities following the completion of the Humboldt-Edmonton line in 1887. This saw the completion of a system which would serve a major portion of the Northwest through the 1890s. Some reorganization took place including the acquisition of the Prince Albert line by the C.P.R. Selected government lines were converted to telephone systems operated on a commission basis. This resulted in saving the telegraph operator's monthly salary, especially in locations of low commercial use, such as N.W.M.P. posts, Indian reserves, and isolated telegraph offices. Immigration to the Northwest had slowed and population growth had not led to major new developments. In southern Alberta, subsidized lines were extended to Cardston by private interests. Elsewhere the Galts made efforts to acquire the government lines serving the coal fields.[45]

The opening of the Canadian Pacific Railway Telegraph for full trans-Canada commerical service in January 1887 brought the Northwest into direct contact with the Pacific coast and brought improved service to eastern Canada. The establishment of a telegraph in connection with a railway between Calgary and Edmonton in 1891 by the C.P.R. was the final major link in a combined government and private telegraph service which joined all major towns and cities in the Northwest.

Telegraph offices in urban areas such as Edmonton in the 1890s were shared by government telegraph operators and C.P.R. operators to facilitate the transfer of messages and to cut costs. Telegraphers, described by the *Saskatchewan Herald* in the 1880s as "pioneers of science and civilization," remained an important part of western communities.[46] In addition to being the first person in the community alerted to major news events, the telegrapher was frequently an observer for the newly established Canadian Meteorological Service, whose weather reports were among the few types of information that travelled over the wires at no cost. Even the N.W.M.P. had to pay cash for telegraph service.[47] The telegraph office was the source of accurate time to the community—standard time was introduced in December 1883—often to the dismay of conservatives among the population who saw no reason to change. The Edmonton *Bulletin* pointed out that there had been some differences within the community. Standard time for Edmonton was thirteen minutes slower than sun time, which was different from the former telegraph time, mill time, fort time, and church time.[48] This development was an additional factor that worked to integrate the separate communities in the Northwest into the larger community of the Territory.

Business use of the telegraph and the economic impact of this use remains more difficult to assess. Certainly, the potential value of the telegraph to merchants in isolated centres in the Northwest was impressive, as an incident reported by the *Saskatchewan Herald* indicates: "at 11 A.M. on 16 January 1885, T.E. Mahaffey and James Clinkskill, general merchants at Battleford, telegraphed Winnipeg for a carload of flour. At 4 P.M. they received a telegram confirmation that the flour had been shipped."[49] The contrast between this new style of merchandising and the very traditional operations of the Hudson's Bay Company was clearly demonstrated when H.B.C. Board member Sir John Rose made an inspection trip of economic conditions in the Northwest in 1882. Rose wrote:

> You have to see with your own eyes what is now going on ...in order correctly to appreciate it...you see independent Traders carrying on a thriving business, many of them under Tents, and with the most complete assortment of goods required as well by the Railway people (of whom there are some 7000) as by the Settlers whose tents and houses are dotted all over the prairie. If any article appears to be specially fancied, or running short,

it is immediately obtained by telegraphic orders from such Emporiums as Winnipeg, St. Paul, or Chicago, and is in a few days on the spot and, immediately sold and paid for.[50]

Rose found the traditional system of trade used by the H.B.C. to be "obsolete and unsuited to the new order of things." Rose concluded that the Company would need to recruit men who could use the new system.[51]

As a communications tool the electric telegraph had application in a broad range of economic activities: banking, marketing of agricultural and ranching products, land speculation, and management of all aspects of railway operation. On the practical side, the telegraph was essential to the land survey system, it permitted the investigation of "national" weather patterns, and occasionally it was used to provide long-distance medical advice. Administrative use of the telegraph can be judged by the increasing amount of communication carried on "by telegraph" as the nineteenth century drew to a close. The impact of all of these activities and others, however, was little short of revolutionary.

When one can, potentially, affect the course of events although they are three hundred or three thousand miles distant – by sending an order, by supplying information, by setting into motion a corrective response – one may be compelled by duty, by responsibility, or by the hope of profit to do so. Thus rapid communication created new options, new duties, new responsibilities, and new anxieties.[52]

The Government Telegraph Service certainly provided "service" to the Northwest at a time when private interests would not have financed such development, but the system proved an ideal tool to facilitate the centralized planning and decision-making favored by both Conservative and Liberal federal governments in the last decades of the nineteenth century.[53]

The number of petitions and offers of community financial assistance that issued forth from western communities seeking improved telegraphic service testifies to the importance of this communications device in the minds of the settlers. Already many from more established regions were familiar with its benefits. In settling the frontier, its ability to bridge distance and lessen the sense of isolation was even more obvious. In reducing isolation, the telegraph permitted westerners to participate in national and regional affairs. Political events, disasters, scandals, and sporting events could be shared with many with whom one was never in face-to-face contact. This union of many dispersed centres through communications services and transportation facilities was an important factor in the creation of a territorial consciousness. While such a consciousness was emerging, the telegraph continued to play a key role in Canadian and western metropolitan-hinterland relationships.

Notes

1. Public Archives of Canada [hereafter P.A.C.], Sir Sandford Fleming Papers, MG29 B1, vol. 40, file 284, Dr. John Rae's Telegraph Survey Report, 1864.

2. Canada, *Sessional Papers* [hereafter C.S.P.], 1872, Paper No. 4; *see also* Provincial Archives of Manitoba, A.G. Archibald Papers, Canada Privy Council Report, 17 August 1870, in Minister of Public Works to Archibald, 9 September 1870; ibid., 29 May 1871.

3. Canada, Order-in-Council (1484), 12 December 1874, which authorized a telegraph line between Ottawa and British Columbia; for additional detail on this contract system in the Northwest, *see* N.A. Ronaghan, "The Pioneer Telegraph In Western Canada," (M.A. thesis, University of Saskatchewan, 1976).

4. P.A.C., Sir Sandford Fleming Papers, MG29 B1, vol. 93, file 3; and ibid., vol. 95, file 9, "Principles of Railway Construction in New Territory," 1863.

5. P.A.C., Records of the Department of Transport, RG12, vol. 2111, file 3920-6, S. Fleming to Min. of Public Works, 19 February 1879.

6. P.A.C., Records of the Department of Public Works, RG11, vol. 3012, 1880–81 Unpublished Estimates, p. 259.

7. P.A.C., RG12, vol. 2112, file 3920-7, part 3, Rowan to Brown, 16 November 1878.

8. Ibid., part 1, Lucas to Smith, [n.d.] November 1877.

9. Ibid., Rowan to Smellie, 10 September 1877; and 9 June 1877. No final inspection of the telegraph line was made after construction since contractors agreed to maintain the line for five years.

10. Ibid., Lucas to Smith, [n.d.] November 1877.

11. Ibid., part 3, R. Tupper to C. Tupper, "Report on Canadian Pacific Railway Telegraphs," 31 January 1881.

12. Ibid., part 1, Lucas to Smith, [n.d.] November 1877.

13. *Saskatchewan Herald* (Battleford), 18 July 1881.

14. Douglas Owram, *Building for Canadians, A History of the Department of Public Works, 1840–1960* (Ottawa: Queen's Printer, 1979), pp. 147–49.

15. For an overview of F.N. Gisborne's contribution to Canadian telegraphy, *see* David R. Richeson, "The Electric Telegraph in Canada, 1846–1902," vol. 52, *Canada's Visual History* (Ottawa: National Museum of Man, 1982).

16. P.A.C., RG 12, vol. 2112, file 3920–7, part 3, F. Gisborne to C. Tupper, 30 November 1880.

17. P.A.C., RG 11, vol. 1993, F. Gisborne to Government Telegraph and Signal Service, Ottawa [hereafter G.T.S.], 26 September 1882, and 28 September 1882. Canada, Order-in-Council (1396), 5 July 1882, transferred all telegraph supplies, the appropriation for telegraph lines and management of telegraphs and cables from the Department of Railways and Canals, with which it had been shared since 1879, to Public Works.

18. Owram, *Building for Canadians*, p. 148.

19. *Saskatchewan Herald*, 18 July 1881.

20. Owram, *Building for Canadians*, p. 149.

21. *Saskatchewan Herald*, 28 April 1883.

22. *Bulletin* (Edmonton), 6 December 1880.

23. P.A.C., RG11, vol. 1993, F. Gisborne to G.T.S., 20 November 1882.

24. *Times* (Prince Albert), 1 November 1882.

25. Canada, *Census*, 1901. This excludes Saskatoon, which also conforms to the dominant pattern of development.

26. *Times*, 22 November 1882.

27. *Saskatchewan Herald*, 24 November 1883.

28. *Bulletin*, 8 December 1883; P.A.C., RG11, vol. 1993, J.F. Betts to G.T.S., 16 November 1883; ibid., T. McKay to G.T.S., 5 December 1883.

29. P.A.C., RG11, vol. 1993, G.T.S. to H. Gisborne, 7 December 1883.

152 / *David R. Richeson*

30. *Saskatchewan Herald,* 12 January 1884. D. Owram uses this incident to illustrate the "resentment that could arise as a result of ignored local interests" meeting centralized planning and control of public works. Owram, *Building for Canadians,* p. 149.

31. *Saskatchewan Herald,* 26 January 1880.

32. Ibid., 8 September 1879.

33. *Bulletin,* 10 January 1881 and 21 February 1881.

34. *Saskatchewan Herald,* 3 May 1884. L. Vankoughnet, Deputy Superintendent General of Indian Affairs, attempted unsuccessfully to have the G.T.S. telegrapher at Qu'Appelle dismissed for sending a "sensational telegram" critical of the government. In this instance the telegrapher had merely sent a message for a private individual. Any type of message except profanity could be sent if the $2.00 or $2.50 for ten words was paid. P.A.C., RG11, vol. 1994, L. Vankoughnet to F. Gisborne, 27 February 1886; ibid., Gisborne to Vankoughnet, 15 March 1886.

35. *Saskatchewan Herald,* 6 September 1884.

36. Ibid., 27 March 1885 and 11 May 1885.

37. Ibid., 20 March 1885.

38. *Bulletin,* 9 May 1885; *see* Desmond Morton and R.H. Roy, eds., *Telegrams of the North-West Campaign, 1885* (Toronto: Champlain Society, 1972).

39. *Bulletin,* 11 April 1885; and P.A.C., RG11, vol. 1995, Order-in-Council, 3 April 1888.

40. P.A.C., RG11, vol. 1994, Minister of Public Works to G.T.S., 22 April 1885.

41. Ibid., vol. 3133, 1887–88 Department of Public Works Unpublished Estimates, Supplementary, p. 380.

42. Ibid., vol. 1994, Strange to G.T.S., 12 May 1885.

43. Ibid., vol. 3127, 1887–88 Department of Public Works Unpublished Estimates, p. 56.

44. P.A.C., Records of the Royal Canadian Mounted Police, RG18, vol. 60, file 108–92, H. Gisborne to F. Gisborne, Report on Telegraph line between Moose Jaw and Wood Mountain, 22 October 1891.

45. P.A.C., RG11, vol. 1996, A.T. Galt to G.T.S., 2 July 1890.

46. *Saskatchewan Herald,* 18 July 1881.

47. P.A.C., RG11, vol. 1995, Auditor General to G.T.S., 29 July 1889.

48. *Bulletin,* 15 December 1883.

49. *Saskatchewan Herald,* 16 January 1885.

50. P.A.C., MG29 B1, vol. 41, file 297, Rose to Colvile, 12 September 1882.

51. Ibid.

52. V.T. Coates and Bernard Finn, *A Retrospective Technology Assessment: Submarine Telegraphy* (San Francisco: San Francisco Press, 1979), p. 117.

53. C.S.P., A1904, Paper No. 19a, "Special Report On The Government Telegraph Service Compiled By The Department of Public Works," presents a complete summary of the telegraph service provided by the federal government in the Northwest. It includes a map of lines (page 21), a summary of rates, and a statement of revenue and expenditure that clearly shows the extent to which these services were subsidized. An indication of the general impact of telegraphy on frontier areas can be found in John A. Irving, *Mass Media In Canada* (Toronto: Ryerson Press, 1962), pp. 3–11; H. Marshall McLuhan, *Understanding Media* (New York: McGraw-Hill, 1964), pp. 217–27; R.L. Thompson, *Wiring A Continent* (Princeton: Princeton University Press, 1947), pp. 127–29; and Richeson, "The Electric Telegraph in Canada, 1846–1902," pp. 4–8.

Population Growth in
Western Canada, 1901–71

_____W. Peter Ward

Since Confederation, the major regions within Canada have had distinctly different regimes of population growth. Rates of increase in the Maritimes have been exceptionally low while those of Ontario and Quebec have stood close to national norms. Western Canada, in contrast, has experienced sustained, dynamic growth throughout most of the period. Consequently, during the early twentieth century it had a highly distinctive demographic profile.[1] Much of the historical literature on western Canada suggests at least an implicit recognition of the region's distinctive demography. Unfortunately, however, the nature of its population structures has never been examined, nor has their general significance ever been explored. In hopes of introducing these considerations to the study of western Canadian history, this essay describes some of the most basic characteristics of the West's modern population and then discusses some of their broader consequences.

The character of population growth in any society is central to its history. The social significance of the two sources of population increase—natural increase and migration—can vary markedly. Populations that grow essentially by reproduction usually display substantially different demographic characteristics than do those in which migration is a major stimulus to growth. The migrant component of any community often possesses demographic features that distinguish it from the host society, and these characteristics, in turn, have wide-ranging social and economic implications for the community at large. Consequently, the modern history of population growth in North America, which has benefitted from prolonged immigration, has differed somewhat from that of much of western Europe, where immigration has been slight and where emigration has subtracted considerably from some national populations. Even within North America, wide regional variation in the character of population growth has occurred over time. For example, the extraordinarily high rate of increase in French Canada before the twentieth century was sustained entirely by reproduction,[2] while successive settlement frontiers have been dominated by migrant populations. The demographic—and hence social and economic—consequences of population growth have differed accordingly.

During the past two hundred years, Canada has had one of the highest rates of population growth among western nations. Since the turn of the nineteenth century, its population has increased fifty-fold. From 1850 onward, natural increase has accounted for about 85 percent of this growth, net migration the balance. Growth rates, however, have not been steady, and the relative contributions of both processes to population increase have varied considerably over time. Births have always exceeded deaths by a wide margin, but immigration has not invariably exceeded emigration. In fact, Canada had a substantial net outflow of population during the last forty years of the nineteenth century, estimated as high as two-thirds of a million.[3] Since then, however, the nation has had a favorable migration balance in every census decade but that of the depression, although its size has fluctuated from one decade to the next.

The most striking aspect of western Canada's population history has been its high growth rate, one which has far exceeded the national average. As Table I reveals, during the first two decades of the twentieth century, the prairies were more expansionist, but after 1921 this position was occupied by British Columbia, which thereafter led Canadian regional population growth. Rates of increase fell sharply on the prairies after 1931, and over the next forty years they lagged significantly behind the national average.

At the same time, the growth profiles of the prairie provinces differed significantly from one another, as indicated by Table II. Having started from a larger population base at the beginning of the century, Manitoba generally experienced much less dramatic rates of increase than her two prairie sisters. Those of Saskatchewan were much more volatile. After extremely rapid expansion in the pre-depression years, it lost almost 10 percent of its population during the 1930s and 1940s, the only western Canadian province ever to experience a decline. Alberta's population history resembles that of British

Table I

Population Growth Rates: Canada, the Prairies, and British
Columbia, 1901–71

		Percent Increase in Population	
Decade	Canada	Prairies	British Columbia
1961–71	18.3	11.4	34.1
1951–61	30.2	24.8	39.8
1941–51	21.8	5.2	42.5
1931–41	10.9	2.9	17.8
1921–31	18.1	20.3	32.3
1911–21	21.9	47.3	33.7
1901–11	34.2	220.7	119.7
1901–71	301.5	755.3	1,122.8
Annual Growth Rate 1901–71	1.6%	2.9%	3.5%

Source: calculated from Canada, *Census of Canada,* 1901–71.

Table II

Population Growth Rates: Manitoba, Saskatchewan, and
Alberta, 1901–71

		Percent Increase in Population	
Decade	Manitoba	Saskatchewan	Alberta
1961–71	7.2	.1	22.2
1951–61	18.7	11.2	41.8
1941–51	6.4	−7.2	18.0
1931–41	4.2	−2.8	8.8
1921–31	14.8	21.7	24.3
1911–21	32.2	53.8	57.2
1901–11	80.8	439.5	412.6
1901–71	287.2	914.7	2,129.3

Source: calculated from Canada, *Census of Canada,* 1901–71.

Columbia in some respects, with growth rates that have always approached national norms closely when they did not exceed them significantly. In recent years similarities between the two provinces have been particularly striking.[4] Nevertheless, the prairies have also shared population characteristics that clearly distinguish the region from the Pacific province and thus they are considered a single entity here.

Over time, natural increase and net migration have made variable contributions to the expansion of the western Canadian population. The extremely high initial rates of growth characteristic of the early twentieth century were largely the result of high population inflows from outside the region, and in later years the net migration balance continued to favor these regions. Nevertheless, a marked contrast distinguishes the history of prairie migration from that of the westernmost province. As Graphs I and II indicate, having passed through the early settlement period, with its characteristic high level of immigration, the prairies came to be peopled by those native to the region. By 1931, just over half of all prairie dwellers had been born on the plains and by 1971 this number increased to more than three in four. Among the incoming population, migrants from outside the country have always predominated. Historically, the foreign-born on the prairies have outnumbered Canadian migrants to the region by two or three to one.

In contrast, British Columbia's population growth has always been sustained primarily through migration. At no time before 1971 was the majority of the provincial population born in the region although, by this time, the numbers of the native-born were fast approaching those of the migrants. As was true on the prairies, during the first forty years of the century, the greater number of these immigrants came to the province from outside the country. But since then the proportion of the foreign-born has dropped substantially while that of migrants from within the country has increased somewhat. In recent years, internal migration has been a more important source of growth than international migration. Overall, immigrants have bulked much larger in the demographic history of British Columbia than they have in that of the prairie provinces, and Canadians from other regions have been a more significant component of the mountain province's population than they have been on the prairies.

The contributions of natural increase to population growth in each region have also differed significantly. As Table III indicates, until

Graph I
Population by Birthplace for Prairies

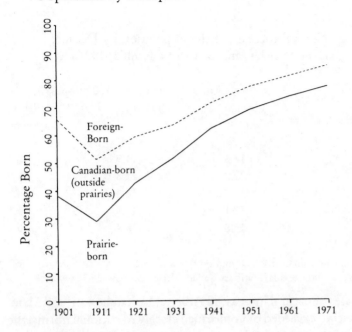

Graph II
Population by Birthplace for B.C.

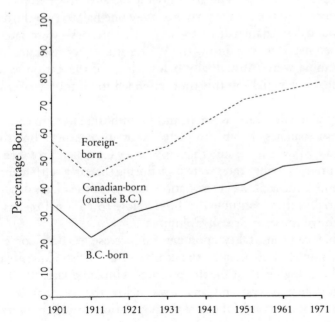

Table III

Average Natural Increase of the Population by Decade:
Canada, the Prairies, and British Columbia, 1921–70

| | Annual Increase per 1000 Population | | |
Decade	Canada	Prairies	British Columbia
1961–70	14.6	11.9	12.0
1951–60	22.2	22.8	18.9
1941–50	17.7	16.4	14.2
1931–40	12.1	13.5	5.8
1921–30	15.9	18.4	9.4

Sources: compiled from Canada, Dominion Bureau of Statistics, *Vital Statistics, 1960,* table 5, and Canada, Statistics Canada, *Vital Statistics, 1970,* table S4.

recently, rates of natural increase in Alberta, Saskatchewan, and Manitoba have either exceeded or conformed closely to national norms, the greatest excess occurring during the 1920s. In British Columbia, however, they have consistently fallen below national means and those of the prairies as well. The great discrepancies of the 1920s and 1930s – when rates in the Pacific province were one-half to two-thirds of Canada's and less than half of those on the prairies – were later reduced somewhat. But even during the 1960s natural increase rates in British Columbia were substantially below those of the nation as a whole, a difference which by this time extended to all four western provinces.

Differential fertility rates were the most significant factor in creating these discrepancies. From the early twentieth century, British Columbia had a lower birth rate than any other Canadian province. In contrast, prairie fertility rates were high during the early settlement years, well above those of the entire nation, and while they later dropped substantially, they continued to hover close to national means, somewhat above those of British Columbia.[5]

The influence of mortality upon natural increase has been somewhat more complex. Historically, the death rate in British Columbia has always been higher than on the prairies.[6] Until the later 1930s, however, mortality in western Canada was below the national average, a reflection of the youthfulness of the population during the early years of the century. Thereafter, the two wests diverged. British Columbia's mortality rate remained high, always surpassing the national mean. On the other hand, those of Manitoba and Saskatchewan fluctuated about the Canadian average while Alberta rates fell sharply below it. The combined influences of fertility and mortality have had rather different effects upon rates of natural increase in the two western regions. On the prairies, relatively high fertility has combined with low mortality to sustain rates of natural increase that historically have either exceeded or closely resembled national norms. British Columbia, however, has had a long history of low fertility and above average mortality, which together yielded the lowest rates of natural increase in Canada during the first seven decades of the twentieth century.

The character of population growth exercises a central influence upon the population structure of any community. In particular, the origins of population increase affect its most fundamental elements: age and sex composition. According to Kalbach and McVey, the age-sex structure of a community is its basic demographic fact:

This is partly true because, at any time, its age-sex structure is the consequence of earlier fertility, migration, and mortality experience, and partly because its structure is simultaneously a determinant of future trends in fertility, mortality, and migration. ... Thus age-sex composition is both a consequence of and a determinant of demographic processes.[7]

Seen in this light, the growth patterns of the settlement years in the West are far more significant than has generally been recognized because they created highly distinctive age and sex regimes with widespread consequences for western Canadian society.

Graphs III to X display the changing age-sex structure of Canada and its two western regions in each decennial census year from 1901 to 1971. Viewed together they reveal three shared general trends in the population history of the western provinces and at least as many contrasts. Perhaps the most obvious of these shared characteristics is the pronounced excess of males over females in the pre-depression West. On the prairies, men aged 20 to 64 outnumbered women of the same age by between 1.3 and 1.7 to one during the first three decades of the century. In comparison, the British Columbia discrepancy was even

Age-Sex Distribution in
Canada and Western Canada 1901–1971

Graph III   1901

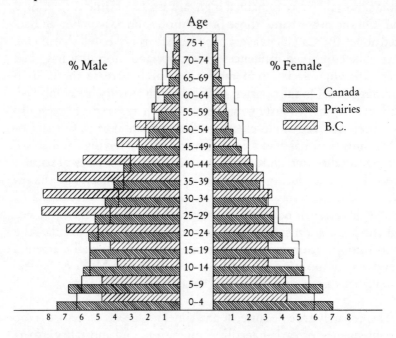

Graph IV   1911

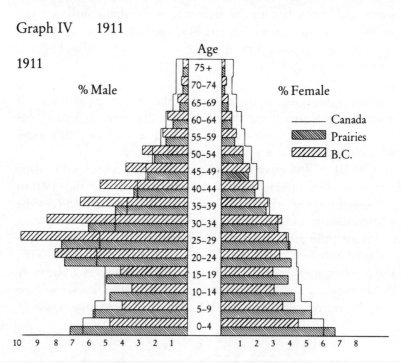

Graph V   1921

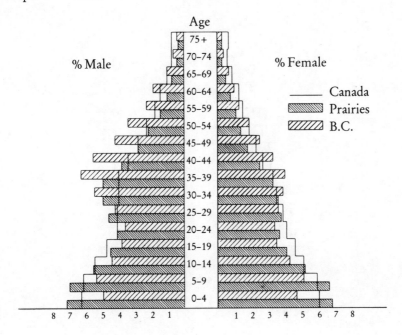

Graph VI   1931

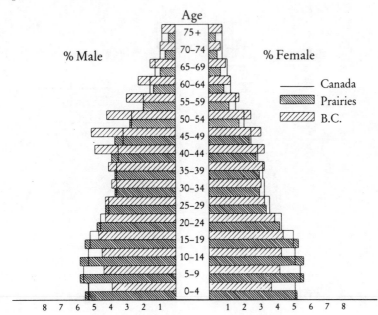

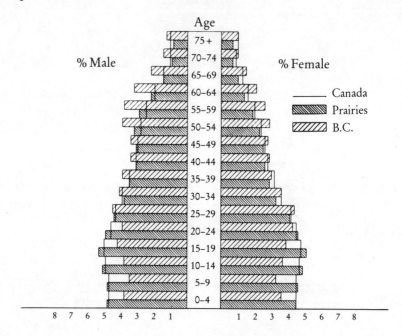

Graph VII   1941

Age

% Male

% Female

——— Canada
Prairies
B.C.

75+
70–74
65–69
60–64
55–59
50–54
45–49
40–44
35–39
30–34
25–29
20–24
15–19
10–14
5–9
0–4

8 7 6 5 4 3 2 1   1 2 3 4 5 6 7 8

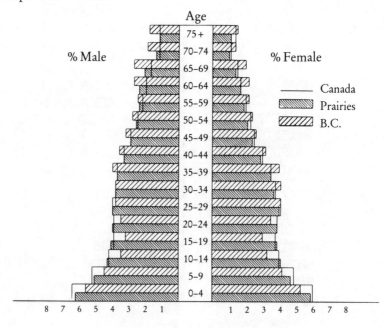

Graph VIII   1951

Age

% Male

% Female

——— Canada
Prairies
B.C.

75+
70–74
65–69
60–64
55–59
50–54
45–49
40–44
35–39
30–34
25–29
20–24
15–19
10–14
5–9
0–4

8 7 6 5 4 3 2 1   1 2 3 4 5 6 7 8

Graph IX   1961

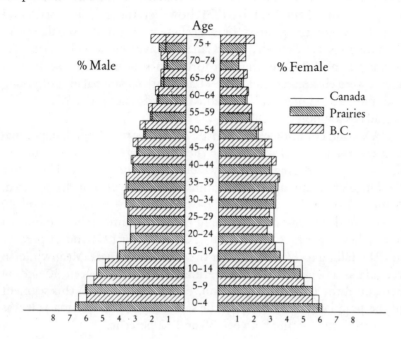

Graph X   1971

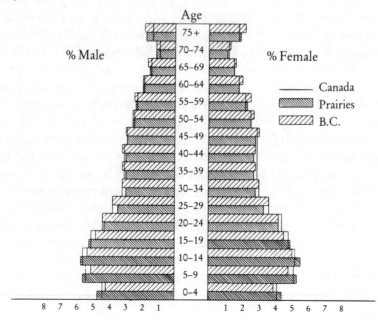

greater; the census records 2.3 times as many men as women in this age group in 1901 and 1911. By 1931, however, the ratio dropped to 1.4 as it also had on the prairies. During these years the sex imbalances in both regions far exceeded the Canadian average, which varied between 1.1 and 1.2. Over the next forty years, however, these discrepancies were eliminated and by 1971 an approximate balance of young and middle-aged men and women could be found in the West and in Canada as a whole.

A second common characteristic of the western Canadian population was the large bulge of men in their prime working years found in the two regions during the first two decades of the century. Thereafter the bulge gradually aged and diminished in size until it disappeared. Before 1941, males aged 15 to 64 constituted between 34 and 40 percent of the prairie population. In British Columbia they amounted to a rather larger part of the total—50 percent in 1901 and 51 percent in 1911, falling to 37 percent over the next thirty years. Meanwhile, in Canada as a whole, working-age men made up between 30 and 34 percent of the national population. From 1951 onward, this segment of the population was roughly the same in western Canada as it was nationally, fluctuating between 30 and 32 percent.

The gradual ageing of both regional and national populations is the third trend indicated by the age-sex pyramids. Table IV, which records the median age of residents in the two western regions and in Canada from 1901 to 1971, amplifies and qualifies the information contained in the graphs. In the earlier decades of the century, the median age of prairie dwellers was somewhat below that of all Canadians. Thereafter the age gap narrowed until it disappeared in 1951 and 1961, only to reappear in the last decade of this survey. The median age of British Columbians, on the other hand, has always been substantially higher than that prevailing elsewhere. Before World War II, on average it exceeded that of the prairies by more than 6.5 years and that of the nation by more than 5 years. Since the war, however, the age gap between British Columbia and the rest of Canada has narrowed considerably. By 1971 the median age for the westernmost province had fallen a full four years from its peak in 1951 (when those in all of Canada were also at their highest); indeed, its population was no older that it had been in 1901. The prairies and central and eastern Canada, meanwhile, had experienced significant ageing since the dawn of the century, though they, too, had grown somewhat younger after 1951.

Table IV
Median Age of the Population by Decade: Canada, the
Prairies, and British Columbia, 1901–71

	Canada	Median Age Prairies	British Columbia
1971	26.3	25.8	28.0
1961	26.3	26.4	29.8
1951	27.7	27.8	32.0
1941	27.1	26.2	32.1
1931	24.8	23.3	30.6
1921	24.0	22.4	29.8
1911	23.8	23.3	28.0
1901	22.7	20.7	28.1

Source: Canada, Statistics Canada, *Census of Canada, 1971, Profile Studies: The Age-Sex Structure of Canada's Population*, 5:1–3, p. 39.

In sum, the primary characteristics of the western Canadian population have closely resembled those of the nation since 1941. But during the earlier years of the century, the populations of the four western provinces had fundamental elements in common that set them apart from the national demographic experience. In particular they shared a pronounced inequality between the numbers of men and women, a disproportionately large number of working-age males, and age structures that departed markedly from national norms. At the same time, however, differences between the populations of the two western regions have been at least as pronounced as those distinguishing the West from the rest of the nation. In any decade before the Second World War, the sex imbalance on the prairies was never as exaggerated as it was in British Columbia, nor was the male working-age segment proportionately as large. Also, the prairies have always had a much younger population than the mountain province.

These differences were due largely to the nature of population growth in the two western regions. Because of British Columbia's greater reliance upon migration as the primary stimulus to growth, its population structure has been influenced more continuously by the character of the incoming population than has that of the prairies, whose growth since 1921 has been sustained primarily through natural increase. The influence of these two different processes upon sex ratios should be readily apparent. Normally, the numbers of male and female children born are roughly equal and for this reason the prairies have had less imbalanced sex ratios than the Pacific province. The substantial sex imbalance of the early twentieth century, a product of extremely high immigration, was sharply reduced by 1941, owing to the region's relatively high birth rate, the onward movement of transient males, and the gradual ageing and death of the remaining surplus male population. Migration patterns, too, may have played an important role in limiting this imbalance. The labor requirements of prairie pioneer agriculture made the employment of family members on the farm highly desirable, if not necessary, and this must have offered significant inducements to family migration and settlement.[8]

In British Columbia, however, where growth has always come primarily from migration, the ratio of men to women was far more out of balance than it was on the prairies before 1921, although from that time onward it generally resembled that of the prairies. Here economic factors had a strikingly different impact upon provincial sex ratios, particularly before the depression. Because the regional economy was based heavily upon frontier resource extraction and construction of a massive physical infrastructure (notably in transportation), the main labor requirements of the province could not be met by women and children. Consequently, the family work unit had a limited role to play in British Columbia. Labor demand selected a migrant population sufficiently strong, vigorous, and mobile—primarily young, single men—to perform arduous tasks in isolated and often impermanent settings. On the prairies, the labor requirements of pioneer agriculture and, perhaps more important, the elaborate mythology of rural family life drew more families than unattached men to the homestead. Since the 1940s, however, migration has increasingly become a family matter in both the prairie and mountain provinces. A much smaller proportion of the transient population has been made up of single migrants. Therefore, even though migration has remained an important source of population expansion it has ceased to promote the growth of imbalanced sex ratios as it once did.

The age composition of the two western regions has likewise been affected by their differing patterns of growth. The prairies, with birth rates significantly above the Canadian average during most of this period, have historically had a relatively young population, particularly before mid-century. And, as Table V reveals, the proportion of the population aged 15 to 64 – the most productive years of life – has seldom strayed far from national norms. Among the elderly, the discrepancies between the prairies and Canada during the early twentieth century were essentially eliminated after World War II. Because of its lower birth and high migration rates, British Columbia, in contrast, has always had an older population. Until the 1930s, however, this was not due to an abnormally high concentration of elderly residents. In fact, it was attributable to the small proportion of the provincial population consisting of children and the large proportion composed of young and middle-aged adults. Only since 1941 has the higher median age of the population owed rather more to the growing numbers of the aged residing in the province.

Table V

Population by Age Groups: Canada, The Prairies, and British Columbia, 1901–71

| | Percent of the Population in Age Group | | | | | | | | |
| | 0–14 | | | 15–64 | | | 65+ | | |
	Can.	Pr.	B.C.	Can.	Pr.	B.C.	Can.	Pr.	B.C.
1971	29.6	30.5	27.9	62.3	60.7	62.7	8.1	8.7	9.4
1961	33.9	34.1	31.3	58.4	57.7	58.6	7.6	8.2	10.2
1951	30.3	30.0	26.1	61.9	62.1	63.1	7.8	7.8	10.8
1941	27.8	28.4	21.4	65.5	66.1	70.3	6.7	5.5	8.3
1931	31.6	33.3	24.7	62.8	62.9	69.9	5.6	3.8	5.5
1921	34.4	37.8	28.5	60.8	59.7	68.0	4.8	2.6	3.5
1911	33.0	33.7	23.3	62.4	64.4	74.5	4.7	1.9	2.2
1901	34.4	38.6	24.9	60.6	59.1	72.6	5.0	2.3	2.5

Source: Canada, Statistics Canada, *Census of Canada, 1971, Profile Studies: The Age-Sex Structure of Canada's Population,* 5:1–3, p. 39.

Occasional references to mine towns and railway construction camps notwithstanding,[9] students of western Canadian history have over-looked the demographic structure of the plains and mountain regions. This can scarcely be set to rights here, for a full account of the West's distinctive population history is far beyond the compass of a single short essay. But a few examples should serve to illustrate something of the range of matters linked to population structure. Consider first the economic significance of the western population profile. The unique age and sex distribution of the early twentieth-century West was at once a consequence of the special labor needs of a rapidly growing frontier economy and a source of manpower especially well-suited to its requirements. The primary task in the West at that time was rapid economic development. Growth was led by vigorous expansion of the agricultural, resource extractive, construction, and transportation sectors. Regional labor needs called for a large pool of unskilled and semi-skilled workers, many of them highly mobile owing to the temporary, cyclical, and speculative character of much frontier enterprise. Young and middle-aged men with no immediate domestic ties were best suited to these tasks, and the West attracted them in large numbers before 1931. In consequence, the presence of a youthful, energetic population presumably enhanced productivity in the western Canadian economy during these years. The resource extractive economy in British Columbia required male labor almost exclusively; correspondingly provincial sex ratios greatly favored men over women, female labor force participation was well below the national average, and birth rates were markedly lower than elsewhere in the country. On the prairies, women and children played a more important economic role in the dominant agricultural sector, though they, too, seldom entered the wage labor market. There the sex imbalance was less pronounced and birth rates stood well above the national average.[10] After the depression, as the two regional economies gradually reduced their earlier specialized labor demands, the western Canadian population structure lost its distinctiveness and the West came to share the same demographic characteristics and trends as the nation. Its population's unique contributions to productivity no doubt diminished accordingly.

The probable influence of demographic patterns upon regional standards of living seems somewhat more complex and ambiguous. In the West, the degree to which the economically productive have been called upon to support the non-productive (i.e. the ratio between those of non-working age and working age) has varied considerably (*see* Table V). Until 1941 British Columbia had a significantly larger population cohort at working age than did the prairies or the rest of the nation. And as has already been suggested, the productivity of this population was enhanced by its youthfulness and its great preponderance of males. At the same time, however, a higher than average proportion of females in the province did not engage in wage labor, thus diminishing somewhat the productive potential of the community. On the prairies, at the same time, the much larger segment of children increased the numbers of the dependent. But this factor was offset to a significant though unknown extent by the lesser disproportion between males and females and the widespread employment of women and children in productive non-wage labor. Comparing the two western regions at this point, it would seem impossible to draw even tentative conclusions about the impact of demographic structure upon the relationship between the productive and non-productive sectors of their respective populations.

These population patterns must also have had marked effects upon the nature of consumption in the West, although to this date the question has been utterly ignored. The case of housing provides a suitable example. Obviously, the housing requirements of married adults with children differ from those without, and the requirements of both differ from those of the unmarried, particularly transient men. Although western Canada experienced several short building booms, and more generally a massive construction program between 1901 and 1930, the housing needs of a large proportion of the burgeoning western population could be met relatively simply. However deficient these dwellings were by contemporary standards—sod huts, bunk houses, and tent cities in frontier areas, and cheap hotels and boarding houses in urban communities—all provided accommodation for a large segment of the adult population. Because construction of these facilities did not require the larger amounts of labor and capital needed to build family housing, productive resources were thus freed for other forms of investment. In this instance the demographic structure of each region must have had a direct effect upon the nature of the demand for housing, one with indirect consequences for general economic development. Later, as the western regions lost their distinctive demographic character and the large surplus of unattached males gradually disappeared, the demand for more substantial, permanent housing presumably increased accordingly, particularly in British Columbia where the sex imbalance formerly had been greatest.

The consumption of social services offers yet another example of the neglected implications of demographic factors. Until at least the 1940s, British Columbia had a significantly lower, and the prairies a somewhat larger, proportion of children than did Canada on average. Consequently, the former needed to allocate a smaller proportion of its financial resources to public schooling than did the latter. With regard to the aged the converse was true, especially from the 1920s onward. The greater proportion of elderly in British Columbia than on the prairies or across Canada established an abnormally high demand for medical and other services required by older people.

Finally, the demographic profiles of the two wests may well have influenced strongly the sense of self-awareness that developed in each region. During the twentieth century the two communities have each developed distinctive identities. There have been two wests of the mind as well as geography. Generally, western Canadians have seen the special character of their respective regions as rooted in an amalgam of unique geographic circumstances, a distinctive ethnic composition, and an ongoing conflict between local aspirations and powerful central Canadian influences. Most often these identities have found their fullest expression in social, political, and economic protest movements. Their demographic basis has long been neglected, however, even though it may well account in large part for pronounced differences between the character of regional awareness in the mountain and prairie provinces.

Populations born outside the region—indeed outside the country—dominated the early West. The proportions of native-born, Canadian-born, and foreign-born were not too dissimilar in the two regions before 1921. From then on, however, growth patterns on either side of the Rockies progressively diverged. Unlike the prairies, the Pacific province remained predominantly a community of migrants. Among the incoming populations, the foreign-born assumed a proportionately larger significance on the prairies than they did further west. In other words, the prairies increasingly came to be peopled by those with no ties to other parts of Canada and with deepening regional roots. By 1941, over 90 percent of prairie dwellers were either native to the region or were foreign immigrants. British

Columbia, on the other hand, has always been rather more cosmopolitan. Far more than the prairies, it has continually been influenced by immigration, particularly by internal migration.

The implications of these demographic patterns for a developing sense of community should be obvious. The prairies have long had a population base in which a strong sense of regional identity could be anchored,[11] if only because they have come to be filled by those with no ties with other parts of Canada (or, increasingly, other parts of the world). British Columbia has not shared this experience. Perpetual renewal primarily through migration has continually hindered the development of a strong regional consciousness with which most residents can identify.[12] The larger numbers of migrants from other parts of Canada have also dampened the strong inter-regional tensions periodically evident on the prairies. British Columbians have never agreed upon as sharply defined a sense of themselves as have prairie dwellers, nor have their intermittent fits of regional grievance against the centre ever been as vociferous, prolonged, or intense. Explanations for these differences are no doubt complex, but arguably they should begin with an account of the demographic histories of the two wests.

This brief overview alone should offer sufficient evidence of western Canada's distinctive population history. British Columbia and the prairies have shared some very important demographic experiences while other characteristics have set them apart from one another. To this point the significance of population structure has been almost entirely ignored by those who have examined western history, despite its obvious influence upon much that has been central to the regional experience. It is to be hoped that, in future, the demographic factor in the history of the West will be paid the regard that most certainly is its due.

Notes

1. Although the first generation of settlers began to build a new society in the West during the last third of the nineteenth century, the amount of reliable demographic information available for the period before 1901 is insufficient to support systematic analysis.

2. J. Henripin and Y. Peron, "The Demographic Transition of the Province of Quebec," In D.V. Glass and R. Revelle, eds., *Population and Social Change* (London: Edward Arnold, 1972), pp. 213–31.

3. The highest estimate is that of Keyfitz, reported in M.C. Urquhart and K.A.H. Buckley, eds., *Historical Statistics of Canada* (Toronto: Macmillan, 1965), p. 22, column 245.

4. At this writing only the preliminary returns of the 1981 census are available. Thus no detailed description of western Canada's recent acceleration in population increase is possible. The 1976 census reflected the continuation of trends existing in the 1960s. The prairie population increased by 6.7 percent between 1971 and 1976, half the rate of growth that occurred in British Columbia (12.9 percent). Prairie growth was concentrated primarily in Alberta, whose rate of increase was identical to that of the west coast province. Saskatchewan experienced a slight decline (−.5 percent) while Manitoba grew slowly (3.4 percent). From 1976 to 1981, however, the prairie growth rate slightly exceeded that of the pacific province (11.9 percent as opposed to 11.3 percent). The most dramatic increase by far occurred in Alberta, whose population grew by 21.8 percent during these years, again reinforcing the impression that the recent population history of Alberta has resembled that of British Columbia more than it has the two remaining prairie provinces.

5. J. Henripin, *Trends and Factors of Fertility in Canada* (Ottawa: Queen's Printer, 1972), chapters II and III.

6. Canada, Statistics Canada, *Vital Statistics, Volume III, Deaths, 1971* (Ottawa: Queen's Printer, 1974), p. 72.

7. W.E. Kalbach and W.W. McVey, *The Demographic Bases of Canadian Society*, 2d ed. (Toronto: McGraw-Hill Ryerson, 1979), p. 158.

8. It is virtually impossible to judge the extent of family migration to the settling West. But little in the memoir literature suggests that men and women often braved the hardships of pioneer life alone.

9. D.J. Bercuson, "Labour Radicalism and the Western Industrial Frontier, 1897–1919," *Canadian Historical Review* LVIII, 2 (June 1977): 154–75; A.R. McCormack, "The Industrial Workers of the World in Western Canada: 1905–1914," Canadian Historical Association, *Historical Papers, 1975*, pp. 167–90. An exception to this comment dealing with the earliest years of the settlement frontier is Frits Pannekoek's "A Probe into the Demographic Structure of Nineteenth Century Red River," in Lewis H. Thomas, ed., *Essays on Western History* (Edmonton: University of Alberta Press, 1976), pp. 83–95.

10. Superficially, it might seem that the striking variation in fertility patterns in British Columbia and on the prairies was the consequence of differing fertility strategies pursued by families in the two regions responding to differing economic circumstances. It is doubtful, however, that this factor alone accounted for the differences experienced. The greater traditionalism of rural dwellers and the marked contrasts in ethnic composition of the two regions no doubt influenced fertility behavior as well.

11. On the prairie identity, *see* H. Kreisel, "The Prairie: A State of Mind," in Eli Mandel, ed., *Contexts of Canadian Criticism* (Chicago: University of Chicago Press, 1971), pp. 254–66; L. Ricou, *Vertical Man, Horizontal World* (Vancouver: University of British Columbia Press, 1973).

12. E.R. Black has emphasized the strong influence of materialism—the lowest common denominator of a sense of community—as a primary influence upon the political culture of British Columbia. "British Columbia: The Politics of Exploitation," in Ronald Shearer, ed., *Exploiting our Economic Potential: Public Policy and the British Columbia Economy* (Toronto: Holt Rinehart and Winston, 1968), pp. 23–41.

Urban Land Speculation in the Development of Strathcona (South Edmonton), 1891–1912

————————————————— John F. Gilpin

The periodic booms in urban real estate between 1891 and 1912 indicate that the creation, promotion, and sale of land was a focal aspect of the early history of the urban prairie West. Urban land promotion in Strathcona, from its creation in 1891 to its amalgamation with Edmonton in 1912, emphasizes a pattern of investment in land development. The subdivision process and initial sale of property, as well as the extent of built-up area in relation to the amount of land created for the purpose of urban development, are major factors in this discussion.

The City of Strathcona was originally established as the townsite of South Edmonton in 1891 by the Calgary and Edmonton Railway Company. The Calgary and Edmonton Railway Company had been incorporated in 1890 for the purpose of constructing and operating a railway "from a point on the line of the Canadian Pacific Railway Company, within the town of Calgary, to a point at or near Edmonton with power to extend southerly to the International boundary . . . and northerly to the Peace River."[1] Immediately upon its completion, the railway was leased to the Canadian Pacific. The provisional directors of the company were not interested in creating a new railway system, but rather in developing a branch line that fed into the C.P.R. main line.[2] Since the Calgary and Edmonton Railway was one of the colonization railways, it was eligible for a statutory land grant.[3] The company received a total of 1,820,685 acres, which was to consist of unoccupied or unclaimed odd-numbered sections or alternative townships within 22 miles on either side of the railway line. Significant adjustments to the location of this grant, however, were made in order that the land the railway received was suitable for settlement. In addition to this property, the railway company also purchased land for townsite development including the site of its northern terminus, South Edmonton. The urban land holdings of the railway company were placed under the jurisdiction of the Calgary and Edmonton Railway Townsite Company, which was in turn to be administered by the firm of Osler, Hammond, and Nanton of Winnipeg, which had extensive links with other western Canadian land development and railway companies.

The negotiations for the acquisition of South Edmonton were conducted in the spring of 1891 before the location of the northern terminus had been officially announced. In the agreements, the original owners of the land were to provide the Calgary and Edmonton Railway with sufficient land to a maximum of thirteen and one-half acres for right-of-way and station grounds, plus a half-interest in the remaining portion of land, in return for the construction by the railway company of a station and engine shed at a specified distance from the various properties involved.[4] The agreements between the company and the various land owners further specified that the survey of the new townsite would be undertaken by the company with the cost being shared equally among the parties, and that following the survey, the land would be divided or jointly sold by an agent. In the case of Thomas Anderson, the railway company later purchased ownership of the entire portion of the two river lots he owned, thus consolidating their ownership of the most valuable property in the townsite since it was located adjacent to the tracks. In August 1891 the property at the railway townsite was divided between the various original owners and the townsite company.

The checkerboard pattern of land ownership that emerged from these agreements is indicated on Map I. The railway company had thus acquired its northern terminus at a very nominal cost. The original owners, no doubt, felt that the increased value of the land they retained would be adequate compensation for virtually donating their property to the railway company.

The survey of the townsite by the Calgary and Edmonton Railway Company was begun in July 1891, the same month that the track-laying crews reached the future community. The survey was registered as plan I at the North Alberta Land Titles Office in September, and conformed to the provisions of the Territories Real Property Act.[5] The provisions of this legislation concerning subdivisions were fairly simple. They required that the subdivision plan provided to the Land Registrar had to be certified by a licenced surveyor and drawn to a specified scale. The owner also had to sign the plan and declare its accuracy before the Registrar or a Justice of the Peace.[6] These simple regulations were to remain largely unaltered throughout the period under study.

Plan I (see Map I), which covered approximately 926 acres, provided for the subdivision of the townsite into 125 blocks of land arranged in a grid pattern. Fifty-five of these blocks were further subdivided into 50-foot lots. A total of 1,280 individual lots were created as

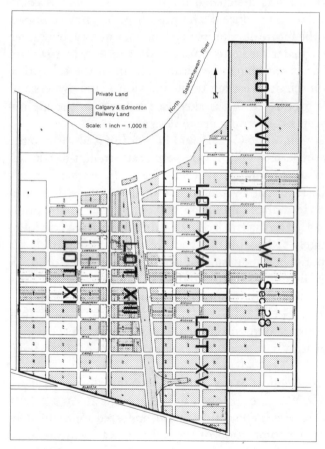

Map I. Plan I, Townsite of Strathcona, 1891, showing the checkerboard pattern of land owned by the Calgary and Edmonton Railway Company.

184 / John F. Gilpin

a result. The plan also provided for two main streets, which extended to the extreme boundaries of the townsite and crossed each other at right angles a short distance northwest of the railway station. The location of the main streets and the subdivision of the individual blocks strongly favored the real estate interests of the railway company, which owned most of the land along the main streets and all the parcels of land with one exception along the railway right-of-way. It was a very ambitious plan that anticipated a phenomenal rate of growth in the district.

No provision was made in the plan for parks or a central square, nor were any of the lots designated for specific uses such as court house, post office, or town office. Plan I was, therefore, not a comprehensive plan for the future development of the community, but rather a mechanism designed to facilitate the sale of the property by townsite company. The decisions about the ultimate form of the town that would emerge on the site were left to the individual land owners and thus would be a product of the marketplace rather than the application of any concepts concerning urban design.

The construction of the Calgary and Edmonton Railway and the location of its northern terminus were part of an attempt to take advantage of the existing commercial development of the area. The railway was to replace the Calgary and Edmonton Trail, while the northern terminus was to replace Edmonton as the emerging dominant urban centre in northern Alberta. By 1891, Edmonton was a community of approximately 650 people that had already established itself as a northern entrepot. The subdivision of land for the purpose of urban development on the north side of the river had been underway since 1881 when the Hudson's Bay Company subdivided the southern portion of its reserve. The Calgary and Edmonton Railway were thus anxious to appropriate Edmonton's economic function in the region rather than dramatically re-orient the existing patterns of commercial development.

The promotional effort of the company was initially aimed at potential investors in Winnipeg through an article in the 26 August 1891 *Manitoba Daily Free Press.* This article, which appeared approximately one month after the completion of the railway, was provided by a "prominent businessman of Winnipeg, who [had] just returned from a trip to Edmonton":

The new town of Edmonton has been established by the Calgary & Edmonton Railway Company at its terminus on the southside of the Saskatchewan just opposite the fort.... The banks of the Saskatchewan at that point are about two hundred and fifty feet high, and the river is about twice the width of the Red so that it has been found necessary to locate the new town permanently on the southside. The present location, however, gives the old settlement easy access to the terminus, and as soon as a traffic bridge, which is to be built, is ready the new place will, it is anticipated, make rapid progress and absorb the business of the district. Great confidence in the new city's future is felt at Edmonton and vicinity....

The local agent of the townsite company, Charles S. Lott, also ensured that encouraging reports appeared in the *Edmonton Bulletin*. Between 22 August and 11 September, the *Edmonton Bulletin* reported that a total of 72 parcels of land had been sold or at least spoken for and that 37 of these sales were made with building conditions as part of the agreement of sale. The majority of the people buying land were identified as being from Calgary, but Winnipeg, Regina, and other locations in western Canada were also represented.

As part of the promotional strategy, Osler, Hammond, and Nanton approached the Dominion Government with a request that certain government offices be located at the new townsite. They suggested that the immigration hall and other public buildings proposed for the Edmonton settlement should be constructed at the railway townsite:

From the rapid progress made at the Railway town and because of the advantages of the location and the great improbability of the line ever being carried across the River at what is known as the former Edmonton Settlement, it is altogether likely that the present terminal point will be the business centre of that district. Any Public Buildings to be conveniently situated, be located within convenient distances of the Railway Station and on the Southside of the River.[7]

This request met with some success: an immigration shed was constructed at the railway station in the spring of 1892. The initiative taken by the townsite administrators was followed by Thomas Anderson, Crown Timber and Land Agent, who suggested that it would be advisable to have the government offices adjoining the immigrant shed at the station.[8] Only a portion of the records were transferred because of strong protests from Edmonton. The location of the Dominion Government offices was resolved in July 1892 when the Dominion Government accepted an offer of land from the Hudson's Bay Company.[9]

The townsite company also began a limited program of public works, including the grading of various streets, the construction of a bridge across Mill Creek, and a road from Saskatchewan Drive near the rail head to the upper ferry crossing. These developments clearly gave the northwest quarter of the townsite, where the railway land was concentrated, distinct advantages in terms of future development.

The townsite company also offered incentives to local groups. The company constructed a hotel near the railway station and donated land for various institutional and industrial purposes.[10] In 1893 the company provided the Methodist Church and Anglican Church with land for construction purposes for the nominal fee of one dollar. On 9 November 1897 land valued at $900 was sold for one dollar to John A. Jackson and William Jackson, who operated an iron foundry and machine shop on the site.

The promotional efforts of the townsite company were complemented by the efforts of the local boosters. The most active of these in the 1890s was the *South Edmonton News,* which was established in 1894. The primary function of the newspaper as stated in the first edition was to promote the interests of the town:

> We are desirous of letting outside people know of our excellent farmlands, of what kind of grain, vegetables, etc., can be produced, and of the many advantages the farmers in this district have over those in other parts.... We are here in the interests of this town and the people of the district.... [11]

By the end of the first year of publication, the *South Edmonton News* was a staunch guardian of, and spokesman for, Strathcona's civic pride. Subscriptions were solicited from the citizens on the grounds that they would be contributing to the welfare and promotion of their town:

When we cast our lot with this town some thirteen months ago, a good deal of confidence in the place was required as here seemingly was no room for a newspaper. But as before stated in these columns a newspaper does a great deal to promote a town's interests. ... And by keeping your local newspaper up to the standard you create a feeling to the outside public that you are a progressive and busy people.[12]

Throughout its history, this newspaper consistently promoted the idea of Strathcona as a separate metropolitan community whose best interests would be served by remaining independent of Edmonton.

In the view of the *South Edmonton News,* the site represented an ideal combination of aesthetic as well as practical advantages that would ensure the creation of a great city. The aesthetic advantages included the heavily wooded slopes of the North Saskatchewan River valley, which presented a magnificent view for those citizens driving along Saskatchewan Avenue. The topography of this area, including many "plateaus... and miniature mountains... which are very picturesque and placid,"[13] provided additional opportunites for the development of "some fine drives... winding about in the shade of the forest which in some places is so dense as to create a feeling of gloom and a premonition as of the presence of wild beasts ready to spring... from the jungles around you."[14] The editor of the *South Edmonton News* also expressed the wish that this "wilderness" be preserved to serve as a contrast to the large-scale industrial development of the townsite proper:

Long may a true touch of nature exist so near our settlement so that even though the air should resound to the shrill call of many factory whistles and the busy hum of industry, we may yet find true solitude, which is so restful to overburdened human nature, within easy reach.[15]

The area that had escaped the subdivision process was the most interesting part of the townsite. The proximity of the townsite to this parkland area may explain the lack of concern for the formal incorporation of parks in the townsite plan until well after the turn of the century.

Another source of local boosterism was the real estate fraternity of Strathcona-South Edmonton. In September 1891, South Edmonton's

188 / John F. Gilpin

first resident real estate agent arrived in the person of William Wilkie.
In addition to his real estate business, he circulated a petition requesting the construction of a road from the rail head to the rural settlements east of the townsite. These types of improvements were critical to the townsite's future as an independent community, since they
would permit access to these areas without having to go through
Edmonton.

Efforts toward self-improvement taken by the community as a
whole included fund raising for road improvements and the creation
of a statute labor district in April 1896. The affairs of these districts
were in the charge of an overseer elected by the resident owners or
occupants of land, who was responsible for such matters as road improvements. Work on Whyte Avenue, for example, was undertaken
in this way in June 1898. These instruments of local control were,
however, inadequate to the development needs of the Strathcona
townsite. The townsite residents also tried to prod the townsite company into taking various initiatives on their behalf.

At one of the general meetings of the townspeople in March 1894,
a motion was passed requesting that Messrs. Osler, Hammond, and
Nanton meet with an Edmonton delegation in Ottawa in order to
obtain a traffic bridge.[16] The construction of this bridge had originally
been suggested by the townsite company as a means of consolidating
the influence of the new townsite in the Edmonton Settlement. The
townsite company, however, was not very responsive to these requests; it felt that the other land owners should also assume some responsibility toward site improvements.[17]

The promotional activities of the townsite company as well as its
local boosters were concerned primarily with encouraging land sales.
Despite the encouraging reports in the *Edmonton Bulletin*, an examination of land title records for the period up to 1899 indicates that
railway land was being disposed at a more modest pace than newspaper reports would indicate.[18] These documents fail to confirm a
number of land sales noted in the *Edmonton Bulletin* articles as well as
the requirement that buildings be erected on the property. A number
of non-residents may have simply taken options on land pending resolution of the townsites future before actually completing the purchase
of property. No building conditions were indicated in the land sales
agreements. The purchases included non-residents from England,
India, and Ireland, and the majority of those who purchased land for
speculative purposes retained ownership until the turn of the century.

The rapid turnover of property did not begin until after 1900. The net result of the townsite company's efforts was that by 1899, less than half of its land was sold.

Land owners who made a concerted effort to compete with the townsite company during the 1890s included Joseph McDonald and F.H. Sache. Of the original owners, Joseph McDonald was in the best position to compete because his land was close to the main streets of the townsite. This competition was noted by the *Edmonton Bulletin*:

> There has been a side boom in South Side Town property this week.... The Company's price was $100.00 a lot and upward. Joseph McDonald, the owner of Lot 11, came to the conclusion that the alternative blocks in his 200 acre claim would pay him very well at $50.00 a lot and proceeded to offer them for sale at the figure, with excellent financial results to himself, but somewhat disheartening to the Company.[19]

Other land owners also suffered from the same economic decline, identified as a North American-wide depression, as well as from special problems derived from the location of their land in the townsite plan.

Frederick Sache, also active in the disposition of his real estate holdings, operated at a disadvantage, however, because only a portion of his land had been fully subdivided into lots, and the majority of it was located some distance from the principal roadways of the townsite. Of his 160 lots, only 25 were sold between 1891 and 1899.[20] Sache, like many other land owners, had tried to remedy his situation by subdividing his land. The intense competition and the total lack of any restrictions extended the subdivision process at an accelerating rate and contributed further to the creation of South Edmonton's urban land glut. By 1899, a cumulative total of 1,837 lots had been created. Of this total, only 10 percent were actually developed.

The problems encountered by the various townsite owners in disposing of their property were further complicated by the fact that Edmonton had not withered away as predicted. Land in the various Edmonton subdivisions continued to be sold at comparable prices regardless of proximity to the railway.[21]

The development of the townsite of Strathcona in the 1890s had taken place without the influence of a municipal government. This situation had been deliberately allowed by the local citizens, who viewed the townsite as not yet ready to support such an institution. This point of view was strongly supported by the large land owners, who would have provided the major portion of the taxes. Of particular significance was the position of the townsite company, which had not anticipated or encouraged a long-term commitment to the development of the community. In August 1895 the company explained in a letter to F. Sache:

> While we do not wish in any way to hinder the advancement of the Town and in fact would do anything in our power to assist them, we do not consider that the place is yet large enough to make Incorporation advisable and it certainly would not be in the interests of the large land owners. The taxes would certainly increase tremendously and there would be very little gained by the increase. We fancy that this cry of Incorporation is worked up by two or three very small property holders and that it would be advisable for you to consult with the other Townsite owners and do what you can in a quiet way to prevent anything being done towards Incorporation.[22]

The large land owners attempted to prevent the establishment of the type of political institutions required to deal with the development issues presented by the townsite.

The incorporation debate was finally resolved in 1898 when the Territorial Government intervened under section three of the North-West Territories Village Ordinaire, which allowed it to establish a village with an elected overseer who would collect taxes and deal with such issues as public health and road improvements. The citizens responded with a petition for the incorporation of the townsite into the Town of Strathcona.

The economic decline of the 1890s after the early real estate boom of the 1880s perpetuated a very cautious approach to civic affairs. Strathcona's first mayor, Thomas Bennett, specifically stated that his policy was to prevent sudden town debt due to "mushroom growth."[23] Bennett's slow-growth philosophy, however, did not survive the spirit of optimism that pervaded the West after the turn of the century. This optimism was a result of the construction activities both real and anticipated of the Canadian Northern and the Grand Trunk Pacific Railways and a new wave of investment in urban land. This change in municipal policy in terms of land development is evident in the extension of Strathcona's incorporated boundaries, the increased pace of the land subdivision process, and its ambitious program of public works.

Strathcona's municipal boundaries were first extended in 1903 and thus marked the first step toward the mushroom growth that Bennett had specifically pledged to avoid in 1899. It was initiated by the Strathcona Board of Trade, which had been established in May 1901. The land annexed was not developed with the exception of a creamery, soap factory, steam laundry, packing house, and brickyard located on the river flat, which had been established by Edmonton businessmen following the completion of the Edmonton, Yukon and Pacific Railway. The extensions were, therefore, not undertaken to accommodate growth within the existing townsite.

The second extension of Strathcona's municipal boundaries took place in 1907 when Strathcona acquired a city charter. The campaign for a city charter began in September 1906 when the *Strathcona Plaindealer* pointed out that Strathcona's destiny as a metropolis required this new status:

> While these special powers might prove injurious to a town that has nothing but ambition to back it up in the race for big population still they are necessary to the town holding a favored position on the map in working its destiny of future greatness.[24]

On 10 October 1906 a delegation from the Board of Trade brought the matter of a city charter to the attention of the town council. Council took action on the proposal on 18 November when a committee on the city charter question was established. The report of the committee presented on 28 December 1906 included a number of recommendations concerning the future operation of the city. With regard to boundaries, it recommended, "Present boundaries be retained: adjoining territory to be added by Lieut.-Governor by order in council upon petition of certain proportion of property owners and city council."[25] This report served as the basis for action on the question of a city charter by the new council, which took office in January 1907. The new council, however, did not endorse the recommendation concerning city boundaries. At the 17 January 1907 meeting of council, the mayor and councilmen MacKenzie and Hulbert were appointed to a committee concerning the boundaries of the proposed city of Strathcona with power to act. Their boundary recommendations appear to have been accepted with little discussion. Other issues, such as the possible use of the single tax and the introduction of the ward and commission systems of municipal government, were the major concerns during the charter debate.

Commensurate with the rapid extension of Strathcona's municipal boundaries was the almost total subdivision by 1912 of all the land that had been annexed. This process was facilitated by the co-operation of the town/city council, which passed all applications for subdivision approval without delay. This co-operation was no doubt a product of the fact that a number of land developers and real estate agents were also on council.[26]

Between 23 July 1907 and 3 January 1912, the city council approved twenty subdivisions, which created in excess of 5,000 addi-

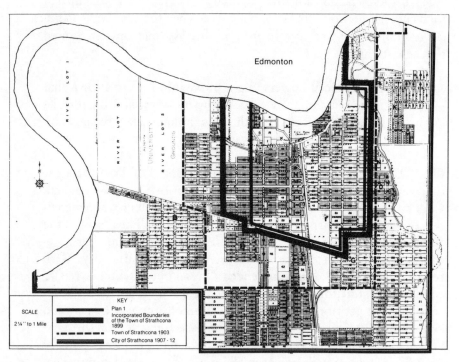

Map II. Strathcona from 1891 to 1912, showing the growing boundaries from townsite to town to city. The shaded portions represent subdivided lots as of 1907. By 1912, however, the entire area shown had undergone thorough subdivision.

tional lots. As in the case of 1903, these extensions were not undertaken in order to accommodate growth in the built-up area. They were designed to expand the real estate market and expand the opportunities for land speculation (*See* Maps II and III). The major land owners had thus overcome their apprehensions about incorporation and had clearly learned how to use the municipal government for their own purposes. Subdivisions created at this time included Hulbert, Strathcona Place, Beau Park, Parkdale, Martin, Allendale, Irvine, Richmond Park, Rosedale, Hazeldean, River Heights, Knob Hill, Shelburne, Bonnie Doon, Brackman-Kerr, University Place, Windsor Park, Windsor Terrace, and Mayfair Park. Land developers' names or localities in England were used to name these various subdivisions.

Real estate activity during this era, however, was not restricted to the creation of new suburbs. Between 1899 and 1912 a total of twenty subdivisions were carried out in the original townsite, a portion of which was contributed by the Calgary and Edmonton Townsite

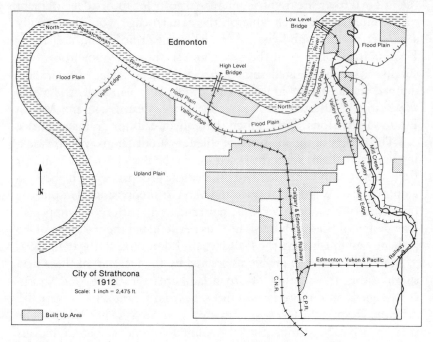

Map III. The City of Strathcona, 1912, showing the actual extent of built-up or developed area in relation to the mass of subdivided land left undeveloped.

Company in 1909. During this era, the original townsite was subject to sky-rocketing land values. The trend toward higher land values was evident as early as 1906 when two lots on Whyte Avenue and West Railway Street near the station were purchased by Messrs. Duggan and Sache from the estate of S. Parrish for $20,000, who resold the property a year later to Pat Burns for $35,000.[27] By March 1911 the *Strathcona Plaindealer* was advising the citizens that "a boom is threatened and it behooves every man with money in his big pocket to refrain from getting excited and intoxicated with large profits and quick returns."[28] Local residents viewed these real estate trends in a highly favorable light. Land speculation, if undertaken by local citizens, was a civic virtue. Profits derived from this activity were a reward for having faith in the future of the community.

Despite the contemporary view that the large number of new subdivisions and the escalation in property values were manifestations of the fulfilment of Strathcona's metropolitan destiny, this era produced a number of potential problems. The extensive annexation of land to the original townsite involved increased costs for future development to the municipality. A ravine on the eastern edge would eventually separate the new subdivisions of Shelburne, Knob Hill, and River Heights from the rest of the town, and so the development of these subdivisions necessitated the construction of a bridge. This ravine drained the adjacent sloughs that dotted the upland plain. Two of these sloughs affected the Strathcona Place, Beau Park, and Martin Estate subdivisions, and resulted in frequent calls for drainage works.

The design of the majority of the new subdivisions was also lacking in imagination. With the exception of the Beau Park and Windsor Park subdivisions, the majority utilized the grid pattern. The best examples are the Windsor Terrace and Mayfair subdivisions. Despite the opportunity for a creative street pattern, a grid pattern was imposed. The design of these subdivisions thus perpetuated the tradition of expediency established by the Calgary and Edmonton Railway in 1891.

In addition to the problems created by the location of these new subdivisions, the amount of urban land created was beyond Strathcona's needs and, more importantly, beyond its capacity to actually develop. Despite the fact that municipal services were not required for these paper subdivisions, the city council commenced an ambitious program of public works. In August 1910, by-law 350 was passed to provide $38,000 for a steel bridge over the Mill Creek Ravine. By-law

397 was passed in May 1911 to provide $5,500 for the purchase of fire hall sites and equipment for the fire department. Extensive expansions to the city's water and sewage systems were also undertaken. All of these improvements were strongly endorsed by the *Strathcona Plaindealer:*

> the extension of electric light and power lines have been very great in the last year owing to the very scattered location of population and industries in the city. This has meant a large expenditure to accommodate the several industrial and residential communities. It will bring large revenue in the future but must be paid for now.[29]

These public works were built to the detriment of the original townsite where the built-up area of the town was concentrated.

Despite the public works program undertaken, the City of Strathcona was faced with an overwhelming task, given the number of subdivisions that had been created. Delays in providing services to the new districts and opening the road allowances were inevitable. One subdivision in this situation was Richmond Park. In May 1911, various Richmond Park land owners petitioned the city council for the improvement of the streets because:

> the said properties are assessed at prices beyond those at which it is possible to sell the said property in the present condition of the streets... without almost no exception the streets are in such a condition that access to the lands owned by us... is almost impossible and it is not possible for heavy vehicles in any way to have access to our lands.

> That no civic improvements have been made on the said Richmond Park, save by the clearing of the trees on a few streets and even in those cases the streets have been left in such a condition as to be very little better than they were when the trees were standing.[30]

Strathcona's decision to approve a large number of subdivisions as well as to embark on a program of public works to serve the needs of a series of empty suburbs had serious financial implications, evident in the statistics concerning rateable property and debenture debt provided in Table I. The value of Strathcona's rateable property took a phenomenal jump of approximately $7 million between 1907 and 1908. This increase cannot be attributed to the expansion of the commercial activities, but rather to the annexation and subdivision of land when Strathcona was incorporated as a city.

The increased value in Strathcona's rateable property was matched by higher tax arrears, which by 1910 amounted to slightly over $100,000. This deficiency in tax revenue was made up by periodic loans from the local branch of the Imperial Bank. The first of these loans was obtained in August 1899 when $500 was borrowed to allow the town to continue operation pending the collection of the taxes for 1899. As the value of the tax arrears increased, Strathcona was required to increase the amount of money borrowed to cover current expenses. In May 1910, it borrowed $155,000 from the Imperial Bank for this purpose. The problem of non-payment of taxes should have alerted the citizens to the dangers of allowing the tax base to be artificially inflated by land speculation. Despite the obvious need for Strathcona to restrain expenditures on public works and subdivision approval, debentures debt increased by over $1 million between 1907 and 1912.

Table I

Year	Value of Rateable Property	Debenture Debt
1899	Not Available	No Debt Incurred
1900	$437,990.00	$24,000.00
1901	461,880.00	50,000.00
1902	468,027.14	59,000.00
1903	Not Available	59,000.00
1904	671,590.00	79,000.00
1905	927,865.00	183,000.00
1906	1,141,014.00	205,000.00
1907	2,161,594.00	211,700.00
1908	8,829,560.00	382,489.19
1909	6,995,071.00	454,935.62
1910	6,861,730.40	639,140.71
1911	6,777,011.60	920,191.05
1912	7,280,273.75	1,293,926.07

The Strathcona city council responded to this situation in the traditional way by undertaking a massive sale of land in order to recover the back taxes. It ignored the most obvious step of attempting to slow down the subdivision process and thereby reduce or at least stabilize the need for new services. This land sale clearly illustrates how these new subdivisions had become liabilities rather than assets capable of generating tax revenue. Despite the success of the sale, the problem of basing public policy on boosterism and land speculation remained; the people who purchased this property were also land speculators, as were those who had defaulted on the taxes. This basic weakness in the city of Strathcona's financial position did not become evident until after amalgamation and the crisis of 1913.[31] A total of 44,348 lots or parcels of land reverted to the Greater City of Edmonton between 1918 and 1921. Strathcona subdivisions made a major contribution to this total.

Land development in Strathcona was characterized by a high rate of investment in the creation and promotion of urban land in comparison to the investment in its actual utilization. This discrepancy reflects Strathcona's position on an investment frontier that was dominated by other urban centres as close as Edmonton and as far away as London, England. The rate of investment, therefore, depended on investor confidence in the area and was irrelevant to the actual needs of the community. The combined effects of local boosterism and the availability of capital for real estate investment created a very bloated urban community that symbolized, along with Laurier's railway policy, a high degree of overconfidence in the West. Excessive investment in urban land fueled the boosters' imaginations but served to create only the illusion of growth. The rhetoric of the boosters that stressed permanence and progress was contradicted by the fact that the majority of people involved in the real estate trade were simply anxious to make a profit before the speculative bubble burst. This situation represented a conflict between the short-term goals of the major land owners, who were interested in a quick turnover of property, and the long-term goal of building a viable urban community. In Strathcona, however, the overriding trend was to ignore this conflict and persist in viewing land speculation as being in the public interest.

Notes

1. Canada, *Laws, Statutes, etc.*, An Act to Incorporate the Calgary and Edmonton Railway Company, 1890, 53 vic., ch. 84.

2. The provisional directors of the Calgary and Edmonton Railway Company were James Ross, Edmund B. Osler, Herbert C. Hammond, William MacKenzie, Nicol Kingsmill, Herbert S. Holt, and Donald B. Mann. Members of this group who were the most active in western land development were Osler and Hammond. Osler was one of four Canadian directors of the Canada North West Land Company, which administered a number of townsites owned by the Canadian Pacific Railway. In 1882 he established a partnership with Herbert C. Hammond, who had previously been employed by the Bank of Hamilton. Augustus Meredith Nanton, who had joined the company in 1883, became responsible for the Winnipeg office in 1884. This firm was the Canadian agent for the North of Scotland Canadian Mortgage Company, Winnipeg Western Land Corporation, Canada Saskatchewan Land Company, as well as the Qu'Appelle Long Lake and Saskatchewan Railroad and Steamboat Land and Townsite Companies.

3. Chester Martin, *"Dominion Lands" Policy,* ed. Lewis H. Thomas (Toronto: McClelland and Stewart, 1973), p. 57.

4. North Alberta Land Titles Office, Edmonton Transfer Documents 769 A, 800 A, 808 A, and 870 A.

5. North Alberta Land Titles Office, Edmonton Plan I, 25 September 1891.

6. Canada, *Laws, Statutes, etc.,* "An Act further to Amend Chapter Fifty-one of the Revised Statutes of Canada, The Territories Real Property Act," 51 vic., ch. 20.

7. P.A.C., "Records of the Dominion Immigration Branch," Record Group 76, vol. 24, file 531, Nanton to Carling, 18 September 1891.

8. P.A.C., "Records of the RCMP," Record Group 18, A1, vol. 68, file 492, Anderson to Burgess, 3 May 1892.

9. The attempt to relocate the land titles office resulted in the formation of a vigilante committee that physically prevented the documents from being removed. The "great land office steal incident" demonstrated Edmonton's militance with respect to the defence of its metropolitan interests.

10. North Alberta Land Titles Office, Edmonton Transfer Documents 2065 A, 2480 D, and 2533A.

11. *South Edmonton News,* 8 November 1894.

12. *South Edmonton News,* 7 November 1895.

13. *South Edmonton News,* 9 May 1895.

14. Ibid.

15. Ibid.

16. *Edmonton Bulletin,* 8 March 1894.

17. *South Edmonton News,* 29 September 1895.

18. North Alberta Land Titles Office, Edmonton Certificates of Title: 749, 768, 793, 848, 854, 867, 976, 23E 169E, 234E, 237E, 65F, 77F, 171F, 190F, 707G, 152G, 229G, 40H, 137H, 148H, 19I, 42I, 185J, 219J, 75K, 80K, 111K, 221K, 5L, 107L, 162L, 182L, 118N, 131P, 227Q, and 138R.

19. *Edmonton Bulletin,* 5 September 1891.

20. North Alberta Land Titles Office, Edmonton Certificates of Title: 787, 788, 51E, 94E, 95E, 194F, 59H, 115J, 128M, 237M, 225N, 128P, 44I, and 3M.

21. *Edmonton Bulletin,* 28 August 1891.

22. City of Edmonton Archives, Sache Papers, Osler, Hammond, and Nanton to F. Sache, 2 August 1895.

23. *Alberta Plaindealer,* 16 June 1899.

24. *Strathcona Plaindealer,* 7 September 1906.

25. *Strathcona Plaindealer,* 1 January 1907.

26. Prominent land developers on Council included J.G. Tipton, J.J. MacKenzie, and Russell A. Hulbert.

27. *Strathcona Plaindealer,* 5 March 1907.

28. *Strathcona Plaindealer,* 31 March 1911.

29. *Strathcona Plaindealer,* 3 May 1911.

30. City of Edmonton Archives, MS 290, file 175.

31. John C. Weaver, "Edmonton's Perilous Course, 1904-1929," *Urban History Review,* no. 2 (October 1977): 28.

The Location of Experimental Farms and Illustration Stations: An Agricultural or Political Consideration?

_____W. Leland Clark

In 1886, the federal government enacted legislation that provided for the establishment of the Central Experimental Farm at Ottawa and for branch stations, which were subsequently located at Nappan, Nova Scotia; Brandon, Manitoba; Indian Head, N.W.T.; and Agassiz, British Columbia. These farms were to conduct experimental work in agriculture, horticulture, stock raising, dairying, and forestry. Arising out of the rapid settlement of western Canada in the early 1900s, there was a widely expressed need for additional experimental farm sites. The pleas presented to the federal government by farmers, community leaders, and politicians in support of particular sites were as varied as they were numerous. The arguments of these lobbyists are of considerable historical interest in that they illuminate the varying agricultural conditions that existed in the several Saskatchewan regions under consideration, the perceived need for substantial improvements in "farming practices," and the relevance of political considerations to the decision-making process.

The federal government had conceded the need for an additional experimental farm in northern Saskatchewan by 1906; the Indian Head farm was deemed to meet the needs of only the southern portion of the province. Several northern communities including Yorkton, Humboldt, Melfort, Saskatoon, Warman, Rosthern, Duck Lake, Prince Albert, and North Battleford were examined as possible sites. Initial reports indicated that suitable land—which meant, in part, that "the proposed site should be clearly seen from the line of railway passing through the country, also it should be within walking distance of a railway station"[1]—was available for purchase at or near Yorkton, Melfort, Saskatoon, Rosthern, and Duck Lake.

In the opinion of William Saunders, Director of Experimental Farms, Yorkton was an undesirable site because it was situated within 72 miles of the Indian Head farm and the two farms would be "too near to each other to produce satisfactory results."[2] Duck Lake was equally unsatisfactory because it was "near the northern limits of the present wheat-growing district and on the borders of the timbered country, and having a large Indian reserve, has comparatively few settlers within reach."[3] It would appear that Saunders's assessment was shared by others in that there is no evidence of further consideration of those two communities.

A significant factor in the federal government's site selection process was the potential expense of any proposed land acquisition. In fact, the Honorable Sydney Fisher hinted rather strongly to one advocate that such land should be made available free of charge:

> I am not prepared, at the present moment, to say I will not pay anything, but the feeling I have ... is that the place which wants this station, and which is suitable in other respects for the work, ought to be glad to supply a quarter section for the purpose; and I am quite sure there are places all through the province – quite suitable in other characteristics – which would do this.
>
> The only station yet established is that at Lethbridge, where we have received a large area of land free. The Galt Irrigation Company has given us water supply, also free, for irrigation purposes.
>
> Mr. Saunders was informed at Saskatoon that it was quite likely they would supply land there.... You, of course, well understand that Saskatoon is very favourably situated, from its being a great railroad centre, and consequently would serve most excellently visitors....[4]

While the supporters of what would prove to be the unsuccessful Saskatoon bid did agree to subscribe privately "the difference between $50 per acre and the [asking] price [i.e., $65 per acre] of the quarter section ... for the Experimental Farm,"[5] the advocates of the ultimately selected Rosthern site were unmoved by the minister's thinly veiled threat. Both Saunders and Angus MacKay, the superintendent of the Indian Head Experimental Farm, reported moreover that "the Saskatoon farm was much the more desirable of the two [i.e., than Rosthern]."[6] The Saskatoon site was extremely well situated in that it was bound by the C.P.R., the Grand Trunk Pacific railway and "the Goose Lake Trail, one of the most important and heavily-used trails in that part of the country."[7] Although Dr. Saunders agreed that Rosthern "would serve the purpose very well,"[8] the community was much less accessible, served by "only one railway and that a branch line of the C.N.R."[9] In contrast with the supportive claims of a local Member of Parliament who repeatedly stressed Rosthern's merits as an agricultural centre ("Rosthern is one of the largest wheat shipping points in the world"),[10] Dr. Saunders unenthusiastically conceded that "Rosthern would be a convenient point for a fairly large area of settlement."[11] Saskatoon, on the other hand, was "in the centre of an immense area in every direction where settlement has been pouring in very rapidly for some years past and where a large acreage has already been broken."[12]

Advocates, meanwhile, of the less popular Melfort proposal argued primarily in political terms, indicating, perhaps, that they understood the current decision-making process more clearly than others. Although the secretary of the Melfort Liberal Association did stress the need for a "northern" experimental farm, he significantly reminded his local Member of Parliament of the frequent complaints that the Laurier government had done nothing for the Melfort district:

We need a Judicial District and Registry Office badly and have been trying for a long time to get them built with no satisfaction whatever. Humboldt, however, has secured various government offices whilst nothing has come to Melfort. So the indifferent ones say why work for a party when it does nothing for the district.[13]

Another prominent Melfort resident was equally direct when communicating with the local M.P.'s son:

Last week Dr. Saunders of Ottawa and Angus Mackay [sic] of Ex. Farm Indian Head paid Melfort a visit...they found several choice farms along the C.N.R. that would suit the purpose admirably and their report will be favourable of some, but as they told me it now rests with the Government and I should beg your father to interest himself in the matter, it is so often thrown up to me when taking up the cudgels on his behalf that he has done nothing for Melfort and it would be a good answer to them if he had the farm placed here ... as apart from all other considerations Melfort is a most suitable and central spot for a farm of that kind.[14]

The inference that the investigative team of William Saunders and Angus MacKay would present a "favourable" report on behalf of a Melfort site is interesting in light of Dr. Saunders's subsequent dismissal of Melfort as having as "yet very poor railway service, a train [only] three times a week." [15] Perhaps the Saunders-MacKay team, for their own "political" reasons, were diplomatically reassuring wherever they travelled.

Why then was Rosthern selected as the site of Saskatchewan's second experimental farm, a site which would prove so unsatisfactory that a future Liberal administration would propose to abandon it by the early 1920s? [16] All of the available evidence indicates that the decision in favor of Rosthern was blatantly political. Reginald Beatty, a Melfort area pioneer, recalled in later years his journey to Ottawa in 1906–7 to lobby on behalf of the Melfort Agricultural Society:

> Poor Adamson[17] (a personal friend of mine) was feeling rather uncomfortable as he had made some political promises to his Rosthern supporters that they should get the farm. I then kept on at [Minister of Agriculture] Mr. Fisher pointing out plainly that if Rosthern was selected it would only be duplicating Indian Head [due to similarities in soil type]. ... the usual formula was given me that the matter would receive every attention and so on, while really it was and had been a foregone conclusion that Rosthern should get it from political reasons pure and simple.[18]

To suggest that the decision in favor of the Rosthern site was "a foregone conclusion" may be unjustified in that the Honorable Frank Oliver, the recently appointed Minister of the Interior, felt compelled to write to the Minister of Agriculture at some length in support of the Rosthern site as late as September 1907. While he repeatedly stressed that Rosthern was "the farthest northerly point in Saskatchewan at which wheat raising has been made a success," [19] Oliver began that letter by noting pointedly that G.E. McCraney, M.P. for Saskatchewan, was "very urgent on the location of the proposed farm at Rosthern,"[20] and continued by saying that he himself "very strongly"[21] supported this recommendation despite the fact that he was "unable to go fully into all the reasons."[22]

A subsequent director of the Central Experimental Station, Dr. E.S. Archibald, provided—many years later—a more detailed explanation for that particular land transaction. The farm site in question had been purchased

> from the Rosthern Realty Company at the very high price of $50 per acre. Rumour has it that this company was the liberal organ for the district and the area sold by them to the Government for the Experimental Station had been purchased by them a few days before for a very much lower figure.[23]

When the federal Conservatives decided to enlarge the Rosthern Experimental Farm in 1913 by purchasing an additional 480 acres at the again somewhat exorbitant sum (for that area) of $52 per acre, "$10,000 [of the total purchase price]... was [reportedly] rebated to the Conservative organization of the district."[24] According to Dr. Archibald, the governmental decisions that led to both of these land transactions were both political and partisan in nature as the respective parties seized in turn the opportunity to divert tax dollars into their campaign chests.

Although political arguments were on occasion presented in support of specific requests for additional sites in the "post-Rosthern" era,[25] there is no evidence to indicate that politics so blatantly influenced the decision-making process thereafter. While supplicants certainly continued to engage in home-town "boosterism," agricultural factors were primarily stressed. As an example, many petitioners, including W.R. Motherwell, Saskatchewan's Commissioner of Agriculture, argued that there was a particular need for experimental work in the drier southwest region:

> Between the 3rd and 4th Meridians, or in what is known as the pre-emption area, it is admittedly drier and more difficult for growing grain crops, unless under approved methods of tillage. ... This is the district to which the large majority of the new settlers are going at the present time.... Many of them having no

experience and with no older settlement nearby to take example from, I fear that, should a dry year recur, as it may at any time, all these new settlers will experience great disappointment and loss.... It is astonishing, what may be, and has been, done to offset a light precipitation, in the way of storing up moisture by ... "dry farming" ... this system of good tillage is all the more necessary in the pre-emption area. Summer-fallowing in a new district, to the settler unfamiliar with the object in view, is simply to him the rankest kind of nonsense ... unless he sees with his own eyes or hears from practical men the good results that have emanated and may emanate from this system.[26]

While Motherwell noted that he and his own department were actively promoting the adoption of improved agricultural methods at Farmers Institute meetings and "by distributing winter wheat and alfalfa, believing that that area will grow these crops successfully,"[27] he argued that these limited efforts could not equal "the great education work that an Experimental Station of similar proportion to your Rosthern one would do in the locality, which is, be it remembered, an immense area, capable of great development."[28]

In addition to the problem of insufficient rainfall, the farmers of the semi-arid southwest were faced with a

dangerously deficient surface humus supply which is a feature of the soils of the arid belt where our conditions do not admit of plowing under a green crop, since that robs the land of its equally deficient moisture, or turning under long stubble or spread straw, for that rots very slowly with us and may only do harm, or that sovereign remedy, the application of well-rotted manure, since we find it impossible to raise stock profitably on the sort of grazing that our low and uncertain rainfall and high evaporation rate afford.[29]

This petitioner, who was experiencing his "third dry year,"[30] furthermore repeated the oft-expressed argument that "Rosthern, Saskatoon [i.e., the university farm] and Indian Head might as well not exist ... [because] for demonstration purposes they are out of reach of us and out of touch."[31] Although agricultural experimentation and the demonstration of improved farming practices were clearly different and distinct functions, most observers assumed that they were synonymous and their petitions were drafted accordingly.

Ironically, the very success of the federal government's immigration policies was contributing to the need for additional experimental farms as new immigrants were encouraged, if not required, to settle in areas previously deemed to be unsuitable for cultivation. As two Maple Creek agricultural spokesmen explained,

> Owing to these adverse growing conditions the greater part of this district is sparsely settled, it being considered that farming could not be carried on successfully. However, as other parts of the west are fast being filled, incoming settlers are now taking up the available lands in this district, and are endeavouring to farm them. As most of these settlers are unfamiliar with such conditions as are here met, they are at a loss to know just what methods of cultivation to pursue.... [32]

That the newly arrived settlers were encountering disappointingly severe agricultural problems as early as 1915 was reported by one Radville district farmer: "There are now about 14 resident farmers in this township [which was part of the "burnt-out" area situated southwest of Weyburn] whereas six years ago there were 45, all of those who have gone were unable to continue as they did not make enough out of their crops to begin to pay expenses." [33]

That many of these recent arrivals felt neglected and even betrayed by the federal government was evident in the plea of the South Cypress Union of Grain Growers Association for additional experimental stations:

> We can only think that it is due somehow to a failure [by government]...to appreciate the exceptional nature of these conditions...that we have been left so long to do our own experimental work, we, who as working farmers, have not the training nor the time or the means to devote to it. Our rainfall over ten years averages eight inches, badly distributed. We are accustomed most of us to a precipitation of three or four times this amount.... [34]

By 1918, the arguments presented in favor of the establishment of an experimental farm in the semi-arid southwestern region had been altered somewhat by changing circumstance. Although a Swift Current spokesman bemoaned the growing history of unsatisfactory crop results in that area,[35] he stressed particularly the fact that 25.4 percent of the soon-to-be-returning soldiers who had filed for homesteads prior to or at the time of their enlistment had no previous farm experience while an additional 41.8 percent had less than three years.[36] Society, it was argued, owed these veterans more than land per se; they must be shown how to farm successfully.

It was also evident that the agricultural future of the southwest was very much in doubt by 1918. Although an earlier petitioner from the Maple Creek area had boasted of the bountiful and varied crops that the area had produced—"alfalfa has and is being tried, apples[!] grow in profusion, rye was cut on the ninth day of June and stood between five and six feet high,"[37] subsequent correspondents were more pessimistic. Even though the Cypress Hills Water-Users Association requested that the federal government establish a demonstration facility in the Maple Creek area "where both irrigation and dry farming can be practiced,"[38] the Saskatchewan Stock Growers Association perceptively petitioned for a station that would scientifically examine the future of ranching in that same region.[39] Perhaps the southwest was not, in fact, suitable for agriculture.

The decision to establish an experimental farm in the Swift Current area in 1920 was based upon several factors. It was a large region not served by any other experimental station. Soil and climatic conditions were substantially different from other regions in that the "light loam ... requires special methods of handling"[40] and the entire area "is subject to drying winds and a somewhat lesser rainfall"[41] than found elsewhere in the province. This area, furthermore, was newly settled by relatively inexperienced farmers. While not publicly acknowledged as such, the decision in favor of Swift Current reflected Ottawa's awareness that there was a severe agricultural crisis in the southwest. In the words of the minister, "Agriculture must be carried on under dry farming conditions or the land must be allowed to revert to ranching."[42] Although some observers such as W.R. Motherwell had argued that experimental stations should be established in advance of settlement so that relatively inexperienced farmers could be assisted in dealing with agricultural problems unique to that region,[43] the federal government established the Swift Current farm in 1920 largely as the result of the failure of local farmers to resolve the agricultural problems of the area. The Swift Current station constituted, therefore, a "rescue" attempt by the federal government.

As noted earlier, many petitioners made little or no distinction between experimental stations and demonstration farms, a confusion which was compounded by the fact that the federal government, under the provisions of the Agricultural Instruction Act, provided the provincial departments of agriculture with financial assistance "for instruction and demonstration purposes." [44] As the federal minister explained,

> Where the Federal and Provincial Departments are working along similar lines, as they do in Agriculture, some division must be recognized, and hitherto the Dominion has confined its work to carrying on experiments and investigations, leaving to the provinces the duty of demonstrating to the farmers the methods best suited to the conditions obtaining in their district. Applications for Experimental Farms have come in from all over the Dominion. In the great majority of instances they are really for Demonstration farms. [45]

The distinction between the federal and the provincial role was largely indiscernible to many petitioners as in the example of the Humboldt town council, who offered the federal department the free use of 75 acres of land so that "something should be done to demonstrate to the farmers the extraordinary advantages derived from mixed farming." [46]

Due to the widespread need to publicize improved agricultural practices among local farmers, the federal department decided in 1915 to establish illustration stations at which approved farmers would demonstrate recommended practices under the supervision of the nearby Experimental Farm. Such illustration stations were relatively inexpensive to maintain; they were easily accessible to local farmers; and they could be offered—somewhat as a consolation prize—to those whose requests for an experimental farm could not be granted. [47]

One of the arguments used to promote the establishment of an illustration station in certain communities was the fact that the residents, by virtue of ethnic origin, were in special need of agricultural instruction. For example, the executive officers of the Canora Liberal association stressed the fact that their community was "composed largely of Ruthenians whose methods are sadly in need of improvement if they are to become valuable citizens of the country. They are, however, a class of settlers who imitate readily and . . . if proper ideals of farming are given them, will, without doubt, become expert farmers."[48] Fourteen years later, spokesmen for this same community continued to stress this particular argument (in addition to the habitual explanation of differing soil and climatic conditions):

> A majority of our farmers are from Central Europe and have not inherited the general knowledge of Canadian farming methods that the settlers from Eastern Canada possess. Living in little communities they have not the advantage of observation and imitation of the practices of the prairie bred farmer, they in many cases, either adopt costly and impractical experiments of their own, or fall into a discouraged and discontented mood and farm in a rough and ready, rule of thumb fashion that usually results in a bare existence with scrubby, inbred stock, weedy farms, primitive buildings and sheriff's writs, the main features of their career. The outlook for the next generation brought up under these conditions is not promising. . . . [49]

It was that petitioner's hope that the provision of an experimental farm (or, more logically, an illustration station) would aid this particular region where, even during the war years, "the proportion of prosperity enjoyed by the farmers . . . was much less than that of other portions of the province where intelligent work and educative ideas have been employed."[50]

Some eight years later, a Yorkton area spokesman provided some indirect evidence that such "educative work" could indeed succeed with East European immigrants, those whom he described as a "very cosmopolitan type of settler."[51] In support of his plea for more "instruction" in the art of cattle raising, he emphasized the fact that considerable progress had already been made in poultry raising, thanks to the work of the Extension Department of the University of Saskatchewan:

> The Shippers of live poultry some two or three years ago com-

plained that it was impossible to keep the poultry from the foreign born settlers in the crates because of the fact that they resembled pigeons more in size than hens, but there has been a wonderful change in this connection during the last few years, and the Board [Yorkton Board of Trade] feels that there is fertile ground here for the planting of ideas and instructions with regard to keeping, raising of and improving of other forms of livestock.[52]

Unfortunately, the financially troubled federal government was determined, by the 1920s, to lessen rather than increase the federal role in agriculture.[53] As W.R. Motherwell, the federal Minister of Agriculture as of 1921, stated: "If I could do it, I would like to get rid of some of [the twenty-three experimental stations] rather than establish more, as ... a considerable portion of the work they are doing is distinctly provincial in nature."[54] What Motherwell had implied was that the task of discovering how to produce larger cattle was properly within the jurisdiction of the federally financed experimental farms: teaching farmers how to apply that knowledge was not.

It is interesting to note that some farmers actually opposed the establishment of additional experimental farm sites. As an example, the Belle Plaine Municipal Agricultural Society was very critical of a proposed experimental farm for the heavy clay area near Regina:

Our farmers are not in favour in any way of increasing white collared costs in agriculture by means of taxation. There is too much attempting to cure the ills of the land on the part of men who are not of the land, thereby throwing the pro-erty [poverty?] and the so-called stupidity of the practical farmer in his face....
    You estimate the cost of the Experimental station at $50,000 per year ... it means ... there would be $50,000 less of the farmers' production to stay in his pockets.... Re: Weed and Pest Control; our municipality is already spending increasing amounts to control menace of this kind. Duplication of public ser[v]ice and organization at a cost of rapidly increasing rate of taxation is the ruin of this age.
    Re Damage from Soil Drifting in 1930. Our farmers are one and all in accord that crop damage occuring this season was not due to soil drifting but from ensuing hea[v]y frosts and lack of sub-

soil moisture. Our experienced farmers disco[v]ered this without the help in any way whatsoever on the part of Tax-eating B.S.A. Johnnies.[55]

While other farmers undoubtedly shared that writer's reservation about the practical utility of "Tax-eating B.S.A. Johnnies," there is no additional evidence to indicate that such skepticism led to openly expressed opposition to the location of experimental farm stations in any given district. Most farmers—at least those who wrote letters to Ministers of Agriculture—wanted more, rather than fewer, such farms.

While the arguments presented both in support of and in opposition to the many requests for additional experimental farm sites varied substantially, there was one very predominant theme. There existed on the prairies—in this case primarily Saskatchewan—such marked variations in the quality of the soil, in the amount of rainfall, and in wind patterns that it was impossible to establish standard cropping and/or agricultural practices. What was agriculturally sound in one district might well be largely unsuccessful in another. In addition, the "cosmopolitan" (to use the words of one petitioner) nature of the farm community meant that prairie farmers themselves were anything but uniform in terms of the amount of knowledge and experience they could apply to the agricultural problems they encountered. An examination of the problems encountered in the selection of experimental farm sites and illustration stations even within Saskatchewan alone demonstrates the danger of considering the prairies as a region; of describing agricultural problems in general terms; and of considering farmers as a homogeneous group. It is also evident that severe agricultural problems were arising in specific areas of Saskatchewan at a time and in a manner not generally appreciated by historians. For example, many farmers in the southwest were encountering alarming difficulties even prior to the Great War and those depressed agricultural conditions (with 1915 being a welcome exception) generally continued into the 1920s. Fortunately, those who were responsible for locating experimental farms and illustration stations were well aware of such variations in agricultural conditions, and were primarily influenced by those varied conditions—with the probable exception of the 1908 decision in favor of Rosthern—during the period under examination.

The decisions to establish specific experimental farms, politically important though they may have been, were properly based on agricultural considerations.

Notes

1. P.A.C., Department of Agriculture, v. 2747, f120331, Wm. Saunders to Hon. Minister of Agriculture, n.d. [received 4 June 1908].
2. Ibid.
3. Ibid.
4. Ibid., 187753, Hon. Sydney Fisher to G.E. McCraney, M.P. (for Saskatchewan), 12 October 1906.
5. Ibid., 188356, J.H.C. Willoughby to Wm. Saunders, 22 March 1907.
6. Ibid., Wm. Saunders to Hon. Minister of Agriculture, n.d. [received 4 June, 1908].
7. Ibid.
8. Ibid.
9. Ibid.
10. Ibid., G.E. McCraney, M.P. to Hon. Sydney Fisher, 16 March 1907. McCraney, who resided in Rosthern, was M.P. for the constituency of Saskatchewan in which Rosthern was then located.
11. Ibid., Wm. Saunders to Hon. Minister of Agriculture, n.d. [received 4 June 1908].
12. Ibid.
13. Ibid., 187754, F.B. Goodwillie to A.J. Adamson, M.P., 10 September 1906.
14. Ibid., f120331, Reginald Beatty to F.A. Adamson 11 September 1906.
15. Ibid., Wm. Saunders to Hon. Minister of Agriculture, n.d. [received 4 June 1908].
16. Ibid., v.2898, f19–8 part 1. W.R. Motherwell [Minister of Agriculture] to W.O. McDougall [Secretary, P.A. Agricultural Society], 20 March 1923. "However, the location of the Farm undoubtedly was not what it should have been. It is on a

single line of railway, and is not in a very large or very thickly settled agricultural area or territory, is cut off on the north and east sides from the nearest good farming territory by land not suited to agriculture, and is as relatively close to Saskatoon on the south that our Farm and the College naturally overlap in their territory and work ... why the Farm was not originally placed in the Melfort district, in the centre of a very large area excellently suited for agriculture, is more than I can understand." Ibid., v2843, f1–30 – part 1, 287934, E.S. Archibald [Director, Experimental Farm] to Dr. Grisdale [Deputy Minister of Agriculture], 14 November 1922.

17. A.J. Adamson, the Liberal M.P. for the Humboldt constituency, resided in Rosthern, Saskatchewan.

18. Ibid., v2898, f19–8 part 1, Reginald Beatty to Hon. Mr. Motherwell, 16 March 1923.

19. Ibid., v2747, f120331, Frank Oliver to Hon. Sydney Fisher, 3 September 1907.

20. Ibid.

21. Ibid.

22. Ibid.

23. Ibid., v2843, f1–30 – part 1, 287934, E.S. Archibald to Dr. Grisdale, 14 November 1922.

24. Ibid.

25. "I may add that Aneroid [i.e., a proposed Experimental Farm site] is very close to the line (one mile) of Moose Jaw and Maple Creek constituency and that the favourable considering of the petition cannot fail to have a desireable [sic] effect on future elections." Ibid., v2762, f199701, 247066, R.B. Lloyd to Minister of Agriculture 14 February 1916. In contrast with the above, a local M.P., who wrote to the Minister of Agriculture in reference to a proposed station in the Peace River district, declared that he was "not going to make any suggestion as to where this farm should be located. I think that the officials of your Department ... are thoroughly capable and trustworthy in making selection of land for the farm." Ibid., v2898, f19.9 part 1, D.M. Kennedy to Hon. W. R. Motherwell, 9 February 1923. Perhaps, Kennedy, as a Progressive M.P., was either affirming his (and his party's) disinterest in the political patronage system or he was demonstrating his awareness that he, as an opposition member, had no influence.

26. Ibid., 202073, W.R. Motherwell to Honorable Sydney Fisher, 2 September 1909.

27. Ibid.

28. Ibid. The federal government's decision to establish an experimental farm at Scott, southwest of North Battleford, did not meet the needs of the dry southwest.

29. Ibid., 267733, David Steinhouse to Minister of Agriculture, 8 July [no year indicated].

30. Ibid.

31. Ibid.

32. Ibid., 220906, W.R. Abbott (President, Maple Creek Agricultural Society) and Geo. C. Stewart (Secretary) to Hon. Martin Burrell, 9 March 1912.

33. Ibid., v2762, f199701, 245703, Percy B. Calladine to The Minister of Agriculture, 15 November 1915.

34. Ibid., 267733, David Steinhouse to Minister of Agriculture, 8 July [no year indicated].

35. "In the past fifteen years the only years in which a good crop was obtained were those in which we had an abnormal rainfall in June." Ibid., 264556, Geo D. Arnott [city clerk, Swift Current] to Hon. Minister of Agriculture, 10 December 1918.

36. Ibid.

37. Ibid., 234235, Theo. C. Armstrong to J.H. Grisdale, 14 August 1913.

38. Ibid., v.2762, f199701. Cypress Hills Water-Users Association to Hon. Minister of Agriculture, n.d.

39. Ibid., v2850, f1.44.1, part 1, 273204, Memorandum prepared by Minister of Agriculture for the Privy Council, [25 May 1920?]

40. Ibid., 273205, Report of the Committee of Privy Council, 29 May 1920. It should also be noted that different soil types produced separate and distinctive weed problems. As the Director of the Experimental Farm system explained, "Weed control Experiments are being conducted at Indian Head and Swift Current but on different soil types. Moreover, at those two stations Yellow Mustard and Canada Thistle are not difficult weeds, yet these are most prevalent in the heavy soil area, and cultural methods now practised for control induce soil drifting." Ibid., v.2898, f19-8 part 1, 336064, E.S. Archibald to Hon. Robert Weir, 12 March 1931.

41. Ibid.

42. Ibid., 273204. Memorandum prepared by Minister of Agriculture for the Privy Council [25 May 1920?].

43. For example, Motherwell sought the establishment of an experimental farm station in northeastern Saskatchewan in 1910 because the acquisition of available land elsewhere meant that this area of Saskatchewan would be settled next. Ibid., v.2762, f199701, 207758, W.R. Motherwell to Hon. Sidney Fisher, 14 July 1910.

44. Ibid., 233504, M. Burrell to L.H. Good, 5 January 1914.

45. Ibid., 232282, M. Burrell to C.C. Smith, 25 October 1913.

46. Ibid., 231225, W.H. Stiles to Hon. Minister of Agriculture, 1 August 1913.

47. W.R. Motherwell had to deny the request of the Carrot River Board of Trade for an experimental station in that area, owing in part to budgetary restrictions. The minister promised instead "to establish one of those forty acre plots in some suitable, frontier locality in your riding." Ibid., v.2898, f19-8 part 1, 307640, W.R. Motherwell to Malcolm McLean, M.P., 27 April 1926.

48. Ibid., v.2762, f199701, 203167, R.W. Cumming and P. Douglas to Dr. Cash, M.P., 12 October 1909.

49. Ibid., v2898, f19-8 part 1, H.M. Sutherland to W.R. Motherwell, 21 April 1923.

50. Ibid.

51 Ibid., J.M. Clark to Hon. Robert Weir, 12 January 1931.

52. Ibid.

53. Motherwell should have been suitably impressed by a supporter of a Prince Albert location who noted: "In matter of economy we have prison labour for any amount of rough work." Ibid., v2898, f19-8 part 1, Chas. W. McDonald to Hon. W.R. Motherwell, 18 April 1923.

54. Ibid., v2831, f1-12-11 part 1, 307801, W.R. Motherwell to Honorable C.M. Hamilton, 12 April 1926.

55. Ibid., v2898, f19-8 part 1, Chas. Horlton (secretary) to Regina Board of Trade, 10 December 1930.

J.J. Maloney:
How the West was Saved
from Rome, Quebec,
and the Liberals

_____ Raymond J.A. Huel

The name John James Maloney still arouses mixed and passionate responses in Canada in general and western Canada in particular, although it has been over four decades since he excited audiences with his fiery oratory. Catholics have regarded Maloney as a shameless apostate who deceived the public with his incredible comments on their church and its doctrines. Militant Protestants, on the other hand, have viewed Maloney as an echo of the Reformation, warning them to be on their guard against Romish threats to cherished liberties and traditions. During his speaking tours Maloney was identified as "The Protestant Lecturer," "the Canadian Lecturer," "Ex-Cleric of the Church of Rome," or as an agent of the Ku Klux Klan. Maloney might be described as hot-tempered, unable to manage his affairs in a responsible manner, and predisposed to substituting fantasy for reality. He was a volatile but otherwise lovable individual who appeared to be suffering under the delusion that there was a sinister conspiracy against him and his work.

A captivating public speaker, Maloney derived optimum benefit from salesmanship and showmanship techniques. Furthermore, he incorporated contemporary regional moods and sentiments into his lectures to produce a more meaningful and effective presentation. He began his career in Ontario by denouncing the machinations of Catholicism before audiences whose upbringing had predisposed them to respond positively and emotionally to such declarations. Moving to the West, he found another receptive audience for his anti-Catholic animus as a result of long-standing controversies over the existence of separate schools.

Maloney also delivered an impressive indictment against eastern influences on western life and institutions. He demonstrated how the French Catholic, Quebec "bloc" in Parliament had used its influence to withhold provincial jurisdiction over natural resources and Crown lands, to impose separate schools and French language instruction on the West, and to prevent the status of these schools from being altered by provincial legislatures. He showed how the Liberal party was only too happy to cater to the demands of Quebec. Maloney also struck a responsive chord when he denounced the unconstitutional use of the French language on the radio, in administrative circles, and on the labels of articles sold in the West. Maloney's more refined and secular version of the dialectic between the Dominion's purpose and the West's interests took the form of a plan to merge the western provinces into a single administrative unit. Then, and only then, could the West, a community of individuals sharing common occupations and interests, free itself of eastern domination and work out its own destiny.

Maloney simultaneously raised and represented some of the fundamental issues that have constituted Canadian communal life. He began his career in the 1920s with activities that contributed to the national debate concerning the extent of cultural dualism in Canada. At a more regional level, he tapped the fear that the Liberal government in Ottawa was attempting to create a second Quebec in the West contrary to the desires of the majority of the West's population, which was neither French-speaking nor Roman Catholic.

John James Maloney was born in Hamilton, Ontario, on 13 February 1895 or 1896. He attended St. Mary's Separate School and served as an altar boy prior to entering St. Jerome's College in Kitchener, where he devoted himself to "eight straight years of study and constant work" in preparation for the priesthood. While at St. Jerome's he registered for military service because he planned to enlist at the end of his studies in June 1918. He was granted an exemption but it was subsequently cancelled. Feeling that he had been "treated unfairly," Maloney went to Ottawa, where he met Wilfrid Laurier and "received some advice from him." Afterward, Maloney spoke to the Minister of Justice, C.H. Doherty, in his private office. Maloney surprised Doherty by saying that he had met his son, whose whereabouts was supposedly a closely guarded secret, at the Jesuit noviciate in Guelph. This disclosure had the desired effect; within five minutes Maloney received his exemption.

After graduating from St. Jerome's, Maloney went to the Grand

Séminaire in Montreal to complete his studies for the priesthood. He willingly accepted the life of a seminarian until he became ill during the flu epidemic of 1918 and was taken to l'Hôtel Dieu, where one of the sisters, a very pretty maiden, took a liking to him. Maloney quickly discovered "that the iron walls and cold gray walls of a Convent did not securely encase the ideas of popery." He then began to doubt his vocation, rejected the concept of clerical celibacy, left the seminary, and returned to his native city.[1]

In September 1919, Maloney became a subscription agent for the *Catholic Register* in the Hamilton area. Allegedly advised by the journal's editor, Father T. O'Donnell, that his expenses would be reimbursed, Maloney borrowed money from family and friends to continue his canvassing operations. When his financial situation became desperate, however, he retained some of the funds he had collected. In April 1921, Maloney was dismissed, and a short while later he initiated a civil suit against Father O'Donnell and the *Register,* contending that his dismissal had "injured his character and reputation." In the meantime, O'Donnell, on behalf of the *Register* and the Catholic Church Extension Society, laid a charge of theft against Maloney. Maloney pleaded not guilty, and suggested that the proceedings were motivated by his civil action against the clergyman. In his defence, Maloney declared that Archbishop McNeil of Toronto had asked him to investigate the *Register*'s editorial policy. Maloney claimed that many Catholics objected to the journal's Sinn Fein views and had earned O'Donnell's displeasure. Furthermore, Maloney declared, he had been threatened with arrest if he did not withdraw his action against O'Donnell. Maloney then "collapsed and fell forward against the railing crying out that he wanted only the justice of a British court."[2]

After the trial, Maloney went to Toronto where he "fell into irreligion." Wandering into Cooke's Presbyterian Church one day, he met Dr. William Patterson, who understood his state of mind and instructed him in the Bible. Maloney joined the congregation and was later asked to speak publicly on his conversion. Thus, on 20 August 1922, Maloney began his career as a Protestant lecturer by denouncing the errors of Romanism to a capacity audience in Cooke's Church. This debut was characterized by a style that Maloney would refine and embellish in the years to come. He began by castigating Father O'Donnell, not so much for the hardship he had caused Maloney, but for his unpatriotic attitude toward the British Empire. The Catholic church was described as a commercialized religion that ruled by fear and oppression. Maloney hinted that the hierarchy had placed spies in the audience and that attempts would be made to suppress and silence him but, he declared, he was not afraid of such tactics.

After this address, "the wheels of the Inquisition were set in motion" against him. Friends deserted him, his parents suffered, and Catholics boycotted him, but Maloney continued to enlighten Ontario against the popish conspiracy until December 1925.

His next effort was to campaign for the Conservatives in the federal election of 1925 because he felt that Quebec dictated the policies and actions of Prime Minister Mackenzie King. Maloney went to Saskatchewan in February 1926, where he campaigned against Mackenzie King in the Prince Albert constituency by-election. He claimed to be a Conservative from eastern Canada and did organizational work for the Independent Conservative candidate, saying that he wished to remain in Saskatchewan as a party organizer. Most of his activities, however, were directed toward Orangemen, who were most receptive to his message.[3]

From Saskatchewan, Maloney went to British Columbia. While in Victoria, he spoke at Orangemen's meetings and gave radio addresses. His return to the prairies in May 1927 coincided with the establishment of the Ku Klux Klan in Saskatchewan. Maloney subsequently became a prominent speaker at Klan rallies. As could be expected, his denunciation of various facets of the Catholic faith before Klan audiences was "punctuated with frequent outbursts of applause." A few days after the fiery cross was raised for the first time in Saskatoon, Maloney began a series of lectures in the old Knox Church. One of his addresses was broadcast over a local radio station. In this broadcast, Maloney quoted scripture to support his contention that confession and the dogmas of the Catholic faith were not necessary for salvation. He also affirmed that the Catholic religion was "man-made" and that it was detrimental to progress. Maloney then reiterated a challenge to a local parish priest to debate the merits of Catholic beliefs.[4]

As could be foreseen, some individuals took exception to Maloney's remarks. One such person was Gerald Dealtry, editor of *The Reporter,* a small Saskatoon weekly. In October 1927, he referred to Maloney as a fomenter of hatred, a disseminator of putrid propaganda, and a coward who had studied for the priesthood in order to avoid military service. An indignant Maloney responded by pressing three charges of defamatory libel against Dealtry. The case was heard on 24–25 January 1928, and the *Saskatoon Star* described the proceedings as "one of the greatest legal battles fought in the Saskatoon court house." Dealtry was found guilty and fined two hundred dollars.[5]

Maloney got away with many questionable tactics. Premier J.E. Brownlee of Alberta was informed by a Protestant pastor, the Reverend H.D. Ranns of Biggar, that Maloney was using Brownlee's name to give some respectability to his dubious activities, claiming that the premier and members of the Alberta cabinet had subscribed money to his campaign.[6] Brownlee then wrote to Premier J.G. Gardiner of Saskatchewan asking for information on Maloney, admitting that he had met Maloney some years ago "at the instance of certain friends" and had given him a donation "in a moment of weakness." Gardiner replied that Maloney claimed to be an ex-priest, delivered his lectures in a "capable" manner, and charged fifty cents' admission to his meetings. According to Gardiner, Maloney would use the name of any individual or organization to create the impression that he had their encouragement and support.[7]

In the meantime, Premier Gardiner denounced the Klan and its activities on the floor of the Legislative Assembly. Two weeks later, at a public meeting in Regina attended by two thousand people, Klan organizer J.H. Hawkins declared that the Klan would no longer remain silent when it was attacked. Challenging Gardiner's statement that Maloney had registered in a Prince Albert hotel under an assumed name, Hawkins affirmed that "none knew the dangers which faced Mr. Maloney and others who went about the country rousing Protestants to do their duty." Hawkins related an incident in an Ontario hotel where acid had been added to Maloney's shaving water, burning his hands. Hawkins claimed that when Maloney discovered that no attack would be made on him in Prince Albert, he re-registered under his real name.[8]

A few weeks later, Maloney informed a Regina audience that a "pernicious effort" was being made to get rid of him. He declared that "letters galore" were being sent to Ontario asking whether he had stolen money or been involved with women. Turning to Gardiner's address, Maloney claimed that it had insulted every member of the Klan who was a Liberal. Furthermore, Maloney stated, he had received letters from "700 or 800" prominent Saskatchewan Liberals expressing regret for Gardiner's atttack on him.

In the days that followed, Maloney galvanized Saskatchewan audiences with his revelations. At Alsask, for example, he disclosed that eighty percent of the funds budgeted for orphanages in Saskatchewan went to Catholic institutions, while the Protestant orphanage at Indian Head received only a "miserable six hundred dollars." After citing other examples of the administration's preferential treatment of Catholics, Maloney concluded by affirming: "Perhaps this in part explains why Mr. Gardiner prefers a black shirt to a white robe." In Wilkie, Maloney spoke for almost four hours, charging the Catholic church with "commercializing the sentiment of the heart." He also stated that the Grey Nuns had "one hundred million more property wealth than the CPR." In Nokomis, he delivered "The Jesuit Lecture," in which he described how the Jesuits used trickery to place Wilfrid Laurier in power and how they had used the same techniques to defeat Arthur Meighen. In Kerrobert, he discussed Rome's stance on celibacy. He declared that nuns should not be isolated from the world and denied "the joys of motherhood." He went on to inform his audience that the Catholic church had 82,000 orphans and 62,000 nuns. Making a passionate plea on behalf of the nuns who were cut off from the world, he stated: "Oh Rome, let them come out! Let them give significance to the words 'Let your light so shine'." In Regina, he combined another volatile issue in his denunciation of insidious papal plots. He charged that the federal government was withholding jurisdiction over natural resources from the western provinces until Catholics could be promised the same type of separate schools as those in Quebec.

Despite the fact that Gardiner was not a Roman Catholic, Maloney had no difficulty in depicting him as a puppet of Rome and Quebec. Speaking in Biggar following Gardiner's visit the previous day, Maloney declared that when he began his crusade to enlighten Catholics he never imagined that the political leader "of a great party, mostly supported by Protestants" would become his outspoken opponent. Maloney claimed that Gardiner obtained his information from Catholic priests, the same vicious individuals who attempted to obstruct his own campaign. In Regina, Maloney quoted Gardiner as having declared that all good comes from Rome. Maloney solemnly stated that the premier was attempting to usurp Henry VIII's title as "Defender of the Faith." Needless to say, this declaration was followed by laughter and applause.[9]

The life of a dedicated Protestant lecturer, however, was not without its tribulations. While speaking at Meota, for example, Maloney was greeted with a shower of overripe eggs. As he left the platform, the meeting degenerated into a minor riot. According to *The Sentinel and Orange and Protestant Advocate*, a journal which gave widespread coverage to Maloney's activities, the local Catholic priest in Luseland deliberately tore one of Maloney's posters from the post office bulletin board. Furthermore, the proprietor of the local hotel, a Roman Catholic, refused to provide accommodation for Maloney and his secretary. During the meeting, a papist heckler intensified matters but "Maloney soon made the troublemaker look sick." According to *The Sentinel*, the heckler riposted with a "dirty oath" and Maloney, who "resented such cowardice ... jumped clear over the piano and made for the individual who suddenly disappeared." In Macklin, Maloney was denied the use of a community hall, in which he was scheduled to speak, after the parish priest started a petition. *The Sentinel* reported that the meeting was held in Evesham instead and that practically all of Macklin came to hear the lecturer. They were so indignant at what had transpired that, the following day, the Macklin hall was offered to Maloney free of charge. *The Sentinel* also disclosed a startling incident in this affair. Apparently the priest had threatened an individual in the district by declaring: "You brought Maloney here. I will get you. We have ways and means. I will get you."[10]

In addition to town meetings, Maloney also utilized the radio to reach a wider audience. In two lectures broadcast over station CHUC in Saskatoon in January 1928, Maloney slandered the Catholic church. The station's licence was held by the International Bible Students' Association, and when its director was made aware of the contents of the broadcast, he issued instructions that no more were to be aired. In the meantime, the International Bible Students' Association applied to have its broadcast licence renewed, but was refused on the grounds that their programs had contained "religious matter of a controversial nature." The Regina *Standard* hinted that the explanation was flimsy and said that there was "clearly a desire on the part of someone or some influential body to put a check on free speech." Maloney sent a telegram to Prime Minister King stating that petitions with 200,000 signatures were being circulated in Saskatchewan, a "province which is 80 percent Protestant," to protest the government's refusal to renew the licence. For good measure, Maloney informed King that he was bringing the matter to his attention on the "advice of the President of the Liberal Executive."[11] Maloney presented the petition at Klan meetings and some eighty copies circulated throughout the province. The issue was also taken up by various organizations and churches, not on behalf of the International Bible Students' Association, but to defend the principle that religious groups should be allowed to broadcast.

Another of Maloney's activities was as publisher of the *Western Freedman*, a weekly journal. In November 1927, Maloney announced that he had sold his paper to a syndicate of Regina businessmen. In his lectures, Maloney urged his listeners to subscribe to the *Freedman* and to buy shares in the Freedman Publishing Company, "which was to be incorporated in the near future." He also asked his audiences to canvass for subscribers and advertisers.[12] The 5 April 1928 issue listed Maloney as director, and claimed that the circulation of the journal was 12,000. The *Freedman* was "uncompromisingly opposed to the Roman Catholic Church as a system," but not to individual Catholics, and spoke out for

> God and Christianity, pure and undefiled; secondly for the Protestantism for which our fathers bled and died; and lastly for loyalty to our Sovereign Lord the King, for Canada and the whole Empire which it has pleased the Almighty to call our King to reign over.[13]

Maloney was convinced that Catholic domination would imperil the development and interests of Canada and the British Empire.

As a result of the politicization of the school and language issues by the Conservative party and the publicity generated by the Klan, 1929 was a banner year for Maloney. In anticipation of a provincial election that year, Maloney and the Klan introduced a significant modification in their propaganda. While they continued to denounce the conspiracies of Catholicism, they adopted a more pragmatic approach by emphasizing the relationship between Quebec, the Catholic Church, and the federal and Saskatchewan Liberal parties. This variation on a theme was evident in the lecture Maloney delivered in Biggar on 7 March, which was titled, "Is it true that the Roman Catholic Church runs the Liberal Party?" The editor of the Biggar *Independent* claimed that the topic and the large audience indicated that things were warming up and predicted that "as soon as official announcement is made of an election, the fireworks will begin in earnest."[14]

As events were to prove when the election was called, the editor's prediction was correct. Speaking before a large audience in Saskatoon, Maloney created a sensation when he affirmed that nuns were teaching in the Tramping Lake Public School and that in another school, Protestant children were being taught by a Catholic teacher in the basement of a Catholic church. A few days later in Purdue, Maloney contended that for two years the government had "utterly ignored" the protests of Protestants in districts where there were school problems, and that the Liberals were stating that they had resolved all such difficulties. Maloney concluded his address by stating that the Liberal party was being ruled by Quebec.[15] Klan and Conservative candidates reiterated and embellished these accusations.

Even after the defeat of Gardiner's government on 6 June, Maloney continued to expose the Quebec conspiracy. On 24 June, for example, he spoke in Moose Jaw and related how an individual from Lacadena had applied for a gasoline permit and had received bilingual forms. Maloney claimed that the French element in Saskatchewan was being given preference over the English despite the fact that there were twice as many Germans and Scandinavians. Maloney asserted that the Postmaster-General was a French Canadian who hated everything British. In a three-hour address in Regina in February 1930, Maloney exposed the political propaganda and teachings of the Catholic church. Citing a recent pastoral letter written by Bishop J.-H. Prud'homme of Prince Albert dealing with the status of Catholic teaching orders, Maloney claimed that it was an attempt to overthrow Premier J.T.M. Anderson's Saskatchewan Co-operative government. Maloney asserted that seventy-five percent of priests in Saskatchewan were "foreign born" and, hence, did not understand the "principles of British liberty." Maloney also revealed that, as a seminarian in 1918, he had been told by a French priest that plans were being prepared to make Saskatchewan a second Quebec.[16] When Armand Lavergne, a prominent Quebec M.P. and nationalist, resigned from the Quebec Conservative Association when that body refused to censure the Co-operative government's proposed educational policy, Maloney, on behalf of the Western English Language League, sent a telegram to the party's national executive in Ottawa. He congratulated the Conservatives on Lavergne's "accidental departure" from their ranks and described him as a traitor and firebrand "whose only object was the disruption of the Empire."[17]

In late 1929, there were rumors that Maloney would enter federal politics and contest the Rosetown constituency as an independent candidate. In May 1930, Maloney was in Ottawa conferring with officials of the Conservative party and seeking financial aid for his campaign to run against Mackenzie King in Prince Albert. Maloney argued that the local Conservative candidate, John Diefenbaker, had run three times and lost three times. According to Maloney, Diefenbaker would not run again and had a lesser chance of winning than himself. The Prince Albert Conservative Association was surprised by this news because Maloney's candidacy had never been discussed. Diefenbaker was not aware that Maloney sought the nomination.[18]

It was obvious that Maloney was becoming disenchanted with events in Saskatchewan. He believed that he had played a crucial role in defeating the Gardiner administration. He had anticipated a reward for his services and when this failed to materialize, he became very bitter. Maloney later wrote that he had risked everything for a sacred cause but the Anderson government forgot him when it came to power: "In their pride and conceit they wanted to believe they did it all."[19]

Since the papist menace had been checked in Saskatchewan and his presence was no longer required, Maloney looked to Alberta as the land of opportunity. He spoke in the Vermilion district and then went to Vulcan, where he was arrested by the R.C.M.P. for violating customs regulations. After visiting the Hanna area, he arrived in Calgary to begin a five-month crusade in the fall of 1930. He transferred the *Freedman* from Saskatchewan to Alberta and changed its name to the *Liberator*. The climax of his Alberta sojourn, however, occurred between 6 September to 25 December 1931 when he spoke in Edmonton, which he ominously described as the "Rome of the West." During this interval, Maloney claimed to have sounded the clarion call to 100,000 sleepy Protestants, speaking three times on some evenings. Consequently, many Catholics left their churches, while Protestant ones were better attended. The Klan was inaugurated and "over 700 boys and girls were saved from the dangers of mixed marriages."[20]

According to Maloney, Edmonton had 165 Roman Catholic properties, and was "the strongest Roman Catholic centre for its size outside of Quebec." In addition, he argued that the huge untaxed estates of the church were throwing the burden of municipal taxation on the little homes of the "poor struggling workingmen." To support his contention, Maloney cited the example of a fire that had devastated a Catholic building. Firemen had worked for many hours to extinguish the blaze but no taxes were forthcoming from that property to pay for such services. Attacking city politics, Maloney charged that no one could be elected alderman without the approval of the Catholic hierarchy. More significantly, northern Alberta, which was under Catholic domination, looked to the "Rome of the West" for direction. The Catholic leader was Archbishop H.J. O'Leary, "whose personality, brain power and acts of finesse are unquestioned" by the citizens of Edmonton.[21]

In the 1931 civic elections in Edmonton, Maloney's favorite target was Mayor Jim Douglas. In the pages of the *Liberator,* Douglas, "the son of a Protestant minister," was depicted as a puppet of Rome because, for example, he had attended a Catholic banquet at the Macdonald Hotel and had not objected to remarks that Columbus Day should be a national holiday. On the day that the Masonic Temple was opened in Edmonton, the mayor left the city to attend a Catholic function at Wainwright and appointed a Catholic alderman to replace him at the ceremonies.

On the day before the civic election, Maloney ran a special issue of the *Liberator* that recounted the mayor's faults. The newspaper also contained a unique interpretation of the origins of "O Canada," claiming that it had been written by "a French Canadian Jesuit priest some time prior to 1834" and that it had been sung by French-Canadian rebels in 1837. After exposing these facts, the *Liberator* concluded that it was

> easy to understand why our federal government is predominantly French Canadian; why the agitation to destroy our Union Jack and replace it with the Tricolor and Fleur-de-Lis of France; why the French language is a compulsory subject in our schools and why the English language is a forbidden subject in French Canadian schools in Quebec.[22]

Joseph A. Clark, an Edmonton barrister, commented on Maloney's tactics in a letter to Senator G.P. Graham of Brockville, Ontario. He began by stating that Maloney came to Alberta because the Saskatchewan Conservatives had no use for him. Prior to arriving in Edmonton, Maloney had gone to the Crowsnest Pass but had starved there; he had received little attention in Lethbridge, whereas Calgary

was "too Tory and too Orange." Clark affirmed that Maloney's activities in Edmonton were "a shame and a disgrace." Maloney had
rented the Memorial Hall and large audiences turned out to hear his
attacks on Mayor Douglas. According to Clark, "the most brazenly
manufactured bunk...was fed audiences of 1,000 or more, 75% of
them women." On the last two nights before the municipal election,
Maloney had three or four women in the audience read a set of questions to the mayor. Clark described the questions as "so foreign to
politics and so ignorantly insulting that if it had been a man who was
reading the filth, he would have [had] his block torn off."[23]

In addition to this involvement in Edmonton municipal politics,
Maloney also organized the Ku Klux Klan in Alberta, to which he
attributed Mayor Douglas's defeat. On 7 September 1932, Maloney
signed an application to incorporate "The Invisible Empire Knights
and Ladies of the Ku Klux Klan, Realm of Alberta." On 16 September,
fifteen pages of constitution and by-laws were submitted and Maloney
again signed the application. The objects of the Klan were:

> To inculcate principles of Protestantism, Racial Purity, Gentile
> Economic Freedom, Just Laws and Liberty, Separation of Church
> and State, Pure Patriotism, Restrictive and Selective Immigration,
> Freedom of Speech, Press and Radio, Law and Order, Higher
> Moral Standard, Freedom from Mob Violence, One National
> Public School and One Flag, the Union Jack; One Language, the
> English Language.[24]

The organization of the Klan marked the apex of Maloney's accomplishments in Alberta. Soon afterward, although he remained a public
figure, fortune no longer favored him. Early in January 1933, H.A.
Mackie, an Edmonton barrister, launched a $26,000 suit for injuries to
his character and reputation resulting from allegations Maloney had
made. A few days later, Maloney, in his capacity as Imperial Wizard of
the Alberta Klan, was arrested and charged with administering
seditious oaths to new members.

In late January, Maloney and two associates appeared in court
charged with conspiracy and theft of legal documents from the office
of an Edmonton barrister. The documents concerned a case that was
pending against Maloney. Testifying on his own behalf, Maloney
declared that the charges were a frame-up perpetrated by "Liberal

heelers." He also claimed that opposing interests were attempting to "make the Klan a political catalogue," while he had tried to keep the Klan neutral as well as Protestant. The judge, however, was not impressed with Maloney's passionate oratory. Referring to Maloney's associates as the "worst liars in the witness box I have ever heard," he added that the charges against Maloney were more serious because he was more intelligent than the others. The judge found Maloney guilty of conspiracy and sentenced him to serve one hour in jail and pay a hundred-dollar fine. On the theft charge, Maloney was given a one-year suspended sentence. His two associates were also found guilty and given suspended sentences. In handing down his decision, the judge stated that "the case reminded him of boys who go into the woods to play Indians."[25]

In the meantime, more serious charges arose out of an incident that occurred at the Mayfair Golf Club on 31 December 1932. After driving his auto into a snow-bank, Maloney broke into the club's tool-shed and, once inside, tried to light a fire with papers and blueprints. He had damaged his car while attempting to free it from the snow, and later submitted a claim to an insurance company alleging that the damage had been done by thieves who had stolen his vehicle. Maloney appeared in court on 26 January and surprised everyone by pleading guilty to submitting a false insurance claim. This time, he did not revert to the turbulent style that had characterized the conspiracy and theft trials, and his comments were barely audible. In addition, it was evident that his supporters had diminished considerably.

On 31 January 1933, Maloney appeared in court for sentencing on the Mayfair charges. He was in a "highly nervous state," his hands "trembled visibly," and he broke into tears. As the judge began speaking, Maloney interjected: "Please, please give me one more chance, just one more chance. I'll show the world what I can do. I was trapped. My parents are sick in Hamilton. Please give me a chance. I have Bright's disease." The judge adjourned the proceedings in order to investigate Maloney's allegations of a frame-up, but when questioned further, the accused could offer no additional evidence to substantiate his claim. When court reconvened, Maloney was sentenced to serve two months in jail, pay a hundred-dollar fine and fifteen dollars in damages. As Maloney was led away to the cells, seventeen Klanswomen were denied their request to shake hands with him through the bars. Fifty Klansmen came to the police station to see Maloney before his transfer to the Fort Saskatchewan penitentiary. On the afternoon Maloney was transferred, the Chief Constable was informed by two men that their mother had died earlier that day in Vancouver and that she had requested her body be sent to Edmonton and the funeral service be performed by Maloney. The men asked that Maloney begin his sentence after he had officiated at the services, but they were advised that this could not be done.[26]

Despite these manifestations of solidarity by Klan members, it was obvious that the relationship between Maloney and the Klan had deteriorated. In 1934, Maloney filed a statement of claim against the Klan seeking $3,926, allegedly owed him for salary, rent, and expenses. The Klan in turn pressed charges of theft against Maloney. According to testimony given at the trial, the Klan had given Maloney two bonds valued at two thousand dollars each. This money was to be left as security with a firm of publishers for the production of Maloney's book, *Darkness, Dawn and Daybreak,* yet the book had not been published and the bonds had not been returned to the Klan. The case was heard in the Supreme Court of Alberta in late March 1934, but the judge later declared a mistrial when Maloney's counsel, in addressing the jury, prejudiced his client when he mentioned that Maloney had been convicted previously and had served a jail sentence.[27]

The Crown did not present a particularly strong case. When the proceedings were resumed, a charge of conversion was substituted for the original charge of theft. On two separate occasions, Maloney failed to appear in court to answer to the charge, and a bench warrant was issued for his arrest. Maloney's lawyer produced a doctor's certificate stating that Maloney was in a Calgary hospital, having opened an old wound while cranking his auto. The judge responded by stating that if police had the warrant, they might be able to get to Maloney before he encountered more accidents.[28]

In his autobiography, Maloney asserted that his court cases in Edmonton were "pure frame-ups activated by forces whose wrath I had incurred through fighting for principle and right." He claimed that new evidence was surfacing but that he would not disclose it prematurely and allow his enemies to turn it to their advantage. Claiming that he had suffered personally as a result of the litigation, Maloney characteristically added: "But that's nothing; I knew what to expect when I entered Edmonton, the Rome of the West."[29]

Maloney claimed in a letter to Prime Minister Bennett that the events in Edmonton were caused by the Liberal machine, in retaliation for his part in Gardiner's defeat in Saskatchewan. Turning to more pressing matters, Maloney claimed to have brought in $100,000 at political meetings in Saskatchwan, and that he had paid out over $50,000 for hall rents, salaries, and other expenses. In addition, he had published a paper every two weeks at a cost of $7,000 an issue. Maloney estimated that he had lost $7,000 as a result of his efforts in Saskatchewan and that "friends" there had advised him to turn to Ottawa for help.[30] As could be expected, Bennett's secretary replied that the prime minister was ignorant of the issues raised in Maloney's letter and, furthermore, "Mr. Bennett has no knowledge by whom you were told to present your bill or to whom it was to be presented."[31]

In the meantime, Maloney continued his struggle against the forces destroying Canada. In 1933 he organized a petition protesting against the use of French, a "foreign language," over the radio. He commented later that ten thousand signatures had been collected and sent to Ottawa and that the petition had "caused a stir."[32] Maloney argued that the presence of the French language on items sold in western Canada was "the thin edge of the wedge." He appealed to Ontario manufacturers, who were apparently unacquainted with the true state of affairs in the West, to end this abuse: "Remember, the French are negligible out West and the people of many nations and bloods whose children were born on these Prairies and British Columbia want a united Canada through one language."[33] Commenting on developments in Saskatchewan, Maloney stated that the Anderson government could not overcome certain factors that were partial to Quebec. In desperation, Maloney exclaimed: "Quebec! Quebec! Quebec! One would think that at least in B.C. one could not appoint a Provincial Mosquito Inspector without finding out how Quebec feels." Maloney also asserted that Quebec feared the West after Saskatchewan put Bennett in power, and promised to discuss this point in a forthcoming book on the proposed union of the three prairie provinces.[34]

During this period, Maloney's autobiography, *Darkness, Dawn and Daybreak,* was published. A short volume of forty pages, it recounted the highlights of his career. An advertisement in the book indicated that a second volume would be available for $2.25. This second volume was to include a chapter on mixed marriages, convents and their abuses, and the role of the Orange order in the natural resources issue in Alberta. It would also include a lengthy discussion of a new political structure for western Canada.

While the second volume of *Darkness, Dawn and Daybreak* was never published, some time later, probably in 1935, Maloney's *Rome in Canada* was released by Columbia Protestant Publishers in Vancouver. The foreword stated that because Canada "was the strongest and fastest growing Roman Catholic country in the world" and probably was one of the few countries that would receive the pope, Canadians had to know something about that religion. *Rome in Canada*, a 168-page book, contains 48 chapters including: "Edmonton's Untaxed Acres," "Keep Your Eye on the Confessor," "Why the King of England Must be a Protestant," "Who are the Jesuits?" and "Is Rome a Religion?" Chapter 47, entitled "Autobiography of the Author," is a reproduction of *Darkness, Dawn and Daybreak*. Some of Maloney's revelations were astounding, for example, the concluding statement in "She was made a Bride of the Church": "Rome is a mystery. They have never answered the Roman Catholic woman at Dinsmore, Saskatchewan, who asked why there are no red-headed priests."[35]

Rome in Canada is punctuated with short excerpts from Maloney's speeches, some of which were composed after the fact for effect. For example, in a lecture in Cooke's Church on 22 August 1922, Maloney allegedly declared: "I am starting tonight on a career which will bring me many heartaches, disappointments, etc.; and I will be the target for frameups, even attacks will be made on my life." In a prophetic declaration before the 12 July celebrations at Brampton in 1925, Maloney stated: "Some day I will leave for the West and make my presence felt for this cause."[36]

In view of contemporary political disenchantment in western Canada, the most interesting chapter of *Rome in Canada* is the one dealing with the union of the three prairie provinces. Maloney claimed that Canadians were overgoverned and overtaxed, and his "sensible and practical solution" was to unite the three prairie provinces under one government. This administrative unit would be more efficient and stronger because it would represent individuals with common occupations and interests. Furthermore, union would reduce "the army of governmental parasites and their friends who rely on patronage." Maloney's plan called for the closure of the legislative buildings, official residences of the lieutenant-governors, in Regina and Edmonton, and the universities in Saskatchewan and Manitoba. Provincial jails would be closed as would one normal school in each province. Winnipeg would emerge as the capital of the larger western province, Edmonton would become the university city, the legislative buildings in Regina would be transformed into a training centre for the R.C.M.P., the university buildings in Saskatoon would house a central reformatory for the prairies, and one normal school in each province would be retained for wayward girls. Redistribution would create one provincial constituency for each existing federal one, thus reducing the total number of M.L.A.s from 173 to 55.

Maloney argued that union would not only result in important financial savings but it would also allow westerners to decide whether or not they wanted a dual school system, "for remember Westerners never yet have had a vote on this issue, and it is long overdue." He urged provincial governments to act quickly on the question of union before they became bankrupt, so that "the West can speak with a united voice in all matters of public concern."[37]

The precise nature of Maloney's activities after his departure from Edmonton in 1934 is unknown. He spent some time in British Columbia before returning to Alberta in 1938 as an anti-Social Credit campaigner. In May of that year, Maloney wrote J.A. MacKinnon, Liberal M.P. for West Edmonton, asking for information on the number of Catholics, Protestants, and Jews in the western provinces. Maloney also wanted to contact someone in authority concerning the forthcoming provincial election in Saskatchewan. He claimed to have been campaigning in that province against the Social Credit party and assured MacKinnon that Conservatives were going to vote Liberal rather than elect the C.C.F. or Social Credit. He urged MacKinnon to speak in Regina and Saskatoon and inform people that Social Credit was a "real fizzle."[38]

A few months later, Premier William Aberhart was informed by a supporter in Daysland that Maloney would be speaking on the radio and that his talk would be critical of Social Credit and Aberhart. The Premier received a letter from a correspondent in Saskatoon informing him that Maloney was making arrangements with others to go to Alberta. According to Aberhart's informant, Maloney was being paid by the Liberal and Conservative parties in Alberta with funds coming from Toronto and Ottawa, and his object was to bring about Aberhart's downfall.[39]

In this new facet of his career, Maloney had no difficulty in exposing the secular pope. In an editorial in the *Expositor*, a paper published in Calgary, Maloney charged that Aberhart was building up a corporate state. While Hitler lived in a palace high on a mountain, the premier resided "at the palatial MacDonald [sic] Hotel being conveyed wherever he wants to go in a high priced Buick car, and Mr. Aberhart proceeds further in the Nazi love of the spectacular by recently decking his chauffeur in an elaborate uniform." According to Maloney, Aberhart's legislation was an imitation of Hitler's policies and like the latter, the premier was attempting to silence the press, exterminate his enemies, and use "shock" troops. The real head of state in Alberta was the lieutenant-governor, but Aberhart closed his official residence before the Royal Visit "thus forcing our Sovereign to take the MacDonald, [sic] Aberhart's quasi residence."[40]

In August 1939, Maloney accepted a challenge issued by Norman Jacques, M.P. for Wetaskiwin, to debate the merits of Social Credit and orthodox monetary policy before an Edmonton audience in September. Maloney stated that after expenses were deducted, the proceeds should be given to the poor in order that they might obtain food, clothing, and shelter.[41] It is not known whether the debate took place. Maloney left Alberta shortly afterward.

The high point of Maloney's career and appeal had long passed. Subsequent developments confirmed his decline. In January 1940, Maloney was in Melville, Saskatchewan, where he created the impression that he had been sent there by R.B. Bennett to ensure the defeat of J.G. Gardiner, Minister of Agriculture, in the federal elections.[42] The following month a warrant was issued in Winnipeg for Maloney's arrest on a charge of false pretences. He was arrested in Delburne, Alberta, a short time later but the charges were dropped because of insufficient evidence.[43] In March 1941, Maloney was given a suspended sentence in magistrate's court in Kitchener, Ontario, on six charges of false pretences. He had been held in custody since 25 December 1940. The charges had been laid against him by Cornwall police in connection with the sale of a book attacking the Catholic church. He was also wanted in Cornwall for cashing a worthless cheque.[44]

An exhaustive search has not revealed any information on Maloney's subsequent activities and demise. He reportedly died at the end of World War II. Legend has it that his death occurred on Good Friday and that he called for a priest and reconciled himself with the church he so bitterly denounced during his lifetime.

As a Protestant lecturer, Maloney was neither unique nor

original. He imitated and improvised upon themes that were hallmarks of the anti-Catholic tradition and had been popularized by other notables. Maloney's forte was that he succeeded in linking these prejudices more intimately to contemporary concerns. At the political level, for example, there was a fear that federal politics were being dominated by Quebec. In western Canada, this suspicion was aggravated by the belief that Quebec, a geographically remote and, worse yet, a French-speaking and Catholic province, was using its influence in Ottawa to impose bilingualism and separate schools on the West, regardless of regional needs and aspirations. In this respect, Maloney reinforced the traditional suspicion of the West vis-à-vis the East.

Maloney's career is difficult to assess objectively. There is no doubt that he had a profound impact on his audiences and that he contributed significantly to the establishment of the Ku Klux Klan in Saskatchewan and Alberta. In *Rome in Canada,* Maloney described his vocation in the following terms: "I preached the doctrine of British connection as well as upholding Protestant principles. ... The work that I have done and am doing is only the same as that of Luther and Knox."[45] Despite this altruistic self-evaluation, it is clear that Maloney was an opportunist who was able to turn the issues of the day to his advantage and profit in a public forum. Maloney represents a particular form of militant Ontario Protestantism crusading for the supremacy of Anglo-Saxon norms and traditions in the West. Maloney's denunciations found a receptive audience in a West where people were convinced that they never had the opportunity to work out their own destiny, and that their legitimate needs and goals had been subordinated to the interests of eastern Canada.

Notes

1. J.J. Maloney, *Rome in Canada* [hereafter cited as *Rome*], (Vancouver: Columbia Protestant Publishers, 1935), pp. 130–38.

2. *The Sentinel and Orange Protestant Advocate* [hereafter cited as *The Sentinel*], 14 March 1922. This journal was the official organ of the Orange Lodge of Canada.

3. Archives of Saskatchewan [hereafter cited as A.S.], Papers of the Rt. Hon. J.G. Gardiner [hereafter cited as Gardiner Papers], Gardiner to Ranns, 15 February 1928, 12091.

4. *Morning Leader* (Regina), 5 October 1927; *Saskatoon Star*, 19 October 1927.

5. *Saskatoon Star*, 25 and 26 January 1928.

6. A.S., Gardiner Papers, Gardiner to Brownlee, 28 February 1928, 12149.

7. Ibid., Brownlee to Gardiner, 21 February 1928, 12146; Gardiner to Brownlee, 28 February 1928, 12144–45.

8. *Morning Leader*, 17 February 1928.

9. The newspaper file in the Gardiner Papers contains numerous reports on Maloney's activities as reported in the rural weekly press. The daily papers in urban centres also carried reports.

10. *The Sentinel*, 13 December 1928.

11. Public Achives of Canada [hereafter cited as P.A.C.], Marine Branch, RG42, vol. 493, file 209-32-101. Clipping from the Regina *Standard*, n.d.; Maloney to Mackenzie King, 15 March 1928.

12. A.S., Gardiner Papers, Fleishacker to Gardiner, 28 May 1928, 12227.

13. Ibid., *Western Freedman*, 5 April 1928, 12858.

14. *Independent* (Biggar), 7 March 1929. Clippings from this newspaper were provided by the Biggar Museum and Gallery.

15. *Daily Star* (Regina), 14 May 1929; 18 May 1929.

16. *Evening Times* (Moose Jaw), 24 June 1929; *Daily Star*, 8 February 1930.

17. P.A.C., Papers of the Rt. Hon. R.B. Bennett [hereafter cited as Bennett Papers], MG26 K, Maloney to Executive Liberal-Conservative Association, 27 January 1930, 19043.

18. *Leader-Post* (Regina), 14 May 1930.

19. *Rome*, p. 148.

20. Ibid., pp. 157–59.

21. Ibid., pp. 124, 157.

22. *The Liberator*, Extra Edition, n.d.

23. P.A.C., MG26 J, Papers of the Rt. Hon. W.L. Mackenzie King, Clark to Graham, 13 November 1931, 157292-293.

24. Registrar of Joint Stock Companies, Edmonton. Application for incorportion as a society, 17 September 1932.

25. *Edmonton Journal*, 25 September 1933.

26. Ibid., 26 January to 1 February 1933.

27. Ibid., 15 February 1934; 27 March 1934.

28. *Leader-Post,* 29 May 1934.

29. *Rome,* pp. 161, 165.

30. P.A.C., Bennett Papers, Maloney to Bennett, 12 October 1933, 351220–221.

31. Ibid., Millar to Maloney, 31 October 1933, 351222.

32. *Rome,* p. 164.

33. Ibid., p. 24

34. Ibid., pp. 152–53.

35. Ibid., p. 57.

36. Ibid., pp. 10, 31.

37. Ibid., pp. 126–29.

38. A.S., Gardiner Papers, Maloney to MacKinnon, 16 May 1938, 55820.

39. Provincial Museum and Archives of Alberta, Premier's Papers, Social Credit, 404(c), Rollesfson to Aberhart, 12 October 1938; Murcheson to Aberhart, 11 November 1938.

40. Glenbow-Alberta Institute, Circulars re: Social Credit, 1936–38, RB4 M165 f3, *Macleod Gazette.*

41. *Edmonton Journal,* 17 August 1939.

42. A.S., Gardiner Papers, Stevenson to Gardiner, 19 January 1940, 44543.

43. A. Appleblatt, "J.J. Maloney and the Ku Klux Klan," *The Chelsea Journal* (Jan.-Feb. 1976), p. 48.

44. *Edmonton Journal,* 24 March 1941.

45. *Rome,* p. 159.

C.A. Dunning, 1916–30:
The Rise and Fall of a
Western Agrarian Liberal

_____J. William Brennan

The western political career of Charles Dunning ought to interest historians of western Canada for at least two reasons. He was, as David Smith has recently noted, one of those agrarian leaders trained and tested by the Grain Growers' organizations during the first two decades of the twentieth century "whose later contribution to regional and national politics proved exceptional."[1] Among his contemporaries, however, Dunning was among the few who remained loyal to the Liberal party at a time when thousands of prairie farmers and many of their leaders, notably T.A. Crerar, were abandoning the old parties for a new political organization of their own creation.

Dunning's career also merits attention because he was one of the many distinguished politicians from the West who sought the larger stage at Ottawa and became a spokesman for the western region's interests in the federal cabinet. His entrance into federal politics was certainly deemed to have great significance at the time. His political success as Premier of Saskatchewan made him in some Liberal eyes the heir apparent to Mackenzie King. Western farmers saw him no less as a savior. "There is no greater need in the cabinet," the *Grain Growers' Guide* declared at the time of Dunning's appointment as Minister of Railways and Canals, "than a real fighting western minister who will be able to convince the powers that be that the prairie provinces are a part of Confederation, and entitled to be treated as such." Mackenzie King's official biographer has concluded that Dunning was never more than a pretender to the throne, if that,[2] but this should not preclude a fuller examination of the accomplishments of this "real fighting western minister" who sat in the House of Commons as the M.P. for Regina from 1926 to 1930.

Little is known of Dunning's early life. He came to Canada from Great Britain in 1902 as a lad of seventeen with hardly any formal education, little money, and poor health. He had not even the practical knowledge of agriculture so often held to be a necessary preparation for settling on the Canadian prairies. Dunning managed to find work on a farm near Yorkton at ten dollars per month. With a year's experience, and his health restored, he filed for a homestead of his own near Beaverdale, not far from Yorkton, and sent for his family to join him. In partnership with his father, who had worked for the railway in Britain, Dunning set out to make a success of farming on the prairies.

Within a few years, Dunning joined the Saskatchewan Grain Growers' Association, and it was through this farmers' organization that he rose to public prominence, first as a district director and then as vice-president. A much more significant milestone in Dunning's career, however, was his appointment as general manager of the Saskatchewan Co-operative Elevator Company. This farmer-owned grain concern, incorporated by provincial statute in 1911, was empowered to construct or purchase elevators at local shipping points; and the Saskatchewan government advanced 85 percent of the cost. Dunning played a major role in the preliminary organization of the new firm, and was elected secretary-treasurer at the company's first general meeting in July 1911. His ability was further recognized when, at a subsequent meeting of the directors, he was appointed general manager.[3]

Although Dunning lacked any practical training in the new business (he was later to remark that "when I went to the Winnipeg Grain Exchange I was looked on as the green kid from the farm and laughed at"), the board of directors' confidence in him was amply justified. Starting with only 46 elevators in 1911–12, the company's network grew to 137 elevators in the second year of operation, 192 in the third, and 215 in the fourth. By 1916 the company boasted 230 country elevators ready for operation, and construction of its first terminal at the Lakehead was nearing completion. Similarly, the volume of business grew from 3,250,000 bushels in the first year to 28,000,000 bushels in the fifth. The number of shareholders also rose dramatically, from 8,000 in 1911 to more than 18,000 in 1916. The story of the company's success during its first five years of operation was the story of Dunning's success as general manager. Nowhere was this more apparent than in the last balance sheet he presented to the shareholders, one that showed a record profit of more than $757,000 on the company's operations during the 1915–16 crop year.[4]

Dunning's business ability early brought him to the attention of both the Saskatchewan and federal governments. In 1913 Dunning accepted a provincial invitation to serve on a royal commission appointed to investigate the related problems of cheaper agricultural credit and higher prices for Saskatchewan's staple crop. Three years later, the federal government offered him a directorship on the board of the Grand Trunk Pacific Railway. Parliament had authorized a loan of $8,000,000 to the foundering line, and the government was anxious to secure "public spirited and representative citizens of high standing in Canadian affairs" to represent it on the board. Dunning declined the honor, pleading that the pressure of his duties as general manager of the Saskatchewan "Co-op"[5] prohibited his participation.

Dunning did not, however, refuse an offer to enter the provincial government made some months later. He assumed the portfolio of Provincial Treasurer, and for the next ten years this "successful farmer and ... successful businessman"[6] applied his considerable talents to the administration of Saskatchewan's finances. Dunning was the third prominent Grain Grower to enter the cabinet, joining W. R. Motherwell and George Langley as spokesmen for farmers in the councils of the government. An interlocking of personnel between the leadership of the Saskatchewan Grain Growers' association (S.G.G.A.) and the leadership of the government at Regina had long been a feature of Saskatchewan politics, and over the years it had proven to be a mutually beneficial arrangement. The presence of prominent Grain Growers in the cabinet had assured Saskatchewan farmers of a sympathetic consideration of their wishes. Resolutions adopted at annual S.G.G.A. conventions quickly found their way into the statute books of the province, and government policies generally followed the lines advocated by the organized farmers. For the Liberals, the arrangement had been equally beneficial, assuring as it did the continued support of rural voters.

Prior to 1916, Dunning does not seem to have been an active member of any political party, or even to have taken much interest in politics, save for his involvement in the Saskatchewan Direct Legislation League. As a Grain Grower, Dunning nevertheless professed to find the Liberal party more to his liking than the Conservative party.

"The great distinction between real Liberalism and real Conservatism in this Dominion," he declared to readers of the *Grain Growers' Guide* in 1916,

> lies principally in the attitude of each toward the fiscal or trade policy of the Dominion. I have felt for many years that the true Liberal attitude toward this question was not being taken by the Liberal party in the Dominion.
>
> In the West, the grain growers' movement has been the greatest fighting agency against the Protective Tariff and I believe that from the West, with its increased representation, it is possible to develop such a force for true Liberalism as will affect the whole of the party, and so render easy reform, which, without that influence developed in that way, would be impossible.[7]

Dunning's open identification with liberalism came at a time when prairie farmers were showing a new impatience with both of the national parties. In Saskatchewan, a new party, the Nonpartisan League, appeared in 1916 appealing to farmers as a class to take the reins of government into their own hands. Liberals did not take the new party lightly, and on the eve of the 1917 provincial election stole one of the League's most attractive planks by inaugurating a scheme of low-cost agricultural credit. In their country meetings, the Liberals laid great stress on the fact that theirs had been a "farmers' government" in all but name, and pointed to the presence of Motherwell, Langley, and now Dunning as proof. Only one Nonpartisan candidate was elected, by acclamation (having received the endorsement of all three parties), but he left the League within a few months and sat in the Legislature as a Liberal.[8]

The Nonpartisan League soon disappeared, but the farmers' enthusiasm for independent political action grew more intense with the collapse of wheat prices after the war. Farmers' governments came to power in Alberta and Manitoba, but not in Saskatchewan. In that province the government remained solidly Liberal, though the political militancy of Saskatchewan farmers was to challenge all the ingenuity and resourcefulness of Premier W. M. Martin and his successor, Charles Dunning.

The Liberals early recognized that political survival could only be assured by playing down all ties with the federal wing of the party and showing an even greater solicitude for the wishes of the organized farmers. Martin publicly severed the link with the federal Liberal party in a speech at Preeceville in May 1920, and Dunning made the rounds of farmers' picnics and the annual S.G.G.A. conventions, stressing his past involvement in the farmers' organization and urging that there was no need to upset a Liberal government of farmers simply to put in a "farmers' government."[9]

Martin was determined to leave nothing to chance, and in 1921 he persuaded J.A. Maharg to join the cabinet as Minister of Agriculture. Maharg had served as president of the Saskatchewan Grain Growers' Association and the Saskatchewan Co-operative Elevator Company since 1911, and had taken a leading role in the formation of the new Progressive party. One of three supporters of the "Farmers' Platform" elected to Parliament from Saskatchewan as Unionist candidates in 1917, Maharg was one of the first to join T. A. Crerar on the cross-benches after the latter's celebrated resignation from the Union government. It was a bold stroke, intended to demonstrate the Liberals' sympathy for the views of organized agriculture, and it enabled Martin to avoid defeat in the provincial election of June 1921.

From this point onward, Martin's political position steadily deteriorated as the close relationship between his government and the organized farmers began to disintegrate. Ever since the premier's Preeceville speech in May 1920, the farmers had assumed (incorrectly as it turned out) that at the time of the next federal election they would have nothing to fear from W. M. Martin or his government. To be sure, the premier no longer held any official responsibility for federal party matters, but Ottawa and Regina Liberals continued to co-operate through the National Liberal Organization Committee, a body that counted among its Saskatchewan members such party stalwarts as W. R. Motherwell and a young M.L.A., J.G. Gardiner, who was rapidly rising to a place of influence in party ranks.

In January, months before it was known there would be a federal election in 1921, the Saskatchewan executive of the National Liberal Organization Committee began to consider the possibility of reaching an understanding with the Progressives in order to avoid a three-cornered contest in the province. The appropriate overtures were made, but were rebuffed. Premier Martin took no part in these negotiations, of course, but he, too, was anxious to see the Liberals and Progressives work together, particularly in his own home riding of

Regina. Martin made a trip to the East early in September, after the Meighen government had made up its mind to go to the country, and left at least one Ottawa Liberal in no doubt as to what his intentions were:

> I am satisfied that Martin is most anxious and willing to do all he can to further our cause, but of course he must act discreetly. He is not without hope that with a little tact, he might send from his Province four to six supporters, some will win their seats by election, and others, he hopes to arrange by a saw off with the Farmers.[10]

Even this proved impossible to arrange, for, in September, the Saskatchewan executive of the National Liberal Organization Committee defiantly published its earlier correspondence with the Progressives and declared that "the flag of Liberalism" would not be hauled down in that province. Nevertheless, Martin and Dunning continued to work quietly behind the scenes, attempting to make a bargain with the new farmers' party whereby they would throw their weight behind the Progressives elsewhere in the province if W.R. Motherwell was not opposed in Regina. T.A. Crerar was agreeable, but the local Progressive organization in Regina would have nothing to do with it and proceeded to put up a candidate there.

Co-operation with the Progressives had proven fruitless, even in Regina. Little now appeared to be lost by taking the offensive, and in the last weeks of the campaign the provincial Liberal organization was quietly thrown into the fight in every constituency where the Liberals were thought to have a chance of success. Martin and Dunning campaigned for W.R. Motherwell, and the premier publicly called for the election of a Liberal government a week before polling day. This precipitated Maharg's resignation from the provincial cabinet and drew the S.G.G.A. into provincial politics.

Martin's sudden and, from the farmers' point of view, unexpected attack on the Progressive party made political sense only if it limited the farmers' electoral success in Saskatchewan and if he was prepared to accept the consequences. The Progressives virtually swept the province, taking fifteen of the sixteen seats, with W.R. Motherwell the only Liberal returned in Saskatchewan and one of only two elected anywhere on the prairies.[11] Martin realized that he had lost the support of the farmers, and the Liberals moved quickly to repair the damage resulting from his renewed embrace of the federal party. To replace Martin, who retired to the bench, the Liberals chose Charles Dunning, confident that he alone could stem the rising tide of agrarian unrest that threatened to sweep them away.

Dunning met the threat from the farmers' political movement head on, denying that he was out to fight the Grain Growers and pointing to his own record of service in the agricultural community. His former prominent association with the organized farmers served him well. Dunning, the former Grain Grower leader, could attack the farmers' political movement without appearing to criticize its foster parent, the S.G.G.A. It was not simply fear of schism and a weakening of the farmers' organization that prompted Dunning to act as he did, of course, but also a desire, as a good party man, to keep the Liberal ship afloat in heavy seas. Political necessity dictated that the new premier again put some distance between himself and the federal Liberals in order to mollify the Grain Growers, and by words and deeds Dunning sought to demonstrate after 1922 that his government had the farmers' best interests at heart. When Saskatchewan voters again went to the polls in 1925, the farmers failed to dislodge the Liberals from power.[12] It was not, however, Dunning's adroit political manoeuvring alone that saved Saskatchewan Liberals from the fate that befell their Alberta and Manitoba counterparts. Changes in the nature, leadership, and philosophical underpinnings of the farmers' movement in Saskatchewan during the 1920s were also important.

It was no accident that the farmers' entrance into provincial politics was so hesitant in Saskatchewan. The close association between the government and the Grain Growers had served to enhance the reputations of a group of men who came to dominate the highest echelons of organized agriculture in Saskatchewan, and they, no less than the Liberals, were determined to preserve it for their own benefit. These farm leaders—J.A. Maharg, J.B. Musselman, A.G. Hawkes, Thomas Sales, John Evans and H.C. Fleming—had found a power base in the Saskatchewan Co-operative Elevator Company. Its phenomenal success (due in no small degree to the solid financial support provided by the Liberal government at Regina) ensured that their views would carry great weight within the ranks of the farm movement in Saskatchewan. By 1919, Maharg and his cohorts occupied six of the nine seats on the board of the 21,000-member Saskatchewan

252 / J. William Brennan

Co-op. All but one were also members of the executive of the S.G.G.A., whose 36,000 members made it the largest and most representative organization in the province.[13] The Grain Growers controlled the political destinies of Saskatchewan, and it was this "interlocking directorate," firmly entrenched in power, that controlled the farmers' organization.

In 1920 and 1921 this small group of men, and particularly Maharg and Musselman, managed to thwart all efforts to commit the S.G.G.A. to provincial political action. Not until after the 1921 federal election, and Premier Martin's full and open endorsement of the federal Liberal party, was the entrenched leadership of the S.G.G.A. finally compelled to take the farmers' organization into provincial politics. After 1922, however, Maharg, Musselman, and their associates found themselves increasingly on the defensive within their own organization. Maharg had already incurred the wrath of those rank and file members of the S.G.G.A. who objected to the close liaison in personnel and views between the Grain Growers' executive and the Liberals, and wished to see a true "farmers' government" in Regina.[14] Antagonism toward the practice of holding multiple offices grew more widespread as time passed. The 1922 farmers' convention provided an ominous portent of the years of feuding that lay ahead.

A.J. McPhail, a Ladstock farmer who was to play an increasingly prominent role in the S.G.G.A., introduced an amendment to the constitution providing that "no one having held the office of President or Vice-President for four consecutive years immediately preceding shall be eligible for re-election." It was defeated by a large majority, but another motion barring members of the federal or provincial government from office in the association nearly carried. More dramatic was the defeat of A.G. Hawkes in his ninth bid for re-election to the vice-presidency of the S.G.G.A. In his place, the delegates chose George F. Edwards, another rising star in the farmers' movement, who, by his own admission, had agreed to run chiefly because he "felt it would be necessary to get rid of the sinister influence exercised by J.B. Musselman.... [15] Musselman soon abandoned his post as secretary of the S.G.G.A. for a safer haven in the Saskatchewan Co-operative Elevator Company.[16] He was succeeded by A.J. McPhail, one of those most strongly opposed to the practice of holding multiple offices. The insurgents, or "Ginger Group" as they were popularly known, increasingly dominated the executive.

This internal struggle acquired a new dimension in 1923 with the inauguration of the Wheat Pool campaign, which eventually sounded the death-knell of the farmers' political movement in Saskatchewan. George Edwards, A.J. McPhail, and Violet McNaughton, the recognized leaders of the insurgent element within the S.G.G.A., had initially favored provincial political action, but they also became ardent champions of the Wheat Pool. They were caught in a dilemma. Their first goal, the creation of a provincial Progressive party, could only be realized by working with Maharg and the other Co-op men who remained on the Grain Growers' executive, most of whom were antagonistic toward the pooling concept. On the other hand, if Edwards, McPhail, and the others placed their influence firmly behind the Wheat Pool campaign, they would have to develop a close working relationship with the chief foe of the Grain Growers' political movement, Charles Dunning.

Faced with such a choice, the insurgents opted to devote their energies to dislodging Maharg from the S.G.G.A. executive and working with the provincial government to make the Wheat Pool a success. By 1924 the Ginger Group had triumphed. In January 1924, J.A. Maharg was defeated in his bid for re-election for a fourteenth term as president of the S.G.G.A., and the Grain Growers decided to leave the provincial political field. By the middle of June more than half of Saskatchewan's crop acreage was signed up to the five-year Wheat Pool contracts and the Saskatchewan Co-operative Wheat Producers Limited was formally organized. With the Ginger Group firmly in control of the S.G.G.A., the Dunning government no longer had anything to fear from that quarter.

With the emergence of the Farmers' Union of Canada (F.U.C.), the farmers' movement was no longer a single monolithic organization. Founded at Ituna, Saskatchewan, in December 1921, the F.U.C. modelled itself upon the One Big Union, adopting whole sections of the latter's constitution, and eschewed active participation in politics in favor of economic action. No one but an "actual dirt farmer" could join its ranks, which numbered 10,000 by 1923. Since the Farmers' Union considered political action futile and divisive, it offered no aid or comfort to the provincial Progressives, and instead directed all of its energies into the organization of the Wheat Pool.[17]

The provincial Progressive party in Saskatchewan was clearly hampered by the unwillingness of either the S.G.G.A. or the F.U.C. to support it at the critical time. Once the S.G.G.A. withdrew from politics, Dunning's appeal to an agrarian electorate ensured that the Liberals would win the 1925 provincial election with ease. With the Progressives no longer a threat, he could now seek to accomplish what Martin had tried and failed to do in 1921: reunite the federal and provincial wings of the Liberal party. Beyond that was to lie a post in Mackenzie King's cabinet and a career in federal politics.

Dunning's success in provincial politics had early marked him as a bright prospect for the larger stage at Ottawa. He was sympathetic to the demands of western farmers, and Liberals were quick to recognize that his presence in the federal cabinet would help to revive the political fortunes of the King government on the prairies. King began wooing Dunning in 1924 and, fresh from his triumph in the provincial election a year later, the Saskatchewan premier seemed on the verge of coming to Ottawa. Within a few days, however, Dunning began to waver, and on 22 August advised King from Regina:

> The unanimous feeling is that I could wield a great influence Federally, without impairing the solidarity of the Provincial party, by remaining here at the present time. The strong belief also exists that matters will probably develop in such a way as to leave me as Premier of Saskatchewan in a position to be a strong influence towards the unification of Liberalism, after the Federal election is over, especially if the results made it necessary for elected members of Liberal mind to stand together or, in the alternative, allow a Conservative minority to rule.[18]

Why had Dunning changed his mind? King apparently felt that Dunning wished to play it safe: if the Liberals did win the impending general election, he could still enter the cabinet, but if they lost he would still be Premier of Saskatchewan. In fact, Dunning had serious reservations about Liberal chances on the prairies, believing that without some reconciliation between Liberals and Progressives a large number of Conservatives would be returned in three-cornered contests.[19] Dunning may also have calculated that if the Liberals again fared badly at the polls, Mackenzie King's continued leadership of the party might be in jeopardy. In that case, Dunning would be ready and waiting in the wings.

His misgivings about the Liberals' prospects notwithstanding, Dunning had promised to lend his active assistance once the writs were issued. He was at King's side as the prime minister toured Saskatchewan, and he also spoke outside the province. Saskatchewan Liberals also assisted in the campaign in a more practical way, as Dunning threw the full force of his political machine behind Liberal candidates in the province. This, coupled with the appeal of King's promise to complete the Hudson Bay Railway, a project much favored in Saskatchewan, had the desired result. While the Liberals had carried only one of the province's sixteen seats in 1921, they won fifteen of twenty-one in 1925.

In other parts of Canada, the Liberals were not as fortunate. King and eight of his cabinet colleagues were defeated, and the Conservatives emerged from the election as the largest party in the House of Commons. Some Liberals seriously began to consider replacing him as leader, and Dunning seemed the logical successor. He was a politician with a winning reputation, a distinction Mackenzie King could hardly claim. With Dunning as leader, these disgruntled Liberals believed the party could win back the support it had lost in English Canada, especially in the West, and with solid support from Quebec virtually assured, again become the dominant party in the country.[20]

The Saskatchewan premier himself took no active part in the plot to unseat King. Shortly after the election, Dunning had apparently made up his mind to accept King's offer of a cabinet portfolio, and informed the prime minister that he would enter the government when he was called. It would have been awkward, not to say embarrassing, for him to have done so and at the same time be seeking to propel himself into the federal Liberal leadership at King's expense. Political usurper or not, Charles Dunning was the key to King's plans. King envisaged Dunning becoming the leader of a western Liberal bloc within the federal party, much as Ernest Lapointe served as King's chief lieutenant in Quebec. Senator Andrew Haydon went west in mid-November to convey King's views to the Saskatchewan premier. The plan was outlined to Dunning, who gave his approval. He would come to Ottawa after the Legislature had prorogued, and would take the portfolio of Railways and Canals because he felt he lacked the federal experience necessary for Minister of Finance.[21] Dunning resigned as premier late in February, and on 1 March became the third Saskatchewan representative in the federal cabinet, joining King and W.R. Motherwell. The immediate problem, to find a seat in Parliament, was swiftly resolved. Frank Darke obligingly resigned, opening a seat in Regina, where Dunning had resided since 1912, and the new minister entered the House of Commons unopposed.

With Dunning in the federal cabinet, the old comfortable relationship between Regina and Ottawa Liberals seemed firmly established again. The outward appearance of harmony was deceiving, however, for the party increasingly found itself troubled by a feud between Dunning and his successor as premier, J.G. Gardiner. It was perhaps inevitable that such an intense and sometimes bitter rivalry should have developed between these two men. Dunning had received most of the credit for the Liberals' success in Saskatchewan and by all accounts he was not one to share the limelight. His government was, in the opinion of one observer, "purely a one-man Government. Nobody counts in it but Dunning and privately I may say I do not think anybody will be allowed to count in it but Dunning as long as he is there." King had formed a similar impression of the Saskatchewan premier during the 1925 federal campaign. "He is a difficult sort of person to work with," King had noted in his diary, "being so self-centred, vain and self conscious.... Should be most helpful and efficient in a Govt. but inclined to boss the show." [22]

Gardiner naturally resented this. Since entering the provincial cabinet as Minister of Highways in 1922, he had demonstrated a considerable talent for political organization, and had ambitions to enter the federal field as well. "G[ardiner] would like to go to Ottawa," Andrew Haydon had reported to King in November 1925,

> but prefers Saskatchewan and yet if he were in the Federal field bossing the organization of the three Provinces he would be happy. He talked to me privately. He thinks D[unning] is pretty ambitious—that he seeks to be Premier—that it is wrong to ask him to be the only thing on the Prairies—not that G. will not follow him, but that if other Ministers are to come to Ottawa they come not because D. says so but because the Premier calls them. [23]

Disagreement over questions of party tactics, particularly as they related to the Progressives, further sharpened the rivalry between the Saskatchewan premier and his chief lieutenant. Dunning had adopted a rather flexible attitude. He had criticized the farmers for entering politics and had not been afraid to meet them head on in a provincial election, of course, but he had also been prepared in 1921 to seek an accommodation with the federal Progressives to avoid division among what Liberals so often referred to as the "low tariff forces." Gardiner's view was quite different. There was only one attitude to take toward the Progressives, he had written to Mackenzie King in 1924,

and that is to recognize in them the real opposition to your Government. If I had to make a choice tomorrow between voting and working for Progressive or Conservative candidates, I would have no hesitation in saying I would support the Conservative. We are in a position here now to clear the Progressive movement from this province and elect Liberals in practically every seat.... [24]

When the provincial Liberals threw their full support behind the King government in the 1925 federal election, Gardiner was able to put his theories into practice. The sweeping Liberal victory in Saskatchewan doubtless enhanced Gardiner's reputation as a skilful political organizer, but it also made him more than ever the *bête noire* of the Progressives.[25]

King had been anxious to see Gardiner come into the federal cabinet as well, so impressed was he with the latter's organizing abilities. Gardiner's unpopularity among the Progressives, however, whose support was vital to the beleaguered Liberals, created complications. By early February, King had been obliged to conclude that it would be unwise "at the present time" for both Saskatchewan men to come even if, as had been arranged, Gardiner was to take Motherwell's place in the cabinet. Naturally, Gardiner was not pleased.[26] His talents would have been an invaluable asset to the disorganized federal Liberals, but he did not have Dunning's appeal among western farmers. King needed the support of those farmers, and their political representatives in Parliament, if he hoped to remain in power. He had wanted both men, but Dunning was the key to King's plans in 1926.

Distance did not lessen the "unfortunate bitterness and cleavage," as King termed it, between Dunning and Gardiner. It complicated the selection of a successor to Dunning as party leader and premier. There were two serious aspirants: C.M. Hamilton, whom Dunning would have preferred, and Gardiner. The caucus opted for Gardiner, largely, it would seem, on account of his work as head of the party machine. Dunning's role in the whole affair continued to be a matter for speculation long after he had left for Ottawa. In some quarters it was alleged that Dunning had actively supported Hamilton's candidacy in opposition to Gardiner; others were of the opinion that, notwithstanding his well-known preference for Hamilton, Dunning had taken no active part in the selection of a successor.[27] Whether Dunning had interfered or not, Gardiner was certainly aware of his rival's ambition and of the need to protect his own position. This may well explain why Gardiner kept control over party organization in his own hands after he assumed the premiership when his predecessors had entrusted the work to others.

The government Dunning joined in March was out of office by the end of June, and the Customs scandal still hung over its head. The succeeding Conservative government was in turn defeated within a few days, and the nation plunged into another campaign for a general election. Liberal preparations for that contest revealed that Dunning and Gardiner remained poles apart in their attitudes toward the Progressives. Gardiner, of course, wished to fight them one and all, and was supported by a fellow partisan, W. R. Motherwell. Others, including Dunning and King, disagreed, believing that Liberals and Progressives "sh[ou]ld keep together on constit'l issue, and not permit the Customs matter to come to the fore as it w[ou]ld if they as well as tories began fighting us."[28] Co-operation was made more difficult in Saskatchewan by Progressive suspicions of Gardiner's uncompromising attitude, but eventually three-cornered contests were avoided in more than half the constituencies in Saskatchewan. While the Liberals publicly stressed the need for unity among the low-tariff forces in Saskatchewan, Gardiner concentrated on trying to defeat the three Progressives, M.N. Campbell, W. R. Fansher, and A.M. Carmichael, who had supported Meighen during the recent parliamentary session.[29]

Saskatchewan showed no great interest in either the constitutional issue or the Customs scandal. Local issues still dominated federal elections there, and the hustings once more resounded with well-worn arguments on the tariff, freight rates, and the Hudson Bay Railway. Again, as in 1925, the federal and provincial Liberal organizations worked as one. The continued recovery of Saskatchewan's farm economy also augured well for the Liberals. There had been a marked improvement in wheat prices and yields in 1925; the outlook for the agricultural machinery business, ever a reliable barometer of the state of the Saskatchewan economy, was said to be better than at any time since 1920, and newspapers were reporting the first signs of a renewed influx of immigrant farmers and farm laborers into the province. The result was a near total Liberal sweep in Saskatchewan: sixteen Liberals and one Liberal-Progressive were elected against only four Progressives. Dunning was re-elected in Regina, though his majority was less than half of what Darke had polled in 1925. The particularly good showing of their candidate in a straight two-way fight left Regina Conservatives elated; among Liberals Dunning's reduced majority was attributed to his unselfish contribution to the national campaign at the expense of his own.[30]

Mackenzie King's triumphant victory in 1926 put an end to the intrigues against him and dashed Dunning's hopes, however fanciful, of succeeding to the leadership of the Liberal party. King had no particular liking for Dunning as an individual but admired his administrative abilities, confiding to his diary on one occasion that he found Dunning to be "head and shoulders over the other ministers."[31] In the new cabinet, which was sworn in ten days after the election, Dunning again assumed the portfolio of Railways and Canals, joining King and W. R. Motherwell once more as federal ministers from Saskatchewan.

Dunning was the first westerner to hold the Railways and Canals portfolio. Clearly, his most significant accomplishment for western Canada was his resolution of the long-standing controversy over the Hudson Bay Railway. Prairie farmers had long desired a direct rail link with Hudson Bay, and construction of the line had commenced in 1908. By 1917, when the work was stopped on account of World War I, 332 miles of track had been laid and the grading completed to within 92 miles of Port Nelson on Hudson Bay. There the line stood, and although prairie farmers took up the cry for its completion in 1919, it drew no closer to Port Nelson. Politicians from Ontario, Quebec, and the Maritimes showed no interest in the scheme; indeed, many were vehemently opposed to it, and the wisdom of selecting Port Nelson as the terminus of the line was questioned in Parliament and the press. Alberta farmers' enthusiasm began to cool as well, for the completion of the Panama Canal opened a new and cheaper route to British markets for their grain. Manitoba and Saskatchewan farmers and businessmen remained enthusiastic boosters of the Hudson Bay Railway, however, and in 1924 organized an On-to-the-Bay Association to lobby more effectively for the completion of the line.[32]

Proponents of the Bay route were encouraged by Dunning's appointment as Minister of Railways and Canals, since he supposedly favored the scheme. Their confidence began to waver, though, when he announced in November 1926 that the government would engage an impartial expert to examine the relative merits of Port Nelson and Churchill as the terminus of the still unfinished line. The President of the On-to-the-Bay Association declared that there could be no possible excuse for such a change, unless it were to appease foes of the scheme. The Saskatchewan Legislature could see no reason for any further delay either, and demanded that "construction of the Hudson Bay Railway ... be carried on without interruption so that the line may be completed to Nelson, and work ... commenced on the Port terminals during 1927." [33]

The expert Dunning engaged for the task was Sir Frederick Palmer, a consulting engineer employed by the British government and the ports of Glasgow and London. Palmer visited the two sites in July 1927, accompanied by Dunning and several senior departmental officials, and pronounced himself in favor of Churchill, largely on the strength of its fine natural harbor. Commissioning Palmer, though regarded with suspicion at the time, proved to be a bold stroke. Palmer's definitive report cleared the air; even the On-to-the-Bay Association readily concurred with his recommendations. Construction of the additional 150 miles of track necessitated by the change began almost at once, and Dunning's courage in abandoning Port Nelson and choosing Churchill strengthened his stature in the West. [34]

On all fronts, the political prospects seemed entirely favorable for the federal Liberals, and no more so than on the prairies, basking again in the warm glow of prosperity. Immigrants were again streaming to the West, the result in large measure of the relaxation of the federal government's immigration regulations, and especially the so-called Railways Agreement of 1925. The Canadian Pacific and Canadian National Railways were building new lines, particularly in central and northern Alberta and Saskatchewan. Prairie farmers were harvesting record crops and receiving good prices.

Dunning's urban constituents felt the effect of bumper crops and higher prices, too. There was a dramatic resurgence in construction activity in Regina, symbolized by the erection of a new Canadian Pacific hotel opposite Victoria Park. The prairie city was the nation's leading distribution point for farm implements, and its population jumped from 37,329 in 1926 to 53,209 in 1931. Regina was becoming more than just a market centre for the surrounding agricultural community; during the late 1920s it also began to develop a wider industrial base. Among the new industries established, none drew more attention, or more civic pride, than the General Motors assembly plant, which began turning out 150 Chevrolet cars a week in December 1928.[35]

The good times did not restore harmony within the ranks of liberalism in Saskatchewan. In the months following Gardiner's elevation to the premiership, rumors began to circulate that he was "carrying on a knifing campaign against Dunning, both at Ottawa and in Regina," with the knowledge and support of Mackenzie King and the Saskatchewan organization.[36] Evidence of a vendetta or purge is difficult to find, but it is clear that there were a number of irritants that continued to trouble relations between Dunning and Gardiner after 1926. One arose out of their differing attitudes toward a syndicate of Regina businessmen, headed by George M. Bell. Bell and his associates had extensive newspaper interests in the province, including the four Regina and Saskatoon dailies, and Bell's insurance firm enjoyed a monopoly of the government's business. Bell was apparently not above using his newspapers to further his business interests and attempted to make deals with the government at Regina.[37]

In 1922, shortly after his appointment to the Highways portfolio, Gardiner had been approached by Bell's syndicate with the request that the company be guaranteed a sizeable percentage of culvert sales to the Department of Highways. The transaction was similar to others, in which Bell and his cronies had been acting as brokers for companies doing business with the government. While Gardiner had no scruples about using patronage for political purposes, he was, as Andrew Haydon had once remarked to Mackenzie King, "somewhat of a Puritan," and expected the same degree of personal rectitude that he practiced himself from others. Gardiner bluntly rejected Bell's suggestion, thereby sowing the seeds of a lengthy feud between the two men. Gardiner believed that, in retaliation, Bell sought to influence party members to choose Hamilton as Dunning's successor in 1926, though not a Hamilton's instigation.[38]

At the same time, Bell was also involved in a struggle with the Meilicke family of Saskatoon for control of the *Leader* group of newspapers. It culminated in a reshuffling of the board of directors in

April 1926, in which Bell was removed from the board by the majority shareholders, the Meilicke brothers and Burford Hooke. The former were known to be close friends of the new premier and there were some who suspected that "it was Gardiner who induced the Mellickes [sic] to break with Bell and put him out of control of these newspapers."[39] In turn, Bell attempted to buy out the Meilickes with the assistance of a group of Conservative businessmen in Regina. He eventually failed in these efforts, sold his share of the newspapers to Hooke and the Meilickes, and moved to Calgary, where he acquired control of the *Albertan.*[40]

Bell's newspapers periodically featured articles on the supposed falling-out between the premier and the federal Minister of Railways. Gardiner may well have suspected that these articles were inspired by Dunning, since he and Bell continued to be good friends. Dunning, who candidly admitted on one occasion that he could not see completely eye to eye with either Bell or Gardiner, sought to effect a reconciliation, but without success. By January 1929 local Liberals were becoming "somewhat alarmed" over the whole situation with a provincial election in the offing.[41]

Their conflicting attitudes toward the Progressives constituted another source of continuing friction between Dunning and Gardiner. In his only recorded direct attack on Dunning, over the too friendly attitude of the federal Liberals toward the Bracken government in Manitoba, Gardiner complained to Mackenzie King early in 1928 that he was

... growing tired of having the political situation in the west in the hands of man who treats us like a group of school boys ... [Dunning] tries to take all credit for things which turn out right and throw the blame on one of the other western ministers, myself or yourself, for everything which goes wrong.... The whole provincial organization here are becoming restless under the treatment we are receiving from this man who takes at every turn and gives nothing.

Now it was King's turn to assume the role of peacemaker, urging Gardiner not to "attribute to Mr. Dunning any motives or actions other than those wholly friendly to both yourself and myself, without at least giving us all a chance to talk over the situation together."[42]

Whether such a frank discussion ever took place remains unclear, but by the end of the year a measure of harmony seems to have been restored between the two Saskatchewan Liberals. Gardiner sought Dunning's assistance during the 1929 provincial election campaign, and the latter agreed to come without hesitation. As it turned out, though, first the pressure of parliamentary business and then an attack of appendicitis prevented Dunning from taking any direct part in that campaign. No less than local Liberals in Saskatchewan, Dunning was nevertheless confident that the party would again emerge victorious.[43] When the ballots were counted on 6 June, the Liberals were still the largest group in the Legislature, but with twenty-six seats, they were six short of a clear majority. The Conservatives increased their representation from four to twenty-four, and the balance of power was held by the six Independents and four Progressives elected.[44]

Saskatchewan Liberals generally attributed the outcome to the rise of the Ku Klux Klan and its blatant appeal to racial and religious bigotry, but an obviously bitter Dunning confided to Mackenzie King that Gardiner also ought to bear some of the blame for the party's poor showing at the polls. Gardiner's antagonistic attitude toward the Progressives had "driven them into the opposition camp"; he had been "too cocksure," and had erred in calling the provincial election at a time when Parliament was still in session, thus preventing federal M.P.s from taking part in the campaign.[45]

Dunning's bitterness is understandable, for the results of the 1929 election had implications that extended beyond the narrow confines of provincial politics. In Saskatchewan, as in the United States, the Ku Klux Klan had been able to find, and feed upon, racial prejudice and religious bigotry of long standing. Its message was attractive to those concerned about the "menace" of sectarian influence in public schools and unrestricted immigration from continental Europe. The latter was an issue of particular concern in Regina and other Saskatchewan cities. Among urban dwellers, no less than among farmers, the notion that more immigrants were needed to fill up Saskatchewan's remaining vacant lands had come to be regarded with skepticism. Urban opposition to unrestricted immigration was based on the fear that newcomers from continental Europe would displace British and Canadian workers already in the province.

Such concern was not without foundation, for many central and eastern European immigrants who had come to the province intending to farm soon drifted into the towns and cities, where they competed for jobs. Seasonal unemployment had always been a problem in Saskatchewan, and it became more serious during the 1920s. Farm labor was being replaced by machines and, except at harvest time, Regina and the other cities harbored large numbers of unskilled men seeking work. Many of the immigrants from central and eastern Europe lacked the capital to buy farms and experienced difficulty in finding work as agricultural laborers because established farmers preferred English-speaking workers. The continued drift of immigrants from the farms to the cities was one of the main reasons for the growing clamor for a policy restricting immigration. The Klan and the Conservative party were quick to respond, and the result was not lost on Dunning: all three provincial ridings within his federal constituency, including the two Regina seats, went to the Conservatives in 1929.

Notwithstanding the growing political uncertainty at home, and the warnings of some that he should find another, and safer, seat before the next election,[46] Dunning's star continued to rise. He had, as King's biographer has noted, "ability, energy and experience," and when James Robb died suddenly of pneumonia in November 1929, opening the Finance portfolio, Dunning succeeded him. In King's eyes, Dunning was the obvious choice, not only because of his considerable administrative talents, but because of his views on the tariff. Robb had relied too much on his departmental officials and was tainted by high tariff leanings; Dunning's "Western (free trade) point of view" ensured that the government would be stronger with him as Minister of Finance.[47]

The task facing Dunning was not an enviable one, for the nation was beginning to feel the effects of slumping wheat sales and the stock market crash. Dunning's remedy was to lower the tariff on a wide range of goods imported from other parts of the Empire in the hope that this gesture would in turn open up markets for Canadian wheat and other farm products. The Dunning budget became the centrepiece in the Liberals' campaign for re-election in the summer of 1930, but it was soon overshadowed by R.B. Bennett's bold promises to blast his way into foreign markets. The King government was soundly defeated, losing almost forty seats mainly on the prairies and in Quebec. Dunning was among the fallen, losing to a Conservative, Frank Turnbull, by 3,700 votes.

Dunning's fate was not unique. Half of the Liberal losses in the West were in urban ridings, where unemployment had become an even more serious problem, and the federal government was regarded as the culprit for allowing too many immigrants. A survey conducted in Regina early in August 1930 showed a total of 3,756 men without jobs. At the end of the summer the last of the 850 employees of the General Motors plant were laid off. Unemployment, however, was not the only factor responsible for the outcome in Regina. The old issues that had contributed to the Liberal collapse in 1929 were still alive in 1930, thanks to the Anderson government's efforts to eliminate religious garb and emblems from public schools. On election night the Klan marched in triumph through the streets of Regina celebrating Dunning's defeat.[48]

For Dunning, 1930 was as significant a watershed as 1916 had been. "I feel sometimes," he confided to a friend scarcely a month after the election, "that I am at the crossroads of life, – deciding whether to definitely abandon politics for a business career or to accept some arrangement ... to enable me to remain in public life."[49] More than one Saskatchewan M.P. offered to vacate his seat so that Dunning might remain in federal politics. There were also rumors that he intended to return to the provincial field. In the end, Dunning did neither, and instead became vice-president of the Ontario Equitable Life Insurance Company and manager of a Canadian Pacific resort hotel in Quebec.[50] Though he would sit again in the House of Commons and hold the finance portfolio in a Liberal government after 1935, the voters of Regina had brought Dunning's western political career to an end.

In attempting an assessment of Dunning's accomplishments as a farm leader and politician, one is inevitably influenced by the knowledge that he slipped easily into the world of big business after 1930 and "was soon more at home on St. James Street than in a prairie village." An early biographer has noted that to some of his contemporaries, Dunning

... was a sheer opportunist, an ambitious man absorbed in his own advancement, whose principles were, to put it mildly, flexible. These critics satisfied themselves by saying that a man who begins life as a dedicated agrarian and ends it as a tycoon in St. James Street is just one more man on the make.... [51]

Such criticism ignores the fact that while Dunning was a product of the farmers' movement, the world of business was not foreign to him. At the age of twenty-six, after all, he had become general manager of the newly-formed Saskatchewan Co-operative Elevator Company. The company showed a profit from the beginning, due in great measure to Dunning's skilful handling of its affairs. This business ability, more than anything else, brought Dunning to the attention of the Martin government, and explains his appointment as Provincial Treasurer in 1916.

Now embarked upon a second career, Dunning tied himself and his fortunes to the Liberal party at a time when a latent revolt against both of the old parties was spreading through the farmers' movement. Dunning might have forsaken the Liberal party, as other prominent farm leaders did, but he chose not to. It was not some mystical attachment to Liberalism that prompted Dunning to remain loyal to the party of Laurier and Mackenzie King, but the practical view that prairie farmers could accomplish more through the collective influence of their votes upon the existing political parties than through the creation of a third party.[52]

The list of Dunning's own accomplishments lends a good deal of credibility to this view. Few other western politicians of his generation could claim to have worked harder to improve the lot of the farming community. Dunning sought to obtain a higher price for western grain through the re-establishment of the Canada Wheat Board in the early 1920s and then, when those efforts failed, through the Wheat Pool. [53] He pushed for the completion of the Hudson Bay Railway as an alternative shipping route for prairie grain, and was finally successful after he joined Mackenzie King's cabinet. As for the Dunning budget of 1930, while it did not effect the dramatic changes in national fiscal and tariff programs the western farmer desired most of all, it did lessen the protective features of such policies. Charles Dunning's career typified the close relationship that developed between the farmers' movement and the Liberal party during the early decades of the twentieth century. No less than T.A. Crerar, another illustrious farm leader of the period, who left and then rejoined the Liberals, Dunning served the agricultural community well.

Notes

1. D.E. Smith, *The Regional Decline of a National Party: Liberals on the Prairies* (Toronto: University of Toronto Press, 1981), p. 37.

2. *Grain Growers' Guide* [hereafter *Guide*], 3 March 1926; H.B. Neatby, *William Lyon Mackenzie King: The Lonely Heights, 1924–1932* (Toronto: University of Toronto Press, 1963), pp. 87–88.

3. J. Nelson, "How I Found in Canada My Land of Opportunity: Premier Dunning of Saskatchewan," *Maclean's Magazine*, 1 January 1925, p. 14; *Guide*, 19 July 1911, 6 December 1911; Archives of Saskatchewan [hereafter A.S.], Saskatchewan Sessional Papers, Session 1912, no. 12.

4. *Guide*, 16 and 23 February 1916; *Saskatchewan Co-operative Elevator Company Annual Report, 1916*, pp. 11–13.

5. *Morning Leader* (Regina) [hereafter *Leader*], 28 March 1913; Queen's University Archives [hereafter Q.U.A.], C.A. Dunning Papers, F. Cochrane to Dunning, 10 June 1916; Dunning to F. Cochrane, 20 June 1916.

6. *Leader*, 19 May 1922.

7. Ibid., 10 May 1912; *Guide*, 25 October 1916.

8. P.F. Sharp, *The Agrarian Revolt in Western Canada: A Survey Showing American Parallels* (Minneapolis: University of Minnesota Press, 1948), pp. 77–93; J.W. Brennan, "A Political History of Saskatchewan, 1905–1929" (Ph.D. dissertation, University of Alberta, 1976), pp. 364–70.

9. *Leader*, 6 May 1920; *Guide*, 4 August 1920; A.S., S.G.G.A. Papers, *Minutes of the Twentieth Annual Convention of the Saskatchewan Grain Growers' Association* [hereafter *Convention Minutes*], pp. 56–57.

10. Public Archives of Canada [hereafter P.A.C.], W.L.M. King Papers, J.A. Robb to King, 5 September 1921, p. 56894. For a fuller account of these negotiations and the 1921 federal campaign in Saskatchewan, *see* Brennan, pp. 505–13.

11. See *Directory of Members of Parliament and Federal Elections for the North-West Territories and Saskatchewan, 1887–1966* (Regina: Saskatchewan Archives Board, 1967) for these and other federal election results for Saskatchewan.

12. J.W. Brennan, "C.A. Dunning and the Challenge of the Progressives, 1922–1925," *Saskatchewan History*, vol. XXII, no. 1 (Winter 1969), pp. 1–12.

13. L.D. Courville, "The Saskatchewan Progressives" (M.A. thesis, University of Saskatchewan [Regina], 1971), pp. 107–9.

14. P.A.C., J.W. Dafoe Papers, Dafoe to C. Sifton, 2 May 1921; *Guide*, 1 June 1921; *Saskatoon Daily Star*, 1 June 1921; A.S., S.G.G.A. Papers, Bickleigh G.G.A. to J.B. Musselman, 13 June 1921.

268 / J. William Brennan

15. A.S., S.G.G.A. Papers, *Convention Minutes*, 1922, pp. 87–91, 117; H.A. Innis, ed., *The Diary of Alexander James McPhail* (Toronto: University of Toronto Press, 1940), p. 23; K. Edwards, ed., *Memoirs of George F. Edwards* (Ottawa: n.p., 1968), p. 18.

16. Q.U.A., G.F. Chipman Papers, Chipman to T.A. Crerar, 31 March 1922; P.A.C., J.S. Woodsworth Papers, E.A. Partridge to Woodsworth, 31 August 1922.

17. D.S. Spafford, "The Origins of the Farmers' Union of Canada," *Saskatchewan History*, vol. XVIII, no. 3 (Autumn 1965), pp. 89–98.

18. *The Mackenzie King Diaries, 1893–1931* [hereafter *King Diaries*] (Toronto: University of Toronto Press, 1973), 3 November 1924, 10 and 14 August 1925; P.A.C., W.L.M. King Papers, C.A. Dunning to King, 22 August 1925, p. 97169.

19. *King Diaries*, 14 August 1925; P.A.C., J.W. Dafoe Papers, Dafoe to C. Sifton, 30 June 1925; A.K. Cameron Papers, T.A. Crerar to Cameron, 11 August 1925.

20. Neatby, pp. 74–75, 86–88. A fuller account of the "plot" to unseat King may be found in S.P. Regenstreif, "A Threat to Leadership: C.A. Dunning and Mackenzie King," *Dalhousie Review*, vol. XLIV, no. 3 (Autumn 1964), pp. 272–89.

21. Neatby, pp. 92–93; P.A.C., W.L.M. King Papers, A. Haydon to King, 23 November 1925, pp. 98531–32.

22. Q.U.A., T.A. Crerar Papers, C.E. Gregory to Crerar, 13 September 1922; *King Diaries*, 30 September 1925.

23. P.A.C., W.L.M. King Papers, A. Haydon to King, 23 November 1925, p. 98535.

24. Ibid., J.G. Gardiner to King, 15 November 1924, p. 84872.

25. P.A.C., A.K. Cameron Papers, T.A. Crerar to Cameron, 26 January 1926.

26. Neatby, pp. 93–95; A.S., J.G. Gardiner Papers, W.R. Motherwell to Gardiner, 29 January 1926, p. 2636; Gardiner to W.R. Motherwell, 15 February 1926, pp. 2640–41; P.A.C., W.L.M. King Papers, King to C.A. Dunning, 6 February 1926, p. 111150.

27. *King Diaries*, 31 January 1926; P.A.C., A.K. Cameron Papers, T.A. Crerar to Cameron, 27 February 1926; *Western Producer*, 21 October 1926; P.A.C., J.W. Dafoe Papers, Dafoe to C. Sifton, 26 October 1926.

28. *King Diaries*, 5 July 1926.

29. Neatby, pp. 163–64; *Leader*, 19 August 1926; *Western Producer*, 26 August 1926; A.S., J.G. Gardiner Papers, Gardiner to W.L.M. King, 31 August 1926, pp. 8059–61.

30. P.A.C., A. Meighen Papers, H.W. Laird to Meighen, 16 September 1926, pp. 87979–80; *Leader*, 15 September 1926.

31. *King Diaries*, 4 June 1926.

32. H.A. Fleming, *Canada's Arctic Outlet: A History of the Hudson Bay Railway* (Berkeley: University of California Press, 1957), pp. 64–83.

33. *Leader,* 25 November 1926; *Manitoba Free Press,* 5 February 1927; Saskatchewan, *Journals of the Legislative Assembly, 1927,* p. 36.

34. Fleming, pp. 84–86; P.A.C., J.W. Dafoe Papers, Dafoe to A.G. Dexter, 12 April 1927; *Western Producer,* 18 August 1927; P.A.C., A.K. Cameron Papers, T.A. Crerar to Cameron, 8 February 1928.

35. E.G. Drake, *Regina: The Queen City* (Toronto: McClelland and Stewart, 1955), pp. 181–82.

36. P.A.C., J.W. Dafoe Papers, Dafoe to C. Sifton, 26 October 1926; A.K. Cameron Papers, T.A. Crerar to Cameron, 21 December 1926; *Western Producer,* 15 December 1927.

37. P.A.C., A. Meighen Papers, J.H. Leech to Meighen, 4 March 1926, pp. 75866–67; J.W. Dafoe Papers, Dafoe to C. Sifton, 26 May 1926.

38. P.A.C., W.L.M. King Papers, A. Haydon to King, 23 November 1925, p. 98535; *Leader,* 23 October 1928.

39. P.A.C., J.W. Dafoe Papers, Dafoe to C. Sifton, 26 October 1926.

40. P.A.C., Meighen Papers, F. Somerville to Meighen, 10 July 1926, pp. 87435–37; J.W. Dafoe Papers, C. Sifton to Dafoe, 4 November 1926.

41. Q.U.A., C.A. Dunning Papers, J.G. Gardiner to Dunning, 21 February 1927; W.M. Martin to Dunning, 13 Janaury 1929; Dunning to W.M. Martin, 19 January 1929; Dunning to G.M. Bell, 13 September 1929.

42. P.A.C., W.L.M. King Papers, J.G. Gardiner to King, 17 January 1928, pp. 129730–35; King to J.G. Gardiner, 3 March, 1928, p. 129741.

43. A.S., J.G. Gardiner Papers, Gardiner to W.L.M. King, 3 January 1929, p. 8201; Q.U.A., C.A. Dunning Papers, Dunning to J.G. Gardiner, 13 May 1929, 1 June 1929.

44. *Saskatchewan Executive and Legislative Directory, 1905–1970* (Regina: Saskatchewan Archives Board, 1971), pp. 49–50. Two deferred contests in the far northern ridings of Ile à la Crosse and Cumberland increased Liberal representation in the sixty-three-seat Legislature to twenty-eight.

45. *King Diaries,* 7 June 1929.

46. Q.U.A., C.A. Dunning Papers, G.M. Bell to Dunning, 9 June 1928, 10 September 1929.

47. Neatby, p. 296; *King Diaries,* 26 November 1929.

48. Neatby, p. 340; *Leader-Post* (Regina), 15 August 1930, 3 September 1937; Q.U.A., C.A. Dunning Papers, Dunning to W.A. MacLeod, 4 August 1930.

49. Q.U.A., C.A. Dunning Papers, Dunning to J.A. Cross, 22 August 1930.

50. Q.U.A., C.A. Dunning Papers, Dunning to E.W. Stapleford, 10 October 1930; P.A.C., J.W. Dafoe Papers, G. Dexter to Dafoe, 25 October 1930.

51. Neatby, p. 358; G.V. Ferguson, "Charles Avery Dunning," *Queen's Quarterly,* vol. LXV, no. 4 (Winter 1958): 572.

52. Q.U.A., C.A. Dunning Papers, Dunning to J. Evans, 3 April 1925; Dunning to T.A. Patrick, 12 December 1925.

53. Brennan, "Political History," pp. 540–67.

"Misfits," "Malingerers," and "Malcontents": The British Harvester Movement of 1928

_____W.J.C. Cherwinski

Before the depression the prairie farmer's single most pressing problem, outside of the weather, the protective tariff, and interest rates over which he had no control, was to acquire a sufficient number of satisfactory workers to see his year's work through to a profitable conclusion. He pursued a variety of courses to solve this problem. Individual attempts at recruitment in Canada, the United States, and Europe were combined with vigorous lobbying in Ottawa. The federal government eventually responded by establishing a high priority on the recruitment of farm labor outside the country.[1] As experienced farm hands became increasingly hard to attract, however, farmers and the Dominion government resorted to a variety of training schemes, designed to create practiced "sons of the soil" from men whose hands bore the grime of the city. Unfortunately, most of these plans produced indifferent results.[2]

While year-round farm hands required training and experience, at harvest time, when the farm operator struggled to get his crop in before freeze-up, laborers mainly needed brawn and endurance. Since the grain ripened during the same four-week period across the region, the total number of men required often reached into the tens of thousands. To meet the seasonal demand of the harvest, immigration authorities usually tried to co-ordinate the arrival of newcomers with the ripening of the grain crops. In other cases, prairie provincial governments released public servants to help with the harvest, a practice emulated by military officials who furloughed soldiers during World War I when the labor shortage was particularly acute. Similarly, holidays for school children were extended so that the youngsters could help where they were capable. One of the more long-lasting expedients, designed to meet the requirements of the prairie harvest, was the annual harvest excursion sponsored by the railways in conjunction with the provincial and federal governments from 1890 to 1929. Cheap railway fares, usually less than half the regular price, were offered as an incentive for men in the Maritimes and in central Canada to avail themselves of the opportunity to earn "big money" in return for sun-up to sun-down labor, stooking sheaves at the beginning of the season, and later assisting with the threshing.[3] When the supply of men from the East proved inadequate, railways offered reduced fares at various times to prairie urban dwellers, British Columbians, and American farm workers. Although it was often suggested that steamship companies should co-operate with the railways to offer similar deals to British workers plagued by unemployment, only in 1906, 1923, and 1928 were significant numbers of men from the "Old Country" recruited.

The most extensive of the harvester movements from Britain occurred in 1923 when twelve thousand men were called. While there were problems at the time, this migration did not prove to be the most difficult to administer; nor did the 1923 migrants cause the most trouble. That distinction went to those of 1928. A special set of circumstances created the appearance of a manpower crisis sufficiently grave as to justify an exceptional drive to recruit harvesters, causing a considerable impact on individuals, institutions, and the region.

The problem of providing adequate harvest labor was never simply one of supply and demand. If wages had been high enough, a sufficient number of Canadians would most likely have offered their services. Other considerations, however, always clouded the situation. One such major consideration was the persistent myth that in the prairies, the land of opportunity, tenacity and hard work would ultimately be rewarded. The publicists who worked for the Immigration Branch of the Department of the Interior (later the Department of Immigration and Colonization) and the railway companies appeared to dedicate their lives to propagating this myth. During the 1920s, they directed their major efforts at potential immigrants from the British Isles. This policy reflected a sense of transatlantic Anglo-Saxon solidarity and a concomitant negative view of Canada's changing ethnic and cultural mix. These fears, derived from the pre-war emphasis on continental European and American recruitment, forced federal and provincial political leaders to press their bureaucratic subordinates for greatly increased immigration from the "Old Country."[4] Thus, the Anglo-Saxon race would be preserved and its values, based on hard work and determination, would be strengthened in Canada's vigorous northern climate.

At the same time, economic conditions in England, characterized by excessive post-war unemployment, provided a ready supply of labor. "Thousands of men... looking abroad for the betterment of their state"[5] could be satisfied while consolidating imperial ties. As a result, the Empire Settlement Act of 1922 committed the British government to subsidize half the cost of approved training and emigration schemes designed to send useful, stable settlers to the Dominions. Because the agreement with Canada called for subsidies for farm workers and domestics only, it was hoped that many would choose the Canadian prairies and, while they were becoming established, that they would help to satisfy the region's insatiable demand for agricultural workers. In addition, authorities in London made repeated attempts to convince Canada to accept short-term labor as well, particularly for the annual harvest.

The prairies should have been responsive to offers of labor in the first post-war decade. The farmers' need to increase production and profits in the light of slumping grain prices after 1918 meant a commensurate increase in acreage put to crop. Moreover, high interest rates led many farmers to reject the war-time innovation of gas-powered tractors, despite the fact that horse-drawn equipment was more labor-intensive.[6]

Bureaucrats, senior and junior, federal and provincial, were not at all enthusiastic about the prospects of hordes of untrained, emaciated British "factory fodder" descending on the prairies every autumn. They dealt with requests for, and complaints about, labor from farmers almost daily and realized that many prairie farmers, themselves former British residents, preferred English-speaking workers. Other employers, however, had acquired a suspicion of the work habits of the British urban dispossessed, perpetrated by stories about experiences with slum children from Dr. Bernardo's homes, remittance men, and recipients of unemployment insurance.[7] Moreover, in the long run, farmers placed the willingness to work earnestly for long hours with a minimum of supervision above considerations of national origin.

Officials responsible for immigration and labor matters were well aware of the problems that the conventional harvest excursions caused each year. Workers from elsewhere in Canada often refused to go home after the crop was off and drifted to the cities, arousing considerable criticism from organized workers with whom they competed for work, from civic officials who were forced to grant them relief when they fell on hard times, and from law enforcement officers concerned with the increase in crime that often resulted when too many idle men gathered in one place.[8] Consequently, government policy emphasized permanent British family settlement, while harvest help was to be recruited from within the country as much as possible. If absolutely necessary, Canada could solicit for short-term labor in the United States. Not only could the American harvesters be assembled faster and more cheaply, after the harvest, they promptly returned home where, no doubt, they would be quick to advertise Canada's boundless potential.[9] By comparison, similar movements from overseas held a much greater risk of generating bad publicity, which could endanger Canada's whole immigration strategy.[10]

Despite government policy, transatlantic solidarity and pressure from shipping sources won out in 1923 when a bumper crop created a critical need for 50,000 to 60,000 harvesters. When it appeared that North American sources could not meet the demand, the two major Canadian railway companies made an agreement with the British government to transport 12,000 British workers to the prairies, promising wages of $4.00 per day plus board. When the relevant statistics were compiled early in 1924, proponents of imperial migration pointed proudly to their accomplishments as a result of the experiment: the 11,871 migrants had paid their own reduced fares, the harvest had been completed, and the 80 percent of the harvesters who had remained in western Canada were "successfully assimilated."[11]

Immigration officials, however, tended to view the 1923 harvester scheme differently. Seven hundred physically defective men who slipped through a cursory inspection were an ongoing problem, as were those who refused to work for less than the promised $4.00 per day and had to be supported while awaiting deportation. When many of the immigrants drifted to the cities for the winter, the Department of Immigration and Colonization heard many complaints from city dwellers and organized labor.[12] When forty-six unemployed harvesters, allegedly spurred on by British agitators brought over with the group and abetted by Canadian Communists, marched from Toronto to Ottawa to demand work and wages from the prime minister, the department was forced to allocate men to follow them and offer them work at every stop on the way.

The most difficult task, however, was to deflect the criticism levelled at Canada and Canadians in the British press and Parliament. Stories of workers oppressed by callous employers, unfeeling officials, and a hostile environment jeopardized the recruitment of British families who had a desire to settle and farm on the prairies. As a result, the Immigration Department discouraged subsequent short-term harvester movements from overseas.[13] Undeterred, advocates of imperial migration pressed on, identifying immigration of any kind with national progress and prosperity. From 1924 to 1927 the department was able to resist such pressures, and specific harvest movements were very selective and limited to small groups of university students.[14]

Some of the responsibility for the decision to organize a full-scale British harvester movement in 1928 rests with the atmosphere of uncertainty and miscalculation that prevailed during the 1927 harvest. Early spring rains suggested only moderate crop prospects that year. Therefore, immigration officials were able to deflect pressure from the British government and steamship companies about another harvester movement and pointed to adequate local labor resources enhanced by a slow economy in central Canada and the Maritimes, which promised a well-subscribed harvest excursion.[15] The manpower surplus of late July 1927 turned into a manpower crisis by early September. The rush from the East had not materialized; late rains in the two previous years had made harvest work unprofitable for the migrants. Officials had also overestimated the number of local men willing to pursue harvest work. Compounding the problem further, the railways were able to secure only a fraction of the anticipated number of regular European immigrants who were expected to help out that year.[16] With pressure mounting from farmers demanding government action, officials contemplated extra harvest excursions. Meanwhile, an appeal went out to potential harvesters in the United States. Special permission was granted Americans to enter Canada with their cars and to follow the harvest for sixty days.[17] The harvest labor supply problem, which one senior government official called the "hardy annual," had again baffled everyone involved.[18]

There were early indications that 1928 would be no better. Increased crop acreage was reported throughout the region with the result that spring labor requirements would be high. The members of the provincial offices of the Employment Service of Canada again considered the possibility of importing labor from overseas specifically for the harvest.[19] Simultaneously, the suggestion was expressed even more emphatically on the other side of the Atlantic by British M.P. and former chairman of the Overseas Settlement Committee, William Lunn. His argument was familiar: there were thousands of unemployed in Britain and

> Canada needs British settlers. They are the best, Canada desires to remain British. Her loyalty is undoubted. The Canadian harvest will soon be due. . . . I am sure that three months' work in the healthiest of climates with good wages would be a blessing to all.

In his opinion, three-quarters of the harvesters would eventually settle, with their families, in the Dominion.[20]

Another person quick off the mark was Lord Lovat of the Overseas Settlement Committee (O.S.C.), who cabled Immigration Minister Robert Forke late in June to indicate that in light of the "exceptionally encouraging" reports from the prairies, he was prepared, with the department's permission, to approach the steamship companies to ascertain a special rate for a possible movement of British harvesters. The deputy minister, W.J. Egan, in an obvious effort to deflate the idea, replied that such a movement was unnecessary since the farm labor supply was adequate. Lovat persisted, however, and approached Prime Minister King, as did L.S. Amery of the Dominion Office at Whitehall, with a similar request. In the meantime, the shipping companies pressed the Immigration Department's London office "for harvest excursions at a special rate."[21]

Suggestions from men of influence notwithstanding, nothing could be decided until the actual harvest labor requirements had been determined at the annual labor conference held for that purpose in July. On 19 July, the representatives of the railways, farm organizations, provincial governments, and the federal government brought down their verdict based on all the available information. In all, 75,000 harvesters would be required: 12,000 by Manitoba, 40,000 by Saskatchewan, and 23,000 by Alberta. The three provinces could each supply an estimated 25,000 men from within, and another 6,000 could be expected from British Columbia. Since interest in harvest excursions from the East had declined, officials doubted they could fill the remaining 44,000 slots from the rest of Canada. The number of recruits from the United States was also an unknown quantity since bad weather in South Dakota, Illinois, and Wisconsin could delay harvesters there past the time when they were needed in Canada. Moreover, the desirability of American harvesters was undermined by reports that on the West Coast, farm workers were "becoming infested with members of the I.W.W. who were endeavouring to organize the workers in order to demand a higher scale of pay."[22]

No matter how the statistics were interpreted, there appeared to be a shortfall of some ten thousand workers. The Immigration Department explored all the possible alternatives. First, the maritime and central provinces were canvassed to get up-to-date information on labor sources. Except in Quebec, however, healthy local economies meant less than usual interest in harvest excursions. Meanwhile, the Minister of Labour counselled the three prairie governments to avoid a repetition of the 1923 experience. In late July, with the harvest less than a month away, prairie governments indicated grave concern. Saskatchewan, which needed the greatest number of harvesters, urged Ottawa to be "prepared to meet any crisis which might arise." With no alternatives apparent, the Immigration Department finally cabled Lord Lovat that "10,000 British harvesters might find temporary employment in Canada." But first, the railway companies had to agree to distribute them, to take full responsibility for arranging winter work for them, and to provide a "substantial reduction" in the return fare for those who desired to go home.[23]

Knowing full well that Deputy Minister of Immigration, W.J. Egan wished to avoid possible criticism of his department should the movement go awry, the railway companies refused to take sole responsibility, particularly for winter work. Negotiations continued for another ten days. To his credit, Lovat sought to break the deadlock by setting aside £5000 to pay the companies up to £6 per man to cover the difference between the reduced rate and the regular one-way return fare. He cautioned, however, that any publicity given to the offer could scuttle the objective of permanent settlement; it "would be tantamount to offering inducements to return."[24]

While the Department of Immigration and the railways remained adamant in their respective positions, news of the movement began to spread on both sides of the Atlantic. The necessary documents and posters were distributed, Canadian medical men and civil examiners were dispatched to designated centres in Britain, and hundreds of men awaited the process of selection. Pressed by the need for haste, threatened by the Immigration Department with a possible drastic reduction in the movement, and assured by the O.S.C. that "misfits" and the unemployed would be returned at British expense, on 4 August the railways agreed to co-operate with Ottawa.[25]

The terms of the harvester movement were simple. The men would be moved at a rate of £12 each way from the port of embarkation to Winnipeg. The O.S.C. was to pay an additional £3 per man and also agreed to provide each harvester with £1 on landing and another £1 in Winnipeg to cover expenses for those who needed it. The subsidies for returning men remained a secret. To guarantee that Canada received physically fit harvesters, each applicant had to pass a full medical administered by appointed doctors and a civil examination to determine his employment history and marital status. Harvesters had to be between eighteen and forty years of age. To ensure that indigents were eliminated, harvesters had to be single; if married, they had to have their spouses' permission to leave. In addition, they had to prove they had held a job in the previous twelve-month period.[26]

There is no doubt that the posters promised hope for many: "10,000 Harvesters for Canada Wanted Immediately, Special Fare £12 to Winnipeg, Work Guaranteed—Wages from £3 to £5 per week and free keep, Harvesters must sail at once, Last sailing August 18, 1928." Members of what was known as Britain's Heartbreak Army of 1,305,000 unemployed came in droves to the twelve examination and selection centres scattered throughout England, Scotland, and Wales. If the popular press's description of the men in the queues are to be believed, many were in desperate straits: "One man had no shirt to take off, many had no collars and some were dressed in little more than rags. One man had walked [to London] all the way from Scotland." Others had not eaten for days; still others bore obvious scars from the war fought a decade earlier.[27]

The O.S.C. exerted "quiet, but nevertheless persistent" pressure for Canada to look kindly on the victims of industrial society; instead, the Immigration Department opted to enlist miners, who, having been unemployed only since the General Strike of 1926, were of "generally splendid physique" owing to a lifetime spent with pick and shovel.[28] Those who were not miners came from the ranks of the unskilled and semi-skilled.

Whatever their place of origin or background, most of the applicants saw the harvester movement as an opportunity to make a considerable amount of money with limited expenses; if they could prove their need, their fare would be paid for them. Others were allegedly told by relief agencies to apply and if accepted to go on pain of having benefits withdrawn from their families. There were also some who used the occasion to escape burdensome family responsibilities by declaring themselves single to civil examiners.[29] Still others went for positive reasons, having long held an image of Canada as an exciting and romantic place, as one young immigrant, enticed to Canada somewhat later, described:

> Just one thing filled my whole life and that was to get to Canada and then, who knows, see America. I would stand for hours in front of the shipping offices and look at the big posters that showed a sunburnt farmer with a Stetson hat and a big red shirt looking over miles and miles of golden corn, where huge threshing machines and laughing happy gangs of men were at work.[30]

Harvesters who shared this young man's views were more likely to settle in Canada and take up farming after the harvest. No doubt most of the British recruits shared this image of the Canadian prairies in varying degrees.

In the eight days devoted to recruiting, half of the 25,000 applicants were rejected immediately and about one-quarter of the remainder failed the medical examination. This left approximately 9,900 hopefuls. When it was announced that the C.N.R. was only able to take 6,000 and the Canadian Pacific 2,500, there was considerable grumbling about the "disappointment to the unemployed."[31] Many applicants, however, changed their minds, some when they learned they would have to work hard from dawn to dusk, and "in the case of some married men—had their minds changed for them."[32] When the hectic selection process was completed, the Immigration Department's senior official in London, J. Bruce Walker, proudly but prematurely concluded that most of the problems experienced in the past would be avoided: "the mentality and the physical qualities of the men sent forward will be found of a very high order," and "malingerers, time servers and indolent men" had been kept to a minimum.[33]

Space on twenty-six vessels was set aside by the Canadian Pacific,

White Star, Cunard, and Anchor-Donaldson lines to transport the British harvesters. Most of the ships, such as the *Montclare,* the *Calgaric,* the *Letitia,* and the *Laconia,* had long been plying the North Atlantic in the interests of the immigrant trade. Their crews took little notice of their exuberant, excited passengers. The crossings were generally uneventful except for some illness, possibly caused by predeparture revelry. Passage grants from the O.S.C. apparently contributed to the availability of liquor and the frequency of gambling encountered on board the ships. Although the men inevitably grumbled about the food and accommodation, the more adaptable among them judged both as satisfactory. The men spent most of their time speculating on their fate and the nature of the work they were sent to do. To better face the unknown, a number of them gathered into groups and vowed not to separate no matter what happened en route. They learned more of what to expect when they marched off the ship at Halifax or Quebec City, often to the whine of bagpipes, and joined harvest excursionists from the maritime and central provinces on colonist cars for the trip to Winnipeg. Except for one incident, when the excursionists descended on a store run by two blind men at Mattawa, Ontario, and "cleaned them out of everything they took a fancy to and left without paying a cent for what they took," the two-day trip did not compare with earlier harvester excursions, which were characterized by wholesale theft and destruction of property.[34]

Once the men reached Winnipeg, the railways took charge of distribution. The "assisted" men were given ten dollars each to pay their one-half cent per mile fare to their destinations, and, together with those who paid their own way, were told to assemble according to the province in which they wanted to work. After being reassured that there was plenty of work, they were issued tickets to communities serviced by the railway company that had brought them to Winnipeg. They left in groups of five. Unfortunately, despite years of effort and organization dedicated to streamlining distribution procedures, Winnipeg still remained a bottleneck in the process. The result was that many harvesters, Canadian and British, had to walk the streets of the city and sleep in one of the three Immigration Halls, in some cases for several nights, before they were dispatched.[35]

Some of the British farm labor recruits had no intention of going to a farm; they departed directly to jobs in their own field and an estimated 600 to 800 immediately left for the United States. Others chased rumors of employment, especially to balmy Vancouver, only to discover on arrival that too many others were ahead of them. Stranded and harassed by people who did not want them, they requested help only to be told by the railways that they had to return to their original destination to qualify for cheap fares home or to other parts of the country. Unsuccessful at finding work in urban areas, a number returned to the harvest "as a sort of penalty" with the intention of finding something better later or, failing that, demanding to be sent home.[36]

Of those intent on giving farming a try, the most fortunate were those destined for the farms of friends or relatives. There they encountered a warm welcome, enjoyed a congenial environment, received lengthy explanations on the strange behavior and practices of Canadians, and, perhaps most valuable of all, were given proper instruction in local farming methods, which they could take to the next job.[37] For the remainder, the introduction to prairie life was considerably more trying. On reaching the community named on the sheet of paper they clutched, they were usually met by the railway agent, sometimes accompanied by one or more farmers. If they were lucky and the harvest was imminent, the farmers looked them over, questioned them about their experience, and, if satisfied, offered them jobs. If cutting was still several days away, however, the farmer often offered a holding wage of one or two dollars per day to pick stones or clear brush. Depending on their experience and the demand for men in the area, migrants could expect to earn more for harvesting. Agreements were sealed with a handshake and harvesters scheduled to begin work the next day. Those capable of following instructions about setting up a proper stook were usually assured continuous work in the area until threshing began. After proving themselves satisfactory, they could look forward to more work close by and then move north, where the harvest started later, until the season ended in late November.

There were numerous unfortunate instances in which there was no one at the station to greet the harvesters; or worse, if there was, it was an agent of the railway cursing his employer or the provincial Employment Service for sending more men than he had ordered or could place.[38] Unnerved by this experience, some of the men simply proceeded on to the nearest large community, their harvesting days over. In the short run, those who stayed created a welcome situation for the farmers—a labor surplus with competition forcing down wages. The employers' advantage was brief, however, as most harvesters, British or Canadian, moved to where wages were rumored to be better rather than accept appreciably less than they had expected.

Even when mutually approved verbal agreements prevailed, there were some farmers who took perverse pleasure in exploiting green Englishmen either by inflicting upon them impossible tasks, or by refusing to pay the agreed wage after the work was finished. The harvester had little recourse but to move on; his chances of recovering his money were slim. Such behavior often backfired, however, as a farmer's reputation determined whether he got a sufficient crew when labor was scarce later in the season. Most often the major complaint was not against failure to pay but the discrepancy between the money promised in England by recruiting officials—£3 to £5 per week with free keep—and the wages farmers offered to inexperienced hands. To complicate matters, most British harvesters expected to be paid by the week while the customary practice on the prairies was payment by the day. The harvester received no money on days when he was unable to work due to wet weather or mechanical breakdown. In such instances, the aspiring harvester usually accepted prevailing conditions on the understanding that with experience his circumstances would improve.[39]

There is no doubt that the majority of British harvesters made the best of the situation. They competed adequately with permanent settlers and city dwellers of American, central European, and Canadian antecedents. Less successful were the ones who managed to hide injuries and ailments from the selection officers in Britain. Their first encounter with the back-breaking job of stooking under a hot sun, frequently with clothing and footwear inadequate for the task, resulted in the reappearance of industrial injuries and war-related wounds. For them and for those who suddenly discovered long dormant ailments to avoid work—generally referred to as "malingerers"—the circumstances were intolerable. The only alternative was to flee to the nearest urban centre.[40]

Inexperience and poor physical conditioning were the greatest liabilities the conscientious Britisher took to the harvest fields. Since the farmer was under considerable pressure to get the grain cut and stooked, especially if rain threatened, he had no time to teach a novice the proper techniques nor the patience to wait for untrained muscles to respond without pain. Moreover, farmers and threshing crew operators alike could not afford to hire men who were not suited to the job, since damage to machinery and injury to horses inflicted intentionally or inadvertently caused expensive delays. Therefore, the harvester who lagged behind the rest or adopted a know-it-all attitude when criticized was dismissed, especially when experienced men showed up looking for work. Persistence and perseverance, however, usually brought satisfactory work at good pay from a more sympathetic farmer, particularly when threshing was in full swing and farmers found it necessary to journey into the cities looking for available men, offering $6.00 per day (more than £7 per week) plus board to attract them.[41]

The work and wages enjoyed by harvesters were usually standard throughout a region at any given time. Living conditions, however, were another matter. Homesickness was widespread, and there was one reported suicide. Harvest labor was a short-term expedient for farmers, required for only about a fortnight a year. Consequently, unless the farm was large and equipped for farm hands, only makeshift amenities at best could be provided for the harvesters. Beds were often located in barns, sheds, or other outbuildings, which were extremely cold as the season progressed. Single farmers usually had less to offer than married ones; one Scotsman fed his men salt pork three times a day and roomed them in a straw shack.[42] But in most instances, the farmer realized that he had to maintain the goodwill as well as the strength and endurance of his hands with plenty of wholesome food. Amongst farm wives, serving appetizing meals, frequently in difficult circumstances, became a matter of considerable pride. Evidence would suggest that most British harvesters were truly impressed with the meals they were fed on the job.[43] Complaints were usually directed at the strange concoctions prepared by "foreigners" who did not appreciate the delicate palates of their men. One observer related the following story:

I met one man who had been sent to the farm of a Russian Meninite [sic], and not one person on the farm could talk or understand a word of English. The food was utterly strange; a big basin was set on the kitchen table containing a mess of strange ingredients, and everybody sat round it and attacked it with spoons.

The British harvester was unable to eat it, and by signs he indicated that he would prefer eggs and milk. The Meninite [sic] farmer was very kind and supplied eggs and milk without stint, but after ten days or so on a diet restricted to these, the harvester crocked up and was ordered home by the doctor.[44]

These cases were rare, however, because farmers from the Continent preferred to hire their own nationals whenever possible.

Another source of concern for men far from home, who had anticipated considerable wages to tide them over the winter, were periods of enforced inactivity, especially in the first few weeks of the season. Railway officials did everything in their power to avoid such circumstances, and tried to disperse British harvesters through the southern part of the region where English-speaking farmers predominated and where the harvest was supposed to start early. Their calculations were sometimes wrong when the warm summer that promised an early harvest turned cold and wet in the last half of August. Moreover, some of the harvesters chose to go their own ways rather than journey to where they were directed. Within days reports began to flood into railway and immigration headquarters of towns "glutted with men," most of them out of money and living on the goodwill of local citizens and civic governments. Their difficulties were compounded when other British harvesters were fired as unfit or replaced when the farmers' regular harvesters from the East appeared, many of whom had decided late to come west when they heard that there was a bumper crop to be harvested.[45]

Initially the prairie community was sympathetic to those who, because of circumstances beyond their control, found themselves in dire straits. People provided food, shelter, and clothing, and many farmers were quick to offer the "$1.00 until" rate for odd jobs before the cutting began. Sympathy turned to anger and disgust when it was learned that many of the British men were dissatisfied with the terms of employment long accepted by harvesters from the rest of Canada, and that these novices were demanding an experienced man's pay. Easily recognized by their accents, their shoes, and the cut of their clothing, their attitudes and behavior were the main topic of conversation.[46] A reporter from the *Toronto Star* described the situation:

For three weeks I constantly crossed the trail of these thousands of British miner-harvesters. Indeed, it was impossible in a trip made during the last of September and the first of October to escape visual and oral contact with these homeless nomads of the plains. They were everywhere. Everywhere you heard of them. They cropped up sooner or later in every western conversation. Almost every farmer one spoke to had had experience of them or knew of neighbors who had had experiences with them. Salesmen had met them, observed them and talked with them all up and down the land. In the lobbies of the small hotels they said what they thought of them without reserve.... [47]

What prairie people said about the British miner-harvesters was not complimentary, and this hostility aggravated the problem further. Convinced that the open arms they had been promised were part of the same pack of lies that guaranteed them "£3 to £5 per week and free keep," the miner-harvesters joined ranks and resolved not to work for anything less. If their terms were not met, they demanded to be sent home immediately.

Much of the rhetoric and organization of the "won't works" or "malcontents" was generated by agitators amongst them whose prime objective seems to have been to embarrass everyone associated with the movement, which symbolized the existing system's exploitation of workers. The Communist Party of Great Britain had tried to disrupt the movement before it began, conducting meetings outside of Labour Exchanges to urge men not to go. The Canadian government's decision to emphasize the recruitment of men from mining districts because of their physical endurance played directly into the hands of the Communist party. The legacy of the General Strike gave miners every reason to be militant. The party had little difficulty in sending some of its members, allegedly well supplied with money, to carry on the work overseas. Party activists organized the men into cohesive groups aboard ship, who maintained their unity when they arrived on the prairies. There they adamantly insisted on a "hire all or hire none" position, knowing full well that farmers could not accede to their demand.[48]

Since farm work was obviously not their objective, the militants quickly went to the nearest large centre where they contacted local members of the Communist Party of Canada. Together they organized protest meetings against the harvester movement, citing it as a cruel attempt by the British government to ship its social problems to the rest of the Empire. In Calgary, for example, seven hundred people, consisting of harvesters and local sympathizers, met to demand that the Immigration Department repatriate the fifty men stranded there for refusing "starvation wages" of $1.50 to $4.00 per day and that maintenance be provided for them in the meantime. In Drumheller, another forty "of a similar calibre" gathered and were reported to be "exerting a very bad influence" on other harvesters in the area.[49]

Canadian authorities had anticipated problems with the harvester movement from the beginning, and for this reason Ottawa had been adamant that the railways and the British government take joint responsibility for the consequences. When municipalities appealed for help to maintain stranded harvesters, immigration officials simply instructed them to seek compensation from the railway company which served their community. For their part, British authorities dispatched W.C. Osmond, a senior finance officer with the Ministry of Labour but seconded to the O.S.C., to observe the scheme in operation and facilitate winter work placement. His real role, however, appeared to be that of trouble-shooter, with the responsibility of reviewing and paying any legitimate costs incurred in housing and moving the miner-harvesters.[50]

Since Winnipeg had been the dispersal point for the harvesters, it was also the collection depot for the disgruntled from the region. Two of the city's three Immigration Halls served as refuges for "malcontents" and "misfits." A number of them quickly made contact with local Communists as well as other disappointed harvesters, some of whom had never ventured out of the city. Authorities made every effort to convince them to reconsider their decision. The railway companies promised to pay their fares out to the jobs and guaranteed them $4.00 per day and return transportation to Winnipeg if the work was no longer available. Even outsiders, including members of the City Council, the Winnipeg Trades and Labor Council and the One Big Union tried to persuade them to take jobs, but their efforts proved fruitless as well.[51] The harvesters were convinced that they had been wronged and they were determined to agitate until they got their way.

Two hundred people attended a well-publicized open-air rally organized by the Communist party in Market Square on 28 August where a resolution was adopted demanding free transportation home for the harvesters so they could "become disillusioned ambassadors for the Workingclass [sic]" and full maintenance until they departed. On

2 September a delegation visited City Council to demand that it press the Immigration Department to provide transportation and maintenance. Two days later, again in Market Square, another rally was held, this time attended by five hundred people, and addressed by Tom Ewen (McEwen), the district organizer for the Communist party; W.N. Kolisnyk, a Communist member of City Council; and a man named Lester from the One Big Union. Again the subject was the prompt return of the harvesters.[52]

Initially, immigration and railway authorities wanted to withhold maintenance from those who refused to work, but the organized resolve of the men convinced I. Gelley, Immigration's senior man in Winnipeg, that the situation was far worse than in 1923 and that they had to be accommodated before they caused serious property damage or hurt Canada's reputation. Accordingly, the men were fed two meals a day as a temporary measure. Then, on 4 September, in a move which he hoped would clear up the situation in Winnipeg and save the Department further embarrassment, Gelley ordered a special train for the 328 "misfits," "malingerers," and "malcontents" congregated in the city. It was to depart two days later, avoiding large centres on the way to Quebec City, where the men would be segregated in an Immigration Building until their ships departed.[53]

Gelley's hopes for a speedy return to tranquility were short-lived. At the same time, British delegates to the Empire Parliamentary Association, which was touring the West that fall, arrived and heard of the planned movement of British citizens. Some of the delegates saw an opportunity to make some political hay and hurried down to the C.N.R. station to interview the harvesters, who were placed in an enclosure and guarded by two R.C.M.P. officers. Apparently this was done to prevent the sale of train and boat tickets and food hampers.[54] The response was immediate. Thomas Johnston, the Labour M.P. for Stirling, Scotland, immediately rushed out to report that he had seen British harvesters kept in an underground cage with an armed soldier and a couple of dozen policemen on the door, herded about like sheep and forbidden to leave. "British citizens," he thundered, "are not in the habit of being treated that way." As to the harvesters' plight, he concluded that their grievances were legitimate, that the wages and conditions they confronted had been misrepresented, and that they had not been fairly treated by immigration authorities since their arrival in Winnipeg.[55]

Soon after the train departed, Gelley was requested to meet with the British delegation at the Fort Garry Hotel and, after two hours of questioning, managed to convince them that the harvesters "had been treated with all courtesy, and in the best manner that it was possible to handle a lot of grousing people under the circumstances."[56] The damage had been done, however, as reports of "Harvesters Caged Underground" were headlined in British papers the next day.[57]

The departure of the special train for the East and the parliamentarians for Saskatoon did not signal the end of problems for those associated with the harvester movement. Reports continued to come in of men stranded in communities throughout the West, many of them unwilling to work and holding demonstrations to protest their treatment. Saskatoon had had close to three hundred harvesters on hand early in September, but most of them dispersed, leaving a hard core of seventeen at mid-month who refused work even at $5.00 per day while another nine were reported at Hudson Bay Junction.[58] Meanwhile, in Calgary another group of 57 men had gathered at a rally in the Variety Theatre on 13 September to organize a march on City Hall to demand free passage home. While Calgary civic officials refused, in Regina the provincial government felt obliged to give the men thirty-five-cent meal vouchers only to have them presented as payment for restaurant meals costing considerably more. The miner-harvesters stretched the patience of officials even further when the Deputy Minister of Labour, Thomas Molloy, was roused in the middle of the night to find accommodation for half a dozen men who had been evicted from the Paris Hotel, where they had been placed by the government. The proprietress had been sufficiently provoked to declare: "I wouldn't take those big bums into my house again if the Prince of Wales himself were to ask me to."[59] While such boyish behavior caused prairie people to shake their head in amazement, it did not irritate them as much as the realization that, with the harvest in full swing throughout the region and with men in great demand, there were miner-harvesters around who still refused $4.00 to $6.00 a day, even though the railways offered to transport them free of charge. They continued to insist that they had been deceived and refused to co-operate.

Within a week of the first contingent's departure, the Immigration Halls in Winnipeg were again full. Restless and bored with the prospect of having to wait, the harvesters got involved in potentially ugly disturbances that had to be broken up by police almost daily.

When officials learned that some of them had allegedly purchased guns at local pawn shops, immigration authorities suggested that the railways get rid of them on a daily basis before serious trouble broke out since it was "impossible to reason with them."[60] While this solution was somewhat impracticable, departures nevertheless were considerably speeded up thereafter. By mid-month a total of 725 had left, and by 26 September the number had risen to 1,377.[61]

Most prairie residents had had their fill of the miner-harvesters' antics by that time. The Deputy Minister of Immigration confided that some good might come from an early Canadian winter: "If it takes out of Canada those who are not particular about working and are unwilling to make any effort to adjust themselves to life in a new country, perhaps we will not lose much."[62] By the end of September, most of the "won't works" had long departed. More pressing was the matter of finding winter work for those who chose to remain. As the harvest neared completion in Manitoba and Saskatchewan, municipal governments again passed resolutions to refuse assistance to any non-resident harvesters who wanted to spend the winter within their jurisdictions.[63] While the railways, along with the British government, had accepted responsibility for placement or return of the men, all involved knew that they had to co-operate and co-ordinate their activities to achieve any success. As early as 12 September, Osmond, on behalf of British authorities, had met in Regina with representatives of the Immigration Department, provincial Land Settlement Branches, the two railways, the Employment Service, and the United Farmers of Canada (Saskatchewan Section) to plan "a central clearing house" for miner-harvesters needing winter work.[64] Three weeks later, the railways, the Employment Service, and the Land Settlement Branches for the three provinces agreed to advertise jointly inviting farmers, merchants, bankers, and elevator operators to hire British harvesters at $5.00 to $10.00 per month, depending on experience. Meanwhile, the railways agreed to move harvesters at a one-cent per mile rate to other jobs on the prairies, but not east of Winnipeg while there was still a shortage of workers in the local region. In anticipation, however, the Land Settlement Branch began to make inquiries about possible placements on Ontario farms.[65]

Originally, the plan for the harvester movement had been for the men to find winter work on farms on the prairies, and this remained the principal objective, but everyone realized that the likelihood of

British industrial labor staying on farms was remote, especially when farmers themselves preferred to leave the boredom and isolation of a farm in winter if they could.[66] Harvesters already in urban centres generally refused farm work outright no matter what the consequences. The wages offered by prairie farmers for winter work made it doubly difficult to attract workers. After the harvest was over, wages dropped sharply to between $5.00 and $15.00 per month plus board, and in a great many cases all the farm hand received was board alone for the few chores he had to perform. Even Canadian migrant labor preferred hard work in the northern bush camps to this fate. A few single harvesters who had sincere intentions of becoming farmers accepted these conditions, but the married miner, whose family under British regulations was removed from unemployment benefits to face the stigma of the Poor Law after he had been away two months, could not possibly survive under these circumstances. This alone forced many men who would otherwise have stayed to return home.[67]

Private organizations like the Orange Lodges, which had a particular interest in keeping the prairies British and Protestant, made special efforts to find work for some of the miner-harvesters in smaller centres. However, jobs in the cities, primarily in central Canada, in the bush, in the mines, and on the railways eventually absorbed the vast majority of the estimated 1,200 to 1,400 who were still in Canada past year's end.[68] For the 6,368 transported back to Britain, work in Canada was unavailable, unsuitable, or unacceptable, and the special observer of the 1928 movement, W.C. Osmond, closed the books on them by paying outstanding expenses incurred by the railways. In the middle of January 1929 he left Canada after attending a luncheon in his honor in Winnipeg sponsored by representatives for the immigation, colonization, and transportation groups with whom he had been associated for four months.[69]

Like shopkeepers counting the day's receipts long before closing time, the various interested parties involved in the British harvester movement began to assess its impact some time before Osmond departed. Outside of some blatantly political comments the tally was not encouraging for a similar venture at a later date. A few realists, namely those upon whose shoulders the organization of the venture fell, had known from the beginning that a completely successful movement was impossible because too many things could go wrong. The harvester movement of 1923 had already demonstrated this clearly.

The British government was an obvious loser. With considerable domestic unemployment and an election on the horizon, it had hoped to dispose of a sizeable proportion of the miner-harvesters and their dependents in the Dominions, or at least help them make sufficient money to survive the winter without unemployment insurance. Wanting to dispatch as many men as possible, some British spokesmen initially complained that Canada was being too restrictive in its selection process.[70] British authorities must have had second thoughts, however, when they learned that three-quarters of those who went to Canada returned home, that almost 40 percent of those who returned left with no money at all, and that only a third were able to pay their return fare.[71] As a consequence, Dr. Black, the C.N.R.'s Director of Colonization, admitted:

It is now apparent from the percentage that will be left in the country that the movement will be no credit to any institution which took responsibility for it.... owing to the high percentage who have returned home and the trouble they have given, the Ministry of Labor, who so eagerly sponsored the movement, are now extremely sick of it all, and have indicated... that if anything of the kind is to be undertaken in future, it will have to be carried on under entirely different arrangements.[72]

Canadian imperialists and advocates of stepped-up British immigration were also disappointed. They had been convinced that not only would newcomers stay and enhance the labor force but that they would advertise the bounties they found. In actuality, the exact opposite happened. This movement became a high-profile event with considerable press coverage on both sides of the Atlantic. Sensationalism suppressed the scheme's merits and distorted events such as the "Iron Cage" incident in Winnipeg. Similarly, the suicide of a harvester was interpreted as a common occurrence, and the "$1 until" wage was viewed as the prevailing offer.[73] In the British press, Canada emerged not as a land of opportunity that welcomed the British with open arms but as a hostile place peopled by callous foreigners "determined to keep the British down" and upstart colonials unwilling to give proper consideration to people from the Mother Country. This view was well illustrated by James Dunlop, the Commissioner of the Scottish Board of Education, who complained after touring the prairies that the harvesters "got no time to acclimatize themselves to the un-accustomed climatic conditions and the change of food and water."[74] In short, the publicity generated by the movement did not enhance the reputation of Canada as a potential home for settlers, and in fact created problems in recruiting suitable British immigrants the follow-ing year.

The Communist Party of Great Britain, however, considered their involvement in the 1928 harvester movement a success and planned a conference to feature the returned men who could be used "as an exposure of the whole harvester migration swindle."[75] In a sense, the party was the only real winner in 1928 since it helped to make the movement an event of public interest and in the process embarrassed the authorities responsible. It also received considerable public attention through its superb talent for organizing men and events to demonstrate the deceitfulness of the capitalist system.

For the harvesters a successful or disappointing experience in 1928 depended upon individual objectives and the particular circumstances they confronted. For the immigrant who used the movement as a means to get to the United States, it was an admirable success, while the one who naively believed optimistic promises about wages and working conditions suffered accordingly. The number of "won't works" who demanded early return indicates the degree of failure. As could be expected, immigration and railway authorities assiduously sought, found, and publicized stories of harvesters who had succeeded in the venture or who were delighted with the experience.[76] These exemplaries found the adventure they sought, earned considerable money, made new friends, and either went home to a comfortable winter, or stayed and farmed or worked at their respective callings and later sent for their loved ones.

To the prairie farmers, for whom the entire exercise was osten-sibly staged, the British harvester movement successfully contributed over 16 percent of the work force needed to harvest the bumper crop of 1928. Yet the attitudes and behavior displayed by the harvesters reinforced for a number of Canadians the low regard in which they always held lazy, condescending Englishmen. The complaint made by two of the "imported urbanites," however, that "it was Englishmen who did us the most dirt," reveals the most lasting legacy of the 1928 experiment.[77]

The farmers and political leaders who came to the prairies in the pre-war rush had argued loudest and longest that the alarming ethnic mix had to be righted by stepped-up British immigration. They were the first to order harvesters, but they were also the first to dismiss them. They had hoped to attract men like they imagined themselves to have been when they first arrived. They had crossed the Atlantic using their own resources and in their own minds came armed only with independence, initiative, and a willingness to accept whatever wages and working conditions were offered in order to learn the business of farming. From then on they skimped, saved, and persevered against considerable odds until they prospered. They assumed that the Mother Country still produced men like themselves, who were choice prospects among the harvesters, according to one observer:

He it was who made light of blistered hands and aching back; he who would not be deflected from his objective by Communist agitators who sought to wreck the scheme; he who showed intelligence and accepted work at a dollar a day picking stones when he couldn't get $4 at stooking. He developed a blind eye which refused to see defeat and kept right on working when every part of his anatomy cried out for rest. When one job ran out he lost no time in annexing another, invariably backing up his request for work with "I'll take anything...."[78]

Such men were scarce, however, and misfits, malingerers, and malcontents were terms prairie farmers applied to the British harvesters. To them, Englishmen were products of the dole and unemployment insurance, which sapped their strength and made them unable and unwilling to work. Buttressed by trade union and Communist rhetoric to the point that they were afraid to venture alone, they were unable to cope, even with considerable subsidies. They appeared to be more interested in advertising their plight than in making an honest effort to correct the situation. In short, in the opinion of one respected Saskatchewan observer who tried to sum up prevailing sentiment, assisted immigration had only brought "pussy-footed, spineless people who are not worth salt."[79] For this reason, prairie farmers were forced to give grudging credit to the central European immigrant who, despite his cultural and linguistic shortcomings, had come over on his own and provided a better illustration of independence, and a willingness to sacrifice.[80]

Some prairie dwellers, when confronted with such evidence, attempted to dismiss the 1928 movement as an aberration since "few countries assist in getting rid of their best citizens."[81] Yet the harsh response of the Anglophile farmer to the miner-harvesters indicates disillusion spawned by the realization that a distinct gap had developed between the land of their birth and their vision of it, a gap which had not been obvious until faced with an object of comparison. To them, it seemed that new forces were at work and new values prevailed. That there was too much "mollycoddlin' and pap-feeding" was a common comment, as were: "the Britishers we're getting now are too soft"; "that's not the way we got our pioneers"; "the failure of the Britisher on the land is no disgrace to him since he has become so urbanized"; and "these Britishers have no feeling for the soil."[82]

Doubtless, concerns about urbanized workers who had no feeling for the soil, combined with the attitudes and behavior exhibited by the British harvesters, confirmed farmers' suspicions of the city as the source of undesirable influences and city dwellers as parasites living on handouts, feeding at the trough filled by the country's real producers. Farmers seldom expressed such views with clarity.[83] Nevertheless, as testimony presented to the Saskatchewan Royal Commission on Immigration and Settlement reveals, English-speaking prairie farmers showed no such reticence about offering their opinion on immigration in general and the use of British industrial workers as farm hands in particular. The "problem" of the ethnic make-up of the region notwithstanding, such immigrants were unacceptable in their view.

The 1928 movement fully demonstrated that assisted immigration was conscript immigration and, therefore, worthless. The policy of trying to solve the farm labor supply problem through immigration had backfired. Even with the rapidly rising cost of farm labor during the decade, the supply was unpredictable at best and certainly unreliable. The problem had to be solved by other means than four decades' dependence on outside labor sources. High wheat prices late in the decade encouraged farmers to mechanize their operations; large numbers turned to combine-harvesters drawn by gasoline-powered tractors. In 1929, in part because of a crop failure in certain sections of the region, only 3,592 harvesters came to the West, and in 1930 the idea was completely abandoned, its demise accelerated by the British harvester movement of 1928.

Notes

1. The pressure often became so great that Obed Smith, a senior Immigrant official, was moved to retaliate that "The farmers of the west need not expect the Canadian immigration department, the provincial government, or the railways to make men out of India Rubber." P.A.C., Immigration Branch Records, RG 76 (hereafter I.B.), vol. 38, file 839, part 2, news story, *The Telegram*, n.d.

2. W.J.C. Cherwinski, "Wooden Horses and Rubber Cows: Training British Agriculture Labour for the Canadian Prairies, 1890-1930," Canadian Historical Association, *Historical Papers, 1980*, pp. 133-54.

3. John Herd Thompson, "Bringing in the Sheaves: the Harvest Excursionists, 1890-1929, *Canadian Historical Review* LIX, 4 (December 1978): 467-89; W.J.C. Cherwinski, "The Incredible Harvest Excursion of 1908," *Labour/le travailleur* 5 (Spring 1980): 57-79; George V. Haythorne, "Harvest Labor in Western Canada: An Espisode in Economic Planning," *Quarterly Journal of Economics* V, 47 (May 1933): 533-44.

4. J.A. Schultz, "Canadian Attitudes Toward Empire Settlement, 1919-1930," *The Journal of Imperial and Commonwealth History* I, 2 (January 1973): 237-51; Saskatchewan Archives Board (hereafter S.A.), Dunning Papers, Wilson to Dunning, 31 May 1922, pp. 28, 578-79; University of Alberta Archives, Pearce Papers, file 9/2/5/4-6, Pearce to McGrath, 10 March 1924; *Montreal Star*, 21 February 1928; *Morning Albertan* (Calgary), 12 September 1922.

5. *Agricultural and Industrial Progress in Canada* (hereafter A.I.P.C.), December 1923, p. 232.

6. E.B. Ingles, "Some Aspects of Dry-Land Agriculture in the Canadian Prairies to 1925" (M.A. thesis, University of Calgary, 1973), pp. 87-89; P.A.C., Dept. of Labour Records, RG27, vol. 113, file 600.02-48; S.A., Dunning Papers, Johnson to Dunning, 20 August 1921, p. 14377 and Keller Grain Growers to Dunning, 31 August 1921, p. 14380.

7. I.B., vol. 276, file 218165, part 1, Blair to Stewart, 1 February 1926; Patrick A. Dunae, "Tom Brown on the Prairies: Public Schoolboys and Remittance Men in the Canadian West 1870-1914" (paper presented to the Canadian Historical Association meeting, Saskatoon, Saskatchewan, 1979); Cherwinski, "Wooden Horses and Rubber Cows," pp. 135-37.

8. S.A., Martin Papers, Cook to Martin, 14 July 1921, pp. 30196-98; Public Archives of Alberta (hereafter P.A.A.), Premiers' Papers, file 503, Miller to Greenfield, 20 September 1923.

9. I.B., vol. 276, file 218165, part 2, Memo "British Harvester Movement-1928," 14 September 1928.

10. Ibid., vol. 38, file 839, part 6, Barnett to Freer, 21 March 1925.

11. The C.P.R. concluded that "the movement proved permanently beneficial as an immigration scheme." A.I.P.C., September 1926, p. 176. *See also* December 1923, p. 231 and October 1928, p. 197.

12. Trades and Labor Congress of Canada, *Proceedings,* 1923, pp. 8–9.

13. I.B., vol. 612, file 907095 (1923) contains detailed information on the problems faced by the department. *See also* Schultz, "Canadian Attitudes Toward Empire Settlement", p. 241.

14. The objective was to introduce the "better class" of potential immigrant to the rigors of prairie life. In 1926, forty students from Oxford and from Wye Agricultural College in Kent joined the annual harvest excursion. The next year the program was expanded to include 300 young men selected from thirteen universities plus Wye College. I.B., vol. 276, file 218165, part 3, "Scheme for enabling British University Students to visit and work in Canada during the Harvest Season, 1927"; A.I.P.C., September 1926, September 1927.

15. P.A.C., Canadian National Railways Records, RG 30 (hereafter C.N.), vol. 8390, file 3620–12, Black to Dix, 27 June 1927, Johnson to Black, 26 and 30 June 1927, Dennis Memo, 26 July 1927; file 3620–15, "Extract from Periodical Report...Harvest Arangements, 1927"; P.A.C., Dept. of Labour Records, RG27, vol. 117, file 600.02–133, pp. 16–17.

16. Dept. of Labour Records, RG27, vol. 117, file 600.02–133, p. 17; C.N., vol. 8390, file 3620–15, Black to Robb, 30 July 1927, Black to Johnson, 13 August 1927.

17. C.N., vol. 8390, file 3620–15, Black to Egan, 8 September 1927, Egan to Black, 9 September 1927; I.B., vol. 276, file 218165, part 1, Little to McDonell, 2 July 1928.

18. Dept. of Labour Records, RG27, vol. 117, file 600.02–133, p. 20.

19. Ibid., pp. 18, 29; Glenbow Alberta Institute (hereafter G.A.I.), C.P.R. files (hereafter C.P.), file 714, Kent to Colley, 21 May 1928. Hereafter all dates will refer to 1928 unless otherwise indicated.

20. I.B., vol. 276, file 218165, part I, clipping from *Yorkshire Evening News,* 17 May.

21. Ibid., Lovat to Forke, 27 June, Egan to Lovat, n.d., Skelton to Egan, 19 July; part 2, Memo "British Harvester Movement—1928," 14 September.

22. Ibid., part 1, Gelley to Egan, 19 July, and Broughton to Little, 21 July; P.A.A., Premiers' Papers, file 0491, Heenan to Brownlee, 23 July; C.N., vol. 8390, file 3620–15, McGuire to McNicholl, 4 September.

23. I.B., vol. 276, file 218165, part 1; Rhodes to Heenan, 24 July; Saunders, Molloy, Taschereau, and Godfrey to Heenan, 25 July; Murray to Heenan, 27 July; part 2, Memo "British Harvester Movement — 1928," 14 September; P.A.A., Premiers' Papers, file 0491, Heenan to Brownlee, 24 July.

24. C.N., vol. 8390, file 3620–1, Black to Robb, 19 November; I.B., vol. 276, file 218165, part 1, Lovat to Egan, 31 July.

25. What exactly was agreed was a subject of disagreement. W.J. Black, Director of Colonization for the C.N.R., accused a London official of the company of agreeing to full railway responsibility for winter work placement while Vice-President A.T. Weldon argued that the railways had only agreed to "heartily cooperate in the placing of men in winter farm employment." C.N., vol. 8390, file 3620–1: Weldon to Robb, 7 November; Black to Robb, 19 November; Black to McGowan, 6 September; Black to Egan, 19 September; I.B., vol. 276, file 218165, part 1: McNaughton to Egan, 3 August; Egan to Baird and McNaughton, 3 August; Egan to Forke, 4 August.

26. I.B., vol. 276, file 218165, part 1: Pagé to Jeffs, 23 July; Egan to Dennis, 25 July, Egan to Riddell, 27 July; "Torosus" to Immigration Ottawa, 27 July; Lovat to Egan, 28 July.

27. *The Daily News and Westminster Gazette*, 11 August.

28. I.B., vol. 276, file 218165, part 2, Walker to Egan, 25 August.

29. Of the 2,851 selected from the Glasgow area, employment records showed that 530 were married, although most of them claimed single status to improve their chances of qualifying. Ibid., part 3, Walker to Egan, 22 September.

30. *Empire News* (Manchester), 5 July 1931.

31. I.B., vol. 276, file 218165, part 1, Jeffs to Pagé, 9 August, "Torosus" to Immigration Ottawa, and Immigration Ottawa to "Torosus," 13 August.

32. Ibid., part 2, Walker to Egan, 25 August, part 2, *Yorkshire Evening News* clipping, 3 August.

33. Ibid., part 2, Walker to Egan, 25 August.

34. Ibid., Boyle to Land Settlement Branch (hereafter L.S.B.), Saskatoon, 12 October, A.D.M. to Egan, 11 September; C.N., vol. 5629, file "British Harvesters, 1928," "Harvesting in Canada: Undergraduates' Experience" (hereafter "Undergrads' Experience"); Cherwinski, "Incredible Harvest Excursion of 1908," pp. 66–70.

35. C.N., vol. 5629, file "British Harvesters–1928," "Undergrads' Experience."

36. Ibid., Black to Robb, 4 January, 1929; I.B., vol. 276, file 218165, part 3, Taylor to Forke, 1 November; Blair to Rattray, 2 November.

37. I.B., vol. 276, file 218165, part 3, Findlater Report, 15 October.

38. For example, the C.P.R. agent at Daysland, Alberta, ordered thirty men and got eighty. Ibid., part 2, P.J. Rossiter statement, n.d.

39. C.N., vol. 8390, file 3620–2, European Colonization Manager to McNaughton, 4 October; vol. 5629, file "British Harvesters, 1928," "Undergrads' Experience."

40. Frederick Griffin, "Raw Recruits," *Toronto Star Weekly*, 10 November.

41. C.P., file 729, Colley to Vanscoy, 14 November.

42. Saskatchewan Royal Commission on Immigration and Settlement, Minutes of Evidence (hereafter R.C.I.S.), vol. 33, p. 43; I.B., vol. 276, file 218165, part 2, clipping from *The Citizen*, n.d.

43. "Feeding the Harvesters," *Farm and Ranch Review*, 5 September 1913; C.N., vol. 5629, file "British Harvesters, 1928," "Undergrads' Experience"; *Regina Daily Post*, 28 September.

44. C.N., vol. 8390, file 3620–1, clipping from *Evening News*, 25 September.

45. I.B., vol. 276, file 218165, part 2, Evans to Goldsmith, 24 August, part 3, L.S.B. Field Supervisor's Report, 5 October; *Manitoba Free Press*, 27 December.

46. C.P. file 753, Schmidt to Colley, 17 September. One group protesting low wages was threatened with arrest by a group of Saskatchewan farmers if they did not disperse immediately. R.C.I.S., vol. 43, p. 91. *See also* Lloyd G. Reynolds and Carl A. Dawson, *The British Immigrant: His Social and Economic Adjustment in Canada* (Toronto: Oxford University Press, 1935), p. 207.

47. *Toronto Star Weekly*, 10 November.

48. Ibid.; I.B., vol. 276, file 218165, part 1, clipping from *Ottawa Journal*, 6 August; part 2, Gelley to Jolliffe, 6 September; C.N., vol. 8390, file 3620–1, McGowan to Black, 5 September; *Manitoba Free Press*, 28 December.

49. I.B., vol. 276, file 218165, part 1, Alland Report, 30 August, Gelley to Jolliffe, 6 September, Farmer to Forke and Jolliffe to Gelley, 11 September; C.N., vol. 8390, file 3620–1, McGowan to Black, 5 September.

50. I.B., vol. 276, file 218165, part 1, Egan to Black, 30 August; part 2, McNaughton to Egan, 17 August; C.N., vol. 8390, file 3620–1, Johnston to Creelman, 15 August, Black to McGowan, 6 September.

51. I.B., vol. 276, file 218165, part 1, Gelley to Jolliffe, 14 September.

52. Ibid., "British Harvesters! A Mass Meeting," Alland Report, 30 August, Alland Report, 5 September. *See also* Tom McEwen, *The Forge Glows Red: From Blacksmith to Revolutionary* (Toronto: Progress Books, 1974), pp. 53–54.

53. C.N., vol. 8390, 3620–1, McGowan to Black, 8 September, Johnson to Creelman, 5 September, Macalister Memo, 15 September; I.B., vol. 276, file 218165, part 2, Gelley to Jolliffe, 4 and 6 September.

54. C.N., vol. 8390, file 3620–1, McGowan to Black, 8 September.

55. *Ottawa Citizen*, 7 September.

56. I.B., vol. 276, file 218165, part 2, Bostock to Forke, 7 September, Gelley to Jolliffe, 14 September.

57. C.N., vol. 8390, file 3620–1, clipping from *Evening Standard*, 7 September.

58. Winnipeg Communists sought to co-ordinate operations with their counterparts in Saskatoon to organize the harvesters passing through but failed because "the comrades of Saskatoon are nearly all Ukrainians and are not able to do it." I.B.,

vol. 276, file 218165, part 2, "Communist Activities amongst British Harvesters," 8 September.

59. Ibid., Cardinal to Gelley, and Gelley to Jolliffe, 13 September, Jolliffe to Gelley, 17 September; *Manitoba Free Press,* 28 December. Variations on the meal stunt were quite common. See *O.B.U. Bulletin,* 13 September.

60. I.B., vol. 276, file 218165, part 2, Gelley to Jolliffe, 18 September, Steven Report, 10 September, Green Report, 24 September, Johnson Report, 25 September.

61. Ibid., Gelley to Jolliffee, 14 and 26 September; *Manitoba Free Press,* 12 September.

62. I.B., vol. 276, file 218165, part 3, Blair to Rattray, 2 November.

63. Ibid., part 2, Adshed to Egan, 8 August; part 3, Skinner to Jolliffe, 27 October, Taylor to Forke, 1 November; P.A.A., Premiers' Papers, file 0524, Brownlee to Greenfield, 10 September.

64. *Ottawa Citizen,* 13 September; C.N., vol. 8390, file 3620-1 "Extract from Western Colonization Manager's Report, first half of Sept. 1928."

65. I.B., vol. 276, file 218165, part 3: Gelley to Jolliffe, 27 September; Johnston and Foster to Blair, 28 September; Nixon to Rattray, 18 October.

66. C.N., vol. 5617, file 4031-4, Soldier Settlement Board, "Summary of Agricultural Conditions for period ending Oct. 31, 1929."

67. The fact that a man abandoned his family in Britain and remained in Canada did not ensure success as was the case with one Fred Sharpe, a man with a wife and child on the Isle of Man. Sharpe worked for a year before losing his job. Destitute and in danger of arrest for vagrancy, he sought deportation in October 1930. S.A., Dept. of Labour Records, file LaI6 (1), Sharpe to Merkeley, 24 October 1930; I.B., vol. 276, file 218165, part 3, Dist. Supt. to Gelley, 17 October, Blair Memo, 18 October.

68. C.P., file 753, Ball to L.O.L., Coleman, Alta., 12 September, MacKinnon to Colley, 12 November; Reynolds and Dawson, *The British Immigrant,* p. 79; Allen Seager, "Class Consciousness, Class Anarchy: Three Alberta Coal Towns During the Depression" (Paper presented to the C.H.A. meeting, Saskatoon), 1979, p. 10; C.N., vol. 8390, file 3620-1, Black to Robb, 4 January 1929. Thirty-eight percent of those removed by C.N. were unable to pay their own passage.

69. C.N., vol. 8390, file 3620-1, McGowan to Black, 5 January 1929. Up to the end of December, Osmond had paid out to the C.N.R.: $3051.42 for maintenance, $108.25 for medical expenses, and $2075.77 to cover the cost of transporting stranded harvesters to and from Winnipeg and within the region. *See also Manitoba Free Press,* 3 January 1920.

70. I.B., vol. 276, file 218165, part 3, Adshead to Blair, 3 October.

71. Ibid., Blair to Walker, 3 February 1929.

72. C.N., vol. 8390, file 3620-1, Black to Robb, 19 November.

73. *Manitoba Free Press,* 29 December.

74. C.N., vol. 8390, file 3620–1, clipping from *Evening News,* 25 September; C.P., file 753, *London Star,* 1 October, "Foreigners Favoured in Canadian Harvest."

75. I.B., vol. 276, file 218165, part 3, Starnes to Egan, 28 December.

76. Ibid., Boyle to LSB, 12 October; *Manitoba Free Press,* 31 December; C.N., vol. 8390, file 3620–1, Weir to Black, 28 August; C.N.R. Press Releases: "Miner Harvesters in Canada," 29 August, "Miner Harvesters Settle Down," 21 September, "Miner Harvester Buys a Farm"; A.I.P.C., January 1929, p. 16.

77. *Toronto Star Weekly,* 10 November.

78. Farmers whose families had been in Canada for several generations were recognized by the harvesters as more accommodating than the recent arrivals. *Manitoba Free Press,* 26 and 29 December.

79. Percy H. Shelton, Vice-Chairman, R.C.I.S., Statement vol. 22, pp. 114–19.

80. Ibid., vol. 6, p. 34; vol. 15, pp. 8–9; vol. 26, p. 14, vol. 29, p. 49.

81. Ibid., vol. 22, p. 66; vol. 23, pp. 56–57.

82. *Toronto Star Weekly,* 10 November.

83. Several farmers complained of British harvesters being a bad influence on other workers. In addition, some British farm trainees housed at Alberta's Agricultural Colleges agitated to be sent home on the same terms as the harvesters.

Bankers and Farmers in
Western Canada, 1900–1939

T. D. Regehr

In 1926 a delegation from the Canadian Bankers' Association met with the leaders of the Canadian Council of Agriculture to discuss the problems of rural credit. Both sides approached the meeting with a considerable willingness to compromise and a determination to resolve their differences. Yet, at the end of the meeting, one of the bankers reported rather sadly:

> I should say that the effect of the arguments was to convince each member of the Canadian Council of Agriculture that we had a reasonable answer to every point raised. I am afraid, however, that as a body they will never be convinced... farmer like, they will continue to grumble about all the matters which were brought forward notwithstanding the fact that they know our attitude is not unfair.[1]

The organized farmers came away from the same meeting more convinced than ever that the chartered banks of Canada were not adequately meeting their needs. They were prepared to concede that the bankers could not do some of the things asked of them because of the terms of the Bank Act, but to the farmers, this was merely an argument in favor of legislative amendments to the Bank Act. The bankers' references to sound banking practices left the farmers unconvinced because some of the practices Canadian bankers thought unsound were in fact being followed in other countries.

As long as the farmers talked only about their needs and the bankers about sound banking policies and the requirements of the Bank Act, there was no real meeting of minds, and it was often left to the politicians to sort out and, if necessary, impose working arrangements between the two parties.

The Main Issues

There were four main issues over which farmers and bankers disagreed during the first four decades of the twentieth century. The first was that the banks refused to grant the farmer sufficient credit; second, the interest rates on farm loans were too high; third, the term of usance of loans was too short; and fourth, collection or foreclosure proceedings were often unfair and injurious to the general interests of the country.[2]

Farmers trying to establish themselves on new homesteads in western Canada rarely had enough money to carry on operations without resort to credit for improvements, stock, machinery and supplies, and personal needs until the crop was harvested in the fall. Farmers could be regarded as entrepreneurs trying to establish themselves. In western Canada, however, credit needs very substantially exceeded the savings accumulated and deposited in western Canadian banks. During the pioneer period, at least, the West was a debtor region. The banks often found it impossible to meet the farmers' demand for credit, although they argued that the Canadian branch banking system, unlike the unit banking system in the United States, was remarkably well suited to move money quickly and easily from older regions, where deposits normally exceeded loans, to newer and developing regions where more money and credit were required. Sir Edmund Walker, the President of the Canadian Bank of Commerce, told a parliamentary committee in 1913 that "at a hundred and twenty-two western branches of the Canadian Bank of Commerce, in the middle or prairie provinces, we have farmers' deposits amounting to $2,869,926, and we have loans to farmers amounting to $13,035,784."[3]

Walker admitted that it was not the custom of the banks to break down their loans regionally or into occupational groupings, but there was general agreement that "The savings of the eastern provinces, where the growth of industry and trade is slow and the demand for new capital is not increasing, are sent westward and loaned out to merchants and manufacturers and farmers of the new territories."[4] A Royal Commission in Saskatchewan that examined the problem in

1913 asked the banks to provide statements showing average loans and deposits at each of their Saskatchewan branches. These returns also showed that average loans in the province significantly exceeded average deposits.[5] The impressions thus created have been widely accepted as a reasonably accurate indication of banking operations in western Canada. The farmers of western Canada were getting more credit than the total amount of money saved and deposited in the region. Their complaints about inadequate credit facilities have therefore been regarded as somewhat unreasonable.

Recently the Bank of Nova Scotia has made many of its records available for historical research. Among these records are branch-by-branch annual returns and statistics. These clearly show that, at least in the case of the Bank of Nova Scotia, the situation in 1913 was rather abnormal, and the widespread belief that the West, on balance, owed the banks more money than could be covered by deposits in western Canadian banks is only correct for a comparatively short period of time. Table I gives the total loans and desposits at all Bank of Nova Scotia branches in Manitoba, Saskatchewan, and Alberta, together with a tabulation of the amount by which deposits exceeded loans in the three prairie provinces. Negative figures indicate an excess of loans over deposits. Regrettably, figures for the period from 1928 to 1934 are not available.[6]

The figures given in Table I were greatly influenced by large and significantly fluctuating grain accounts held by the Winnipeg regional head office of the Bank of Nova Scotia. In Table II, therefore, the same calculations are shown, but the returns from the main office in Winnipeg are excluded.

Table I
  Bank of Nova Scotia
  Western Canada Banking Statistics

Year	Loans	Deposits	Surplus
1900	$141,770	$118,665	$−23,105
1901	94,890	183,951	89,061
1902	86,696	278,695	191,999
1903	168,920	350,018	181,098

Table I (continued)

Year	Loans	Deposits	Surplus
1904	400,958	473,215	72,257
1905	437,936	638,321	200,385
1906	745,815	850,474	104,659
1907	1,021,061	949,006	-72,055
1908	928,644	862,664	-65,980
1909	1,270,292	1,157,482	-112,810
1910	2,601,615	1,526,190	-1,075,425
1911	4,104,819	2,055,517	-2,049,302
1912	4,536,694	3,185,142	-1,351,552
1913	6,432,212	3,375,465	-3,056,747
1914	6,268,676	3,300,504	-2,968,172
1915	6,074,619	3,626,983	-2,447,636
1916	6,255,685	4,612,971	-1,642,714
1917	6,714,249	5,342,695	-1,371,554
1918	6,175,001	5,733,910	-441,091
1919*	17,781,596	12,064,057	-5,717,539
1920	16,803,606	13,303,866	-3,499,740
1921	12,632,143	12,322,055	-310,088
1922	14,873,385	11,801,571	-3,071,814
1923	10,826,608	11,121,331	294,723
1924	13,389,544	11,054,943	-2,334,601
1925	11,373,165	11,877,583	504,418
1926	10,398,855	13,647,142	3,248,287
1927	12,267,544	14,599,628	2,332,084
1935	21,504,983	16,899,776	-4,605,207
1936	13,458,299	17,990,369	4,532,070
1937	9,995,129	17,634,429	7,639,300
1938	11,190,282	17,963,874	6,773,592
1939	18,971,366	18,845,383	-125,983

*On 30 April 1919 the Bank of Ottawa was amalgamated with the Bank of Nova Scotia. At the time, the Bank of Ottawa had 17 branches in Manitoba, Saskatchewan, and Alberta and handled one of the largest grain accounts in Winnipeg—an account the Bank of Nova Scotia lost in 1921 but regained the following year.

Table II

Bank of Nova Scotia
Western Canada (excluding Winnipeg) Banking Statistics

Year	Loans	Deposits	Surplus
1903	$17,627	$18,980	$1,353
1904	128,196	89,824	-38,372
1905	166,475	196,912	30,437
1906	267,089	339,345	72,256
1907	384,843	450,960	66,117
1908	255,824	400,509	144,685
1909	348,752	548,536	199,784
1910	823,054	809,160	-13,894
1911	1,758,530	1,181,825	-576,705
1912	1,788,674	2,088,701	300,027
1913	3,143,278	2,232,521	-910,757
1914	3,116,178	2,133,686	-982,492
1915	2,875,496	1,987,588	-887,908
1916	2,518,734	2,790,999	272,265
1917	2,337,349	3,250,054	912,705
1918	2,384,956	3,502,863	1,117,907
1919*	6,393,202	8,444,434	2,057,232
1920	8,078,857	8,529,672	450,815
1921	7,015,322	7,882,293	866,971
1922	6,837,218	7,123,233	286,015
1923	5,326,827	6,966,893	1,640,066
1924	4,892,516	7,060,219	2,167,703
1925	4,396,893	7,611,712	3,214,819
1926	4,842,393	8,927,575	4,085,182
1927	7,070,102	9,714,785	2,644,683
1935	6,801,286	9,225,934	2,424,648
1936	6,935,256	10,931,302	3,996,046
1937	6,926,675	10,981,457	4,054,782
1938	7,464,459	11,390,140	3,925,681
1939	7,890,646	12,714,806	4,824,160

*On 30 April 1919 the Bank of Ottawa was amalgamated with the Bank of Nova Scotia.

The main branches in the other major western cities also included a number of non-farm accounts, and in Table III the same calculations are shown, but with the returns from Winnipeg, Regina, Saskatoon, Calgary, and Edmonton excluded. There is no doubt that some of the loans and deposits in these five cities were made to or by farmers, but

Table III
    Bank of Nova Scotia
    Western Canada (excluding Winnipeg, Regina, Saskatoon,
    Calgary, and Edmonton) Banking Statistics

Year	Loans	Deposits	Surplus
1911	$45,923	$36,795	$ – 9,128
1912	303,517	166,662	– 136,855
1913	526,725	279,413	– 247,312
1914	684,070	322,695	– 361,375
1915	598,999	342,680	– 256,319
1916	519,277	579,152	59,875
1917	549,513	895,285	345,772
1918	625,158	1,011,814	386,656
1919*	4,018,666	5,171,988	1,153,322
1920	4,703,203	4,991,645	288,442
1921	4,223,555	4,507,847	284,292
1922	4,382,827	4,095,624	– 287,203
1923	3,143,631	4,048,636	905,005
1924	2,785,514	4,103,681	1,318,167
1925	2,295,130	4,491,119	2,195,989
1926	2,094,422	5,257,819	3,163,397
1927	2,758,741	5,836,619	3,077,878
1935	4,117,374	5,947,946	1,830,572
1936	3,963,066	6,565,441	2,602,375
1937	3,682,448	6,654,034	2,971,586
1938	4,111,608	6,905,938	2,794,330
1939	4,013,328	7,531,914	3,518,586

*On 30 April 1919 the Bank of Ottawa was amalgamated with the Bank of Nova Scotia.

the loans and deposits outside of these centres were almost entirely made to or by rural people and most clearly illustrate the trend in bank loans and deposits of farmers in western Canada.

These figures show that western Canada as a whole was a significant debtor region, insofar as the Bank of Nova Scotia was concerned, only for the period from 1907 to 1924. They further suggest that for the rural communities in western Canada the period of significant net indebtedness was much shorter—from 1911 to 1915. The wide publicity given the 1913 figures of the parliamentary committee and the Saskatchewan Royal Commission created an impression that was, in fact, only accurate for a short period of time, but they were still the basis on which western banking policies and criticisms were based as late as 1931.[7] For most of the period under consideration, the Bank of Nova Scotia received more deposits in western rural communities than it granted in loans.

This suggests that western farm complaints about unduly restrictive bank credit policies had some validity and that one of the main defences offered by the bankers is of dubious veracity. But such calculations of loans and deposits meet only in part the larger questions involved. The bankers always maintained that farmers with adequate collateral got all the loans to which they were entitled. That, the bankers admitted, was not necessarily all the credit the farmers needed and thought they should get. The problem, however, lay very largely in the nature of the collateral most farmers could offer as security for their loans. It was illegal under the terms of the Bank Act for the chartered banks to take mortgages on real estate as security for loans.[8] Yet, a farmer's main assets were his land and improvements thereon. Other assets the farmer could offer as security for bank loans were his personal chattels and his crops and livestock in various stages of maturation. The prices of grain and other farm products, however, fluctuated a great deal. As a result it was often fairly easy to get a bank loan in years when both yield and prices were high, but next to impossible when there was a crop failure or the international price for grain fell. The sale value of the farmer's chattels was also greatly influenced by the economic prosperity of the district.

A graphic description of the bankers' response to a fall in prices was provided when Prime Minister Bennett called in a number of bankers in 1931 and upbraided them for their rural credit policies. The Secretary of the Canadian Bankers' Association reported the incident:

The Prime Minister said... he understood quite clearly what had happened in the West with reference to extensions of credit to farmers: Without any general instruction with regard to loaning policy it would seem that the branch manager, finding that advances made last year had only been partially cleared up, due to the severe fall in prices, of his own initiative and to maintain his own record had put in force a policy of restriction with regard to future loans; many of the managers in the West were young men just assuming the responsibilities of a career and any of a timid or conservative nature became ultra conservative in the granting of credit, seeing that there was little prospect of improved prices for the 1931 crop.[9]

In 1931 the farmers complained that they were not getting sufficient credit. They had, however, obtained a great deal of credit in the prosperous years before 1929. The comparative abundance of credit in the late 1920s, followed by the severe restrictions of the early 1930s, ruined many farmers. For most farmers it would have been better if the bankers had advanced less credit in the late 1920s and more in the early 1930s, in each case following a policy whereby western farm loans more or less balanced deposits made by the people of that region. The branch banking system that facilitated interregional transfers of funds and the importation of money in prosperous times and stringent collections during difficult times in fact accentuated the already severe economic fluctuations to which the prairie grain economy was susceptible. It also led to the seemingly anomolous situation where farmers vociferously demanded more credit while seemingly drowning in a sea of debt.

The second major point of contention between farmers and bankers related to the high interest rates charged on loans to prairie farmers, contrasted with the low rate paid on deposits. Until the 1930s, bank loans to western farmers generally carried a rate of 8 to 10 percent, which was approximately 2 percent higher than similar loans in other parts of the country and 4 or 5 percent higher than the best rate offered to large corporate borrowers. Interest paid on deposits was usually 1 or 2 percent.[10]

The banks justified these rates by stating that the western business was scattered, risky, and expensive and that, in fact, reducing interest rates to the levels demanded by most of the western farmers would

force the closing of many of the small branches and a general reduction of banking services offered.

Table IV shows, at ten-year intervals, the number of Bank of
Nova Scotia branches shown to be making a profit and the number
suffering losses.[11]

According to the calculations of the Bank of Nova Scotia, most
branches in every region were unprofitable, and the figures in that
regard were no worse for the prairies than for most other regions.

It might be reasonably asked why the Bank of Nova Scotia continued to operate successfully when most of its branches were unprofitable. The answer, quite simply, is that the branch profit and loss
statements did not reflect the real value of a branch to the total operations of the bank. One very important item contributed very substantially to the seemingly dismal showing of many branches. If a branch
had a surplus of deposits over loans, that surplus could be transferred
to the head office to be loaned out where there was a greater demand,
or perhaps only where the senior officers at head office preferred to
lend the money. The branch, of course, had to pay interest on deposits, but head office paid no interest to the branch for monies transferred from the branch to head office. Some of these transferred funds
were admittedly held as reserves earning no interest, or were placed in-
terest-free or at very low rates of interest as call loans in New York or
London, essentially as reserves that could be called at a moment's
notice. It was undoubtedly difficult to calculate precisely what a
branch with substantial surpluses of deposits over loans was worth,
but the failure to include anything in this regard in the profit and loss
statements of the branches meant that those branches that had more
deposits than loans were almost certain to report a loss, while those
that carried far more interest-bearing loans than interest-paying
deposits showed large profits. In fact, the head office in Toronto rolled
up enormous profits, but that would not have been possible without
the numerous branches where deposits exceeded loans. Furthermore,
when the Bank of Nova Scotia prepared statements showing the pro-
fitability of banking operations in the various regions, the figures
from head office were included in the Ontario and Quebec (one region) results.[12] These results then compared very favorably with the
results for the prairie and maritime regions.

The cost of doing business in western Canada may well have been
higher than in some other parts of Canada, and certainly the cost of

Table IV
Bank of Nova Scotia
Profit or Loss of Branch Banks

Year	B.C. + Profit	B.C. - Loss	Prairies Profit	Prairies Loss	Ontario Profit	Ontario Loss	Quebec Profit	Quebec Loss	Maritimes Profit	Maritimes Loss	U.S.A. & London Profit	U.S.A. & London Loss	Caribbean Profit	Caribbean Loss	Newfoundland Profit	Newfoundland Loss	Total + Profit	Total - Loss
1907	0	1	4	1	5	5	1	3	7	34	3	0	3	4	2	0	22	51
1917	2	1	6	5	15	50	2	8	12	59	3	0	3	10	4	15	46	149
1927	1	4	22	12	29	101	3	16	11	73	3	1	10	13	2	10	71	240
1937	1	5	31	2	15	109	3	18	16	63	2	2	3	21	0	12	42	261

+ Number of branches reporting a profit.
- Number of branches reporting a loss.

servicing numerous small farm loans was more expensive than handling one or several large loans in Toronto or Montreal. A differential in interest rates might have been justified, but the basis on which that differential was most frequently justified was as inappropriate as was the manner in which railways at that time calculated the cost of their branch lines. The branches made very substantial contributions to the profits of the head office, which were not shown in the profit and loss statements of the branches.

The high western interest rates were, of course, particularly hard to bear in years when the crops failed or grain prices were low. Many farmers also believed they were illegal. Section 91 of the Bank Act stated that "The Bank may stipulate for, take, reserve or exact any rate of interest or discount not exceeding seven per cent per annum and may receive and take in advance any such rate, but no higher rate of interest shall be recoverable by the bank." [13] In part because of this provision, the banks always deducted the interest at the time the loan was made to the farmer. A farmer borrowing $1,000 at 8 percent for six months actually got only $960 from the bank. This increased the effective rate of interest slightly, but that was not the main reason why the banks resorted to this kind of discounting.

The courts, in series of legal decisions, had offered a rather ingenious interpretation of Section 91. Rates of more than 7 percent could be charged but the amounts in excess of 7 percent could not be recovered in the courts. Discounted notes, however, could be recovered in full because the bank was merely recovering the principle, the interest having been discounted at the time the loan was made. The farmers, it was further ruled, could not recover amounts in excess of 7 percent if these had been discounted. [14]

To many farmers this was a legal sophistry designed to get the banks around the clear intention of the Bank Act—an opinion shared by several finance ministers and by Prime Minister R.B. Bennett. [15] The bankers retorted that any attempt to limit interest rates would simply make it impossible for them to advance credits to many needy western Canadian communities where the cost of doing business would not be covered by a 7-percent rate. [16] Given only a choice between credit available at higher interest rates and no credit at all, most farmers opted for the former, though not without incessant grumbling. [17]

A third serious problem area for western farmers had to do with the length of time, or usance, of bank loans to farmers. Farm indebtedness was generally considered under three categories: short-term (up to six months), intermediate (six month to three years), and long-term (more than three years).[18] Initially the banks were only involved in granting short-term credit, but over the years they gradually became involved in some schemes to advance intermediate credit. They were not directly involved in long-term credit during the period under consideration, nor were the banks the only credit institutions operating in the fields of short- and intermediate-term credits.

The best available scholarly work on the subject of farm credit in Canada states categorically that "the most noticeable feature of farm credit in Canada is the absence of institutions specifically designed to meet the requirements of agriculture."[19] Canadian banking had begun as a service to the commercial community. Merchants needed accommodation to cover the cost of goods from the time they were purchased until they were delivered and sold. This normally did not require loans for priods of more than three months and the goods themselves provided the security for the loans, which rarely exceeded 60 percent of the estimated sale value of the goods. Manufacturers normally sought accommodations to pay for raw materials and production costs, all of which were recovered when the manufactured goods were sold, and again these goods themselves provided the security for the loans. The long-term capital requirements of the merchants and manufacturers normally came from personal investments, the sale of stocks and bonds, or loans from loan and mortgage companies. Bank notes of three months to six months' usance were therefore well suited to the short-term credit needs of merchants and manufacturers.[20]

Farmers needed longer term notes to carry them from spring seeding to the point when the crop was sold. Yet the banks were generally unwilling to provide more than three-month notes. There was rarely any difficulty in having these notes renewed for a further three months if a good crop was in prospect, but the bankers expected the farmer to settle his account at the end of each year. This meant, first of all, that the farmer had to sell at harvest time when grain prices tended to be low. Holding grain beyond the fall in the hope of selling later at a higher price was regarded as speculation. If the farmer owed the bank money he was really speculating with the funds of the bank's depositors and shareholders, and this was not tolerated.[21]

Even more serious problems arose if there was a crop failure or prices fell to a level where the farmer could not repay his loan in full. The banks were then inclined to refuse all further credit, and the farmer could face a forced sale of his chattels, and his land, if pledged as additional collateral. In bad years the farmers needed more flexible repayment schedules than the established banking system provided. The situation was particularly difficult when farmers sought bank credit for operations such as stock raising, where the finished product could be sold only several years hence.[22]

The bankers were very well aware of the problems and certainly tried, within the constraints of what they regarded as sound banking policies, to devise schemes to meet the needs of the farmers. Their official position, however, was unequivocal:

It is a first principle of banking in Canada that the funds of the Banks available for commercial purposes should be employed only for the production and distribution of commodities: that the assets of the Banks should be kept in liquid form and their funds not loaned against fixed assets, or even loaned against liquid assets to under-capitalized businesses. Adherence to these principals requires that a customer shall have sufficient working capital to carry his stock of merchandise at its low point: that advances made to a manufacturer to buy additional raw materials at the beginning of his season shall be fully liquidated from the sale of the manufactured product by the end of the season: and that advances to a wholesaler to purchase seasonal goods shall be cleared off as the goods are sold.... Modification of a banking principle would be justified by the requirements of the situation as a whole. It is my impression that the Banks generally are now disposed to meet this situation in a broad spirit.[23]

The banks' willingness to modify their principles, however, often depended on the willingness of governments to underwrite some or all of the risks involved.[24] In the fields of intermediate and long-term credit, the bankers seriously considered several new schemes, but only those fully protected by government guarantees were implemented during the period under consideration. Here, more than in any other aspect of banking, fundamental banking principles and the basic needs of the farmers were sharply at variance. Farmers and bankers readily

318 / T. D. Regehr

agreed that the situation was unsatisfactory, but they were unable to find a solution to the problems of usance of bank loans to farmers.[25]

The fourth major issue generating a great deal of animosity between bankers and farmers concerned forced sales of the farmer's chattels and foreclosure if his land was pledged as additional security for loans he could not pay as they fell due. The problems in this regard were really twofold. There were farmers who got so deeply into debt that they had no prospect of getting out.[26] Some bankers were inclined to see most such cases as "men with small stakes, shiftless, lazy poor farmers, failures from other provinces and countries" who "must be weeded out."[27] Unfortunately, hard work, virtuous living and astute management were often to little avail against crop failures or low prices and many farmers unable to pay their debts found themselves in that position through no particular fault of their own. The farm organizations and prairie politicians believed that such men and their families must be protected. It was not in anyone's interest to see good men and their families thrown off the land, and provincial governments were persuaded to pass legislation that exempted the home quarter and some of the farmers' chattels from legal proceedings. In particularly difficult years, debt moratoriums and debt adjustment schemes were also put in place.[28]

The banks obviously disliked exemptions, moratoriums, and debt adjustment schemes, saying that the inability to take proceedings made the security against which they could advance loans of no value,[29] and forced them to curtail severely their loans to farmers. The Canadian Bankers' Association was very well aware of the bad publicity generated by foreclosures and at various times urged its members not to disturb farmers doing the best they could to meet their obligations. In several instances the Secretary of the Canadian Bankers' Association also urged the extension of additional credits in order to keep deserving farmers afloat.[30]

Often the bankers' policies toward comparatively well-to-do, but temporarily embarrassed, farmers also created difficulty. The pressure to clean up all loans at the end of each season forced farmers to sell grain or livestock when it was not in their best interest to do so.[31] Furthermore, the banks with their short-term notes were always very eager to get the farmers' money before they paid it to their other creditors—the machinery agents, lumber companies, local stores, and loan and mortgage companies. In difficult years, rural areas were often overrun by collection agents, and it was often the nastiest or the one with the most serious threats who got his money first. A furniture merchant in Herbert, Saskatchwan, for example, complained that on one day no fewer than twenty-three collection agents were in town after it became clear there would be a crop failure.[32] Creditors always seemed eager to give the farmer another kick when climate or markets had laid him low. Certainly the banks were never regarded as a soft touch in such situations, although complaints against them were not as bitter as were the complaints against some locally elected municipal councils, who presumably knew the local situation better and made sure they were paid before anyone else. Foreclosure sales for back taxes were more frequent in many districts than forceclosure proceedings initiated by the banks. The bankers, however, had their own obligations and could hardly afford to take second or third or last place to other creditors. It was often a frustrating business.[33] One Saskatchewan banker wrote gloomily that "a little sympathy sometimes helps even if the request cannot be granted."[34]

Evolution of Relations Between Farmers and Bankers

At various times one or another of the four problems identified above occupied a great deal of attention of farmers and bankers. The intensity of the ongoing controversy generally reflected international financial conditions, although tremors in international finance often had disproportionate and highly disruptive repercussions in western Canada.

The first such agitation in the twentieth century occurred as a result of the comparatively minor financial crises of 1907 when international confidence in major Canadian securities was temporarily undermined. This immediately led to a restriction of farmer credit and a correspondent described the results to Premier Scott of Saskatchewan:

For some time past the Banks... have been getting more and more conservative with their money and have now stopped making advances of any kind and are pressing for cash due them by the public. The farmers in many instances (not having saleable grain) have made application to the various loan companies and these are now being refused right and left. Nothing but disaster can result from this. It is imperative that settlers having the necessary improvements on their places should be able to procure loans.[35]

This was simply the obverse side of the usual and prudent precautions any bank was likely to take in turbulent or uncertain times. Banks must seek to increase the liquidity of their assets if there is a possibility that large numbers of depositors will be making withdrawals.

The crisis of 1907 was fortunately of relatively short duration and farmer demands for government intervention at that time elicited little more that Premier Scott's sympathy and the hope "that the present conditions are but temporary and that restoration of confidence will shortly come."[36] The crisis was nevertheless a harbinger of things to come. In every succeeding crisis the banks sought to batten down the hatches, call in whatever loans they could, and grant as little credit as possible for the shortest possible time, thus ensuring that they had enough cash and liquid assets and reserves to face the uncertain future. Farmers, at the same time, stood in particular need of accommodation and, when unable to get loans from the banks or loan companies, appealed to the government for help. Prairie governments, very sensitive to the political power of the organized farmers, responded with strong statements of support for the farmers and criticism of the banks, but they were often very slow and cautious in actually doing anything to resolve the problems.

The 1907 crisis proved, as Premier Scott had hoped, a temporary disruption and, once passed, led to a period of great optimism and expansion in western Canadian agriculture. The chartered banks participated enthusiastically in this expansion, with Sir Edmund Walker becoming one of the principal spokesmen for more investment in western agriculture.[37] Substantial amounts were advanced on short terms to western farmers.

Prairie farmers at the time, however, stood in particular need of long-term credits that the Canadian chartered banks could not advance. The established loan and mortgage companies charged high interest rates and still could not keep up with the demand. New and different agricultural credit institutions, which would grant long-term credit at reasonable rates and on reasonable repayment schedules, were demanded as alternatives to the commercial banks.[38]

At that time, rural credit societies of various kinds had become very popular in Europe, particularly in Germany, and in 1913 a joint Canadian-American commission travelled extensively in Europe. The commissioners studied the rural credit societies established in various countries and sent long and detailed reports to their respective provincial and state governments. The operations of the Credit Foncier of France (a joint stock company) and of the Landwirtschaften (co-operative loan and mortgage companies), both of which provided long-term agricultural credits, were described in detail, as were the Credit Agricole of France and the Raiffeisen Banks of Germany, which dealt in short- and intermediate-term agricultural credit. The record of the German co-operative rural societies seemed particularly encouraging, and farmers began to exert pressure on their governments to have similar institutions established in Canada and the United States.[39]

Several different schemes were proposed. Some rural credit societies were incorporated and given power to issue debentures to raise funds, and then to loan these funds to farmers in need of long-term credit, usually at a rate of one percent above that paid to raise the funds. Other co-operative credit societies had no power to issue debentures, but made collective loans from the banks. Under this scheme some assets of all the members of the co-operative were pledged as collateral for loans made from the banks. In view of the superior security offered, the banks were expected to advance money at the same low rates of interest as were granted to major corporate borrowers. The farmers actually getting the money paid interest at a rate of one percent above that obtained by the society from the bank, thus providing for the operating costs of the society. Any profits were returned as a credit against interest charges.[40]

The Canadian chartered banks were willing to advance loans to credit societies at lower rates of interest, provided the security offered was really superior to that offered by individual farmers. They pointed out, however, that in Germany there were stable and long established rural communities and farmers with substantial assets might be willing to support the rural societies, but in Canada where communities were newer and less stable, the more successful farmers would probably not be willing to pledge their resources as security for loans to needy, poor, and perhaps improvident neighbors. Some banks were willing, nonetheless, to work with co-operative societies, and even to take a part in their organization. Near Lethbridge, for example, the Canadian Bank of Commerce brought together 60 local farmers, each giving a personal guarantee of up to $150 for loans made to individual members. The affairs of this society were governed by four trustees appointed by the guarantors. Success with this scheme at Lethbridge encouraged bankers to promote similar societies elsewhere.[41] These, however, were exceptions. For the most part, the Supervisor of the Bank of Hamilton was right when he wrote:

> If these cooperative circles come into existence the individuals will consist almost wholly of quarter section men, or of those with larger farms and heavy debts. The better class of larger farmers can borrow at a very slightly greater rate of interest without becoming responsible for other people's debts, and they won't have anything to do with the cooperative associations.[42]

Rural credit societies with power to issue debentures ran into equally serious problems. In Europe the rural areas had established farmers and businessmen with investment funds, which they were willing and eager to invest in their own community. Western Canada, however, had fewer potential investors. In order to raise the very large sums required, Canadian credit societies had to borrow in international markets, but found few investors willing to buy their securities unless these had some security beyond that of the farmers' land. In order to get any money at attractive rates, these societies needed government guarantees, or, alternatively, the provincial governments might borrow the money and then advance funds to deserving rural credit societies. Unfortunately, even the provincial governments, or credit societies whose debentures were guaranteed by provincial governments, found it impossible to raise the required funds after the financial stringency of 1913 and the outbreak of war the following year. As a result, Premier Scott had to inform his constituents that there was "no hope that a new cooperative mortgage association, strange as it would be at first in money markets, could sell a guaranteed bond which the well known railway companies cannot sell."[43]

The situation of the farmers was made worse by the concentrated effort of the banks after 1914 to get their assets into more liquid form. By 1916 members of the Canadian Bankers Association were informed that "The Banks are deriving much satisfaction today from the fact that we are in a more liquid position than we were on the eve of the war."[44] E.L. Pease, the Managing Director of the Royal Bank and author of that report to the bankers, however, also recognized that this was creating very serious problems. He had been gathering information on the operations of the Credit Agricole of France and the Agricultural Banks of Australia and New Zealand and began to urge the adoption of some similar scheme in Canada. He proposed that the chartered banks get together to organize an Agricultural Bank with each bank taking some of the shares of the proposed new bank, which should have the power to issue debentures and to advance loans on the security of farm mortgages. Pease believed the "manufacturers of farm products" should be given credit on terms commensurate with the time required to manufacture the product.[45] He also expressed the fear that if the chartered banks did not act, prairie governments would attempt to set up provincial agricultural banks that would enter into direct competition with the established financial institutions.[46]

Pease's scheme ran into immediate opposition from his fellow bankers. The first point of contention was whether the proposed new bank should be allowed to accept deposits in competition with the established bank, or whether it should rely entirely on long-term debentures. A special Committee on Rural Credits was established by the Canadian Bankers' Association to study the matter further. Members of the committee were very reluctant to get involved in farm land mortgages and charged that Pease's scheme would simply have the banks do indirectly what they were not willing to do directly.[47] The uneven history of Australia's Agricultural Bank was not encouraging and even Pease admitted that the collapse of the Australian Bank in 1893 had proved that "A commercial bank could not at the same time conduct a land loaning company's operations."[48] As a result, after a year's discussion, the proposal that the chartered banks form an Agricultural Bank, which would extend long term credit to western farmers, was quietly shelved.[49]

By that time, however, Pease and his colleagues at the Royal Bank were espousing another cause. In 1914, following the outbreak of war, the federal government had amended its Finance Act in order to protect the credit of Canadian banks while increasing the money supply. The main provisions of the 1914 Finance Act have been summarized:

... the Minister of Finance was permitted to advance dominion notes to the chartered banks upon the pledge of satisfactory securities; the banks could make payments in their own notes rather than dominion notes or gold; the excess circulation privilege of the banks, formerly seasonal to finance wheat exports, was extended to the whole year; the redemption of dominion notes in gold was suspended; and the government could declare a general moratorium.[50]

The bankers expected that these special wartime provisions would be withdrawn once the war was over, but Pease feared this would result in a very severe contraction of the money supply and serious disruption of Canadian trade. The matter was first discussed at the annual shareholders meeting of the Royal Bank, at which Pease was authorized to propose the formation of a Canadian Central Bank of Rediscount. In his Presidential Address to the Canadian Bankers' Association in 1918, three days after the signing of the armistice, Pease proposed the plan to his colleagues. The proposal was immediately referred to a Confidential Committee of the Association for further study and report. The bankers disagreed about the merits of continuing the essentially inflationary provisions of the Finance Act. Some, notably Sir Vincent Meredith of the Bank of Montreal, wanted a complete return to the Gold Standard, from which Canada, in practice if not in theory, had departed in 1914. Others argued that in the uncertain and troubled financial circumstances of the postwar period, any innovations or daring new policies were likely to undermine confidence and were therefore inadvisable. In the end, largely on the urging of Sir Edmund Walker of the Canadian Bank of Commerce, a compromise was reached. The bankers recognized that a hasty return to gold would prove disastrous for Canadian international trade, but that major innovations were also undesirable. Instead they suggested that the wartime provisions of the Finance Act be extended beyond the end of the war, with a view to a more gradual return to gold.[51]

Pease had worked closely with Finance Minister White, who was favorably disposed to the idea of a central bank of rediscount, but White's illness and resignation in 1919 brought to the finance ministry the less able and more cautious H.L.Drayton. Drayton accepted the recommendations of the bankers that the provisions of the Finance Act be extended. A serious controversy, nevertheless, developed over the amount of money individual banks should be allowed to borrow from the Treasury, and the uses they could make of such funds.[52]

Some banks, notably the Royal, thought a fairly expansionist policy was appropriate while others, including the Bank of Monteal, advocated tight money policies.[53] Farmers needing financing to get their produce to international markets, of course, stood to gain more from an expansionist than a tight money policy.

There were, as the bankers expected, serious financial problems after the cessation of hostilities. As early as 1916, E.L. Pease had predicted, "we shall then probably be confronted by serious inflation, by very dear money, a big reduction in the prices of commodities, and by labour troubles." Pease believed concerted action was needed and a Confidential Committee of the Canadian Bankers' Association was established to "watch the general financial situation and communicate with the General Managers of the Banks from time to time."[54] Within the fairly narrow confines of the Bank Act and sound banking principles, the Confidential Committee and the Association's Rural Credits Committee tried to find ways and means of coping with the difficulties of western farmers.

The position of western farmers during the postwar economic recession was somewhat paradoxical. There were, on the one hand, insistent demands for more credit at lower rates. But as grain prices fell, there were also growing fears that farmers would be unable to pay the debts they had already incurred.[55] By 1924 there were pessimistic statements by farm groups suggesting that up to 90 percent of the farmers were in fact insolvent and that they could only be saved if provincial governments continued debt moratoriums established for those who enlisted, and introduced debt adjustment schemes of one sort or another.[56] Voluntary renegotiation and amortization of debts were specific solutions proposed by the organized farmers and several prairie governments passed legislation whereby debt adjustments might be expedited on a voluntary basis.

Comparatively little came of the talk of involuntary debt moratoriums and debt adjustments in the 1920s. The 1923 hearings on the decennial revisions of the Bank Act focused largely on the need for more intermediate credit.[57] Farm loan boards were established or expanded by the provincial governments more or less in accordance with the bankers' view that "for the sake of encouraging immigration, and to get the western country particularly settled by the right type, the Governments, but not the banks, might take a little chance in giving financial assistance to men who really do not have the assets to en-title them to credit, but who are healthy, industrious, anxious to work and eventually to own their own homes."[58] These farm loan boards, however, never had sufficient resources to meet the demand for low-cost long-term farm credit.

Increased prosperity after 1924 reduced the farmers' need for credit somewhat while at the same time increasing the bankers' willingness to extend it. In fact, there was later general agreement that in the period 1925–30 far too much credit had been extended.[59] Throughout the 1920s, however, the farmers' groups talked concurrently and equally vehemently about the need for more credit and the need for protection for those who could not pay their debts.

The collapse of prices for grain and other western Canadian agricultural commodies in 1929–30 immediately induced the banks to restrict credit as much as possible and to collect as many of their outstanding loans as they could. Provincial governments were soon called upon to honor guarantees of loans to farmers or to farmer organizations, particularly the Wheat Pools. In order to carry on, however, the farmers needed far more credit. Much of the needed new credit was no longer available from the banks, and an elaborate system of rural relief financed or underwritten by the government had to be established.[60]

Protection for debtors also became increasingly necessary. Debt adjustment schemes soon became a part of the legislation of every prairie province, and these schemes were amended regularly to make it more and more difficult to initiate proceedings against debtors. These schemes reached their logical conclusion in the late 1930s when repayment schedules in Alberta were tied directly to the "productive capacity" of the farm involved.[61] Both principal and interest could be written down, if necessary without the consent of the creditor, and creditors had to obtain special permits from duly appointed government boards before they could take any proceedings against a farmer. There was a growing fear among many creditors that there would be wholesale repudiations of farm debts and, in part to counteract that threat and in part to provide greater uniformity among the various provincial debt adjustment and debt moratorium schemes, the federal government passed its Farmers' Creditors Arrangement Act in 1934.[62]

The bankers were certainly not happy with this turn of events, but considered it preferable to the radical alternatives suggested by Progressive, Social Credit, and Co-operative Commonwealth Federation orators.[63] In the earlier crises the bankers had advocated some innovative new policies. They made a major propaganda effort in 1931, but otherwise seemed unable to do more than defend sound banking principles, which were obviously not meeting the needs of the farmers.[64]

The major thrust of western farm leaders in the 1930s was the demand for monetary reform. To most farmers this meant very substantial expansion of the money supply. A central bank of rediscount under government control was considered the best means to achieve this. The decennial review of the Bank Act in 1933, a federal Royal Commission, and a number of provincial inquiries and commissions all focused on the need for a central bank. The bankers were as reluctant in 1933 as they had been in 1918, with only the Royal Bank giving the idea qualified support. The bankers recognized that the existing situation was unsatisfactory, and caution rather than uncompromising hostility marked their attitude toward proposals that a central bank be established.[65] Once the necessary legislation was passed, even those bankers who had opposed it quickly indicated their willingness to work with the new institution. Not surprisingly, the first governor came from the Royal Bank, but the policies he and his successors pursued have been a disappointment to those who expected that a central bank would solve the farmers' credit problems.

In debt moratoriums and debt adjustment schemes prairie farmers found a temporary reprieve in the 1930s. At a well-attended western Canadian Interprovincial Debt Conference in 1942, there was almost no talk of monetary reform, but a great deal of discussion about the need for immediate and more effective debt legislation.[66] The bankers complained that any successful attempts by western farmers to evade paying their debts would make it more difficult to advance credit in the future. That, however, was the concern of another day for the politicians and farmers who had just come through the trials and tribulations of the dirty thirties.

No account of farm credit in western Canada, particularly in the 1930s, would be complete without some reference to some of the farm credit schemes developed by western Canada's largest development company—the Canadian Pacific Railway. This railway company, conscious of the need for credit arrangements that would encourage immigration and expedite western development, sold its own extensive land holdings to farmers on long-term repayment schedules that placed comparatively light annual burdens on the farmers. The practice of amortizing farm loans in western Canada was in fact pioneered by the C.P.R., as were ways of dealing leniently with defaults due to crop failure or low prices.[67]

In the 1920s C.P.R. President Edward Beatty advanced innovative and imaginative new schemes to help farmers who generated traffic for his railway. In 1920 he organized the Western Colonization Association, in which various companies and agencies interested in facilitating the settlement and re-establishment of returned soldiers and the settlement of new immigrants to western Canada participated. The association was supported by several banks that subscribed much of its $1,500,000 capital stock. The funds were used to assist soldiers and immigrants in the acquisition and improvement of farm land.[68]

In 1923 the Western Colonization Association was re-organized as the Canada Colonization Association (C.C.A.), with the C.P.R. and the C.N.R. as major partners. The C.N.R., however, soon decided to form its own organization, giving the C.P.R. effective control of the Canada Colonization Association.[69]

One of the important achievements of the C.P.R. and the Canada Colonization Association was the assistance provided to more than 20,000 Mennonites seeking to escape Soviet Russia in the 1920s. The story of that immigration is told elsewhere.[70] Of note here are the unusual farm credit arrangements the C.P.R. and the C.C.A. made to accommodate many of these Mennonites. The C.P.R., on the strength of a very general and probably legally unenforcable contract, advanced millions of dollars to pay the transportation costs of the immigrants. Further funds were advanced by the C.C.A. to assist the immigrants in establishing themselves. In a number of cases, so-called "ready-made" farms were offered to the immigrants on rather peculiar terms, sometimes referred to as the "Mennonite Terms." The C.C.A. sold to the prospective farmers the land with buildings and essential livestock, or provided funds to acquire all that was essential to the operation of the farm. In some cases the C.C.A. handled C.P.R. land. In other cases land owned by others was acquired and resold. The lands and improvements were sold to the immigrants at market value and all debts incurred were subject to interest charges. The repayment schedules, however, were variable. At Coaldale, Alberta, for example, immigrants were placed on 80 acres of irrigated farm land, fully equipped. They were fairly carefully supervised by the C.C.A., and each farmer was required to plant and deliver to the credit of the company the product of ten acres of sugar beets.[71] The beets were delivered to a local factory in which the C.P.R. had also participated but which was operated on a partly co-operative basis. The value of the beets delivered to the factory to the credit of the company was then credited against the interest and principal of the farmer's indebtedness to the company. The loans could be repaid at any time. In this way payments were directly related to the income and the ability of the farmers to pay. Each spring the farmers received further credit to buy supplies and equipment which the regional supervisor of the C.C.A. considered necessary, but they were also prevented from buying on credit things the supervisor thought they could not afford or did not need. Most of these people had no previous experience with irrigation or growing sugar beets and some needed a good deal of advice from the C.C.A., but in the end almost all of them repaid their debts and became successful farmers. Certainly the success rate in that community was greater among those assisted by the C.C.A. than among others working on their own or with other established financial institutions.

The C.C.A. never served a very large number of western Canadian farmers, but those it did serve benefitted from its innovative rural credit policies. It was perhaps unfortunate that Beatty, a director of the Bank of Montreal, was unable to persuade that bank or the Canadian Bankers' Association to substantially expand and participate wholeheartedly in his scheme.

Perhaps the unique nature of the success enjoyed by the C.P.R. and the C.C.A. was best illustrated on 19 September 1937, when Sir Edward Beatty, one of the biggest of the "fifty big shots" then so vehemently denounced by Social Credit and Socialist orators, visited the Mennonite community at Coaldale, Alberta. Elsewhere the dust and the political rhetoric and the hostility of the populace had been most discouraging for the C.P.R. president, but at Coaldale a major celebration of thanksgiving was arranged to honor the C.P.R. officials, who, according to one writer, had been called of God to perform a great service.[72] In that place, in the 1920s and 1930s, the C.P.R. had extended the kind of rural credit the people desperately needed. The records of the C.C.A. clearly show that the company did not escape the usual problems likely to arise between debtors and creditors, and even some farmers indebted to the C.C.A. availed themselves of debt moratoriums and debt adjustment mechanisms. The records also show that the C.C.A. plans enjoyed considerably more success than most other rural credit schemes.

During the first four decades of the twentieth century western farmers often felt they were not getting the kind of credit they needed at reasonable rates. The bankers, however, believed that sound banking principles and the Bank Act did not permit them to advance credit to the extent or in the manner demanded by the farmers. The evidence drawn from the Bank of Nova Scotia records shows that some of the main arguments advanced by the bankers in support of limited credit facilities and high interest rates are at best only partially applicable. The evidence from the archives of the Canadian Bankers' Association indicates that the bankers were very much concerned about western problems and that several imaginative proposals were seriously debated, but any action taken had to be within the confines of established banking policy. Records of the organized farmers strongly suggest that they were generally preoccupied with immediate and short-term problems and that their demands for more credit and also for protection from creditors tended, to a large extent, to nullify each other. The radical alternative of socialization of credit and banking never enjoyed majority support, and it was never made clear exactly how this might solve the problems of farm credit. When farmers voted for Social Credit or C.C.F. candidates in the 1930s, they did so with a very clear opinion that the existing system had failed, but only with hazy notions of how radically new policies would solve their problems. Existing rural credit systems probably exacerbated the wide fluctuations in the prairie economy, but weather and international markets were at the root of those fluctuations. It was left for the provincial and federal governments to seek compromises between farmers and bankers. In the 1910s and 1920s, those compromises were often expedited by provincial guarantees. In the 1930s, debt moratoriums and adjustments, and legislation establishing the Bank of Canada marked the political response to an ongoing controversy.

It is appropriate to give the last word to a politician who was repeatedly called upon to intervene in the relations between bankers and farmers. In reply to a complaint that banks were not assisting farmers to buy twine needed for the harvest, Premier Walter Scott of Saskatchewan concludes,

The position is undoubtedly serious but unless our banking system is more useless from the farmers' standpoint than we have every right to expect, the banks should be looked to to meet it. Another thought is that the situation helps to show the extreme danger of going too far in the direction of protecting farmers in the matter of their debts. Any measure to save people from their debts is a two-edged sword.[73]

Notes

1. Archives of the Canadian Bankers' Association, Toronto (hereafter C.B.A.), carton 1055, file 3463, "Canadian Council of Agriculture, 1923–27," Report by J. Dodds to the President of the Canadian Bankers' Association.

2. Farmers and bankers generally agreed on identifying the problems of rural credit in western Canada. Saskatchewan Archives Board (hereafter as S.A.), Records of the Saskatchewan Grain Growers' Association, Farmers' Union of Canada, United Farmers of Canada (Saskatchewan Section) (hereafter S.G.G.A.), file VIII–18, Memo re: Conference with Bankers' Association, November 1926; file IX–17, Report of Banking Committee, 1922; C.B.A., carton 1046, unnumbered files on Rural Credits, "Rural Banking Credits."

3. Canada, Minutes of Proceedings, Evidence, etc. of the Select Standing Committee on Banking and Commerce during the Parliamentary Session of 1912–13 (hereafter Banking and Commerce Committee, 1912–13), (Ottawa: King's Printer, 1913), p. 484.

4. Ibid., p. 531.

5. Saskatchewan, Agricultural Credit Commission Report (Regina: King's Printer, 1913).

6. These Tables were prepared from detailed information contained in the Archives of the Bank of Nova Scotia (hereafter B.N.S.), Statistics No. 7; Statistics No. 8; Annual Summaries, 1935, 1936, 1937, 1938, and 1939; Rules and Procedure (Revision of 1927). Unfortunately, detailed branch-by-branch information is not available for the years 1928–34 inclusive.

7. In 1931 several Progressives in the House of Commons were disposed to pronounce the position of the great majority of western farmers as hopeless with respect to their indebtedness. Western attacks on the banks became so vociferous that Beaudry Leman, President of the Canadian Bankers' Association, issued a formal statement in defence of the banks. This statement was first sent to all the

general managers and underwent substantial revisions before all the general managers were willing to have it published. It represented the official position of all the banks, not only of the president of the association. C.B.A., carton 1059, has a number of files all dealing with Banking Situation, 1931, in the Prairie Provinces. Mr. Leman's article was widely published and commented on in the press. It first appeared as "The Prairie Provinces and the Banks," *Journal of the Canadian Bankers' Association* XXXVIII, 4 (July 1931): 368–70.

8. E.P. Neufeld, *The Financial System of Canada: Its Growth and Development* (Toronto: Macmillan, 1972), p. 88. Land could be pledged as "additional security" for bank loans, but the banks could not deal directly in mortgages on land. As a result, farmers obtained far more credit from mortgage and loan companies than they did from the banks.

9. C.B.A., carton 1059, file 3908, Banking Situation, 1931–Prairie Provinces (Mr. Leman's article).

10. B.N.S., Statistics 7; C.B.A., carton 1046, unnumbered files on Rural Credits, Memorandum on Rural Banking Credits.

11. Based on information drawn from the same sources as Tables I, II, and III.

12. B.N.S., Statistics 8.

13. Canada, 13–14 Geo v. Cap. 32, Section 91.

14. C.B.A., carton 1059, file 3911, Banking Situation, 1931–Prairie Provinces (Interest Rates in the West).

15. Ibid., file 3908, Banking Situation, 1931–Prairie Provinces (Mr. Leman's Article); Beaudry Leman, President of the Canadian Bankers' Association, to Mr. McLeod, Vice-President, Canadian Bankers' Association, 31 March 1931.

16. Ibid., carton 1046, unnumbered files on Rural Credits, Memorandum on Rural Banking Credits.

17. Ibid., file 3911, Banking Situation, 1931–Prairie Provinces (Interest Rates in the West).

18. Ibid., carton 1055, file no. 3502, "Long Term Credit and Intermedite Rural Credit," F. Williams-Taylor, President of the Canadian Bankers' Association, to members of the Confidential Committee of the Canadian Bankers' Association, 18 July 1923. George Ruff, "Farm Finance," *Proceedings of the Eleventh Annual Convention of the North Dakota Bankers' Association,* 17–18 June 1913.

19. W.T. Easterbrook, *Farm Credit in Canada* (Toronto: University of Toronto Press 1938), p. 161.

20. C.B.A., carton 1046, unnumbered files on Rural Credits, Winnipeg Sub-Section, Canadian Bankers' Association, response to resolution passed by the Joint Committee of Commerce and Agriculture, 1916. J.A. Stevenson, "Agricultural credit systems and the West," *Canadian Political Science Association, Papers and Proceedings of the First Annual Meeting* (Toronto, 1913), vol. 1, p. 55–81.

21. Ibid., Memorandum entitled Rural Banking Credits.

22. Ibid., carton 1000, unnumbered file, "Meeting of Executive Council," 31 May 1916.

23. Ibid., carton 1046, unnumbered files on rural Credits, Memorandum entitled Rural Banking Credits.

24. Ibid., carton 1055, file 3502, "Long Term and Intermediate Rural Credit," J.P. Bell, Bank of Hamilton, to Frederick Williams-Taylor, President, Canadian Bankers' Association, 31 July 1923.

25. S.A., S.G.G.A., file 04–IX–240, "Rural Credit, 1925," Agricultural Credit, Extract from Supplementary Report, March 1925, by H.M. Tory, President of the University of Alberta. C.B.A., carton 1055, file 3502, "Long Term and Intermediate Rural Credit," C.E. Neill, Royal Bank, to Sir Frederick Williams-Taylor, President, Canadian Bankers' Association, 19 July 1923.

26. C.B.A., carton 1055, file 3502, "Long Term and Intermediate Rural Credit," J.P. Bell, Bank of Hamilton, to F. Williams-Taylor, President, Canadian Bankers' Association, 31 July 1923.

27. C.B.A., carton 1046, unnumbered file on Rural Credits, Supervisor of the Bank of Hamilton to F.W.S. Crispo, Union Bank, Winnipeg, 23 May 1916.

28. A detailed outline of debt adjustment legislation in Canada is given in S.A., S.G.G.A., file IX–75, Interprovincial Debt Conference attended by Representatives of the Three Prairie Governments and Various Farm Organizations in Manitoba, Saskatchewan, and Alberta at the Bessborough Hotel, Saskatoon, Saskatchewan, 19 and 30 June 1942.

29. The views of the bankers are clearly expressed in C.B.A., carton 1059, file 3908, Banking Situation, 1931–Prairie Provinces, (Mr. Leman's article). The tone of the article actually published was comparatively mild. Early drafts were more critical of attempts by western governments to provide special protection for farmers. The politicians, however, were very well aware of the problems government intervention could cause. See for example S.A., Scott Papers, pp. 22857–58, Scott to James Kerr, 26 September 1914.

30. C.B.A., carton 1046, unnumbered files on Rural Credits.

31. Ibid., "Winnipeg Sub-Section, Canadian Bankers Association 1916," Response to a Resolution of the Joint Committee of Commerce and Agriculture. See also Memorandum entitled Rural Banking Credits in same file. S.A., Martin Papers, pp. 6360–66, Robert Whiteside to Premier Martin, 19 February 1921, and Martin to Whiteside, 25 February 1921.

32. S.A., Scott Papers, p. 22825, P.P. Kroeker to Scott, 8 September 1914.

33. C.B.A., carton 1000, unnumbered file on meeting of the Executive Council, 31 May 1916, H.O. Powell, General Manager, Weyburn Security Bank to G.W. Morley, Secretary of the Canadian Bankers' Association, 27 May 1916.

34. Ibid.

35. S.A., Scott Papers, pp. 22437–38. Reginald Beatty to Scott, 22 November 1907.

36. Ibid., Scott to Beatty, 25 November 1907. W.E. Greening, "The Canadian Banks and the Crisis of 1907," *Journal of the Canadian Bankers' Association* LXXIII, 2 (Spring 1965).

37. G.P. deT. Glazebrook, *Sir Edmund Walker* (Toronto: Oxford University Press, 1933). University of Toronto Archives, Walker Papers, Walker to Woodhouse, 15 April and 4 October 1913, and Walker to H. Cooper, 19 December 1923. Banking and Commerce Committee, 1912–13, p. 478–535.

38. H. Mitchell, "The Problem of Agricultural Credit in Canada," *Bulletin of the Departments of History and Political and Economic Science in Queen's University* (Kingston: The Jackson Press, 1914). Pamphlet entitled "Cheaper Money for Agricultural Development of Saskatchewan, Speech delivered by the Honourable Walter Scott, Premier of Saskatchewan, in the Legislative Assembly and a Paper on European Systems of Co-operative Agricultural Credit, read before the Standing Committee on Agricultural and Municipal Law" (Regina: Government Printer, 1913).

39. The operations of the various German and French rural credit societes are outlined clearly in George Ruff, "Farm Finance," *Proceedings of the Eleventh Annual Convention of the North Dakota Bankers' Association,* 17 and 18 June 1913.

40. J.A. Stevenson, "Agricultural Credit Systems and the West," *Canadian Political Science Association Papers and Proceedings of the First Annual Meeting,* 1913, vol. 1, p. 55–81.

41. C.B.A., carton 1046, unnumbered files on Rural Credits, Memo re: Lethbridge Livestock Guarantors, 6 January 1916.

42. Ibid., Supervisor of the Bank of Hamilton to F.W.S. Crispo, Union Bank, Winnipeg, 23 May 1916.

43. S.A., Scott Papers, p. 22641, Scott to Aron G. Sawatzky, 5 May 1915.

44. C.B.A., carton 1000, Minutes of the Annual General Meeting, 9 November 1916. C.A. Curtis, "The Canadian Banks and War Finance," *Contributions to Canadian Economics,* vol. 3, 1931.

45. Ibid., carton 1046, unnumbered files on Rural Credits, E.L. Pease, Managing Director of the Royal Bank, to George Burn, President, of the Canadian Bankers' Association, 23 May 1916.

46. C.B.A., carton 1000, Minutes of the Meeting of General Managers, 31 May 1916.

47. Ibid., carton 1046, unnumbered Files on Rural Credits. J.W. Taylor, Bank of Montreal, to George Burn, President, Canadian Bankers' Association, 20 April 1916.

48. Ibid., carton 1040, unnumbered File on Agricultural Bank, E.L. Pease, President of the Canadian Bankers' Association, to F.B. Cockburn, Bank of Montreal, 6 March 1917.

49. Ibid.

50. R.C. Brown to Ramsay Cook, in R.C. Brown, *Canada, 1896–1921: A Nation Transformed* (Toronto: McClelland and Stewart, 1974), p. 228.

51. C.B.A., carton 1040, unnumbered File entitled Bank of Re-discount, 1918–1919. Details of Pease's original proposal, some correspondence, and lengthy memos from several of the senior bankers are included in this file.

52. C.B.A., carton 1001, unnumbered file entitled Meeting of Minister of Finance with Confidential Committee, 17 June 1920, H.L. Drayton, Minister of Finance to C.A. Bogert, President of the Canadian Bankers' Association, 5 June 1920.

53. This issue was discussed extensively in articles and letters appearing in the *Journal of the Canadian Bankers' Association,* particularly when Britain went off the Gold Standard in 1931 and the so-called "Banking Holiday" in the United States seriously undermined the position taken by the Canadian bankers.

54. C.B.A., carton 1000, Minutes of Annual General Meeting, 9 November 1916.

55. It was significant that the S.G.G.A. had both a Banking Committee and a Debt Adjustment Committee, the one advocating expanded credit facilities and the other voicing concerns about the serious problems farmers were having in paying their debts. S.A., S.G.G.A., file IX–17, Report of the Banking Committee, 1922, and file II–11, Report of the Debt Adjustment Committee, 6 August 1924.

56. S.A., S.G.G.A., file II–14, "Information compiled from various reports sent in regarding the financial condition of farmers in different districts in Saskatchewan, 1922–23."

57. *Proceedings of the Select Standing Committee on Banking and Commerce of the House of Commons on Bill No. 83, An Act Respecting Banks and Banking and on the Resultion of Mr. Irvine, M.P., re: Basis, Function and Control of Financial Credit, etc.* (Ottawa, King's Printer, 1923).

58. C.B.A., carton 1055, file 3502, "Long Term and Intermediate Rural Credit," J.P. Bell, Bank of Hamilton, to F. Williams-Taylor, President of the Canadian Bankers' Association, 31 July 1923. S.C. Hudson, "A Statistical Analysis of Long Term Mortgage Financing by the Saskatchewan Farm Loan Board" (Ph.D. thesis, Cornell University, 1939).

59. S.A., S.G.G.A, file IX–77, *Studies of Farm Indebtedness and Financial Progress of Saskatchewan Farmers,* compiled by the Department of Farm Management, College of Agriculture, University of Saskatchewan, December 1934. File IX–75, Memorandum, 1936, "Can Western Agriculture Pay Its Debts,?" Copy of Submission by the Manitoba, Saskatchewan, and Alberta Governments to the Federal Government in connection with Farm Debt Legislation, 1942.

60. D.G. Matheson, "The Saskatchewan Relief Commission, 1931–34" (M.A. thesis, University of Saskatchewan, 1974). H.B. Neatby, "The Saskatchewan Relief Commission, 1931–34," *Saskatchewan History* III, 2 (Spring 1950): 41–56.

61. Alberta, Statutes, 1936 (2), Cap. 3. For a general outline of provincial and federal debt legislation in the 1930s, *see* S.A., S.G.G.A., file IX–75, Inter-Provincial Debt Conference Attended by Representatives of the Three Prairie Governments and various Farm Organizations in Manitoba, Saskatchewan, and Alberta, at the Bessborough Hotel, Saskatoon, Saskatchewan, 29 and 30 June 1942.

62. Alvin Finkel, *Business and Social Reform in the Thirties* (Toronto: Lorimer, 1979), p. 78.

63. C.B.A., carton 1063, file 5017, Loans – Agriculture Saskatchewan.

64. C.B.A., carton 1059, files 3908, 3909, 3910, 3911, 3912, and 3913, all dealing with the banking situation in the Prairie Provinces in 1931.

65. Files 4028, 4042, 5012, 5033, 5035, 5055, 5066, 5080, and 5100 in the C.B.A. archives all deal with the formation of the Bank of Canada.

66. S.A., S.G.G.A., file IX–75, Inter-Provincial Debt Conference Attended by Representatives of the Three Prairie Governments and Various Farm Organizations in Manitoba, Saskatchewan, and Alberta, at the Bessborough Hotel, Saskatoon, Saskatchewan, 29 and 30 June 1942.

67. James B. Hedges, *Building the Canadian West: The Land and Colonization Policies of the Canadian Pacific Railway* (New York: Macmillan, 1939).

68. The action taken by the Canadian Bankers' Association, together with supporting documentation relating to the Western Colonization Association, can be found in C.B.A., carton 1001, unnumbered File, Annual General Meeting, 11 November 1920.

69. A very extensive collection of documents relating to the Canada Colonization Association is available at the Glenbow-Alberta Institute, Archives Division, Canadian Pacific Railway Papers, 1886–1958. The organization and activities of the association are outlined in file 526, S.G. Porter, General Manager, Canadian Colonization Association, to D.W. Hays, Canada Land & Irrigation Co., 8 August 1933.

70. Frank H. Epp, *Mennonite Exodus* (Altona, Manitoba: D.W. Friesen & Sons, 1962).

71. Glenbow-Alberta Institute, Archives Division, Canadian Pacific Railway Papers, 1886–1958, file 646, Memorandum re: Mennonites at Coaldale and surrounding districts, 18 September 1926.

72. *Gedenk und Dankfeier des 25–jaehrigen Bestehens der Coaldale Mennoniten Brueder Gemeinde* (Coaldale, 1951), pp. 76–77.

73. S.A., Scott Papers, p. 22667, Scott to John Dickenson, 30 July 1915.

Appendix
Lewis H. Thomas Bibliography

1. Books

The Struggle for Responsible Government in the North-West Territories 1870–97. Toronto: University of Toronto Press, 1956, 2d ed., 1977.

The University of Saskatchewan 1909–1959. Saskatoon: The University of Saskatchewan, 1959.

Chester Martin. *"Dominion Lands" Policy* (ed.). Toronto: McClelland and Stewart, 1973.

The Renaissance of Canadian History: A Biography of A.L. Burt. Toronto: University of Toronto Press, 1975.

Essays on Western History (ed). Edmonton: University of Alberta Press, 1976.

William Aberhart and Social Credit in Alberta (ed.). Toronto: Copp, Clark, 1977.

The Making of Socialist: The Recollections of T.C. Douglas (ed.). Edmonton: University of Alberta Press, 1982.

2. Chapters in Books

"Saskatchewan," In *Encyclopedia Americana.* Chicago: Grolier, 1955.

"Pioneers of the Western Plains." In Pierre Berton, ed., *The Pioneers: The Picture Story of Canadian Settlement.* The Canadian Illustrated Library. Toronto: McClelland and Stewart, 1968.

"The Mid-19th Century Debate on the Future of the North West." In J.M. Bumsted, ed., *Documentary Problems on Canadian History*, vol. 1. Georgetown, Ont.: Oxford University Press, 1969.

"Milton Campbell, Independent Progressive." In C. Berger and R. Cook, eds., *The West and the Nation: Essays in Honour of W.L. Morton*. Toronto: McClelland and Stewart, 1976.

"Government and Politics in Manitoba and the Northwest Territories." In L.G. Thomas, ed., *The Prairie West to 1905: A Canadian Sourcebook*. Toronto: Oxford University Press, 1976.

"Saskatoon, 1883–1920: The Formative Years." In A.F.J. Artibise, ed., *Town and City: Aspects of Western Canadian Urban Development*. Regina: Canadian Plains Research Centre, 1981.

3. Booklet

The North-West Territories 1870–1905. The Canadian Historical Association Booklet No. 26, 1970.

4. Introductions and Forewords to Books

G.M. Grant. *Ocean to Ocean: Sanford Fleming's Expedition Through Canada in 1872.* Revised ed., Edmonton: Hurtig, 1967.

W.B. Cheadle, *Cheadle's Journal of Trip Across Canada 1862–1863.* Revised ed., Edmonton: Hurtig, 1971.

E.G. Luxton. *Banff—Canada's First National Park: A History and a Memory of Rocky Mountains Park.* Banff: Summer Thought, 1975.

[With L.G. Thomas] Douglas Owram. *The Formation of Alberta: A Documentary History.* Calgary: Historical Society of Alberta, 1979.

5. Articles

"The Saskatchewan Legislative Building and Its Predecessors." *Journal of the Royal Architectural Institute of Canada,* July 1955.

"Provincial Archives in Canada." *The American Archivist,* October 1955.

"Early Combines in Saskatchewan." *Saskatchewan History*, Winter 1955.

"The Hind and Dawson Expeditions, 1857–58." *The Beaver*, Winter 1958.

"Archival Legislation in Canada." *Canadian Historical Association Annual Report*, 1962.

"The Place of Canadian History in the Schools." *One World*, (Social Studies Council, Alberta Teachers Association), vol. V, no. 4 (June 1967).

"Confederation and the West." *Revista de Historia de América*, January-December 1968.

Introduction to "Winter Trip on the C.P.R." *Alberta Historical Review*, Spring 1970.

"The Political and Private Life of F.W.G. Haultain." *Saskatchewan History*, Spring 1970.

Introduction to "Louis Riel's Petition of Rights, 1884." *Saskatchewan History*, Winter 1970.

"From the Pampas to the Prairies: The Welsh Migration of 1902." *Saskatchewan History*, Winter 1971. Reprinted in *The Anglo-Welsh Review*, 1976.

"Alexis Reynard." *Dictionary of Canadian Biography*, vol. X. Toronto: University of Toronto Press, 1972.

"Welsh Settlement in Saskatchewan, 1902–1914." *The Western Historical Quarterly*, vol. IV, no. 4 (October 1973).

"British Visitors' Perceptions of the West, 1885–1914." In A.W. Rasporich and H.C. Klassen, eds., *Prairie Perspectives 2*. Toronto and Montreal: Holt, Rinehart and Winston, 1973.

"A History of Agriculture on the Prairies to 1914." *Prairie Forum*, April 1976.

"Eugene Francis O'Beirne." *Dictionary of Canadian Biography*, vol. IX. Toronto: University of Toronto Press, 1976.

"A Judicial Murder—The Trial of Louis Riel." In H. Palmer, ed., *The Settlement of the West*. Calgary: Comprint Publishing Co., 1977.

"The C.C.F. Victory in Saskatchewan, 1944." *Saskatchewan History*, Winter 1981.

"Louis Riel," *Dictionary of Canadian Biography*, vol. XI. Toronto: University of Toronto Press, 1982.

6. *Official Published Reports*

Reports of the Archives of Saskatchewan, nos. 2 to 7. Regina: Government of Saskatchewan, 1947–56.

Directory of Saskatchewan Ministeries, Members of the Legislative Assembly and Elections, 1905–1953. Regina: Government of Saskatchewan, 1954.

Directory of Members of Parliament and Federal Elections for the North-West Territories and Saskatchewan, 1887–1953. Regina: Government of Saskatchewan, 1956.

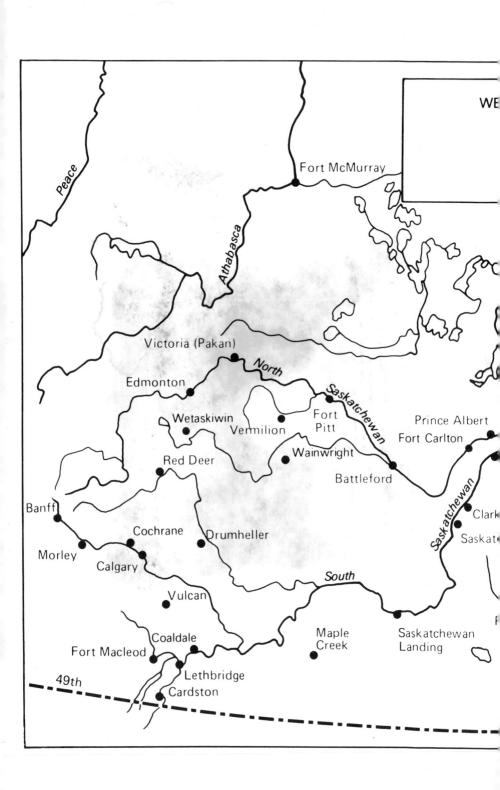

WE

Peace

Athabasca

Fort McMurray

Victoria (Pakan)

North

Edmonton

Saskatchewan

Wetaskiwin

Vermilion

Fort
Pitt

Prince Albert

Fort Carlton

Red Deer

Wainwright

Battleford

Banff

Saskatchewan

Clark

Cochrane

Drumheller

Saskat

Morley

Calgary

South

Vulcan

Coaldale

Maple
Creek

Saskatchewan
Landing

Fort Macleod

49th

Lethbridge

Cardston